Lecture Notes in Computer Science   7831

Commenced Publication in 1973
Founding and Former Series Editors:
Gerhard Goos, Juris Hartmanis, and Jan van Leeuwen

Krzysztof Krawiec   Alberto Moraglio
Ting Hu   A. Şima Etaner-Uyar   Bin Hu (Eds.)

Genetic Programming

16th European Conference, EuroGP 2013
Vienna, Austria, April 3-5, 2013
Proceedings

 Springer

Volume Editors

Krzysztof Krawiec
Poznan University of Technology, Institute of Computing Science
Piotrowo 2, 60-965 Poznań, Poland
E-mail: krawiec@cs.put.poznan.pl

Alberto Moraglio
The University of Birmingham, School of Computer Science
Edgbaston, Birmingham B15 2TT, UK
E-mail: a.moraglio@cs.bham.ac.uk

Ting Hu
Dartmouth College, Geisel School of Medicine
Hanover, NH 03755, USA
E-mail: ting.hu@dartmouth.edu

A. Şima Etaner-Uyar
Istanbul Technical University, Department of Computer Engineering
Masla, 34469 Istanbul, Turkey
E-mail: etaner@itu.edu.tr

Bin Hu
Vienna University of Technology, Institute of Computer Graphics and Algorithms
1040 Vienna, Austria
E-mail: hu@ads.tuwien.ac.at

Front cover EvoStar 2013 logo by Kevin Sim, Edinburgh Napier University.

ISSN 0302-9743   e-ISSN 1611-3349
ISBN 978-3-642-37206-3   e-ISBN 978-3-642-37207-0
DOI 10.1007/978-3-642-37207-0
Springer Heidelberg Dordrecht London New York

Library of Congress Control Number: 2013933136

CR Subject Classification (1998): F.2, F.1, I.2.6, I.2.8, I.5, J.3

LNCS Sublibrary: SL 1 – Theoretical Computer Science and General Issues

Typesetting: Camera-ready by author, data conversion by Scientific Publishing Services, Chennai, India

Printed on acid-free paper

Springer is part of Springer Science+Business Media (www.springer.com)

Preface

The 16th European Conference on Genetic Programming (EuroGP) took place during April 3-5, 2013, in the beautiful city of Vienna, Austria, a world-famous travel destination and a delightful place for the conference. Being the only conference exclusively devoted to genetic programming and the evolutionary generation of computer programs, EuroGP attracts scholars from all over the world.

The unique character of genetic programming has been recognized from its very beginning. Presently, with over 8,000 articles in the online GP bibliography maintained by Bill Langdon, it is clearly a mature form of evolutionary computation. EuroGP has had an essential impact on the success of the field, by serving as an important forum for expressing new ideas, meeting fellow researchers, and starting collaborations. Many are the success stories witnessed by the now 16 editions of EuroGP. To date, genetic programming is essentially the only approach that has demonstrated the ability to automatically generate and repair computer code in a wide variety of problem areas. It is also one of the leading methodologies that can be used to "automate" science, helping researchers to find hidden complex models behind observed phenomena. Furthermore, genetic programming has been applied to many problems of practical significance, and has produced human-competitive solutions.

EuroGP 2013 received 47 submissions from 24 different countries across five continents. The papers underwent a rigorous double-blind peer review process, each being reviewed by at least three members of the international Program Committee from 20 countries. The selection process resulted in this volume, with 18 papers accepted for oral presentation (38% acceptance rate) and five for poster presentation (49% global acceptance rate for talks and posters combined). The wide range of topics in this volume reflects the current state of research in the field, including different genres of GP (tree-based, linear, grammar-based, Cartesian), theory, novel operators, and applications.

Together with four other co-located evolutionary computation conferences, EvoCOP 2013, EvoBIO 2013, EvoMusArt 2013, and EvoApplications 2013, EuroGP 2013 was part of the Evo* 2013 event. This meeting could not have taken place without the help of many people.

First to be thanked is the great community of researchers and practitioners who contributed to the conference by both submitting their work and reviewing others' as part of the Program Committee. Their hard work, in evolutionary terms, provided both variation and selection, without which progress in the field would not be possible!

The papers were submitted, reviewed, and selected using the MyReview conference management software. We are sincerely grateful to Marc Schoenauer of INRIA, France, for his great assistance in providing, hosting, and managing the software.

We would like to thank the local organizing team: Bin Hu, Doris Dicklberger, and Günther Raidl from the Data Structures Group, Institute of Computer Graphics and Algorithms, Vienna University of Technology.

We thank Kevin Sim from the Institute for Informatics and Digital Information, Edinburgh Napier University for creating and maintaining the official Evo* 2013 website, and A. Şima Etaner-Uyar from the Department of Computer Engineering, Istanbul Technical University, for being responsible for Evo* 2013 publicity.

We especially want to express our genuine gratitude to Jennifer Willies of the Institute for Informatics and Digital Innovation at Edinburgh Napier University, UK. Her dedicated and continued involvement in Evo* since 1998 has been and remains essential for the image, status, and unique atmosphere of this series of events.

April 2013   Krzysztof Krawiec
                                                              Alberto Moraglio
                                                                      Ting Hu
                                                         A. Şima Etaner-Uyar
                                                                      Bin Hu

Organization

Administrative details were handled by Jennifer Willies, Edinburgh Napier University, Institute for Informatics and Digital Innovation, Scotland, UK.

Organizing Committee

Program Co-chairs

Krzysztof Krawiec	Poznan University of Technology, Poland
Alberto Moraglio	University of Birmingham, UK

Publication Chair

Ting Hu	Dartmouth College, USA

Publicity Chair

A. Şima Etaner-Uyar	Istanbul Technical University, Turkey

Local Chair

Bin Hu	Vienna University of Technology, Austria

Program Committee

Alex Agapitos	University College Dublin, Ireland
Lee Altenberg	University of Hawaii at Manoa, USA
Lourdes Araujo	UNED, Spain
R. Muhammad Atif Azad	University of Limerick, Ireland
Wolfgang Banzhaf	Memorial University of Newfoundland, Canada
Mohamed Bahy Bader	University of Portsmouth, UK
Helio Barbosa	LNCC / UFJF, Brazil
Anthony Brabazon	University College Dublin, Ireland
Nicolas Bredeche	Université Paris-Sud XI / INRIA / CNRS, France
Stefano Cagnoni	University of Parma, Italy
Pierre Collet	LSIIT-FDBT, France
Ernesto Costa	University of Coimbra, Portugal
Luis Da Costa	Université Paris-Sud XI, France
Antonio Della Cioppa	University of Salerno, Italy
Stephen Dignum	University of Essex, UK

Ender Ozcan	University of Nottingham, UK
Andrew J. Parkes	University of Nottingham, UK
Clara Pizzuti	Institute for High Performance Computing and Networking, Italy
Gisele Pappa	Federal University of Minas Gerais, Brazil
Riccardo Poli	University of Essex, UK
Thomas Ray	University of Oklahoma, USA
Denis Robilliard	Université Lille Nord de France, France
Marc Schoenauer	INRIA, France
Lukas Sekanina	Brno University of Technology, Czech Republic
Yin Shan	Medicare Australia
Sara Silva	INESC-ID Lisboa, Portugal
Moshe Sipper	Ben-Gurion University, Israel
Alexei N. Skurikhin	Los Alamos National Laboratory, USA
Terence Soule	University of Idaho, USA
Lee Spector	Hampshire College, USA
Ivan Tanev	Doshisha University, Japan
Ernesto Tarantino	ICAR-CNR, Italy
Jorge Tavares	Microsoft, Germany
Theo Theodoridis	University of Essex, UK
Leonardo Trujillo	Instituto Tecnológico de Tijuana, Mexico
Leonardo Vanneschi	Universidade Nova de Lisboa, Portugal, and University of Milano-Bicocca, Italy
Sebastien Verel	University of Nice-Sophia Antipolis/CNRS, France
Katya Vladislavleva	University of Antwerp, Belgium
Man Leung Wong	Lingnan University, Hong Kong
Lidia Yamamoto	University of Strasbourg, France
Mengjie Zhang	Victoria University of Wellington, New Zealand

Table of Contents

Oral Presentations

Posters

Adaptive Distance Metrics
for Nearest Neighbour Classification
Based on Genetic Programming

Alexandros Agapitos, Michael O'Neill, and Anthony Brabazon

Financial Mathematics and Computation Research Cluster
Complex and Adaptive Systems Laboratory
University College Dublin, Ireland
{alexandros.agapitos,m.oneill,anthony.brabazon}@ucd.ie

Abstract. Nearest Neighbour (NN) classification is a widely-used, effective method for both binary and multi-class problems. It relies on the assumption that class conditional probabilities are locally constant. However, this assumption becomes invalid in high dimensions, and severe bias can be introduced, which degrades the performance of the method. The employment of a locally adaptive distance metric becomes crucial in order to keep class conditional probabilities approximately uniform, whereby better classification performance can be attained. This paper presents a locally adaptive distance metric for NN classification based on a supervised learning algorithm (Genetic Programming) that learns a vector of feature weights for the features composing an instance query. Using a weighted Euclidean distance metric, this has the effect of adaptive neighbourhood shapes to query locations, stretching the neighbourhood along the directions for which the class conditional probabilities don't change much. Initial empirical results on a set of real-world classification datasets showed that the proposed method enhances the generalisation performance of standard NN algorithm, and that it is a competent method for pattern classification as compared to other learning algorithms.

1 Introduction

In a classification problem, we are given C classes and N training observations. Each training observation x is usually a vector of d features $x = (x_1, \ldots, x_d) \in R^d$ along with the known class labels $y \in \{1, 2, \ldots, C\}$. The task is to predict the class label of a given query instance. The k *Nearest Neighbour* (kNN) classification technique, a popular *instance-based learning* method [14], was originally proposed by Fix and Hodges in 1951 [6]. It determines the k nearest neighbours ("closeness" is usually defined in terms of a distance metric on the Euclidean space) of instance query q, and then predicts the class label of q as the most frequent one occurring among the k neighbours. In contrast to learning methods that induce a function approximation designed to perform well in the entire

K. Krawiec et al. (Eds.): EuroGP 2013, LNCS 7831, pp. 1–12, 2013.

instance space, the kNN method simply stores the training examples (*memory-based* classification); generalisation beyond these examples is postponed until a new instance must be classified.

An important issue that hinders the application of kNN to high-dimensional datasets is the learning algorithm's *inductive bias* – the set of assumptions that a learner uses to predict outputs given inputs that it has not encountered [14] – which assumes that the class conditional probabilities are roughly locally constant, that is, the classification of an instance query q will be most similar to the classification of other instances that are nearby in Euclidean space. This assumption becomes false in high-dimensional spaces, where the nearest neighbours of a point can be very far away, introducing severe bias in the estimates [18].

The method we are developing in this paper deals with the problem of kNN's inductive bias, and falls into the family of methods that employ locally adaptive metrics in order to maintain the class conditional probabilities approximately uniform in the neighbourhood of an instance query. Genetic programming (GP) is employed to learn a model that outputs a real-valued vector, whose components represent individual feature relevances for single features composing a query pattern. This vector is then transformed into a vector of feature weights allowing for a weighted Euclidean distance metric computation, thus enabling a kNN neighbourhood to adapt its shape in different parts of the feature space. This results in enhanced classification performance. We would like to point out that while there exists a plethora of methods for dealing with the *generalisation* of models induced by GP alone (some studies are found in [1–3, 13, 17, 19, 20], this work focusses on hybridising GP and kNN in an attempt to learn even better-generalising models that exploit the power of both learning algorithms.

The rest of the paper is organised as follows. Section 2 formalises the inefficiency that can arise from kNN's inductive bias, and motivates the need to introduce adaptive distance metrics when forming neighbourhoods. Hence, it outlines previous research efforts towards that goal. Section 3 presents the proposed method for dealing with the problem of locally adaptive distance metrics, outlines the experiment setup, the real-world application datasets, and the learning algorithms used to compare against the proposed method. Section 4 analyses the experimental results, and finally Section 5 draws our conclusions and sketches future work.

2   The Need for Distance Metric Adaptation

Formally, in a kNN classification problem, the learner is presented with N training examples $x \in R^d$, each mapped to a corresponding class label y, $y \in \{1, 2, \ldots, C\}$. It is assumed that there exists an unknown probability distribution $P(x, y)$ that generated the training data. In order to predict the class label of an instance query q, we need to estimate the class posterior probabilities $\{P(c|q)\}_{c=1}^{C}$. kNN methods are based on the assumption that the target function is smooth, meaning that the class posterior probabilities $P(c|q)$ are locally constant [4]. That is: $P(c|q + \delta q) \simeq P(c|q)$, for $\|\delta q\|$ small enough. Then,

$P(c|q) \simeq ((\sum_{x \in N(q)} P(c|x)/|N(q)|))$, where $N(q)$ is a neighbourhood of q that contains points x that are "close" to q, and $|N(q)|$ denotes the number of points in $N(q)$. This motivates the estimate:

$$\hat{P}(c|q) = \frac{\sum_{i=1}^{N} 1(x_i \in N(q))1(y_i = c)}{\sum_{i=1}^{N} 1(x_i \in N(q))} \qquad (1)$$

where $1(\cdot)$ in an indicator function that returns 1 if its argument is true, and 0 otherwise.

The assumption of locally uniform class conditional probabilities becomes false when the instance query approaches the class boundaries. We present an example that explains how the choice of a distance measure becomes crucial in determining the outcome of kNN classification. Consider the binary, linearly separable dataset in Figure 1(a), where patterns from each class are represented by the green and yellow circles respectively. Each input pattern resides in a 2-dimensional feature space formed by the horizontal and vertical axes X and Y. The class boundary is represented by the black vertical line and is parallel to the Y axis. The new query to be classified using a 5-NN classifier is shown with the black solid dot. The commonly used Euclidean distance metric assigns equal weight to individual pair-wise feature squared differences, implying that the input space is isotropic or homogenous [14]. This distance metric results in hyper-spherical neighbourhoods – in our 2-dimensional feature space is denoted by the circular strip. We note that the 5-NN neighbourhood has extended into the red-class region, and is dominated by points of the wrong class (3 from the red class and 2 from the green class), thereby causing a misclassification.

If we carefully inspect the dataset in Figure 1(a), we will observe that the class conditional probabilities vary only in the horizontal direction (i.e. a slight move along the horizontal axis may change the class label). In lieu of this knowledge, we should constrict the neighbourhood in the horizontal direction, and elongate it along the vertical direction (direction where the class conditional probabilities do not change), as shown by the vertical strip in the example. This will reduce the bias of the estimate, and leave the variance the same (the neighbourhood is still based on the same number of 5 points). As a result, we observe that the distance metric should not assign equal weights or the same proportions in all directions of the feature space; the weights/proportions during distance computation are query-specific. Capturing such information is of great importance to kNN classification in high-dimensional feature spaces. Figure 1(b) shows examples of different neighbourhood shapes required in different parts of the input space, ranging from circular neighbourhoods, to elliptical ones, and contrasts them against kNN neighbourhoods formed using a standard, unweighted, Euclidean distance metric. Note that the amount of elongation/restriction decays as the instance query moves further away from areas where a decision boundary would lie. The above examples call for locally adapting the distance metric so that the resulting neighbourhood is elongated along the axis direction that provides less class-discrimination information, and is constricted in the opposite case.

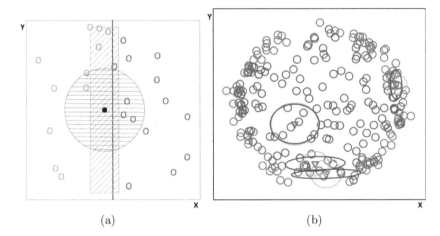

(a)   (b)

Fig. 1. (a) The vertical line represents the class boundaries between classes red and green. The vertical strip denotes the 5-NN region of a neighbourhood for the query instance (solid black dot), which is constricted along the horizontal axis of the feature space. Figure(a) is adapted from the figure found in page 476 in [18]. (b) Different neighbourhood shapes required to minimise the bias of estimates. The little triangles are the instance query points to be classified. The navy-blue ellipses represent the adaptive 6-NN neighbourhoods, while the orange circles are the standard 6-NN neighbourhoods. Note how the shape varies with instance query locations in the 2-dimensional feature space.

2.1 Previous Work

There has been a variety of studies aiming at locally adapting the distance metric so that a neighbourhood of approximately constant a posteriori probability can be produced. The techniques proposed in [5, 8, 10, 12, 15, 23] are based on estimating feature relevance locally at each instance query. The locally estimated feature relevance leads to a weighted metric for computing the distance between the instance query and the training data. As a result, neighbourhoods get constricted along most relevant dimensions, and elongated along less important ones. Although these methods improve upon the original kNN algorithm, the time-complexity cost of such improvement is high due to the local feature relevance being estimated on the fly with costly procedures whenever a new query is to be classified. This makes it difficult to scale up in large datasets.

An improvement to this time inefficiency is presented in the work of [4] that utilises support vector machines (SVMs) to estimate local feature weighting. The global decision boundary is determined offline, leaving only local refinements to be performed online. The proposed technique offers accuracy improvements over the SVMs alone. Additional work [21] attempted to address the time inefficiency issue in online local feature relevance estimation by introducing a very simple locally adaptive distance metric that normalises the ordinary Euclidean or Manhattan distance from an instance query to each training example by the closest distance between the corresponding training example to training examples of a different class. Results showed comparable performance to SVMs.

In addition to the works for determining local distance metrics, there has been considerable research interest in directly learning distance metrics from training examples. The work of [9] proposed a method for learning a Mahalanobis distance measure by directly maximising a stochastic variant of the leave-one-out kNN classification performance on the training data. In [22] the authors developed a method for inducing a Mahalanobis distance metric using semidefinite programming. Both of these methods induce a global distance metric that is employed in every kNN application irrespective of the location of the instance query.

3 Methods

3.1 Supervised Learning of Local Feature Weights

The method we are proposing revolves around the general notion of adapting the shape of the neighbourhood via the computation of a weighted Euclidean distance metric. As discussed in Section 2, a "closeness" criterion that is based on a weighted Euclidean distance metric computation has the effect of stretching/elongating the axis of the feature space. The proposed technique has the potential of scaling up to large datasets, by learning offline a model that outputs a real-valued vector, whose components represent individual feature relevances for every feature describing a query pattern. These relevance values can then be transformed to weights associated with each pair-wise squared feature-value difference in a weighted Euclidean distance computation. Note that the technique is query-based because the learned model outputs a vector of feature relevances for a particular instance query.

Formally, assume that we want to classify patterns defined in a d-dimensional feature space. Each pattern x is a d-dimensional vector of real-valued features, that is, $x = (x_1, \ldots, x_d)$. For every pattern there is an associated class label y, $y \in \{1, 2, \ldots, C\}$. The learning task is to approximate a function $h(x)$ that maps an input vector representing a pattern into an output vector of feature relevances denoted as $x' = (x'_1, \ldots, x'_d)$ driven by an error measure that concerns the classification accuracy as described below. Using the output vector $(x'_1, \ldots, x'_d)$ from $h(x)$, a measure of relative relevance can be given using the following *exponential weighting scheme*:

$$w_i(x) = \frac{exp(x'_i)}{\sum_{i=1}^{d} exp(x'_i)} \qquad (2)$$

We follow [4] and adopt the exponential weighting scheme as it has been shown to be more sensitive in local feature relevance, and in general results in better performance improvement. The weights from Equation 2 can then be associated with features in a weighted Euclidean distance computation:

$$D(x, y) = \sqrt{\sum_{i=1}^{d} w_i(x_i - y_i)^2} \qquad (3)$$

This adaptive distance metric can then be used in the kNN algorithm to form a neighbourhood around query pattern x, and classify it accordingly. The learning algorithm needs to induce a model that uncovers the relationship between an output vector of feature relevances $x' = (x'_1, \ldots, x'_d)$ and the classification accuracy (defined as the number of correct classifications divided by the number of examples in a learning set) of the kNN algorithm that employs the adaptive distance metric accruing from the use of $x' = (x'_1, \ldots, x'_d)$. The goal is to learn to output feature relevance vectors x' that result in high classification accuracy. In summary, once a model for assigning feature weights has been learned, the proposed system is a two-layer classifier: given input x, in the first layer we use the learned model to induce feature weights for x, and in the second layer we invoke the standard kNN classifier that employs the weighted Euclidean distance.

3.2   Multiple-Output Program Representation for GP

We used a supervised learning algorithm, Genetic Programming (GP) [16], to learn such a model. The model needs to output a vector of feature relevances, and for that we used a program representation that was introduced in [24] by the name of a *modi expression-tree*. A *modi* program representation can simulate the effect of a *directed acyclic graph*, and consists of two main parts: (a) an expression-tree, and (b) an associated vector for holding outputs, as shown in Figure 2. Similar to standard GP, a *modi* tree has function nodes representing operations (i.e. arithmetic, conditionals, trigonometry), and terminal nodes representing variables and constants. However, unlike the standard expression-tree structure, which outputs a single value through the root, a *modi* program utilises its output vector, hence producing multiple values, each of which corresponds to a single feature relevance in our case. The two parts of a *modi* program are connected through some special function nodes, called *modi* nodes (grey nodes in Figure 2). A *modi* node has two roles: (1) it updates an element in the output vector that the node is pre-associated with, by adding its node value to the value of the vector element; (2) it passes the value of its right child node to its parent node, so the expression-tree structure can be preserved.

The output vector is in effect an array of memory locations where *modi* nodes are allowed to write into. Figure 2 shows what happens when an example *modi* program is evaluated. Before the evaluation starts, the output vector's elements are all initialised with ones. During the evaluation, each non-*modi* node passes its value to its parent, exactly the same way as in standard GP. On the other hand, each *modi* node firstly uses its node value to update the output vector (shown as curved solid arrows), and then passes on the value of its right child to its parent node (shown as dashed arrows). The side-effect of program evaluation is the update of the output vector – we are not concerned with the value returned at the root of the tree. The value of each output vector's element corresponds to a pattern feature's relevance, so starting from the value of one, the higher a value at the end of the program evaluation procedure, the higher the feature's relevance for a particular input pattern. Once the values of the output vector are set, the exponential weighting scheme of Equation 2 is used to transform each vector element into a weight that will be subsequently used in a weighted Euclidean distance.

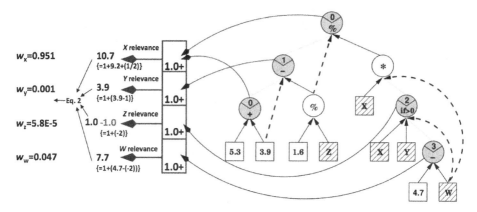

Fig. 2. Example illustration of the way the output vector, representing feature relevances, is updated through the evaluation of a *modi* program, and how this is transformed into a set of feature weights *w* that will be used in the weighted Euclidean distance computation (Equation 3) for determining the neighbourhood during kNN classification. Here we are considering a pattern with four features $[X, Y, Z, W] = [-1.0, 2.0, 1.6, -2.0]$. The output vector allocates a cell index for each of the four features; these are indices 0, 1, 2, 3 for features X, Y, Z, W respectively. Prior to program evaluation, all vector elements are initialised to 1.0. Feeding the input vector $[-1.0, 2.0, 1.6, -2.0]$ into the *modi* program produces the output vector [10.7, 3.9, 1.0, 7.7]. Note that the value of the third vector element resulted in a negative number (-1.0 shown in red font), and has been set back to the lower bound of 1.0. Invoking Equation 2 using the output vector we get a vector of weights w=[0.951, 0.001, 5.8E-5, 0.047] for features X, Y, Z, W respectively. (The figure is adapted from the figure found in page 4 of [24]).

The detailed method for initialising *modi* trees can be found in [24]. It is worth noting that for the case of intermediate nodes, the probability of a node being set to a *modi* node is governed by a parameter $\mu \in [0, 1]$, the *modi* rate. In addition, we are constraining the values that can be held by vector elements within the range of [1.0, 100.0]. During program execution, vector values are incremented by the value returned from a *modi* node, and this can result in certain vector cell indices being assigned very large values – a situation that can degrade the performance of the exponential weighting scheme by zeroing certain feature weights. A very simple check is employed that sets the value of a vector cell back to the lower bound of 1.0 if the last update resulted in a value that was less than the lower bound, and sets the value to the upper bound of 100.0 if the last update resulted in a value that was bigger than the upper bound.

3.3   Experiment Design

In the experiments we used eight real-world datasets (Table 2) obtained from the UCI Machine Learning repository [7]. These were carefully picked to test our method in problems with high-dimensional input spaces. In all datasets, input values were standardised to have zero mean and unit variance. For each dataset we compared the performance of our system *AdaptiveKNN* against the performance of other learning algorithms via stratified 10-fold or 5-fold cross validation (in case data were limited for a particular dataset – see Table 2).

Table 1. GP system setup

EA used in GP system	elitist, generational, *modi* expression-tree representation
modi rate	0.4
Function set	$+, -, *, \%$ (protected), $sin, cos, e^x, log, sqrt$
Terminal set	feature values, 10 random constants in $[0.0, 1.0]$
No. of generations	51
Population size	100
Tournament size	2
Tree creation	ramped half-and-half (depths of 2 to 6)
Max. tree depth	20
Subtree crossover	30% (90% inner nodes, 10% leaf-nodes)
Subtree mutation	40%
Point mutation	30%
Fitness function	classification accuracy

Table 2. UCI Machine Learning Datasets

Dataset	Size	Classes	Input dimensionality	Cross-validation folds
Australian credit appr. (Statlog)	690	2	14	10
Sonar (Mines vs. Rocks)	208	2	60	10
Ionosphere	351	2	33	10
Vehicle Silhouettes (Statlog)	946	4	18	10
Heart (Stallog)	270	2	13	10
Hepatitis	155	2	19	5
Vote	435	2	16	10
Glass	214	7	9	5

The first stage of applying AdaptiveKNN to classification consists of learning a model of feature weights using GP. For each test fold we treat the remaining folds as our learning set. This learning set is further divided into two disjoint sets of *training* and *validation* with proportions of 80% and 20% respectively. The training set is used to fit the model, while the validation set is used for model selection at the end of an evolutionary run. In the second stage, after learning the model, we can assess the generalisation error using the instance queries of the test fold, and using the data in the remaining folds as a *memory* in the standard kNN methodology. Table 1 summarises the setup of the GP system.

We contrasted the performance of AdaptiveKNN against several classification algorithms implemented in the WEKA software [11]:

1. kNN (StdKNN) using the standard Euclidean distance metric. Value of parameter k for number of neighbours was determined via cross validation.

2. SVM with Radial Basis Function kernel (SVM-RBF) trained with sequential minimal optimisation. Values of parameters γ in $K(x,c) = e^{-\gamma\|x-c\|^2}$, and c for soft-margin were determined via cross validation.
3. SVM with Polynomial kernel (SVM-POLY) trained with sequential minimal optimisation. Values of parameters c for soft-margin, and n for polynomial order were determined via cross validation.
4. Naive Bayesian classifier (NaiveBayes).
5. Gaussian Radial Basis Function Network (RBFN). Values of parameters σ^2 in the Gaussian kernel, and k in k-means clustering were determined via cross validation.
6. Feed forward multilayer perceptron (MLP) trained with back-propagation. Network structure determined via cross validation.
7. C4.5 decision tree method (with post-pruning).
8. Classification and Regression Tree (CART) method (with post-pruning).

4   Results

For training the AdaptiveKNN, we performed 30 independent cross-validated runs with each dataset in order to account for the stochastic nature of the GP learning algorithm. The same number of runs were performed for MLP (after parameter tuning) that also exhibits a stochastic element. Thus, is order to calculate cross-validated performance in Table 3, we used the best models out of 30 models learned for each fold, and then average their test-fold performances. For the remaining of the learning algorithms, we first performed parameter tuning and then reported their cross-validated accuracies. Table 3 shows that AdaptiveKNN achieves the best performance in five out of eight datasets. In two cases (Ionosphere and Sonar datasets) it obtained the second best performance following the SVM-RBF. However, in the case of Vehicles dataset, AdaptiveKNN achieved the lowest performance as compared to SVMs and MLP, and it was only comparable with the tree-based methods C4.5 and CART. Looking at the generalisation performance enhancement that AdaptiveKNN offers over StdKNN, we found that this reaches the level of 13.6% (averaged among datasets), with the lowest percentage increases of 3% and 1% obtained for Australian credit and Vehicles datasets respectively. Finally, Figure 3 contrasts the cross-validated

Table 3. Cross-validated Classification Accuracies

	Australian credit	Sonar	Ionosphere	Vehicles	Heart	Hepatitis	Vote	Glass
AdaptiveKNN	**89.1**	88.6	94.5	73.4	**88.5**	**97.8**	**99.2**	**78.3**
StdKNN	86.5	63.6	84.0	72.3	84.4	84.4	92.9	61.7
NaiveBayes	77.1	67.8	82.6	44.7	83.3	87.5	92.7	49.5
RBFN	85.8	87.5	93.7	71.5	84.1	92.5	97.0	70.1
MLP	84.9	82.2	91.4	82.5	78.1	81.2	94.7	67.3
SVM-POLY	86.4	84.6	91.7	84.5	84.8	86.2	97.0	71.5
SVM-RBF	85.5	**89.4**	**94.8**	**84.9**	83.7	86.2	97.0	70.1
C4.5	85.4	71.1	91.4	72.6	76.7	86.2	96.5	67.3
CART	85.6	71.1	89.7	69.4	78.5	82.5	97.0	70.6

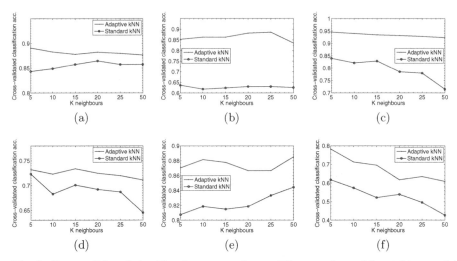

Fig. 3. Cross-validated classification accuracies at different values of k neighbours. (a) Australian credit; (b) Sonar; (c) Ionosphere; (d) Vehicles; (e) Heart; (f) Glass.

classification accuracies at different values of k neighbours for AdaptiveKNN and StdKNN in a sample of datasets. We observe that AdaptiveKNN performs better that StdKNN for all values of k considered.

5   Conclusion

In this work we combined (a) kNN, an instance-based learning algorithm that constructs a local approximation to the target function which then applies to the neighbourhood of each individual query instance, with (b) GP, a very powerful global (i.e. fits a model to the entire instance space) function approximator that is able to learn local relative feature relevances from examples. Transforming these into adaptive distance metrics for use with kNN allows a complex target function to be described as a collection of less complex approximations that are locally tuned to achieve better classification performance.

While there is a cost associated with effective training of GP models (i.e. evolutionary algorithm's parameter tuning through cross-validation, actual cost of performing a significant amount of runs to account for GP's stochastic nature), this process is performed offline once (in contrast to other locally adaptive algorithms that require a considerable amount of online computation), and subsequently allows for a time-efficient computation of local weights. This enhances scalability to large datasets.

Initial empirical results on a collection of real-world datasets showed that (a) the gain in performance over the simple kNN method outweighs this extra cost of offline model learning, and that (b) the proposed method is competent in pattern classification as opposed to other learning algorithms.

There are several avenues for further development of AdaptiveKNN. First, we are planing to compare it against other locally adaptive kNN methods found in literature. Our GP system uses a program representation that hasn't received much attention from the GP community – it falls under the general category of programs with side-effects. We are currently working on optimising two crucial aspects of the system (i.e. *modi* rate, variation operators tailored to this program presentation).

On a more general note, the local feature relevances implicitly touched on the issue of *feature selection*, which can be essentially performed by zeroing certain feature weighs. Adaptive distance metrics for kNN classifiers consist an approach to ameliorate the problem arising from the curse of dimensionality by performing local dimensionality reduction. We plan to investigate this in our future research.

Acknowledgement. This publication has emanated from research conducted with the financial support of Science Foundation Ireland under Grant Number 08/SRC/FM1389.

References

1. Agapitos, A., Brabazon, A., O'Neill, M.: Controlling Overfitting in Symbolic Regression Based on a Bias/Variance Error Decomposition. In: Coello Coello, C.A., Cutello, V., Deb, K., Forrest, S., Nicosia, G., Pavone, M. (eds.) PPSN 2012, Part I. LNCS, vol. 7491, pp. 438–447. Springer, Heidelberg (2012)
2. Agapitos, A., O'Neill, M., Brabazon, A.: Evolutionary Learning of Technical Trading Rules without Data-Mining Bias. In: Schaefer, R., Cotta, C., Kołodziej, J., Rudolph, G. (eds.) PPSN XI, Part I. LNCS, vol. 6238, pp. 294–303. Springer, Heidelberg (2010)
3. Agapitos, A., O'Neill, M., Brabazon, A., Theodoridis, T.: Maximum Margin Decision Surfaces for Increased Generalisation in Evolutionary Decision Tree Learning. In: Silva, S., Foster, J.A., Nicolau, M., Machado, P., Giacobini, M. (eds.) EuroGP 2011. LNCS, vol. 6621, pp. 61–72. Springer, Heidelberg (2011)
4. Domeniconi, C., Gunopulos, D., Peng, J.: Large margin nearest neighbor classifiers. IEEE Transactions on Neural Networks 16(4), 899–909 (2005)
5. Domeniconi, C., Peng, J., Gunopulos, D.: Locally adaptive metric nearest-neighbor classification. IEEE Transactions on Pattern Analysis and Machine Intelligence 24(9), 1281–1285 (2002)
6. Fix, E., Hodges Jr., J.L.: Discriminatory analysis. nonparametric discrimination: Consistency properties. International Statistical Review 57(3), 238–247 (1989)
7. Frank, A., Asuncion, A.: UCI machine learning repository (2010), http://archive.ics.uci.edu/ml
8. Friedman, J.H.: Flexible metric nearest neighbour classification. Tech. rep., Department of Statistics. Stanford University (1994)
9. Goldberger, J., Roweis, S., Hinton, G., Salakhutdinov, R.: Neighbourhood components analysis. In: Advances in Neural Information Processing Systems 17, pp. 513–520. MIT Press (2004)
10. Guo, R., Chakraborty, S.: Bayesian adaptive nearest neighbor. Stat. Anal. Data Min. 3(2), 92–105 (2010)

11. Hall, M., Frank, E., Holmes, G., Pfahringer, B., Reutemann, P., Witten, I.: The weka data mining software: An update. SIGKDD Explorations 11(1) (2009)
12. Hastie, T., Tibshirani, R.: Discriminant adaptive nearest neighbor classification. IEEE Trans. Pattern Anal. Mach. Intell. 18(6), 607–616 (1996)
13. Kattan, A., Agapitos, A., Poli, R.: Unsupervised Problem Decomposition Using Genetic Programming. In: Esparcia-Alcázar, A.I., Ekárt, A., Silva, S., Dignum, S., Uyar, A.Ş. (eds.) EuroGP 2010. LNCS, vol. 6021, pp. 122–133. Springer, Heidelberg (2010)
14. Mitchell, T.: Machine Learning. McGraw-Hill (1997)
15. Peng, J., Heisterkamp, D.R., Dai, H.K.: Lda/svm driven nearest neighbor classification. IEEE Transactions on Neural Networks 14(4), 940–942 (2003)
16. Poli, R., Langdon, W.B., McPhee, N.F.: A Field Guide to Genetic Programming. Lulu Enterprises, UK Ltd (2008)
17. Theodoridis, T., Agapitos, A., Hu, H.: A gaussian groundplan projection area model for evolving probabilistic classifiers. In: Genetic and Evolutionary Computation Conference, GECCO 2011, Dublin, July 12-16. ACM (2011)
18. Trevor, H., Robert, T., Jerome, F.: The Elements of Statistical Learning, 2nd edn. Springer (2009)
19. Tuite, C., Agapitos, A., O'Neill, M., Brabazon, A.: A Preliminary Investigation of Overfitting in Evolutionary Driven Model Induction: Implications for Financial Modelling. In: Di Chio, C., Brabazon, A., Di Caro, G.A., Drechsler, R., Farooq, M., Grahl, J., Greenfield, G., Prins, C., Romero, J., Squillero, G., Tarantino, E., Tettamanzi, A.G.B., Urquhart, N., Uyar, A.Ş. (eds.) EvoApplications 2011, Part II. LNCS, vol. 6625, pp. 120–130. Springer, Heidelberg (2011)
20. Tuite, C., Agapitos, A., O'Neill, M., Brabazon, A.: Early stopping criteria to counteract overfitting in genetic programming. In: Genetic and Evolutionary Computation Conference, GECCO 2011, Dublin, July 12-16. ACM (2011)
21. Wang, J., Neskovic, P., Cooper, L.N.: Improving nearest neighbor rule with a simple adaptive distance measure. Pattern Recogn. Lett. 28(2), 207–213 (2007)
22. Weinberger, K.Q., Saul, L.K.: Distance metric learning for large margin nearest neighbor classification. J. Mach. Learn. Res. 10, 207–244 (2009)
23. Zhang, G.-J., Du, J.-X., Huang, D.-S., Lok, T.-M., Lyu, M.R.: Adaptive Nearest Neighbor Classifier Based on Supervised Ellipsoid Clustering. In: Wang, L., Jiao, L., Shi, G., Li, X., Liu, J. (eds.) FSKD 2006. LNCS (LNAI), vol. 4223, pp. 582–585. Springer, Heidelberg (2006)
24. Zhang, Y., Zhang, M.: A multiple-output program tree structure in genetic programming. In: Mckay, R.I., Cho, S.B. (eds.) Proceedings of the Second Asian-Pacific Workshop on Genetic Programming, Cairns, Australia, p. 12

Controlling Bloat through Parsimonious Elitist Replacement and Spatial Structure

Grant Dick and Peter A. Whigham

Department of Information Science,
University of Otago,
Dunedin, New Zealand
grant.dick@otago.ac.nz

Abstract. The concept of bloat — the increase of program size without a corresponding increase in fitness — presents a significant drawback to the application of genetic programming. One approach to controlling bloat, dubbed *spatial structure with elitism* (SS+E), uses a combination of spatial population structure and local elitist replacement to implicitly constrain unwarranted program growth. However, the default implementation of SS+E uses a replacement scheme that prevents the introduction of smaller programs in the presence of equal fitness. This paper introduces a modified SS+E approach in which replacement is done under a lexicographic parsimony scheme. The proposed model, *spatial structure with lexicographic parsimonious elitism* (SS+LPE), exhibits an improvement in bloat reduction and, in some cases, more effectively searches for fitter solutions.

1 Introduction

A central component of genetic programming (GP) is the use of variable-length representations, which frees the end-user from completely constraining the structure of the problem prior to search [5]. A consequence of using variable-length representations is the phenomenon of bloat, which is best described as the tendency for programs evolved through GP to increase in size at a rate disproportionate to their increase in fitness. Managing bloat is therefore important for the successful application of GP to most problems. However, most solutions to the control of bloat require problem-specific calibration to achieve optimal performance, implying the need for *a priori* knowledge of the problem that may not be available. While there has been some work exploring generalised parameters for prominent bloat control methods [7], there remains a need for effective bloat control methods that do not require excessive problem-specific calibration. One such method is the recently proposed SS+E method, which uses a combination of spatial population structure and local elitist replacement to implicitly control bloat [18]. While the SS+E method has demonstrated useful bloat control properties, its elitist replacement scheme precludes individuals from entering the population when they present no change in fitness but possess a smaller program size. The goal of this paper is to explore a modification to SS+E that

K. Krawiec et al. (Eds.): EuroGP 2013, LNCS 7831, pp. 13–24, 2013.

incorporates lexicographic parsimony [6] into the replacement scheme, thereby allowing smaller individuals with equal fitness to enter the population. The results presented suggest a consistent reduction in program size over SS+E on a range of problems, without compromising the fitness of evolved programs. Indeed, on some problems, the evolved programs are in fact fitter using the revised replacement scheme.

The rest of the paper is structured as follows: §2 presents an overview of bloat and methods used to control code growth in GP; §3 outlines the SS+E model, and introduces the proposed method using lexicographic parsimony within replacement (SS+LPE); §4 discusses the empirical behaviour of the proposed method in relation to its counterparts; finally, §5 draws conclusions and proposes some directions for future work.

2   Bloat Control in Genetic Programming

Initial work on GP attempted to manage bloat by setting an upper bound on the depth of evolved trees [5], or applying a parsimony pressure that adjusts the fitness of individuals by a tradeoff between performance and size [5,19]. Subsequent research into GP has placed a strong emphasis on bloat, and a range of methods have been introduced to manage excessive code growth, including: treating fitness and size as a multi-objective optimisation [1]; applying explicit fitness penalties to above-average sized individuals [10]; analysing and simplifying individuals [13,17]; dynamically extending maximum tree depths in response to fitness [12]; and applying specific genetic operators to reduce the size of large individuals or maintain the size of children to parents [4]. A review and comparison of the most common methods is given in [7], while discussion on the causes of bloat may be found in [14] and the Field Guide to Genetic Programming [11].

2.1   Lexicographic Parsimony Pressure

Applying parsimony pressure in GP is typically achieved through parametric means, whereby fitness becomes a weighted combination of fitness and size. An exception to this is lexicographic parsimony [6], which views fitness as the primary consideration for comparison of individuals, and favours size only in the presence of equal fitness. Implementation of lexicographic parsimony is remarkably simple, and has been shown to provide effective bloat control in many problems. Additionally, lexicographic parsimony requires no parameters over standard GP, and so does not require calibration when applied to new problems.

Empirical analysis of lexicographic parsimony suggests that it provides strong bloat control when the search space presents discrete levels of fitness, upon which many different sized programs may reside. In this situation, the secondary objective of size is considered more frequently, promoting strong control over bloat.

However, in situations where the fitness levels of the search space are fine-grained, such as in symbolic regression, lexicographic parsimony is presented few opportunities to perform size comparisons, and so bloat is poorly controlled. Because of this, lexicographic parsimony is typically not recommended as a general purpose bloat control method [7].

3 Spatial Population Structure and Elitist Replacement

With the notable exception of lexicographic parsimony, bloat control methods typically require some form of problem-specific calibration to achieve good performance. A recent addition to the family of bloat control methods uses a combination of spatial population structure and local elitist replacement to implicitly control bloat [16]. This method, dubbed spatial structure with elitism (SS+E), is particularly interesting as it requires almost no problem-specific calibration beyond standard GP. SS+E has been shown to offer good bloat control in conjunction with strong search capabilities, with particularly good performance on symbolic regression. Recently, SS+E has also been shown to outperform other methods in a complex image analysis problem [18].

The general algorithm for SS+E is shown in Algorithm 1. The operators `InitialIndividual` and `Recombination` are the same as those used in standard GP. Other than the choice of topology, SS+E requires few design choices from the user to be applied to new problems. Previous work on SS+E adopted a torus structure as the basis for its implementation, as previous work has demonstrated the usefulness of this topology over a range of problem domains [3]. Through this topology, the `Neighbourhood` operator identifies the Moore neighbourhood (the eight surrounding locations, along with the current location) around a given location, and then `SelectParent` performs binary tournament selection (without replacement) within this neighbourhood. The operator `PickSurvivor` is used to determine which individual at the current location will pass onto the next generation. The default implementation of `PickSurvivor` (Algorithm 2) is very simple; an offspring is placed at a location under the condition that it is *strictly fitter* than the individual currently residing at that location.

3.1 Lexicographic Parsimonious Elitist Replacement

An important consequence of the default implementation of `PickSurvivor` is that the only trajectory for code growth is through a corresponding increase in fitness (as poor performing large offspring are rejected by the method). However, this implementation of `PickSurvivor` has one weakness in that it does not permit the entry of offspring into the population if they are equal in fitness but smaller than the current occupant. If such a mechanism were in place, then we could expect a direct size pressure to be applied to the population, potentially

Algorithm 1. The basic SS+E algorithm.
Input: A given problem, and a population structure defined by W
Output: A set of evolved candidate solutions to the problem
1: $population \leftarrow \{\}$
2: **for all** locations l in W **do**
3:    $population[l] \leftarrow$ InitialIndividual()
4: **end for**
5: **while** termination condition not met **do**
6:    $generation \leftarrow \{\}$
7:    **for all** locations l in W **do**
8:       $W_l \leftarrow$ Neighbourhood(l,W)
9:       $p_1 \leftarrow$ SelectParent($population,W_l$)
10:       $p_2 \leftarrow$ SelectParent($population,W_l$)
11:       $o \leftarrow$ Recombination(p_1,p_2)
12:       $generation[l] \leftarrow$ PickSurvivor($population[l]$, o)
13:    **end for**
14:    $population \leftarrow generation$
15: **end while**
16: **return** $population$

Algorithm 2. The standard PickSurvivor(c,o) algorithm for determining the program that is copied into the next generation for SS+E.
Input: Two programs, the current occupant c and the candidate replacement o
Output: The program that survives into the next generation
1: **if** Fitness(c) > Fitness(o) **then** //note: assuming minimisation of fitness
2:    **return** o
3: **else**
4:    **return** c
5: **end if**

Algorithm 3. The revised PickSurvivor(c,o) algorithm that incorporates lexicographic parsimony into the replacement process and defines SS+LPE.
Input: Two programs, the current occupant c and the candidate replacement o
Output: The program that survives into the next generation
1: **if** Fitness(c) > Fitness(o) **then**
2:    **return** o
3: **else if** Fitness(c) = Fitness(o) **and** Size(c) > Size(o) **then**
4:    **return** o
5: **else**
6:    **return** c
7: **end if**

improving the bloat control performance of SS+E. The resulting modification to PickSurvivor to achieve this is shown in Algorithm 3, where a secondary comparison of size is performed in the presence of equal fitness. This implementation is in essence an example of lexicographic parsimony, so we refer to this approach as spatial structure with lexicographic parsimonious elitism (SS+LPE).

4   Experiments and Results

To test the performance of SS+LPE, we compared its performance to that of canonical GP, GP using lexicographic parsimony, and SS+E on four benchmark problems used in previous bloat studies [7,16] — the Artificial Ant problem (using the Sante Fe trail), the 11-bit Boolean Multiplexer problem, the 5-bit Even Parity problem, and the Quartic symbolic regression problem. All test problems were run with the typical sets of functions and terminals as defined by Koza [5]. For our analysis, we consider four primary measurements: the fitness of the best individual in the population at each generation, the rate of successful runs against generations ("success" being where an optimal solution was discovered), the mean "effective" size of individuals within the population (that is, the mean number of executed nodes in an individual), and finally the mean "total" size of the individuals. Recent work suggests that measuring the success rate of an algorithm is not necessarily a good measure of performance [8], however we include it here to demonstrate some of the long-run characteristics of the tested algorithms. In §4.2, we explore the performance of the algorithms on problems in which we do not expect the system to find optimal solutions during any run.

The global parameter settings used across all test problems and algorithms are shown in Table 1. In line with recommendations of previous work [7], all the tested algorithms are augmented with tree depth limiting, even when a specific bloat control measure is used. The choice of a run length of 500 generations may seem odd, as it is greater than that used in typical GP tests. However, it has been adopted specifically to highlight some of the properties of the algorithms in long-duration runs. As shown in §4.1, the introduction of the bloat control methods alters the overall search characteristics in ways that may permit the effective use of longer runs.

Table 1. GP Parameter settings

Number of Runs	100
Population Size	500 for canonical GP and lexicographic parsimony, 484 (a 22 × 22 torus) for SS+E and SS+LPE
Initialisation	Ramped half-and-half (depth ranging from 2–6)
Depth Limit	17
Crossover Probability	0.9 for canonical GP and lexicographic parsimony, 1.0 for SS+E and SS+LPE
Mutation Probability	0.0
Max. Generations	500
Selection	Tournament (Size=7) for canonical GP and lexicographic parsimony, binary tournament (without replacement) for SS+E and SS+LPE

Each algorithm was applied to each problem 100 times and the values plotted in the next section are the mean observations of these runs. In the figures that follow, the shaded area around the plot represents the 95% confidence interval of the mean.

4.1   Results

The results of each algorithm applied to each of our four test problems is shown in Figs. 1–4. A general trend can be observed from these results: consistent with previous work SS+E is able to provide good search performance while providing a smaller overall program size than canonical GP. For all the considered bloat control methods, the greatest contributor to bloat control appears to be a reduction in non-executed (so-called "intron", or dormant) subtrees. The introduction of the revised elitism scheme in SS+LPE appears to offer an increased ability over SS+E to prune out these redundant subtrees, without introducing a reduction in fitness. Compared to straight lexicographic parsimony, SS+LPE typically produces slightly larger trees, but the comparison is not entirely straightforward as SS+LPE typically produces trees of greater fitness. The comparison of success rates across the four GP methods is particularly interesting; here, SS+LPE consistently produces the most runs in which an optimal solution is identified. In the case of the 11-bit Multiplexer problem, the number of successful runs using SS+LPE is almost twice that of the next best algorithm (SS+E).

Effect of Bloat Control on Search — Fitness Preserving Operations. The results presented suggest that the introduction of parsimony pressure alters the structure of the evolved trees so that they present fewer non-executed subtrees. This has a potentially useful side-effect: typical runs of standard GP are short, as the evolved trees rapidly gain significant portions of redundant code, so crossover tends to create large numbers of functionally-equivalent offspring, thus stagnating the search process. If the non-executed regions of trees are proactively reduced, then we can expect more function-modifying crossover and mutation to take place, meaning that the search of new regions of the search space can continue for longer. This, coupled with the elitist replacement of SS+LPE, may explain the long-run success of the SS+LPE approach.

To test this, we counted the number of crossover operations that took place within redundant subtrees for each algorithm on each problem. As such crossovers produced offspring that were functionally equivalent to their parents, this measure is referred to as a *fitness preserving operation* (FPO) count [2]. The measured FPO counts for each of the four problems is shown in Fig. 5; as anticipated, the methods using lexicographic parsimony are able to produce functionally-different offspring for longer periods, thus continuing the exploration of the search space. It would be expected that the majority of these functionally-different offspring would in fact be of lower fitness than their parents, but since SS+LPE does not allow these individuals to enter the population, then they should not impact negatively on the search. Essentially, SS+LPE can use this lower FPO count to take a "high-risk" approach to creating offspring in later generations and rely on elitist replacement to prevent poor performing individuals from entering the population.

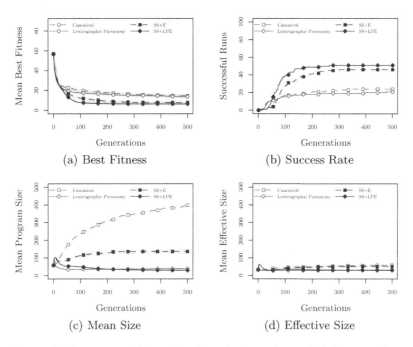

Fig. 1. Performance of the analysed methods on the artificial ant problem

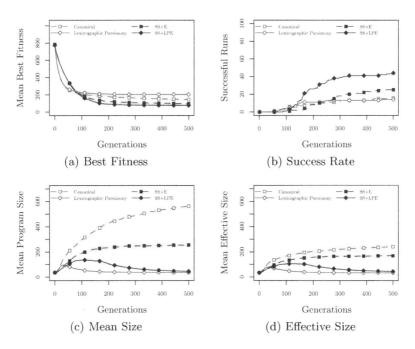

Fig. 2. Performance of the analysed methods on the 11-bit multiplexer problem

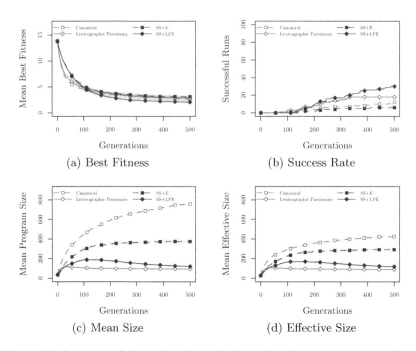

(a) Best Fitness

(b) Success Rate

(c) Mean Size

(d) Effective Size

Fig. 3. Performance of the analysed methods on the 5-bit even parity problem

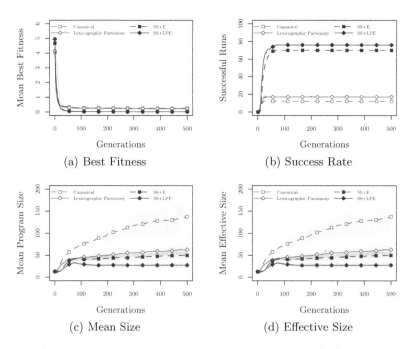

(a) Best Fitness

(b) Success Rate

(c) Mean Size

(d) Effective Size

Fig. 4. Performance of the analysed methods on the quartic symbolic regression problem

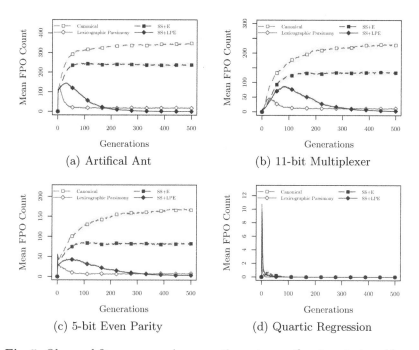

(a) Artifical Ant

(b) 11-bit Multiplexer

(c) 5-bit Even Parity

(d) Quartic Regression

Fig. 5. Observed fitness-preserving operation rates on the given test problems

4.2 Bloat Control on Difficult Problems

The four benchmark problems examined in this paper have a long-established use within GP analysis, dating back to Koza's initial work [5]. Although these benchmark problems offer insights into the different behaviour of the examined methods, they are in some ways trivial and may not reflect the behaviour of a given method on more difficult problems. Recent work has argued the case for testing GP systems on a greater range of problem difficulties [8]. In line with this view, we have tested the examined algorithms under two problems that present a somewhat greater challenge than that posed by our four benchmarks — the "Pagie 1" symbolic regression problem [8,9], and Teller's Tartarus path planning problem [15]. These problems were examined using the parameters outlined in Table 1, and were implemented as described in their respective works, with the exception that automatically-defined functions (ADFs) were not used in the Tartarus problem.

The results for these harder problems are shown in Figures 6 and 7. For both problems, direct comparisons of program size is difficult, as in each case the spatially-structured algorithms produced individuals of greater fitness than the non-spatial methods, but at the expense of greater program size than those produced using straight lexicographic parsimony. However, it is noted that SS+LPE was able to produce smaller programs with equivalent fitness to SS+E, suggesting that the introduction of parsimony into elitist replacement should help to further

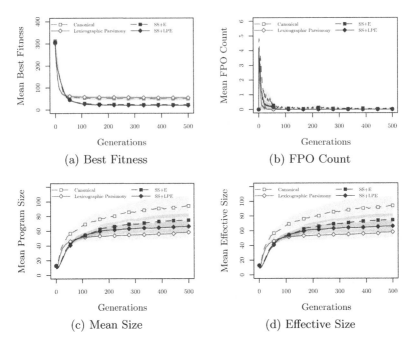

(a) Best Fitness

(b) FPO Count

(c) Mean Size

(d) Effective Size

Fig. 6. Performance of the analysed methods on the "Pagie 1" symbolic regression problem

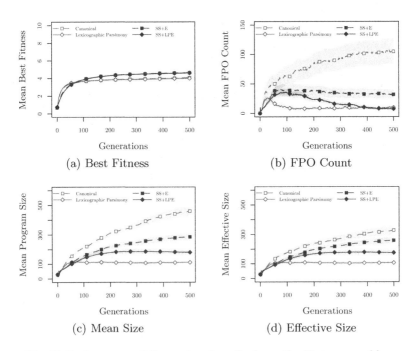

(a) Best Fitness

(b) FPO Count

(c) Mean Size

(d) Effective Size

Fig. 7. Performance of the analysed methods on the Tartarus problem

constrain program growth. It should also be noted that, on both problems, both SS+LPE and SS+E were able to evolve programs that were simultaneously fitter and smaller than those produced by canonical GP. It is also interesting that straight lexicographic parsimony was effective at controlling bloat on the "Pagie 1" problem, despite previous work suggesting that it would fail [6,7].

5   Conclusion and Future Work

Successfully controlling bloat remains an important issue for the application of genetic programming. The most desirable scenario is bloat control methods that do not require excessive calibration to the given problem, such as the recently proposed SS+E method. This paper introduces an extension to SS+E that introduces lexicographic parsimony pressure into the local elitist replacement scheme. This revised approach, dubbed SS+LPE, retains the effective search qualities of SS+E in terms of fitness, and offers an improved level of bloat control, while remaining essentially free of parameters. On the test problems examined, it discovered simultaneously fitter and smaller programs compared to standard GP. When compared to straight lexicographic parsimony, the programs evolved by SS+LPE are generally slightly larger, but this is offset by improved fitness. While testing on more problems is required, the evidence presented here suggests that SS+LPE is a good choice for general purpose GP work.

The results presented in this paper suggest that the introduction of bloat control methods alters the search trajectory to encourage the evolution of programs that present significantly smaller proportions of redundant code. In later generations, this means that crossover and mutation are more likely to take place in regions that will produce functionally-different offspring, meaning that these operators will continue to explore the search space for longer than GP without bloat control. Most analysis on bloat control appears to focus purely on program size, with an implied view that the overall characteristic of the evolved trees does not change. This work demonstrates that the ratio of effective to redundant code in trees is altered through the use of bloat control, suggesting substantial differences in the shapes of trees that are produced. Future work should examine this concept in more detail.

References

1. Bleuler, S., Brack, M., Thiele, L., Zitzler, E.: Multiobjective genetic programming: Reducing bloat using SPEA2. In: Proceedings of the 2001 Congress on Evolutionary Computation, CEC 2001, pp. 536–543. IEEE Press (2001)
2. Jackson, D.: The identification and exploitation of dormancy in genetic programming. Genetic Programming and Evolvable Machines 11, 89–121 (2010)
3. Jong, K.A.D., Sarma, J.: On decentralizing selection algorithms. In: Eshelman, L.J. (ed.) Proceedings of the 6th International Conference on Genetic Algorithms, pp. 17–23. Morgan Kaufmann Publishers Inc., San Francisco (1995)

4. Kennedy, C.J., Giraud-Carrier, C.: A depth controlling strategy for strongly typed evolutionary programming. In: Banzhaf, W., Daida, J., Eiben, A.E., Garzon, M.H., Honavar, V., Jakiela, M., Smith, R.E. (eds.) Proceedings of the Genetic and Evolutionary Computation Conference, July 13-17, vol. 1, pp. 879–885. Morgan Kaufmann, Orlando (1999)

5. Koza, J.R.: Genetic Programming: On the Programming of Computers by Natural Selection. MIT Press, Cambridge (1992)

6. Luke, S., Panait, L.: Lexicographic parsimony pressure. In: Langdon, W.B., et al. (eds.) Proceedings of the Fourth International Conference on Genetic and Evolutionary Computation, GECCO 2002, pp. 829–836. Morgan Kaufmann (2002)

7. Luke, S., Panait, L.: A comparison of bloat control methods for genetic programming. Evolutionary Computation 14(3), 309–344 (2006)

8. McDermott, J., White, D.R., Luke, S., Manzoni, L., Castelli, M., Vanneschi, L., Jaskowski, W., Krawiec, K., Harper, R., De Jong, K., O'Reilly, U.M.: Genetic programming needs better benchmarks. In: Proceedings of the Fourteenth International Conference on Genetic and Evolutionary Computation, GECCO 2012, pp. 791–798. ACM, New York (2012)

9. Pagie, L., Hogeweg, P.: Evolutionary consequences of coevolving targets. Evolutionary Computation 5(4), 401–418 (1997)

10. Poli, R.: A Simple but Theoretically-Motivated Method to Control Bloat in Genetic Programming. In: Ryan, C., Soule, T., Keijzer, M., Tsang, E., Poli, R., Costa, E. (eds.) EuroGP 2003. LNCS, vol. 2610, pp. 204–217. Springer, Heidelberg (2003)

11. Poli, R., Langdon, W.B., McPhee, N.F.: A Field Guild to Genetic Programming, pp. 102–103. Lulu.com (2008)

12. Silva, S., Almeida, J.: Dynamic Maximum Tree Depth: A Simple Technique for Avoiding Bloat in Tree-Based GP. In: Cantú-Paz, E., Foster, J.A., Deb, K., Davis, D., Roy, R., O'Reilly, U.M., Beyer, H.G., Standish, R., Kendall, G., Wilson, S., Harman, M., Wegener, J., Dasgupta, D., Potter, M.A., Schultz, A.C., Dowsland, K., Jonoska, N., Miller, J. (eds.) GECCO 2003. LNCS, vol. 2724, pp. 1776–1787. Springer, Heidelberg (2003)

13. Soule, T., Foster, J., Dickinson, J.: Code growth in genetic programming. In: Koza, J., Goldberg, D., Fogel, D., Riolo, R. (eds.) Genetic Programming 1996: Proceedings of the First Annual Conference, pp. 215–223. MIT Press, Stanford University (1996)

14. Soule, T., Heckendorn, R.: An analysis of the causes of code growth in genetic programming. Genetic Programming and Evolvable Machines 3(3), 283–309 (2002)

15. Teller, A.: The evolution of mental models. In: Kinnear Jr., K.E. (ed.) Advances in Genetic Programming, ch. 9, pp. 199–217. MIT Press (1994)

16. Whigham, P.A., Dick, G.: Implicitly controlling bloat in genetic programming. IEEE Transactions on Evolutionary Computation 14(2), 173–190 (2010)

17. Wong, P., Zhang, M.: Algebraic simplification of GP programs during evolution. In: Proceedings of the Eighth International Conference on Genetic and Evolutionary Computation, GECCO 2006, pp. 927–934. ACM Press, Seattle (2006)

18. Yamaguchi, H., Hiroyasu, T., Nunokawa, S., Koizumi, N., Okumura, N., Yokouchi, H., Miki, M., Yoshimi, M.: Comparison study of controlling bloat model of GP in constructing filter for cell image segmentation problems. In: 2012 IEEE Congress on Evolutionary Computation, CEC, pp. 3468–3475 (2012)

19. Zhang, B.T., Mühlenbein, H.: Balancing accuracy and parsimony in genetic programming. Evolutionary Computation 3(1), 17–38 (1995)

Generation of VNS Components
with Grammatical Evolution for Vehicle Routing

John H. Drake, Nikolaos Kililis, and Ender Özcan

School of Computer Science, University of Nottingham
Jubilee Campus, Wollaton Road, Nottingham, NG8 1BB, UK
{psxjd2,nxk09u,ender.ozcan}@nottingham.ac.uk

Abstract. The vehicle routing problem (VRP) is a family of problems whereby a fleet of vehicles must service the commodity demands of a set of geographically scattered customers from one or more depots, subject to a number of constraints. Early hyper-heuristic research focussed on selecting and applying a low-level heuristic at a given stage of an optimisation process. Recent trends have led to a number of approaches being developed to automatically generate heuristics for a number of combinatorial optimisation problems. Previous work on the VRP has shown that the application of hyper-heuristic approaches can yield successful results. In this paper we investigate the potential of grammatical evolution as a method to evolve the components of a variable neighbourhood search (VNS) framework. In particular two components are generated; constructive heuristics to create initial solutions and neighbourhood move operators to change the state of a given solution. The proposed method is tested on standard benchmark instances of two common VRP variants.

1 Introduction

Optimisation problems often explore a search space which is too large to enumerate and exhaustively search for an optimal solution. Various heuristics and meta-heuristics have been successfully applied to such problems. One drawback of such approaches is the necessity to manually adapt the method used to solve different problem domains or classes of problem. Hyper-heuristics are a class of high-level search techniques which automate the heuristic design process and aim to raise the level of generality at which search methods operate [31]. Hyper-heuristics are broadly split into two main categories, those which select a low-level heuristic to apply at a given point in a search and those which create new heuristics from a set of low level components [5]. Here we are concerned with the second category, those methodologies which generate new heuristics. Whilst most research effort in this field has been on developing heuristics which construct a solution from scratch, a less studied area is the generation of perturbative or local search heuristics. Genetic Programming (GP) [23] has been widely used in the literature to generate heuristics for strip packing [7], bin packing [9, 11, 8], job shop scheduling [18], knapsack problems [24] and boolean

K. Krawiec et al. (Eds.): EuroGP 2013, LNCS 7831, pp. 25–36, 2013.
© Springer-Verlag Berlin Heidelberg 2013

satisfiability [2, 14–16]. Grammatical Evolution [27] is a grammar-based variation of GP which has been used to automatically design local search heuristics for bin packing and stock cutting problems. The vehicle routing problem (VRP) is an NP-Complete [17] combinatorial optimisation problem, which requires the determination of the optimal set of routes to be followed by a fleet of vehicles in order to service the commodity demands of a set of customers. Previously, hyper-heuristic methods [28] have shown to perform particularly well on a number of variants of the VRP. In this paper we explore the potential of grammatical evolution as a method to generate both constructive and perturbative heuristics for the VRP and embed these ideas in a variable neighbourhood search (VNS) framework.

2   Hyper-heuristics

The underlying principles of hyper-heuristics were used as early as the 1960's in the work of Fisher and Thompson [13], where combining job-shop scheduling rules by selecting an appropriate rule for the given state of a problem was shown to outperform using each of the rules individually. The term was first used in the field of combinatorial optimisation by Cowling et al. [12] defining hyper-heuristics as *heuristics to choose heuristics*. Unlike traditional computational search methods which operate directly on a search space of solutions, hyper-heuristics operate exclusively on a search space of heuristics or heuristic components. Burke et al. [5, 4] define a hyper-heuristic as *a search method or learning mechanism for selecting or generating heuristics to solve computational search problem*. This definition distinguishes between the two main classes of hyper-heuristics, those which intelligently select a heuristic to apply to a problem and those which are concerned with automatically generating new heuristics.

The automated generation of heuristics is a relatively new field attracting an increasing amount of attention. Genetic Programming (GP) has been successfully used to evolve heuristics for a wide range of problems. In genetic programming, populations of computer programs are evolved using the naturally inspired notions of inheritance, selection and variation. Unlike Genetic Algorithms which produce fixed-length encoded representations of candidate solutions to a given problem, the evolved program itself when executed is the solution. Geiger et al. [18] used GP to evolve dispatching rules for a job shop scheduling problem. Burke et al. create heuristics for for strip packing [7] and bin packing problems [9, 11, 8] with human-competitive results. Bader-El-Din and Poli [2] also used GP to quickly generate 'disposable' heuristics for the satisfiability problem generating heuristics again with comparable performance to human-designed methods. Fukunaga [14–16] also used GP to generate local search heuristics for boolean satisfiability. Drake et al. [20] managed a constructive heuristic by using GP to evolve the order in which to add items to a knapsack solving the MKP. Further information on using genetic programming as a hyper-heuristic is provided by Burke et al. [6].

3   Grammatical Evolution

Grammatical Evolution (GE) [27] is a recently developed grammar-based form of genetic programming. The evolutionary process in a grammatical evolution system is performed on binary or decimal integer strings of variable length rather than on actual programs. Such strings are then mapped to a sentence (in our case a program) using the production rules of a grammar expressed in BNF (Backus Naur Form). Unlike GP, GE provides a distinction between the genotype and phenotype as is the case in nature. In GE the search process is performed over the genotype (a binary or decimal integer string) and the fitness function evaluates the program (the phenotype) which is obtained. There are a number of advantages to approaching the search process in this way. Any strategy that operates on binary strings can be used to perform the search, this is not strictly limited to evolutionary approaches. The search is also not limited by tree structure and the need to ensure solutions are valid. Within the BNF notation a possible production rule can be defined as:

   <symbolA> ::= <symbolB> | (symbolC)

In the example above, <symbolA> is a non-terminal which expands to either <symbolB> or (symbolC). <symbolB> is also a non-terminal, while (symbolC) is a terminal symbol indicated by brackets. The process typically starts with a single non-terminal start symbol and a set of production rules that define with which symbols this non-terminal can be replaced. A sentence can consist of any number of non-terminal and terminal symbols. Terminals are atomic components of a sentence containing no production rules as they will not be replaced. Each non-terminal is replaced with any non-terminal symbols produced subsequently replaced using their own corresponding production rules. Often there are multiple production rules to replace the current non-terminal symbol in question and a number of choices for terminal symbols. In order to select a production rule at a given point the variable length binary or decimal integer string representing the genotype in the GE system is used. In the case of a binary string, the genome is split into 8-bit portions known as codons. The integer value of a single codon can then take any value between 0 and 255. If the genotype is represented directly as a decimal integer string then this conversion is unnecessary. Each codon is used with the grammar to decide which choice to make when replacing a non-terminal symbol using a given production rule. The first codon is used to select which of the production rules will replace the first non-terminal symbol. This is done by calculating the value of the codon *modulus* the number of production rules to choose from. As an example, for a codon with value 43 given 6 production rules, production rule 1 is chosen (note that the first production rule is at index 0) as 43 *mod* 6 is 1. If this production rule creates a sentence containing further non-terminal symbols the second codon is used to select the production rule for the first non-terminal set in the new sentence. This process is continued until the sentence is made up of only terminal symbols and the mapping process is complete. In this study, the sentences produced take the form of Java code representing portions of low-level heuristics. A more detailed explanation of a GE system is provided by O'Neill and Ryan [27].

Recently, Burke et al. [10] have used Grammatical Evolution to generate low-level heuristics for bin packing. This paper generates heuristics which can consistently obtain solutions which use only one bin more than the optimal lower bound and often the optimal number of bins itself. GE was also seen to be suitably flexible enough to generate different move operators for different classes of bin packing problems as appropriate. Keller and Poli [21, 22] also use a grammar-based genetic programming system to evolve solvers for the travelling salesman problem.

4   Vehicle Routing Problems

The vehicle routing problem (VRP) is an NP-Complete [17] combinatorial optimisation problem where a number of customers are to be serviced by a fleet of vehicles subject to a number of constraints. Different objectives can be considered depending on the goal of the problem. Typical objectives include; minimisation of cost with respect to distance travelled, minimisation of the global travel time, minimisation of the number of vehicles required to service all customers, minimisation of the penalty costs associated with partial service of customers. The objective could also be a weighted combination of such objectives. Real-world commodity distribution in logistics is a complex problem with constrains varying depending on the application. It is therefore natural that many different variants of the VRP exist, each simplifying the problem to a smaller set of constraints which impose the most important restrictions in each specific application of the problem. A large number of exact [25, 33] and meta-heuristic [19, 3] methods have been applied in the literature to solve such problems.

Recently there has been an increasing gain of emphasis on solution methods which operate across different VRP variants. One of the state-of-the-art results obtained by such unified heuristics is the hyper-heuristic approach of Pisinger and Ropke [28]. This work is based on the Adaptive Large Neighbourhood Search (ALNS) framework initially presented by Ropke and Pisinger [30]. The proposed framework is a selection hyper-heuristic which when given a complete solution, traverses the search space through the application of heuristics which remove a number of requests from the solution and subsequently, heuristics to re-insert the removed requests. The selection of the next removal or insertion heuristic to use is based on statistical information gathered during the search. This work also provided a unified model for the VRP allowing five VRP variants to be tested following transformation to the Rich Pickup and Delivery Problem with Time Windows (RPDPTW). Here we will use this model to test our method on the two best known VRP variants. The first is the vehicle routing problem with time windows (VRPTW), this problem requires a number of deliveries to be made at different locations with the added constraint that each delivery has a specific a period (window) of time within which it must take place. The second variant is the capacitated vehicle routing problem (CVRP). In the CVRP, each vehicle in the fleet has the restriction of a limited carrying capacity which must be respected in order to obtain a valid solution.

5   Grammatical Evolution Hyper-heuristics for the VRP

Variable Neighbourhood Search (VNS) [26] is a well studied meta-heuristic methodology for global optimisation. A basic VNS algorithm is outlined in Algorithm 1.

Algorithm 1. Outline of a standard VNS algorithm

N: set of k neighbourhood structures, $\{N_1, N_2,...,N_k\}$;
f: solution evaluation function (minimisation);
$x \leftarrow$ Construct initial solution;
repeat
  $k \leftarrow 1$;
  repeat
    Shaking: $x' \leftarrow$ new point in neighbourhood $N_k(x)$;
    Local Search: $x'' \leftarrow$ result of local search from x';
    if $f(x'') < f(x)$ **then**
      $x \leftarrow x''$;
      $k \leftarrow 1$;
    else
      $k \leftarrow k + 1$;
    until $k = kmax$;
until *stopping criteria met*;

Operating on a complete solution initialised using a chosen method, VNS explores increasingly distant neighbours of the current solution using a predefined set of neighbourhood move operators. This process is known as 'shaking'. Following this, local search is performed to reach a local optimum from the point reached by the shaking procedure. The incumbent solution is replaced by a solution generated by a given neighbourhood move and subsequent local search if such a move will yields improvement in solution quality. This can be considered as a random descent, first improvement method. In the case where an improved solution is not found, the size of neighbourhood move is increased, thus effectively changing the neighbourhood structure used. This ensures the search is diversified sufficiently by performing increasingly larger neighbourhood moves in order to reach more promising areas of the search space when stuck in local optima.

Within this framework we will use grammatical evolution to generate the construction heuristic initialising a solution and ruin and insertion heuristics to perform the shaking procedure. Essentially we will evolve the order in which nodes are inserted into and removed from a solution through the use of a grammar. The grammar used is outlined in Figure 1. From the starting symbol <S>, three heuristic components are evolved using a single genome to select production rules. The set of terminal functions representing information fields which must be retrieved from the current solution state is shown in Table 1. Some of the information fields are not used by some problem variants and will contain null values however it is still important to include such fields to enable the hyper-heuristic to generate heuristics across a broader class of routing problems. Those symbols prefixed 'rqi-' correspond to information about individual requests whilst those prefixed 'rti-' correspond to information information about a route.

```
                         <S> ::= <InitialSolution> <Ruin> <Recreate>
            <InitialSolution> ::= <Recreate> | (empty-solution)
                  <Recreate> ::= <RecreateOrdered> | <RecreateStepwise>
           <RecreateOrdered> ::= <RequestFieldOp> <Order>
          <RecreateStepwise> ::= <Steps> <StepEnd>
                      <Ruin> ::= <RuinOrdered> | <RuinConditional> | <RequestSelection>
               <RuinOrdered> ::= <RouteSelectionLength> <RouteFieldOp> <Order> <RequestSelection>
           <RuinConditional> ::= <RouteFieldOp> <RelationalOp> <RouteFieldOp> <RequestSelection>
          <RequestSelection> ::= <RequestSelectionOrdered> | <RequestSelectionConditional>
   <RequestSelectionOrdered> ::= <RequestFieldOp> <Order>
<RequestSelectionConditional> ::= <RequestFieldOp> <RelationalOp> <RequestFieldOp>
       <RouteSelectionLength> ::= (numroutes-RC) | (percentage-RC)
                        <op> ::= (add) | (sub) | (mul) | (div) | <MaxMin>
                     <Steps> ::= <NextStep> <Steps> | <NextStep>
                  <NextStep> ::= <MaxMin> <RequestFieldOp>
                    <MaxMin> ::= (max) | (min)
                   <StepEnd> ::= (step-cycle) | (repeat-last)
              <RouteFieldOp> ::= <op> <RouteFieldOp> <RouteFieldOp> | <RouteField>
                <RouteField> ::= (rti-iuc) | (rti-d) | (rti-rc)
            <RequestFieldOp> ::= <op> <RequestFieldOp> <RequestFieldOp> | <RequestField>
              <RequestField> ::= (rqi-d) | (rqi-pat) | (rqi-pdt) | (rqi-puc) | (rqi-dat) | (rqi-ddt) |
                                 (rqi-duc) | (rqi-prc) |(rqi-drc) | (rqi-pwt) | (rqi-pindx) |
                                 (rqi-dwt) | (rqi-dindx) | (rqi-pst) | (rqi-ptws) | (rqi-ptwe) |
                                 (rqi-pprevd) | (rqi-pnextd) | (rqi-dst) | (rqi-dtws) | (rqi-dtwe) |
                                 (rqi-dprevd) | (rqi-dnextd)
                     <Order> ::= (ascending) | (descending)
              <RelationalOp> ::= (lt) | (gt) | (lte) | (gte) | (eq) | (neq)
```

Fig. 1. The grammar defining the components and structure of the heuristics

A standard set of non-terminal symbols is used to represent a number of basic binary arithmetic and relational operators shown in Table 2. Instead of the traditional divide function here we use protected divide. As there is always a possibility that the denominator could be zero, protected divide replaces zero with 0.001. In the case of relational operators the comparison is always made from left to right.

The constructive component of the heuristic constructs an initial feasible solution from an empty solution, it is also possible to leave the initial solution empty. The recreate component works in much the same way without the option of leaving the solution empty. Following the RPDPTW model unallocated requests are permitted however they are associated with a high penalty cost. Two methods for selecting the next request to insert are used, ordered and stepwise. *Ordered selection* uses a component composed of binary arithmetic operators and solution state information to rank each unallocated request. The order in which requests are inserted into the solution is derived from this ranking with the direction in which requests are considered determined by one of two terminal symbols, (ascending) and (descending). *Stepwise selection* evolves a sequence of

Table 1. Set of terminal symbols which correspond to information request and route information within a solution

Symbol	Description
rqi-d	Commodity demand of a request
rqi-pat	Arrival time of the vehicle at the pickup node
rqi-pdt	Departure time of the vehicle at the pickup node
rqi-puc	Used vehicle capacity when leaving the pickup node
rqi-dat	Arrival time of the vehicle at the delivery node
rqi-ddt	Departure time of the vehicle at the delivery node
rqi-duc	Used vehicle capacity when leaving the delivery node
rqi-prc	Residual vehicle capacity when leaving the pickup node
rqi-drc	Residual vehicle capacity when leaving the delivery node
rqi-pwt	Time the vehicle must wait at the pickup node
rqi-pindx	The visit index of the pickup node within the route
rqi-dwt	Time the vehicle must wait at the delivery node
rqi-dindx	The visit index of the delivery node within the route
rqi-pst	Service time of the pickup node of the request
rqi-ptws	Opening time of the pickup node time window
rqi-ptwe	Closing time of the pickup node time window
rqi-pprevd	Distance between pickup node and previous node within the route
rqi-pnextd	Distance between the pickup and following node within the route
rqi-dst	Service time of the delivery node of the request
rqi-dtws	Opening time of the delivery node time window
rqi-dtwe	Closing time of the delivery node time window
rqi-dprevd	Distance between the delivery and previous node within the route
rqi-dnextd	Distance between the delivery and following node within the route
rti-iuc	The used capacity when vehicle leaves depot
rti-irc	The residual capacity when vehicle leaves depot
rti-d	Total distance of route

Table 2. Set of non-terminals which represent binary arithmetic and relational operators

Symbol	Description
add	Add two inputs
sub	Subtract second input from first input
mul	Multiply two inputs
div	Protected divide function
max	Maximum value between two inputs
min	Minimum value between two inputs
lt	Less than ($<$)
gt	Greater than ($>$)
lte	Less than or equal to ($\leq$)
gte	Greater than or equal ($\geq$)
eq	Equal
neq	Not equal

different criteria to use at each 'step' when considering which request to insert. If the number of potential requests to insert is greater than the number of selection steps defined one of two options are available, (step-cycle) will return to the first step and cycle through the sequence of criteria again and (repeat-last) will re-use the last criteria in the sequence until all requests are inserted.

As the ruin phase works with a complete solution, selecting the routes from which to remove requests is not a trivial decision. A simple solution is to allow requests to be removed from any route however here we also allow the heuristic to evolve a subset of routes from which to choose. The number of routes to be selected is one of two random constants, either a number between 1 and the total number of routes (numroutes-RC) or a number between 0 and 1 representing the percentage of routes to be selected (percentage-RC). The order in which a subset of routes are considered is either ordered or conditional. *Conditional selection* iterates over the complete set of routes and returns a subset of routes which satisfy a condition set by a criteria evolved in the grammar. If number of routes selected is less than the number specified by the random constant, the remaining routes are selected randomly. The ruin heuristic is parametric with the number of requests to remove determined by the value of k taken from the overall VNS framework. Once the routes are selected the order in which requests are removed must be defined. Two methods for selecting the next request to remove are used, ordered selection as defined previously and conditional selection (as with the selection of routes however the iteration is performed over requests rather than routes). In the case of conditional selection, if less than k requests are selected using the evolved condition the remaining requests are removed randomly.

The parameters of the VNS search algorithm in which the generated construction, ruin and insertion heuristics operate, are set to initial $k = 1$, maximum $k = 30$ with k increased by 1 for each non-improving step. k is reset to 1 when an improving move is made. The local search used is a hill-climber which removes a request from an existing route, and relocates it to a different route so that the best improvement was achieved. Finally the stopping criterion used was 10 consecutive iterations of non-improvement after 30 non-improving steps. All experiments were performed in an offline manner i.e. a separate run of the GE system is performed on each individual instance. The parameters used in the GE runs are summarised in Table 3.

Table 3. Summary of Grammatical Evolution Parameters

Parameter	Value
Generations	50
Population Size	1024
Crossover Probability	0.9
Mutation Probability	0.05
Reproduction Probability	0.05
Maximum Tree Depth	17
Selection Method	Tournament Selection, size 7

6   Results

Table 4 shows the results of the GE hyper-heuristic (GE-PHH) on the first 10 instances for the CVRP from Augerat et al. [1][1]. These instances contain either 5 or 6 vehicles and between 31 and 38 customers. The optimal solution is known for all of these instances and has been obtained by a number of methods in the literature [29]. 'Proximity' is calculated as *Optimal Value/Result Obtained*. To make some assessment of the generality of our method, experiments are also performed on instances taken from Solomon [32] with results shown in Table 5. There are three types of instance in this set; 'R' instances contain customers whose geographic locations have been randomly generated, 'C' instances comprise of clusters of customers and 'RC' instances consist of a mixture of both types of customers.

Table 4. Results of GE-PHH on the first 10 instances of Augerat et al. [1]

Instance Name	Optimal Value	GE-PHH (Vehicles)	Proximity
A-n32-k5	784	811.80 (5)	0.97
A-n33-k5	661	664.79 (5)	0.99
A-n33-k6	742	785.45 (6)	0.94
A-n34-k5	778	828.01 (5)	0.94
A-n36-k5	799	849.22 (5)	0.94
A-n37-k5	669	678.92 (5)	0.99
A-n37-k6	949	1020.06 (6)	0.93
A-n38-k5	730	826.83 (5)	0.88
A-n39-k5	822	905.23 (5)	0.91
A-n39-k6	831	838.75 (6)	0.99
Average			0.95

Table 5. Results of GE-PHH on a selection of instances from Solomon [32]

Instance Name	Optimal Value	GE-PHH (Vehicles)	Proximity
C101.100	827.3	902.64716 (10)	0.92
C102.100	827.3	1198.97254 (10)	0.69
R101.100	1637.7	1766.807 (20)	0.93
R102.100	1466.6	1596.96749 (18)	0.92
RC101.100	1619.8	1871.2241 (15)	0.87
RC102.100	1457.4	1771.4629 (14)	0.82
Average			0.86

In all cases the best solutions obtained for each instance use the optimal number of vehicles. From these results we can see that the generated heuristics are able to reach promising regions of the search space however this does not

---

[1] These instances and optimal solutions were taken from
www.coin-or.org/SYMPHONY/branchandcut/VRP/data/index.htm

necessarily lead to global optima. This limitation may be due to the nature of the local search operator used. As the local search only considers moving a request from one route to another. In some near optimal solutions requests must be exchanged within a single route to reach the global optimum. We observe that the application of the system on VRPTW does not seem to produce as high quality results as for the CVRP. This could be due to the set of components not being well suited to cover the temporal requirements of time window related problems. The system performs particularly poorly on the 'C102.100' instance having a negative impact on the average proximity.

7   Conclusions and Future Work

In this preliminary work we have shown that grammatical evolution shows potential as a hyper-heuristic to generate components of a VNS system to solve the VRP. This method is defined as a hyper-heuristic as it operates on a search space of heuristics rather than directly on a search space of solutions. To our knowledge, this is the first time in literature a GE hyper-heuristic has been used to solve the vehicle routing problem. This method has shown that automatically generating heuristics for the VRP could be an interesting future research direction. We are currently working on evolving each of the components in isolation rather than using a single genome and grammar to evolve the whole system. As mentioned in the previous section this method was restricted somewhat by the choice of local search operator. There are a large number of operators in the literature for the travelling salesman problem (TSP) which could be implemented to also allow request swaps within a route. There are also a variety of standard construction heuristics for the VRP in the literature. These could replace the constructive phase of our method leaving the focus on evolving the ruin and recreate heuristics within the VNS framework.

References

1. Augerat, P., Rinaldi, G., Belenguer, J., Benavent, E., Corberan, A., Naddef, D.: Computational results with a branch and cut code for the capacitated vehicle routing problem. Tech. rep., RR 949-M, Universite Joseph Fourier, Grenoble (1995)
2. Bader-El-Den, M., Poli, R.: Generating SAT Local-Search Heuristics Using a GP Hyper-Heuristic Framework. In: Monmarché, N., Talbi, E.-G., Collet, P., Schoenauer, M., Lutton, E. (eds.) EA 2007. LNCS, vol. 4926, pp. 37–49. Springer, Heidelberg (2008)
3. Bräysy, O., Gendreau, M.: Vehicle routing problem with time windows, part ii: Metaheuristics. Transportation Science 39(1), 119–139 (2005)
4. Burke, E.K., Hyde, M., Kendall, G., Ochoa, G., Özcan, E., Qu, R.: Hyper-heuristics: A survey of the state of the art. Tech. Rep. No. NOTTCS-TR-SUB-0906241418-2747, School of Computer Science and Information Technology, University of Nottingham (2010)
5. Burke, E.K., Hyde, M., Kendall, G., Ochoa, G., Özcan, E., Woodward, J.: A Classification of Hyper-heuristics Approaches. In: Handbook of Metaheuristics, 2nd edn., pp. 449–468. Springer (2010)

6. Burke, E.K., Hyde, M.R., Kendall, G., Ochoa, G., Ozcan, E., Woodward, J.R.: Exploring Hyper-heuristic Methodologies with Genetic Programming. In: Mumford, C.L., Jain, L.C. (eds.) Computational Intelligence. ISRL, vol. 1, pp. 177–201. Springer, Heidelberg (2009)
7. Burke, E.K., Hyde, M., Kendall, G., Woodward, J.: A genetic programming hyper-heuristic approach for evolving 2-d strip packing heuristics. IEEE Transactions on Evolutionary Computation 14(6), 942–958 (2010)
8. Burke, E.K., Hyde, M., Kendall, G., Woodward, J.: Automating the packing heuristic design process with genetic programming. Evolutionary Computation 20(1), 63–89 (2012)
9. Burke, E.K., Hyde, M.R., Kendall, G.: Evolving Bin Packing Heuristics with Genetic Programming. In: Runarsson, T.P., Beyer, H.-G., Burke, E.K., Merelo-Guervós, J.J., Whitley, L.D., Yao, X. (eds.) PPSN 2006. LNCS, vol. 4193, pp. 860–869. Springer, Heidelberg (2006)
10. Burke, E.K., Hyde, M.R., Kendall, G.: Grammatical evolution of local search heuristics. IEEE Transactions on Evolutionary Computation 16(3), 406–417 (2012)
11. Burke, E.K., Woodward, J., Hyde, M., Kendall, G.: Automatic heuristic generation with genetic programming: Evolving a jack-of-alltrades or a master of one. In: GECCO 2007, pp. 1559–1565 (2007)
12. Cowling, P.I., Kendall, G., Soubeiga, E.: A Hyperheuristic Approach to Scheduling a Sales Summit. In: Burke, E., Erben, W. (eds.) PATAT 2000. LNCS, vol. 2079, pp. 176–190. Springer, Heidelberg (2001)
13. Fisher, M., Thompson, G.: Probabilistic learning combinations of local job-shop scheduling rules. In: Factory Scheduling Conference (1961)
14. Fukunaga, A.S.: Automated discovery of composite sat variable-selection heuristics. In: Artificial Intelligence, pp. 641–648 (2002)
15. Fukunaga, A.S.: Evolving Local Search Heuristics for SAT Using Genetic Programming. In: Deb, K., Tari, Z. (eds.) GECCO 2004. LNCS, vol. 3103, pp. 483–494. Springer, Heidelberg (2004)
16. Fukunaga, A.S.: Automated discovery of local search heuristics for satisfiability testing. Evolutionary Computation 16(1), 31–61 (2008)
17. Garey, M.R., Johnson, D.S.: Computers and Intractability: A Guide to the Theory of NP-Completeness. W. H. Freeman & Co., New York (1979)
18. Geiger, C.D., Uzsoy, R., Aytug, H.: Rapid modeling and discovery of priority dispatching rules: An autonomous learning approach. Journal of Scheduling 9(1), 7–34 (2006)
19. Cordeau, J.-F., Gendreau, M., Laporte, G., Potvin, J.-Y., Semet, F.: A guide to vehicle routing heuristics. The Journal of the Operational Research Society 53(5), 512–522 (2002)
20. Drake, J.H., Hyde, M., Ibrahim, K., Özcan, E.: A genetic programming hyper-heuristic for the multidimensional knapsack problem. In: CIS 2012, pp. 76–80 (2012)
21. Keller, R.E., Poli, R.: Linear genetic programming of metaheuristics. In: GECCO 2007, p. 1753. ACM (2007)
22. Keller, R.E., Poli, R.: Linear genetic programming of parsimonious metaheuristics. In: CEC 2007, pp. 4508–4515 (2007)
23. Koza, J.R.: Genetic programming: on the programming of computers by means of natural selection. The MIT Press, Cambridge (1992)
24. Kumar, R., Joshi, A.H., Banka, K.K., Rockett, P.I.: Evolution of hyperheuristics for the biobjective 0/1 knapsack problem by multiobjective genetic programming. In: GECCO 2008, pp. 1227–1234. ACM (2008)

25. Laporte, G.: The vehicle routing problem: An overview of exact and approximate algorithms. European Journal of Operational Research 59(3), 345–358 (1992)
26. Mladenovic, N., Hansen, P.: Variable neighborhood search. Computers and Operations Research 24(1), 1097–1100 (1997)
27. O'Neill, M., Ryan, C.: Grammatical Evolution: Evolutionary Automatic Programming in a Arbitrary Language, Genetic programming, vol. 4. Kluwer Academic Publishers (2003)
28. Pisinger, D., Ropke, S.: A general heuristic for vehicle routing problems. Computers and Operations Research 34(8), 2403–2435 (2007)
29. Ralphs, T., Kopman, L., Pulleyblank, W., Trotter Jr., L.: On the capacitated vehicle routing problem. Mathematical Programming Series B 94, 343–359 (2003)
30. Ropke, S., Pisinger, D.: An adaptive large neighborhood search heuristic for the pickup and delivery problem with time windows. Transportation Science 40(4), 455–472 (2006)
31. Ross, P.: Hyper-heuristics. In: Burke, E.K., Kendall, G. (eds.) Search Methodologies: Intrd. Tut. in Optimization and Decision Support Tec., ch. 17, pp. 529–556. Springer (2005)
32. Solomon, M.M.: Algorithms for the vehicle routing and scheduling problems with time window constraints. Operations Research 35(2), 254–265 (1987)
33. Toth, P., Vigo, D.: Models, relaxations and exact approaches for the capacitated vehicle routing problem. Discrete Applied Mathematics 123(1-3), 487–512 (2002)

Understanding Expansion Order and Phenotypic Connectivity in πGE

David Fagan[1], Erik Hemberg[2], Michael O'Neill[1], and Sean McGarraghy[1]

[1] Natural Computing Research & Applications Group
University College Dublin, Ireland
[2] MIT CSAIL
{david.fagan,m.oneill,sean.mcgarraghy}@ucd.ie, hembergerik@csail.mit.edu

Abstract. Since its inception, πGE has used evolution to guide the order of how to construct derivation trees. It was hypothesised that this would allow evolution to adjust the order of expansion during the run and thus help with search. This research aims to identify if a specific order is reachable, how reachable it may be, and goes on to investigate what happens to the expansion order during a πGE run. It is concluded that within πGE we do not evolve towards a specific order but a rather distribution of orders. The added complexity that an evolvable order gives πGE can make it difficult to understand how it can effectively search, by examining the connectivity of the phenotypic landscape it is hoped to understand this. It is concluded that the addition of an evolvable derivation tree expansion order makes the phenotypic landscape associated with πGE very densely connected, with solutions now linked via a single mutation event that were not previously connected.

1 Introduction

Position Independent Grammatical Evolution[11], or πGE, has been shown to exhibit performance on a par with and in many cases exceeds the performance of Grammatical Evolution (GE)[13] on a wide range of problem domains[2,3,5,11]. πGE is an extension of GE where the order of expansion of the derivation tree is controlled by evolution. It was proposed that this added dimension to the standard GE genotype-phenotype map would allow for search to be performed in the derivation order space of solutions, overcoming the left-most expansion bias exhibited by GE[6].

While there have been many papers dealing with πGE[2,3,5,11], this paper presents the first in depth look into the expansion order in πGE. What orders are actually explored? How does the order of πGE change over a run? Does the algorithm evolve towards a certain order? To answer these questions a metric must be used to determine the distance from a known order. The Order Bias Distance Metric is proposed for this task and then used to examine how πGE behaves. As well as investigating the order behaviour, the first steps are taken to quantify the cost of this order overhead to the search compared with GE.

K. Krawiec et al. (Eds.): EuroGP 2013, LNCS 7831, pp. 37–48, 2013.
© Springer-Verlag Berlin Heidelberg 2013

Another important aspect of πGE is to explore how does a more complex representation effect the connectivity of the algorithm. Does the addition of position independent expansion order provide πGE with a more connected solution space, thus is it easier or harder for πGE to move about the solution space than it is for GE. Previous work by Murphy et al.[9] investigated the connectivity of TAGE compared to that of GE. It was found that the richer representation of TAGE provided it with a much more connected phenotypic space. This is of interest as both TAGE and πGE share a very similar evolution controlled position independent mapping. It has been shown that visualising the program space can be useful in understanding how an algorithm works[7], and through the processes outlined in Murphy's work it is hoped that further understanding of πGE may be gained.

The remainder of the paper is structured as follows. An overview of GE is provided in Section 2, before examining the differences between the GE and πGE genotype-phenotype mappings in Section 3. The new distance metric used in this paper is outlined in Section 4. The results are outlined and explained in Section 5, firstly the order experiments in Section 5.1 followed by the connectivity experiments in Section 6. This is followed by a discussion in Section 6 and finally some conclusions and future work are outlined in Section 7.

2   Grammatical Evolution

Grammatical Evolution(GE)[2,13], is a grammar based form of Genetic Programming(GP)[8]. Whilst GP[14] relies upon the constructing of expression trees, and performing operations on the expression trees, GE takes inspiration from DNA-Protein mapping in its approach to the generation of solutions. GE relies upon the use of a list of integers referred to as a chromosome, or genotype. This chromosome is then mapped to a phenotype, or solution, through the application of a grammar to the chromosome as described in detail in Section 3.

O'Neill[10] presented a series of arguments for the adoption of a genotype-phenotype map for GP, as it can provide a number of advantages. These include a generalised encoding that can represent a variety of structures allowing GP to generate structures in an arbitrary language, efficiency gains for evolutionary search (e.g. through neutral evolution), maintenance of genetic diversity through many-to-one maps, preservation of functionality while allowing continuation of search at a genotypic level, reuse of genetic material potentially allowing information compression, and positional independence of gene functionality.

3   Genotype-Phenotype Maps - GE, πGE

In GE we begin the mapping process by finding the start symbol in the grammar. This non terminal (NT) in the case of the example grammar shown in Fig. 1, <e> is then evaluated using Eq. 1. By taking the first codon value of the GE chromosome (12) and the number of expansions possible for the state <e> (2), we get the first expansion of the tree, where <e> expands to <e><o><e> (12%2).

From this point on the leftmost NT is always expanded first in the derivation process. This action will continue to be performed until no NTs remain to be expanded. An example of this mapping is shown in Fig. 2 based on the example grammar shown in Fig. 1 where the order of expansion is indicated by a set of numbers on the arrows between the blocks on the diagram, in the form of 1(12%2) where 1 is the expansion order and 12%2 is the application of Eq. 1.

$$New\ Node\ =\ Codon\ value\ \%\ Number\ of\ rules\ for\ NT \qquad (1)$$

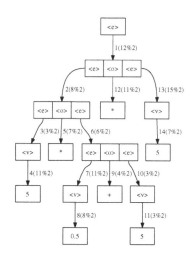

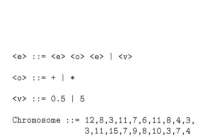

```
<e> ::= <e> <o> <e> | <v>

<o> ::= + | *

<v> ::= 0.5 | 5

Chromosome ::= 12,8,3,11,7,6,11,8,4,3,
               3,11,15,7,9,8,10,3,7,4
```

Fig. 1. Example Grammar and Chromosome

Fig. 2. Standard GE Genotype to Phenotype Mapping

The only difference between standard GE and πGE in its purest form is in the mapping process from genotype to phenotype. πGE's mapping process differs from that of GE in that each expansion of a NT requires two codons. The standard GE chromosome is essentially split into pairs of values where the first codon of the pair is used to choose which NT to expand and the second is used to choose what to expand the NT to, based on the rules available for a NT of that type. The chromosome shown in Fig. 1 can be viewed as a list of paired values such as ((12,8),(3,11)........), where the first value of the pair (The Order Codon) is used to determine the next NT to expand by using Eq. 2 and this will return which NT to choose from a list of unexpanded NTs. Once the NT to be expanded has been chosen, the second codon (Content Codon) is used in conjunction with Eq. 1 (the standard GE expansion rule) to determine what the NT expands to; and if this node happens to be an NT, it is added to the list of unexpanded NTs. Figs. 3 and 4 show the expansion of the example grammar in Fig. 1 using the πGE mapping process. The number associated with each branch of the tree is a reference to the numbered steps shown in Fig. 3 which show how

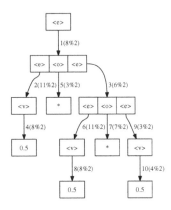

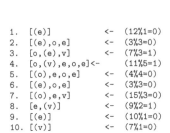

1.	[(e)]	<-	(12%1=0)
2.	[(e),o,e]	<-	(3%3=0)
3.	[o,(e),v]	<-	(7%3=1)
4.	[o,(v),e,o,e]<-		(11%5=1)
5.	[(o),e,o,e]	<-	(4%4=0)
6.	[(e),o,e]	<-	(3%3=0)
7.	[(o),e,v]	<-	(15%3=0)
8.	[e,(v)]	<-	(9%2=1)
9.	[(e)]	<-	(10%1=0)
10.	[(v)]	<-	(7%1=0)

Fig. 3. NT selection process in πGE

Fig. 4. Standard πGE Genotype to Phenotype Mapping

each choice of NT to expand comes about. It is interesting to note the different shape and size of the examples based on just a change in mapping.

$$NT\ to\ expand\ =\ Codon\ value\ \%\ Number\ of\ NT's \qquad (2)$$

4 Order Bias Distance Metric

Order Bias Distance Metric (OBDM) is a measure that shows how far away from a desired derivation order a πGE order is. The metric is measured in terms of the average percentage distance away from the desired order. The metric is very dependent on the πGE algorithms implementation. In πGE, all non terminals are added to a list of possible expansion sites and selection from this list is controlled by the chromosome. When a non terminal is expanded any non terminals generated from the expansion are then placed in the list in the position the parent NT was taken from.

Considering this, it needs to be determined what, if any, orders can an explicit distance from be calculated. Due to the variable length of the list of NTs, selecting a codon value that can always select the correct position in the list means that the only orders that are allowed for comparison to πGE are orders that are constructed by selecting the first NT in the list. As the πGE expansion rule, Eq. 2, can only be set to consistently select the first item in the list and no other position, only orders that rely on using zero codon values for the order codons and select the first codon in the list can be measured.

With this knowledge it can be determined that from the default implementation of the algorithm the only order that can be initialised to and a distance measured from using OBDM is Left-Most Depth First, also known as the standard GE mapping. To ascertain how far from the desired order the current order is, the position selected by Eq. 2, NT Choice, at each step of the πGE derivation is converted into a percentage by using, $(100/|NT\ list|) * NT\ Choice$. The idea is that the desired order, or 0% distance, is always position zero in the list and then 100% distance would be selecting the last item in the list. The distance at each expansion is noted and at the end averaged to provide the percentage distance from the desired order for each individual.

4.1 Alternative Orders

To initialise the initial πGE population to any other desired order requires fundamental changes to the mapping algorithm. *Right Most First Order* can be achieved if the NT list order is reversed so that when the first element is selected in the list it is always the rightmost non terminal. *Breadth First Mapping* can be achieved by appending the new non terminals to the end of the list and then always selecting the first item in the list, allowing the algorithm to process all NT's at the first depth of the tree before moving onto the lower levels. *Breadth First Right Most* can be achieved by reversing the Breath First list above.

The monitoring of any other order becomes far too computationally intensive if a method other than an OBDM style of measurement is used. A metric for any type of non fixed expansion order would have to store all possible outcomes of all possible trees and then see how far away from the original tree the resulting tree was. The branching factor that πGE's order brings makes this task exponentially increasing in difficulty. On a test run trying to monitor all possible valid πGE trees, to a chromosome length of twelve with a simple symbolic regression grammar, the algorithm was using in excess of 20GB of RAM and substantially increased runtime in the order of several hours. OBDM provides a metric that requires zero extra online monitoring and doesn't slow down the algorithm.

5 Results

In this section the result for this study are reported regarding order and connectivity in πGE. Firstly the results for the experiment relating to the understanding of how order works and behaves in πGE is examined. This is then followed by the reporting of the other facet of this study, how does this added order change the connectivity of the πGE representation when compared to GE. For all experiments reported here GEVA v2.0[12] was used and modified as needed to produce the required output.

5.1 Order and πGE

To ascertain what is happening to the πGE expansion order during evolution, a method of recording the expansion process is needed. For this it was decided to store the NT list choice that was taken to first select the parent NT for expansion and the list length when this was taken as well as the tree depth of the parent in every child node. Once this was done the parsing of the data was done and represented using the OBDM above. At each expansion the distance from standard GE order was calculated and then compressed and represented on a population level per generation.

The general setting for the experiments are displayed in Table 1. There were four setups examined of varying population size and generation length. These setups were then applied to three problem domains, *Santa Fe Ant Trail, Even 5 Parity* and *Symbolic Regression*. The experiments were then repeated using a fixed order initialisation, setting every expansion codon to zero so as to guarantee a standard GE order, and then examined to see how the order would change starting from a fixed order. Would it maintain the order or something close to it, or would it follow the behaviour of standard πGE?

Table 1. Parameter settings adopted for the order experiments

Parameter	Value
Setup A	100 Generations 100 Population
Setup B	400 Generations 100 Population
Setup C	100 Generations 400 Population
Setup D	400 Generations 400 Population
Replacement strategy	Generational with elitism (10%)
Selection	Tournament size=2
Mutation probability	0.01 (integer mutation)
Crossover probability	0.0 & 0.9 (variable single point)
Initial chromosome length	200 codons (random init)
Runs	100 per setup & problem

In Fig. 7 the results for Setup D are displayed on the *Even 5 Parity Problem*. Results for other setups and problems where omitted due to space constraints. By examining the figure it can be seen that πGE starts off with a large amount of individuals that have a very GE like mapping order. This anomaly comes from the fact that πGE and GE generate a lot of small individuals at the start of a randomly initialised run and it can be seen that these individuals are greatly reduced after 100 generations. This trend was seen across all setups and problems. Examining Fig. 7, focusing on the left hand side of the figure it shows how the order of the πGE population changes during the run. In fact by the end of the 400 generations it looks like a slightly offset normal distribution of orders is seen. Examining the right hand side of the figure the order of the fixed initialiser is shown. The population starts off with a GE order of expansion but over time this order moves to be more like the order seen in πGE. These findings were seen across all setups and problems. One thing of note was that with a reduced amount of generations the populations drift away from the GE order was reduced but there was no way to stop the drift. The stopping of this drift towards a πGE order is discussed further in Section 6.

5.2   Connectivity and πGE

To fully understand an algorithm it is helpful to visualise the connectivity of the phenotypic space associated with the algorithm. In this experiment the aim is to try and represent a single mutation event in the πGE genotypic space and map the resulting move in the phenotypic space. Through this it is hoped to gain an understanding of how the added search that the evolvable order in πGE causes can lead to results on a par with and in many cases better than GE.

In this experiment GEVA was extended to incorporate the Mutate and Store operation as described in detail by Murphy[9]. Mutate and Store basically starts off with an all zero chromosome and then iterates along the chromosome finding all valid chromosomes and storing them in a neighbourhood. The operator then calls these neighbours and does the same process finding all valid genotypes. This continues until all valid genotypes have been mapped and explored. Once this process is done all the individual neighbourhoods are compressed into a single neighbourhood. The operator removes all degeneracy in the genotypes by only allowing the codon values at each point of the chromosome to represent the choices available thus removing the neutral mutations that GE can take advantage of. For example a GE codon valued 62 is mutated to 64 and this codon is applied to a binary grammar rule, the mutation results in no change to the expansion of the tree. The grammar used for this experiment is similar to the one shown in Fig. 3 except now $< o >::= + \mid -$ and $< v >::= x0 \mid x1 \mid 1.0$. Mutate and Store was run on GE and πGE and was setup in such a way as to limit both algorithms to the same phenotype space.

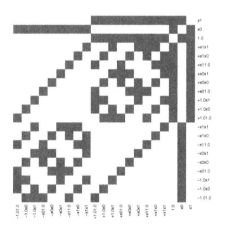 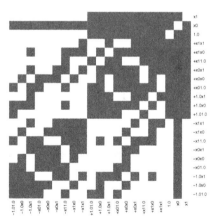

Fig. 5. GE Adjacency Matrix. The x-axis and y-axis are the same and display the phenotypes attainable from the available chromosome length

Fig. 6. πGE Adjacency Matrix. The x-axis and y-axis are the same and display the phenotypes attainable from the available chromosome length.

The first examination of the connectivity of πGE versus GE was performed by converting the connections to a graph and representing the graph as an adjacency matrix or connectivity map as in the Murphy study. Adjacency matrices are good for showing how connected the valid phenotypes are. An algorithm whose phenotype space has a densely populated adjacency matrix will have an easier time moving from phenotype to phenotype and thus it can more easily search the space. Fig. 5 shows the adjacency matrix for GE and Fig. 6 the adjacency matrix for πGE. It is obvious when the two figures are compared that πGE's phenotype space is more densely connected than GE's phenotype space, also worth noting is how GE has no neutral mutation but with the addition of order πGE exhibits neutral mutation. A phenotype of $x1$ cannot exhibit neutral mutation as the NT list for such a tree never exceeds a size of one thus the left-most nonterminal is always picked.

The adjacency matrix representation is good for quickly showing connectivity but it lacks the ability to show multiple connections between the same phenotypes. By examining Fig. 8 and 9 and the actual graph of the neighbourhood for both algorithms it becomes very clear how connected both are. From these figures a couple of interesting things can be seen. Firstly we can see the density of the connections is far more in πGE, also the neutral mutation are clearly displayed. Finally it is also clear that there are multiple edges between the same vertices. These edges are distinct in that they represent clearly different ways to make the same transition, this feature is not seen in GE's graph. A more detailed comparison is done in Table 2 where it is shown that πGE has a much larger total graph degree, the amount of connections to the vertices in the graph, as well as more edges and that every vertex in the graph has a degree, the number of connections coming from a vertex, on average double that of GE.

Table 2. Table outlining features of the connectivity graphs shown in both Fig. 5 and Fig. 6. Of note is the more than double increase in connections for πGE.

Graph Features	GE Graph - Fig. 5	πGE Graph - Fig. 6
$\sum_{i=0}^{n} Vertex\ Degree$	98	198
$\sum_{i=0}^{n} Edges$	49	99
$\sum_{i=0}^{n} Vertices$	21	21
$\overline{Vertex Degree}$	4.67	9.43

6   Discussion - Restricting Order Drift in πGE

It has been shown in the experimental section of this paper that with πGE, evolution does not evolve towards a specific mapping order. πGE instead evolves to a population of individuals with a distribution of mappings orders. However is there a way to limit this drift and force πGE to maintain a mapping order?

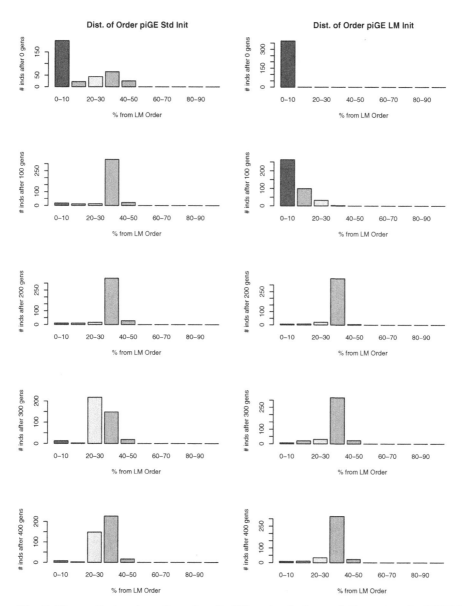

Fig. 7. Figure displays how the order of πGE varies during evolution using the OBDM. For each sub graph the x-axis shows the distance from the fixed order, while the y-axis shows the number of individuals

In previous work[4], a mutation operation was proposed that could focus on order codons or content codons of a πGE chromosome and the algorithm could be setup in such a way as to turn off mutation of the order codons completely. Upon further inspection of how the mapping process works for πGE, even if the

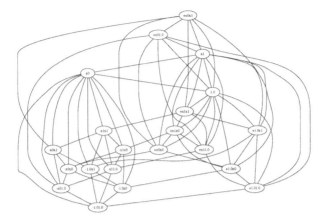

Fig. 8. GE - Single Mutation Graph

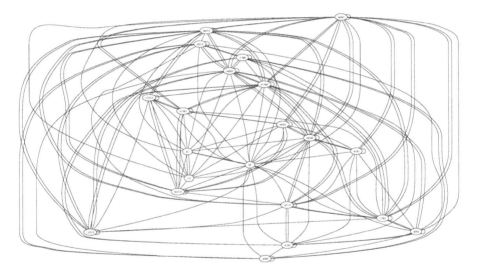

Fig. 9. πGE - Single Mutation Graph

mutation of order codons is not allowed the order of the individual will change with the mutation of the content codons. In πGE the order of the individual is linked to not only the order codon but also the number of NT's left to be expanded. So if a content mutation changes the number of NT's in the list then this may change the expansion order that follows from that point on. This is a similar ripple effect to that noted in standard GE mutation[1], but in this case the ripple is caused by the change in the number of NT's to be expanded.

Consider the following example, there is a section of chromosome and the algorithm is currently pointed at the codon with the value 5, *Chromosome* : [3, 5̲, 9, 7, 8] , and a current NT list mid run: $NT's = [e, o, e, o, v]$. Applying the πGE order rule, 5%5 = 0, leads to the mapper selecting NT zero in the list to expand, $NT's = [\underline{e}, o, e, o, v]$. Applying the GE expansion rule, $9\%2 = 0$, results in this e being replaced by v and sets the NT list for the next expansion in the derivation tree, $NT's = [v, o, e, o, v]$. Next the mapper selects index 2, $7\%5 = 2$, and continues on from there. However if the codon valued 9, that controls what the first e expanded to, is mutated to 4 the list now looks drastically different, $NT's = [\underline{e}, o, e, o, e, o, v]$ and so when we apply the πGE NT selection equation to choose the next codon, $7\%7 = 0$, the NT at position zero is now selected and thus the ripple is started and all the following order choices will be effected.

In general it can be shown that if a content codon is mutated and this mutation results in the number of NT's available for expansion being changed then a resulting ripple will change the order of expansion for πGE.

7 Conclusions

The main aim of this paper was to further investigate what goes on within πGE with regards to the expansion orders used in the algorithm. The orders of πGE individuals during evolution was recorded, from a random order initialisation and a fixed order initialisation, on a range of setups and problems. It was shown that πGE drifts towards a distribution of orders rather than one particular order, this exhibits behaviour similar to that of crossover in GP whereby crossover causes evolution to a distribution of tree sizes. However the drift away from a fixed order can be reduced if a shorter number of generations are used during evolution. The monitoring of other orders was also discussed and some other fixed order initialisations for πGE were discussed, but they would require fundamental changes to the algorithm due to the sensitivity of the order to the size of the NT list. Finally the idea of trying to constrain the order was discussed but again the sensitivity to the NT list size makes this a computationally prohibitive idea.

Given the search overhead the order gives to πGE it was decided to investigate if the order added anything to πGE and try to gain further understanding into how πGE works. By creating graphs of the neighbourhood of single mutation events in GE and πGE it was shown that with the addition of order a significant increase in connectivity was seen. A more densely connected algorithm has the benefit of easier movement within the search space. The order also added pure degeneracy and neutral mutation unlike GE that relies upon codons to provide this, while πGE benefits from both GE's neutral mutations and the ones it gains from the use of variable order. In conclusion it can be said that the overhead of the added search space could represent a problem for πGE to search the solution space, but the increased connectivity could be said to counteract this.

In the future, further examination of the order with πGE is desirable focusing on the behaviour of the elites in the population. It would be good to see how big an impact mutation and crossover would have on fitness and order. The connectivity of πGE presented in this paper while clearly greater than GE presents some interesting ideas. Firstly a more efficient way to explore the connectivity needs to be investigated to allow for much larger phenotype space. Finally repeating this study using crossover may provide more insight into πGE.

Acknowledgments. This research is based upon works supported by the Science Foundation Ireland under Grant No. 08/IN.1/I1868.

References

1. Byrne, J.: Approaches to Evolutionary Architectural Design Exploration Using Grammatical Evolution. Ph.D. thesis, University College Dublin, Ireland (2012)
2. Dempsey, I., O'Neill, M., Brabazon, A.: Foundations in Grammatical Evolution for Dynamic Environments. SCI, vol. 194. Springer, Heidelberg (2009)
3. Fagan, D., O'Neill, M., Galván-López, E., Brabazon, A., McGarraghy, S.: An Analysis of Genotype-Phenotype Maps in Grammatical Evolution. In: Esparcia-Alcázar, A.I., Ekárt, A., Silva, S., Dignum, S., Uyar, A.Ş. (eds.) EuroGP 2010. LNCS, vol. 6021, pp. 62–73. Springer, Heidelberg (2010)
4. Fagan, D., Nicolau, M., O'Neill, M., Galvan-Lopez, E., Brabazon, A., McGarraghy, S.: Investigating mapping order in piGE. In: WCCI 2010, July 18-23, pp. 3058–3064. IEEE Press, Barcelona (2010)
5. Galvan-Lopez, E., Fagan, D., Murphy, E., Swafford, J.M., Agapitos, A., O'Neill, M., Brabazon, A.: Comparing the performance of the evolvable pigrammatical evolution genotype-phenotype map to grammatical evolution in the dynamic ms. pacman environment. In: WCCI 2010, pp. 1587–1594. IEEE Press, Barcelona (2010)
6. Hemberg, E.: An Exploration of Grammars in Grammatical Evolution. Ph.D. thesis, University College Dublin, Ireland (September 17, 2010)
7. Koza, J.R., Poli, R.: Genetic programming. In: Search Methodologies: Introductory Tutorials in Optimization and Decision Support Techniques, ch. 5, pp. 127–164. Springer (2005)
8. McKay, R.I., Hoai, N.X., Whigham, P.A., Shan, Y., O'Neill, M.: Grammar-based genetic programming: a survey. Genetic Programming and Evolvable Machines 11(3/4), 365–396 (2010), Tenth Anniversary Issue: Progress in Genetic Programming and Evolvable Machines
9. Murphy, E., O'Neill, M., Brabazon, A.: Examining Mutation Landscapes in Grammar Based Genetic Programming. In: Silva, S., Foster, J.A., Nicolau, M., Machado, P., Giacobini, M. (eds.) EuroGP 2011. LNCS, vol. 6621, pp. 130–141. Springer, Heidelberg (2011)
10. O'Neill, M.: Automatic Programming in an Arbitrary Language: Evolving Programs with Grammatical Evolution. Ph.D. thesis, University Of Limerick (2001)
11. O'Neill, M., Brabazon, A., Nicolau, M., Garraghy, S.M., Keenan, P.: πGrammatical Evolution. In: Deb, K., Tari, Z. (eds.) GECCO 2004. LNCS, vol. 3103, pp. 617–629. Springer, Heidelberg (2004)
12. O'Neill, M., Hemberg, E., Gilligan, C., Bartley, E., McDermott, J., Brabazon, A.: GEVA: Grammatical Evolution in Java. SIGEVOlution 3(2) (2008)
13. O'Neill, M., Ryan, C.: Grammatical Evolution: Evolutionary Automatic Programming in a Arbitrary Language. Genetic programming. Kluwer (2003)
14. Poli, R., Langdon, W.B., McPhee, N.F.: A field guide to genetic programming. Published via `http://lulu.com` and freely available at `http://www.gp-field-guide.org.uk` (2008), (With contributions by J. R. Koza)

PhenoGP: Combining Programs to Avoid Code Disruption

Cyril Fonlupt and Denis Robilliard

Univ Lille Nord de France
ULCO, LISIC, BP 719
F-62228 Calais, France
{fonlupt,robilliard}@lisic.univ-littoral.fr

Abstract. In conventional Genetic Programming (GP), n programs are simultaneously evaluated and only the best programs will survive from one generation to the next. It is a pity as some programs might contain useful code that might be hidden or not evaluated due to the presence of introns. For example in regression, $0\times$ (perfect code) will unfortunately not be assigned a good fitness and this program might be discarded due to the evolutionary process. In this paper, we develop a new form of GP called PhenoGP (PGP). PGP individuals consist of ordered lists of programs to be executed in which the ultimate goal is to find the best order from simple building-blocks programs. If the fitness remains stalled during the run, new building-blocks programs are generated. PGP seems to compare fairly well with canonical GP.

1   Introduction

Genetic Programming (GP) is a technique aiming at the automatic generation of programs. It was successfully used to solve a wide variety of problems, and it can be now viewed as a mature method as even patents for old and new discovery have been filled. GP is used in fields as different as quantum computing [12], software engineering, classification [6] and even for finite algebras in mathematics [13].

The most widely used scheme in GP is the tree paradigm also known as Tree Based GP where each evolved program is coded as a Lisp-like tree. Different alternatives to the tree based schemes were devised in recent years. For instance, one of the most successful paradigm is Linear Genetic Programming (LGP) [2] where individuals in the population are sequences of high-level languages instructions. The representation (or genotype) of programs in LGP is usually a bounded-length list of integers. This list is subsequently mapped into a sequence imperative instructions.

Unfortunately all these population-based schemes have a significant weakness inherent to their structures. An individual (*i.e.* a program) score which determines its presence in future generations is only based on its own features regardless of any combinations it may form with other programs or good code it may have inside. Another way of seeing this weakness is the disruption of

K. Krawiec et al. (Eds.): EuroGP 2013, LNCS 7831, pp. 49–60, 2013.

program structure caused by the application of genetic operators. Main genetic operators like crossover in the GP paradigm work by modifying the tree structure in case of Tree based GP or by swapping instruction or parts of instruction in case of LGP. There is disruption when use of genetic operators has a negative impact on the execution.

Many researchers have tackled this problem as code disruption may retard the evolutionary process because it may completely make "good code" disappear. Some clever schemes have been proposed these last years to limit the impact of disruption either by limiting the disrupting power of the crossover (size fair crossover,...) or by controlling it.

In this work, we make the following assumption that as the disruption is inherently present in the evolution process, we must use it to our benefit. In this work, we propose to reverse the use of disruption. Instead of watching the evolutionary process to monitor the disruption process, we believe that many if not all individuals in the population might give birth to "good" code.

Another weakness in the GP approach is that while all high-level languages (like C, Java, ...) support loop constructs that allow iterations over data structures, loops are still regarded as difficult instructions to manipulate during the GP evolution even if many problems require repetitive tasks to be solved.

Loops or iterations have received some attention over the last years but, as using loops in GP remains relatively complex and requires Boolean condition, the use of loops and recursion in GP is still uncommon. Even if loops were introduced by Koza in [7], only a few papers were dedicated to the use of loops in GP. Chen and Zhang in [3] showed than using a while-loop structure improved the performance of GP on some classification problem. In the same way, Ciesielski and Li [4] showed that for some modified problems, the for-loops structure can reduce the complexity of the solution. Lately, Larres et al [9] proposed to introduce the concept of unrestricted nested loops for image classification. Even, if all these works proved that using loops provides new and interesting results in the GP field, loops or iteration in GP is still rarely used due to its complexity.

To cope with the above issues this paper aims to investigate a new GP approach where disruption is controlled and iteration is implicitly available, without needing complex modifications to the GP scheme. Instead of using a pool of programs and making them evolve, this approach seeks to combine the programs of the pool and to possibly repeat some of the best building blocks of this pool. This may look superficially similar to the GP teams of [10], but it is different since we construct a composition of functions, while [10] combine not the functions but their results.

The rest of this paper is organised in the following way. Section 2 briefly describes the Linear Genetic Programming (LGP) principles and the disruption process. Section 3 describes our new GP approach called PhenoGP (PGP). Section 4 presents the experiments and results on a set of benchmarks: regression problems, the artificial ant problem and the tower of Hanoi problem. Finally, we conclude in Section 5 and give future research directions.

2   Background

2.1   Linear Genetic Programming

Basically LGP is a subset of GP. Unlike canonical GP [7] also called Tree-GP where programs are coded as trees, in the LGP paradigm, individuals in the populations (*i.e.* programs) consist of a sequence of imperative instructions [2], usually expressed in a high-level language like C.

Each imperative instruction is a 3-register instruction. This means that every instruction consists of an operation on two operand registers, one of them (and only one) could be holding a constant value, and a destination register that the result is assigned to :

$$r[i] = r[j] \text{ op } (r[k]|c_k)$$

where $r[i]$ is the destination register, $r[j]$ and $r[k]$ are the calculation registers and c_k is a constant.

Constants are typically initialized at the beginning of the run with values in the range $[-1.0, +1.0]$. A subset of the registers contains the inputs to our problem, that means that if the solution is a n-dimensional vector, registers $r[0]$ to $r[n-1]$ will be used to hold the inputs values. As explained in [2], besides the required minimal number of registers, an additional set of registers is sometimes used for calculation purpose and storing constants. In the standard case, the output values are stored in the registers $r[0] \dots r[n]$ according to the dimensionality of the problem. Figure 1 gives an overview of an LGP program execution on a 2-dimensional problem.

2.2   Disruption

As explained in the first section, it is not our intention to exhaustively describe all the ways to prevent the disruption process in GP. Many interesting schemes were devised these last years to diminish the disruption process

In [5], Downey and Zhang introduced a clever way to cope with the disruption process. In their work, called Parallel LGP (PLGP), a program consists of n LGP programs which are evaluated independently and provide n results vectors. These vectors are then summed to produce a single results vector. The idea behind LGP is that by separating the program into multiple *independent* small blocks of program, the final program will be much more insensitive to the disruption process. Experiments on some classification problem chosen from the UCI machine learning repository showed that PLGP gave rise for most problems to better fitness solutions than LGP.

3   PhenoGP (PGP)

3.1   Motivation - PhenoGP Scheme

As explained in section 1, PhenoGP (PGP) is devised to combine programs in an effective way and thus to limit the code disruption and to allow the reuse of the same program several times.

PGP is an LGP system where two populations evolve. The first population (called LGP pool) consists of n LGP programs which are evaluated in the usual way while the second population (called master pool) consists of n lists of integers that indicate the **sequence** of LGP programs to execute.

Program Inputs	LGP program	Program Outputs
r[0] r[1]	r[0] = r[1] + 1.27	r[0] r[1]
1.0 2.0	r[1] = r[0] + r[1]	17.23 5.27
	r[0] = r[1] × r[0]	

Fig. 1. LGP overview. $r[0] = 1.0$ and $r[1] = 2.0$ are the two input values to the problem. After execution of the LGP program, results are stored in the same registers ($r[0] = 17.23$ $r[1] = 5.27$)

Let us have a look at a basic example to explain our topic: the aim of the problem is to solve a classic regression problem, for instance $x^2 + x - 1$. Suppose there are two individuals (namely **program1** and **program2**) in our LGP pool. Suppose, the $r[0]$ and $r[1]$ registers are inputs of our program while output is obtained through the $r[0]$ register.

```
    program 1              program 2

    r[0] = r[0] - 1        r[0] = r[0] * r[1]
    r[1] = r[0] + 3        r[0] = r[0] + 1
```

These two programs are moderately fit (the first program is equivalent to $x + 2$ while the second one is $x^2 + 1$) and may or may not be kept in future generations due to the evolutionary process. But if we look closely at these two programs, it is straightforward that executing **program2** just after **program1** will provide a perfect solution to the problem.

$$
\begin{array}{ll}
r[0] = r[0] - 1 & r[0] = x - 1 \\
r[1] = r[0] + 3 & r[1] = x + 2 \\
r[0] = r[0] * r[1] & r[0] = x^2 + x - 2 \\
r[0] = r[0] + 1 & r[0] = x^2 + x - 1
\end{array}
$$

Execution in sequence of program1 followed by program2

Actually, we do not want to avoid the disruption process. As we think disruption is central to GP, the programs will not evolve as in any GP scheme but be part of a larger structure that can use any of the individuals zero time, once, twice or as many times as needed to find a good solution.

On the implementation level, an individual will be a list of integers that indicates which and when to execute each program. For instance, if the list of integers is equal to $\{1\,5\,1\,1\,0\,6\}$, the programs in the LGP pool that will be executed in sequence are: $1\,5\,1\,1\,0\,6$. Note that in this example, the first program to be executed is the program labelled 1 and that outputs of this program will be inputs of the program labelled 5 and so on... Iteration or repetition of the same program is possible and can easily be evolved.

Another problem that might occur in GP is the tendency to bloat (programs have significant amounts of non-effective code that tends to increase during evolution). The GP community is divided, some argue that bloat might be useful to protect good portion of code as others believe it is only harmful. Note, that in the case PGP, bloat cannot occur during evolution as the size of programs remains fixed during the run.

3.2 Program Structure

An example of an PGP program is given in figure 2. In PGP, each program may be executed zero, once, twice or as many times according to the evolution process. An individual in the master pool decides which program in the LGP pool to execute and in which order. All programs are executed in sequence and outputs of the nth program are the inputs of the $n + 1 th$ program.

Pool of LGP Programs:

Program 1	Program 2
r[0] = r[1] + 1.27	r[1] = r[1] / 0.5
r[1] = r[0] + r[1]	r[0] = r[1] * r[1]

PGP program execution list: {1, 1, 2}

Combined PhenoGP Program:

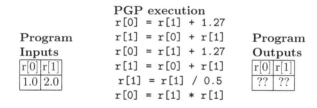

Fig. 2. PhenoGP principles

In this approach, if an LGP program owns a portion of "efficient" code even if it is moderately fit, there is a probability that this program will be used in future generations and will not disappear during evolution.

The heart of our scheme is a $(\mu + \lambda)$-ES (Evolution Strategy) that makes the master pool evolve. An important issue in the case of an ES is how mutation will be performed. In our case, the mutation operator works on a list of integers and is used to modify which sequence of programs to execute in the LGP pool.

We decided to allow the mutation of any integer so that any LGP program of the LGP pool may have the chance to appear zero, once or as many times as needed. Moreover, we decided to allow the mutation operator to have a "no-operation" effect. In other words it means that the mutation can turn one integer of the list into a "do the number of executable program is dynamic. In our opinion this is an advantage over standard LGP where the size of the program is fixed offline and that if smaller programs are needed to solve a problem it might be a more difficult challenge for evolution to get rid off useless code.

For example, before being mutated, programs 1, 2, 1 and 4 are executed in sequence. After mutation, programs 1, 4 and 4 are executed in sequence (-1 means "do nothing").

$$\boxed{1\,|\,2\,|\,1\,|\,4} \qquad \longrightarrow \textbf{Mutation} \longrightarrow \boxed{1\,|\,\text{-}1\,|\,4\,|\,4}$$

Table 1. PGP algorithm

Initialize LGP pool $P_{\mu 1} = \{a_1, \ldots, a_{\mu 1}\}$ // population of LGP programs
Initialize master pool $M_{\mu 2} = \{m_1, \ldots, m_{\mu 2}\}$ // population of lists of integers
Initialize constants
while (termination criterion not fulfilled)
begin
    Randomly select $\lambda 1$ parents from $P_{\mu 1}$
    Mutate these $\lambda 1$ parents to form the offspring population $P_{\lambda 1}$
    Select new parent population from the offspring $P_{\lambda 1}$
        and parent $P_{\mu 1}$ based on the fitness of individuals
    if best fitness unchanged **then**
        //make a diversification on the LGP pool (see section 3.3)
        assign a fitness score to each individual of the LGP pool based on its frequency
            in the 10% best lists of integers
        Randomly select $\lambda 2$ parents from $P_{\mu 2}$
        Mutate these $\lambda 2$ parents to form the offspring population $P_{\lambda 2}$
    Select new parent population from the offspring $P_{\lambda 2}$
        and parent $P_{\mu 2}$ based on the fitness of individuals
    end if
end while

3.3   Diversity for PhenoGP

An important issue to consider in our new scheme is how diversity will be preserved during evolution. If the LGP pool is created during the initialization and does not evolve during the run, we may face a problem of a lack of diversity in the LGP pool.

To solve this problem we chose to make the LGP pool evolve after a few generations of unchanged best fitness. Each LGP program inside the LGP pool will be assigned a fitness that is directly dependent on the number of times it is used in the master pool.

The higher the fitness, the more frequently it is used in the master pool.

In our case we chose to only look at the best 10% individuals in the master pool to give a reward. Figure 3 explains how fitness is assigned. Once fitness has been evaluated, an ES is used inside this pool to evolve a new LGP pool.

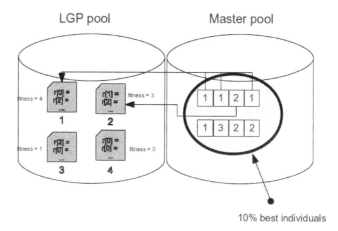

Fig. 3. Overview of the diversification scheme. Fitness is assigned to individuals in the LGP pool based on their frequency in the 10% best individuals of the master pool.

It is clear that this approach might induce a bias towards LGP individuals that are already good and there is a risk that evolution will never change these individuals which provide a good fitness. However our experiments show that this approach seems quite robust. Pseudo-code of our algorithm is presented in table 1.

4 Experiments

In order to validate our scheme, a series of classic experiments were conducted: 6 symbolic regression problems, the famous Santa Fe artificial ant problem and the tower of Hanoi problem. For all problems we measured the average best fitness of 40 independent. The ratio of so-called "hits" was also computed. For regression problems, fitness is evaluated by computing the sum of deviations over all points while for the Hanoi tower problem fitness is simply 4 minus the number of rows on the last peg (a perfect solution is reached when 4 rows are on the last peg).

All problems were also run with standard GP, using the well-known *ECJ* library [1].

The main parameters for standard GP and for our new scheme PGP are :

– the ES PGP is based on is a canonical version of the $(\mu + \lambda)$-ES where μ denotes the number of parents and λ the number of offspring. The parents are deterministically selected using a tournament selection. Child is inserted in the parent of the next generation, only if its fitness is better than the parents fitness, otherwise it is discarded. The parameters for our ES are:

---

[1] Evolutionary Computation in Java, http://cs.gmu.edu/~eclab/projects/ecj/

$\mu = 50$ and $\lambda = 5$. This means that in our case in the master pool, 50 list of integers were evolving in parallel.

- the number of individuals in the LGP population was arbitrarily set to 10 times the size of the LGP population. (*i.e.* 500 LGP programs are available).
- the size of each list in the master pool was set to 10. This means that each individual in the master pool will execute at most a sequence of 10 programs. In order to avoid execution of very large programs, each program in the LGP pool was limited to 12 instructions
- for all regression problems and the tower of Hanoi problem 50,000 evaluations were permitted and 200,000 for the Santa Fe trail problem.
- for regression 10 read/write registers were used for calculation purpose (from $r[0]$ to $r[9]$), $r[0]$ being the output register. They were all initialized for each training case (x_k, y_k) with the input value x_k.
- in the symbolic regression problems the constant probability was set to 0.20 meaning that on average 20% of the instructions will use a constant value.
- the GP parameters were set to 50 generations, 1000 individuals for the regression problem, and 4000 individuals for the artificial ant. Genetic operators were tuned according to the usual practice: 80% for crossover, 10% for subtree mutation and 10% for duplication. The maximum tree depth was set to 11, and we kept the best (elite) individual from one generation to the next. For the regression problems, we defined 4 input terminals against only one ephemeral constant (ERC) terminal.

4.1 Symbolic Regression

The aim of a symbolic regression problem is to find some mathematical expression in symbolic form that associates input and output on a given set of training pairs. In our case, 20 evenly distributed data points x_k in the range $[-1.0, +1.0]$ are chosen as inputs, the outputs being given by the following test functions :

$$\begin{aligned}
f_1 &= x + x + x & f_2 &= x + x + x + x \\
f_3 &= x^5 + x + x + x + x & f_4 &= x^4 - 2x + x \\
f_5 &= \pi & f_6 &= \frac{x}{\pi} + \frac{x}{\pi} + 2x\pi
\end{aligned}$$

The set of operators is $\{+, -, \times, \div\}$ with $\div$ being the protected division (*i.e.* $a \div b = a/b$ if $b \neq 0$ else $a \div b = 0$).

Evaluation is done in the typical way, that is computing the sum of deviations over all points, *i.e.* $fitness = \sum_k |f(x_k) - P(x_k)|$ where P is the evolved program and k the number of input/output pairs. A hit means that the fitness function is less than 10^{-4} on each training pair.

Results can be seen in Table 2 and as it can be seen results are mitigated. On one hand for the first 3 problems (f_1 to f_3) GP clearly provides the best results with the overall most precise approximation, on the other hand PGP provides the best results for the last 3 problems (f_4 to f_6).

It is interesting to see that GP outperforms PGP for the easiest regression problems while for the most difficult problems involving finding non trivial constant values PGP provides very good results and even delivers in some cases a 100% perfect hits program for f_5 and f_6.

Table 2. Results

Problem	PGP		standard GP		Problem	PGP		standard GP	
	Fitness	% hits	Fitness	% hits		Fitness	% hits	Fitness	% hits
f_1	0.04	82.5%	0.002	98%	f_4	0.12	30%	0.33	23%
f_2	0.15	45%	0.0	100%	f_5	0.017	47.5%	0.07	0%
f_3	0.28	22.5%	0.02	93%	f_6	0.177	2.5%	0.21	0%

In our opinion this can be explained by noting that the first three regression problems can be solved using short programs. And as it was noted in [5] short programs will not suffer from code disruption or non-effective code in the way larger programs do. This means that it is not very useful to limit the disruption process as the target program can be expressed in a compact way. Another weakness of PGP for finding short programs it that the list of programs to execute was set to ten and each program held 12 instructions. Even if in the list sequence could be filled with the nop value, on average 120 instructed were executed and this represents too many instructions for finding a short program.

However in the case of more difficult problems when discovering constants is needed PGP clearly outperforms standard GP and is even able to find perfect solutions for f_5 and f_6. These results confirm that PGP is an interesting heuristic particularly when longer programs are needed.

4.2   Santa Fe Ant Trail

The Santa Fe ant trail is one of the most famous problem in the GP field and often used as a benchmark. The objective is to find a computer program that is able to control an artificial ant so that it can find all 89 pieces of food located on a discontinuous trail within a specified number of time steps. The trail is situated on a 32×32 toroidal grid. The problem is known to be rather hard, at least for standard GP (see [8]), with many local and global optima.

Only a few actions are allowed to the ant that each consumes one time step. A maximum time steps threshold is set at start (either 400 or 600). If the program finishes before the exhaustion of the time steps, it is restarted. The fitness function is simply the remaining food (89 minus the number of food pellets taken by the ant).

We do not need mathematical operators nor registers, only the following instructions are available:

MOVE: moves the ant forward one step in the direction the ant is facing, retrieving an eventual food pellet in the cell of arrival; LEFT: turns the ant on place 45 degrees anti-clockwise; RIGHT: turns the ant on place 45 degrees clockwise; IF-FOOD-AHEAD: conditional statement that executes the next instruction or group of instructions if a food pellet is located on the cell in front of the ant, else the next group of instruction is skipped; PROGN2: groups the two instructions that follow in the program vector, notably allowing IF-FOOD-AHEAD to perform several instructions if the condition is true; PROGN3: same as the previous operator, but groups the following three instructions.

Table 3. Results for the artificial ant problem and the tower of Hanoi

Artif. ant	PGP		standard GP	
# steps	Fitness	% hits	Fitness	% hits
400	21.28	15%	8.87	37%
600	9.06	40%	1.175	87%

Hanoi	PGP		standard GP	
#	Fitness	% hits	Fitness	% hits
	0.81	17.5%	1.18	15%

Each MOVE, RIGHT and LEFT instructions require one time step.

Programs are just list of integers. Each integer represents an instruction that is decoded sequentially, and the virtual machine is refined to handle jumps over an instruction or group of instructions, so that it can deal with the IF-FOOD-AHEAD, PROGN2 and PROGN3 instructions. Incomplete programs may be encountered, for example if a PROGN instruction is decoded for the last value of a program vector. On this case incomplete instruction is simply dropped and we consider that the program has reached normal termination.

Results are given in Table 3. It is clear in these results that our scheme PGP is not ease with the artificial ant problem and that standard GP clearly outperforms PGP. We think that once again short programs are better for solving this problem. To test if this was correct, we decided to drop the size of each LGP program from 12 to 3. In this case, the average fitness was slightly better and the number of hits increased from 40% to 66%. Even if PGP is still outperformed by standard GP, the results are closer to those provided by standard GP and show that the size of each LGP program is a sensitive parameter.

When looking closely at the results provided by PGP, we saw that the diversity scheme we add to PGP to avoid being trapped in local optima has sometimes a bad side-effect. Some runs were not very far from the perfect solution with a few pellets remaining when the diversity scheme triggered and delivered bad results. We think that the lack of elitism is a probable cause of PGP bad behavior, on a very chaotic fitness landscape.

4.3   Tower of Hanoi

This problem consists of three pegs, labeled by position, and 4 uniquely sized disks. The initial state has all disks on the first peg such that no disk is on top of a smaller disk. The goal is to reconstruct the tower of the initial configuration on the third peg by moving the disks, one a a time, such that a larger disk never rests on a smaller disk.

We used the same primitive language for the genotype that was introduced in [1] The possible moves for this problem consist of the 6 possibles moves from one peg to another (*i.e.* from peg 1 to 2, from peg 3 to 1,....). A solution is then simply a sequence of single disk move in an order that reconstructs the tower on the third peg. Additionally a limit of 32 time steps was chosen, each move requires one time step.

The following parameters were used for the tower of Hanoi problem: a limit of 32 time steps was fixed, each move requires one time step (This means that the evaluation of the program was stopped after 32 moves either legal or illegal); illegal moves (moving a larger disk on a smaller disk) were not executed but consumed one time step; 50,000 evaluations were allowed; the fitness function was proportional to the number of disks on the last peg after 32 time steps (*i.e.* 4− the number of disks on the last peg).

The results for the tower of Hanoi problem are shown in Table 3. Unlike the artificial ant problem, PGP provides the best performance among the two methods: an average fitness of 0.81 and 17.5% of perfect solution. This shows that PGP is an interesting approach for complex solutions.

5   Conclusion and Future Works

The goal of this paper was to investigate a new GP approach where moderately fit individuals were not systematically discarded during the evolution. The goal was partly successfully achieved and this new scheme was examined and compared with the standard GP approach.

The results show that PGP is an interesting heuristic and that can be favorably compared to canonical GP for the most difficult problems. For problems with short solutions (first three regression problems and the artificial ant problem) GP seems to perform better while PGP achieves reasonable performance for the most complex problems (difficult regression problems and the tower of Hanoi problem).

The disadvantage of PGP over standard GP is that this is a new scheme and that many parameters need to be tuned to achieve good performance. This is particularly true in the case of the artificial ant problem where decreasing the size of each LGP individual increased a lot the overall performance of PGP.

We think that there are some connections between this work and Cartesian Genetic Programming (CGP) [11] as CGP tries to create links between a set of functions, the set of input nodes and the set of output nodes. It remains to see if PGP is some kind of super-set to CGP.

For future work, we will apply this new approach to more complex problems like classification problems. It will also be interesting to investigate how PGP behaves if LGP programs are not randomly generated during the initialization but are tuned according to the problem.

References

1. Angeline, P.J., Pollack, J.B.: Coevolving high-level representations. In: Langton, C.G. (ed.) Artificial Life III, Santa Fe, New Mexico, June 15-19. SFI Studies in the Sciences of Complexity, vol. XVII, pp. 55–71. Addison-Wesley (1992, 1994)
2. Brameier, M., Banzhaf, W.: Linear Genetic Programming. Genetic and Evolutionary Computation. Springer (2007)
3. Chen, G., Zhang, M.: Evolving While-Loop Structures in Genetic Programming for Factorial and Ant Problems. In: Zhang, S., Jarvis, R.A. (eds.) AI 2005. LNCS (LNAI), vol. 3809, pp. 1079–1085. Springer, Heidelberg (2005)

4. Ciesielski, V., Li, X.: Experiments with explicit for-loops in genetic programming. In: Proceedings of the 2004 IEEE Congress on Evolutionary Computation, Portland, Oregon, pp. 494–501. IEEE Press (2004)
5. Downey, C., Zhang, M.: Parallel Linear Genetic Programming. In: Silva, S., Foster, J.A., Nicolau, M., Machado, P., Giacobini, M. (eds.) EuroGP 2011. LNCS, vol. 6621, pp. 178–189. Springer, Heidelberg (2011)
6. Kadar, I., Ben-Shahar, O., Sipper, M.: Evolution of a local boundary detector for natural images via genetic programming and texture cues. In: Proceedings of the 11th Annual Conference on Genetic and Evolutionary Computation, GECCO 2009, pp. 1887–1888. ACM, New York (2009)
7. Koza, J.: Genetic Programming II: Automatic Discovery of Reusable Programs. The MIT Press (1994)
8. Langdon, W.B., Poli, R.: Why ants are hard. In: Genetic Programming 1998: Proceedings of the Third Annual Conference, University of Wisconsin, Madison, Wisconsin, USA, July 22-25, pp. 193–201. Morgan Kaufmann (1998)
9. Larres, J., Zhang, M., Browne, W.: Using unrestricted loops in genetic programming for image classification. In: Proceedings of the IEEE Congress on Evolutionary Computation, pp. 1–8 (2010)
10. Lichodzijewski, P., Heywood, M.I.: Managing team-based problem solving with symbiotic bid-based genetic programming. In: Proceedings of the Genetic and Evolutionary Computation Conference, pp. 363–370. Morgan Kaufmann (2008)
11. Miller, J.: Cartesian Genetic Programming. Springer (2011)
12. Spector, L.: Automatic Quantum Computer Programming: A Genetic Programming Approach. Springer (2006)
13. Spector, L., Clark, D.M., Lindsay, I., Barr, B., Klein, J.: Genetic programming for finite algebras. In: Proceedings of the 10th Annual Conference on Genetic and Evolutionary Computation, GECCO 2008, pp. 1291–1298. ACM, New York (2008)

Reducing Wasted Evaluations
in Cartesian Genetic Programming

Brian W. Goldman and William F. Punch

BEACON Center for the Study of Evolution in Action,
Michigan State University, U.S.A.
brianwgoldman@acm.org, punch@msu.edu

Abstract. Cartesian Genetic Programming (CGP) is a form of Genetic Programming (GP) where a large proportion of the genome is identifiably unused by the phenotype. This can lead mutation to create offspring that are genotypically different but phenotypically identical, and therefore do not need to be evaluated. We investigate theoretically and empirically the effects of avoiding these otherwise wasted evaluations, and provide evidence that doing so reduces the median number of evaluations to solve four benchmark problems, as well as reducing CGP's sensitivity to the mutation rate. The similarity of results across the problem set in combination with the theoretical conclusions supports the general need for avoiding these unnecessary evaluations.

Keywords: cartesian genetic programming, mutation.

1 Introduction

In Genetic Programming (GP) the most common metric for measuring algorithm complexity is the number of fitness evaluations required to solve a black box problem. This metric assumes that the cost of evaluating an individual will dominate search times on real world problems. Under this metric, search algorithms that best exploit evaluation information and avoid unnecessary evaluations will receive the best results. Cartesian Genetic Programming (CGP), a branch of GP, has a particular structure that allows for the detection of some phenotypically identical genotypes without requiring fitness evaluation. No previous work has investigated if this property can be exploited to meaningfully improve CGP efficiency. After discussing the potential theoretical gains of avoiding these evaluations, we propose and investigate three novel techniques designed to improve CGP's search.

2 Cartesian Genetic Programming

Cartesian Genetic Programming is a variant of genetic programming in which individuals encode directed acyclic graphs (DAG). An in-depth explanation of CGP is provided in [4], but for our purposes the important features are:

K. Krawiec et al. (Eds.): EuroGP 2013, LNCS 7831, pp. 61–72, 2013.
© Springer-Verlag Berlin Heidelberg 2013

- DAGs are represented by a collection of nodes and genes specifying output locations.
- Nodes contain genes describing both what function they perform and how they connect to other nodes.
- Offspring are created using mutation.
- Offspring replace parents if they are of the same or greater fitness.

CGP's encoding method does not require a node to connect to an output location, which is required for it to affect the phenotype of the individual. These unconnected nodes and their genes are commonly called "inactive" and the connected nodes and their genes are called "active." As the topology of the DAG is constantly evolving, the number and location of active nodes can change from parent to child. There have been numerous studies on the usefulness of inactive nodes [7,9] including an argument that it is desirable to have up to 95% of the genome inactive [5].

CGP's canonical variation operator is point mutation. Unfortunately the details of this operator are often ambiguously stated. For instance, in some papers this operator chooses a set number of genes at random to be mutated [4], while in other papers each gene can be mutated with a certain probability, allowing any number of genes to be mutated at once [2]. Also, mutation in CGP can either force a mutated gene's value to change [2,4], or randomly reset it to any valid value including the genes previous value [5]. As much of our analysis hinges on the behavior of mutation, we specify mutation as follows: when performing mutation, all genes use the mutation rate as the probability that they are changed to a different value.

The most common form of CGP uses a $1 + \lambda$ strategy, where all offspring are mutants of the parent. The most fit offspring replaces the parent only if its fitness is no worse than the parent. Ties between offspring are broken by random selection and ties between the offspring and the parent are awarded to the offspring: in this manner inactive genes are allowed to drift, which has been shown to significantly improve performance [9]. We will refer to this standard form of mutation and replacement as *Normal.*

3   Wasted Evaluations

Preventing search from repeatedly evaluating the same search point can improve any search that is limited by the number of evaluations it can perform. In an evolutionary search employing indirect phenotype encoding, as CGP does, the same search point can be represented by multiple different genotypes making duplicate detection more difficult. While it does not catch all identical phenotypes, if two CGP individuals are actively identical (contain the same active genes) then their phenotypes must be identical. Miller [4] theorized that this may lead to wasted evaluations as any number of actively identical individuals can be evaluated even though they will receive identical fitnesses. He did not, however, provide any analysis for how frequently these unnecessary evaluations may occur.

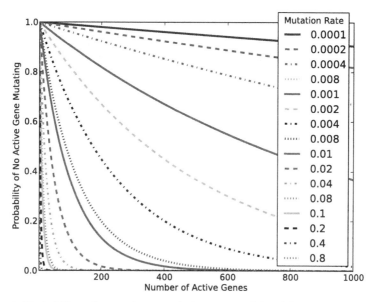

Fig. 1. Probability of no active gene being mutated for different mutation rates

3.1 Detection

Before evaluating a CGP individual, it is common practice to determine which nodes are active allowing inactive nodes to be ignored during evaluation, leading to a reduction in runtime [6]. By storing the set of active genes as part of the individual, it is trivial to determine when active genes are mutated. More generally, it takes $O(N)$ additional time to determine if two randomly chosen individuals contain different active genes, where N is the number of active nodes, assuming at least one of the individuals has been evaluated.

A reasonable heuristic to avoid duplicate evaluations is to determine if a parent's active genes are identical to its offspring. This will catch the majority of cases, as the probability of two individuals being actively identical decreases as the number of mutation applications between them increases. This also has the advantage that extra individuals need not be stored in memory. Due to these advantages, we only compare an offspring against its parent to detect unnecessary evaluations.

3.2 Frequency of Offspring Actively Identical to Their Parent

Using the definition of point mutation given in Section 2, it is possible to quantify the probability that an offspring is actively identical to its parent.

$$(1 - mutation\_rate)^{active\_genes} \tag{1}$$

Equation 1 shows the probability that none of the active genes are mutated at the given mutation rate. To help display the effects of this relationship, Figure 1 illustrates the probability that an offspring is actively identical to its parent for various mutation rates and number of active genes. Figure 1 shows that as the mutation rate and the number of active genes decreases, the probability of an offspring being actively identical to a parent greatly increases. While the other versions of mutation discussed in Section 2 will change the details of this equation, the overall relationship between the variables will be the same.

4   Methods to Avoid Wasting Evaluations

4.1   Skip

The most straightforward method to use existing evaluation results is to set the offspring's fitness to the parent's if they are actively identical. This method will be referred to as *Skip*. As *Skip* makes no modification to evolutionary mechanisms, any problem solvable by *Normal* will be solvable by *Skip*, and vice versa. The primary difference is only that *Normal* will always use at least as many evaluations as *Skip*, with the potential to use significantly more. As a result, *Skip* may solve problems *Normal* cannot if given a maximum number of evaluations.

A significant theoretic advantage to this technique is that it lowers CGP's sensitivity to the mutation rate. In *Normal*, as the mutation rate decreases the potential for wasted evaluations increases creating an evaluation penalty. As the mutation rate increases the expected number of modified active genes increases making small changes in phenotype less probable. From this, *Normal* will likely be most effective when the mutation rate is high enough to expect at least one active gene to be modified by mutation, but low enough to allow the small phenotypic moves required to reach optimal values. Unlike *Normal*, *Skip* can use mutation rates expected to produce frequent offspring that are not actively different from their parents without penalty. As such *Skip* can use very fine grained mutation allowing it to potentially hill climb much more effectively.

4.2   Accumulating Mutation

As was stated in Section 2, some of CGP's success stems from allowing genetic drift of inactive genes [9]. This raises the following question: will evolution in CGP improve if inactive genes are allowed to change at an increased rate?

To test this possibility we propose a method of mutation called *Accumulate*. The primary concept behind this technique is to allow inactive genes to drift multiple generations worth of distance in a single actual generation of CGP. For our example we will refer to one of the offspring produced by the parent as F_0. If F_0 is actively identical to its parent, F_0 produces a mutant offspring F_1 in the same generation. This chain continues with F_i mutating to produce F_{i+1} until an individual is produced that has one or more active genes different from the original parent. This actively different individual is called F_n. F_n is then evaluated. If F_n is no worse than the original parent, it replaces F_0 and CGP continues evolution and selection as normal. If F_n is worse than the original parent F_{n-1} replaces F_0. Thus accumulate's offspring can have zero to multiple active genes changed.

By chaining mutations each F_i will probabilistically have more changes to inactive genes than F_{i-1} when compared with the original parent. By using F_{n-1} or F_n instead of F_0, *Accumulate* can drift faster than *Normal* and *Skip*. This can be advantageous on problems that benefit from high exploration of the neutral space, with the potential drawback that previously active useful structures are less likely to survive to be reintegrated.

4.3   Single Active Mutation

Skip and *Accumulate* have the potential, similar to *Normal*, to generate large numbers of individuals with no active differences, which can be computationally expensive even if they are not evaluated. To avoid this potential overhead, we propose a method to ensure a *Single* active gene is mutated every time an offspring is generated. Creating an offspring using *Single* is an iterative process. Until an active gene has been mutated, select a gene at random in the individual and mutate its value. This has the following properties:

- Exactly one active gene is mutated for all offspring.
- Zero or more inactive genes can be mutated.
- A gene that is active will be mutated more frequently than one that is not.
- No mutation rate is required.

Many of these properties make *Single* distinct from the other described mutation methods. By forcing only a single active gene to change, *Single* may have better results on problems where incremental improvements are possible with single gene changes and worse results on problems where larger changes are necessary. This is in contrast to all of the other methods that have the potential to change multiple active genes. Limiting mutation to a single active gene change does not, however, prevent *Single* from making large phenotypic changes, which are still possible by connecting in inactive nodes.

Single has the property that the effective mutation rate is always $\frac{1}{a}$ for active genes and $\frac{1}{a+1}$ for inactive genes, resulting in $\frac{n-a}{a+1} + 1$ expected mutations, where a is the number of active genes and n is the total number of genes. This means that the number of inactive genes does not affect the probability of an inactive gene being mutated, just the expected number of inactive genes that are mutated. Furthermore, as the number of active genes approaches zero, the expected number of mutations increases dramatically, even though it is still limited to changing a single active gene. As the evolved number of active genes is likely to be highly problem dependent, the behavior of *Single* will likely change significantly from problem to problem, with some problems having very little changes to inactive genes, and others changing a great deal. It is also possible that this will create a selective pressure on the number of active genes which may only become apparent if multiple parents are used.

In comparison with *Skip*, *Single* is even easier to apply to new problems as it completely removes the need to set the mutation rate, but does so at the potential expense of lower maximum effectiveness. In comparison with *Accumulate*, *Single* mutates inactive genes less often with respect to active genes, making it better at preserving useful inactive structures but worse at exploring the inactive space.

5   Experimental Setup

In order to empirically test the suggested benefits of *Skip*, *Accumulate*, and *Single* in comparison with *Normal*, we evaluated their performance on four benchmarks: Parity, Multiplier, Binary Decode and Binary Encode. Both Parity and Multiplier have been used extensively to test CGP [8,5]. The 3-bit even parity is included as it is the most commonly used benchmark for CGP and to help provide some level of comparability with previous work. In order to try a more challenging binary problem, we chose to do the 3-bit multiplier, which has 6 inputs and 6 outputs.

Binary Decode is effectively a demultiplexer, where N input lines specify which of the 2^N output lines should have a value of one, with all others set to zero. For example, if 101 is the input to a 3-bit Binary Decode problem, the output is 00100000. Binary Encode is the reverse of Binary Decode. Given 2^N input lines, where exactly one line has a bit set to one and all others are zero, the binary value index of the one bit is output using N lines. An example of this mapping is that 00100000 should return the output of 101. The reason we use Binary Decode and Binary Encode as benchmarks is their asymmetric number of inputs to outputs and their relatively small number of test cases. For example, on the 16 to 4 Binary Encode and the 4 to 16 Binary Decode (the instances we use) only 16 test cases are needed.

All problems used the operators {and, or, nand, nor} and determine fitness as the average percentage of correct bits across all possible inputs. While this is a common function set used by CGP for these problems, [8] used a different set of operators for Multiplier. Preliminary testing shows our operator set makes Multiplier harder than theirs, but, as always, conclusions drawn by comparing experiments using different operator sets should be minimal.

While a few of these benchmarks may be overly simple, with parity especially being considered for obsolescence [3], they are used here for the specific reason of their simplicity. The primary difference between *Normal* and *Skip* is not that one can solve harder problems than the other, rather it is that *Skip* is thought to solve problems in less evaluations than *Normal*. Being able to compare each method's median number of evaluations until success makes for the most logical metric in this case, so these problems are useful in that they can be solved often. While much of the previous work on CGP uses Koza's *computational effort* to analyze experimental results, [1] explains how that can introduce significant underestimates, especially when using small population sizes.

In order to compare with the effective standard CGP, we use the $1 + 4$ evolutionary strategy. We use a genotype size of 3000 nodes, similar to those found optimal in [5]. Each run was allowed up to 10 million evaluations before being terminated, and 50 runs of each experiment were performed. To help focus the differences between each mutation method, all starting individuals on the same problem were identical for the same run number, meaning that the 50 different individuals *Normal* started with were identical to the 50 starting individuals for *Skip, Accumulate,* and *Single.* For statistical purposes this means all results should be compared as paired tests. As the number of evaluations to success is likely not normally distributed, we choose the Wilcoxon signed-rank test to compare each mutation method with *Normal.* As an attempt to cover a wide range of mutation rates, the 16 mutation rates listed in Figure 1 were used for each method. These cover from 0.0001 to 0.8 on a log scale, and should encompass all previous levels of mutation used with CGP.

6   Results

To summarize the results of testing each mutation rate, Figures 2, 3, 4, and 5 show the median number of evaluations required over 50 runs to solve the Parity, Multiply, Binary Encode, and Binary Decode problems. Note that both axes are presented on a log scale. In the event that the median run of a configuration did not find the optimal value before termination, the value is not displayed in the graph. This can be clearly observed in Figure 3 for mutation rates greater than 0.01. As *Single* does not use a mutation rate, its data is assumed constant for all mutation rates. Table 1 shows fine details about the best configurations found for each mutation method. This includes the mutation rate with the lowest median evaluations until success and the median evaluations it required, the median absolute deviation from that median, the single tailed P-value received from comparing with the best *Normal* configuration using the Wilcoxon signed-rank test, and the median number of active genes in the solution. Note that the number of active genes is a different measure from the number of active nodes, which has been reported in other work, and is used here for compatibility with Equation 1. A complete package of our results as well as the source code used in testing is available from our website.[1]

7   Discussion

Even though the Parity, Multiplier, Binary Encode, and Binary Decode problems have very different numbers of inputs and outputs, different input to output ratios, different evolved numbers of active genes (see Table 1), and different levels of difficulty, Figures 2, 3, 4, and 5 present surprisingly similar results. The steep increases in median evaluations for *Normal* corresponds with the prediction that overly high mutation rates will significantly increase the number of evaluations until success, while low mutation rates will create a significant portion of wasted evaluations. On Multiply, Binary Encode, and Binary Decode,

---

[1] https://github.com/brianwgoldman/ReducingWastedEvaluationsCGP

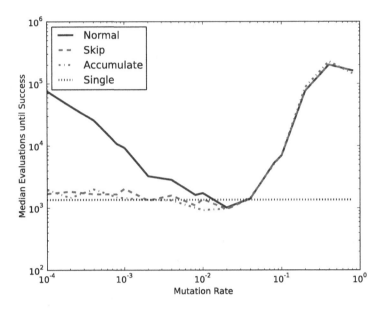

Fig. 2. Median evaluations to success for each method on the Parity problem

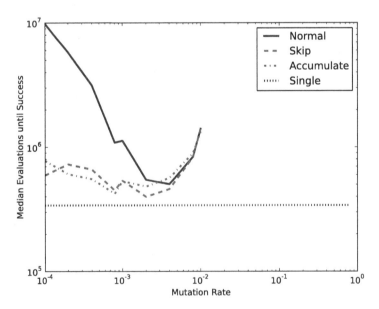

Fig. 3. Median evaluations to success for each method on the Multiply problem

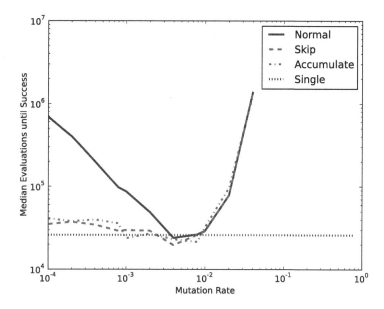

Fig. 4. Median evaluations to success for each method on the Binary Encode problem

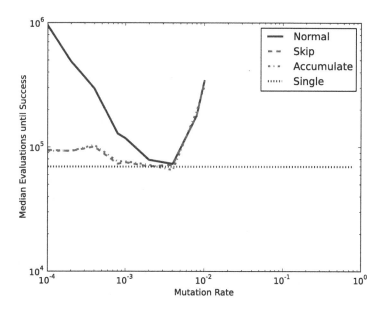

Fig. 5. Median evaluations to success for each method on the Binary Decode problem

overly high mutation rates prevent *Normal* from reaching the optimum. Parity is the only problem CGP could solve using exceptionally high mutation rates, with even a slight improvement at the very top of the tested range. This likely happens as the Parity problem we are using is so simple that a CGP using effectively random search is able to solve it. *Skip* and *Accumulate*'s tendency to mirror *Normal*'s effectiveness as the mutation rate increases is because the probability of creating actively identical offspring approaches zero. As the divergence point is always near *Normal*'s optimum mutation rate, it can be inferred that *Normal*'s significant decrease in quality when using lower mutation rates is likely caused by wasted evaluations. As *Skip* also decreases somewhat in quality, some of the impaired fitness can also likely be attributed to improbability of making large enough genotypic changes to escape local optima with small mutation rates.

All four figures suggest that *Skip* and *Accumulate* have a lower sensitivity to the mutation rate than *Normal*. As the mutation rate goes below the optimal value, *Skip* and *Accumulate* encounter a relatively minor increase in their median number of evaluations when compared with *Normal*. As confirmation of Equation 1 we recorded the predicted number of wasted evaluations and found the aggregate predicted waste was nearly identical to the differences between *Normal* and *Skip*.

Single, the only method without a mutation rate, is clearly not as generally effective as the other methods where mutation rate can be optimized. However, when the optimal mutation rate is not known, *Single* does show significant advantages. When compared against the entire space of tested mutation rates, *Single* almost always requires the least number of evaluations to succeed. Below the optimum mutation rates for each, *Skip* and *Accumulate* are reasonable approximations of *Single*, but come with the disadvantage that they are more computationally expensive. As the number of evaluations required to solve a problem increases, *Single* appears to improve in performance relative to *Normal*. Parity required the least number of evaluations to be solved, followed by Binary Encode and Binary Decode, with Multiply requiring by far the most. This ordering mirror's *Single*'s relative scaling with *Normal*, as it goes from a lower peak performance than *Normal* on Parity and Binary Encode to surpassing it on Binary Decode and Multiply.

Using Table 1, it is clear that *Normal* is never the best option. In all cases *Skip* and *Accumulate* can obtain better results, with even *Single* doing better on Binary Decode and Multiply. Furthermore, *Skip* always had a lower median absolute deviation than *Normal*, with *Accumulate* lower on all problems except Binary Decode. The statistical analysis is less clear as the deviations are so large, but *Skip*'s improvements are definitely significant on all problems except Binary Decode, with *Single* statistically better than *Normal* on Multiply. As support that our configuration for *Normal* is valid to compare against, our peak quality is approximately 6 times better than results published in [8] for their standard CGP and ECGP on Parity.

While the true complexity measure for a GP implementation is how many evaluations it requires to solve a problem, we also performed preliminary timing tests to ensure our new techniques were less computationally complex than the

Table 1. Comparisons of Best Mutation Rate for Each Mutation Method on Each Benchmark. All results are from 100% successful configurations.

		Normal	Skip	Accumulate	Single
3-bit Parity	Mutation Rate	0.02	0.02	0.01	N/A
	Median Evaluations	1,018	959	928	1358
	Median Absolute Deviation	614	564	416	733
	P value	N/A	0.0000	0.4875	0.0790
	Median Final Active Genes	250	250	262	223
3-bit Multiplier	Mutation Rate	0.004	0.002	0.0008	N/A
	Median Evaluations	503,424	398,354	421,859	340,165
	Median Absolute Deviation	191,037	184,979	165,218	151,063
	P value	N/A	0.0212	0.3632	0.0065
	Median Final Active Genes	627	629	684	620
16 to 4 Encode	Mutation Rate	0.004	0.004	0.008	N/A
	Median Evaluations	24,057	19,732	21,563	26,031
	Median Absolute Deviation	8,829	7,425	7,449	10,170
	P value	N/A	0.0000	0.0864	0.3578
	Median Final Active Genes	472	472	499	510
4 to 16 Decode	Mutation Rate	0.004	0.002	0.004	N/A
	Median Evaluations	73,351	70,023	65,347	69,564
	Median Absolute Deviation	17,889	17,036	18,411	21,131
	P value	N/A	0.415	0.3276	0.2398
	Median Final Active Genes	1,117	1,027	1,050	1,090

evaluations they avoid. When using the best found mutation rate on Multiply, *Normal* required the most time (4597 minutes) to complete all 50 runs, with *Skip* using 9% less time, *Accumulate* 16% less, and *Single* 29% less.

8   Conclusions and Future Work

CGP's current mutation operator has the potential to create offspring which can be identified as phenotypically identical to their parents without invoking the evaluation function. Evaluating these offspring creates waste, as we can assign their fitness to be identical to their parent. Through careful definition of how the mutation operator works, we have shown how the probability of having wasted evaluations is dependent on the mutation rate and the number of active genes. We predicted and then provided empirical evidence that avoiding this waste can reduce how many evaluations CGP requires to solve problems as well as reduce CGP's sensitivity to the mutation rate parameter.

We proposed *Skip* and *Accumulate* as two methods for what to do when actively identical offspring are detected, and *Single* as a method to ensure they are never created. On four fairly diverse benchmark problems we showed that *Skip* and *Accumulate* do at least as well as *Normal* using a variety of mutation rates and are frequently vastly more efficient than *Normal*. As there was little discernible difference in their overall quality, for now we suggest *Skip* be used as a replacement to *Normal*, as it is less complex than *Accumulate*, although future experimentation may suggest otherwise. In situations where the mutation rate cannot be optimized, we suggest *Single*, as while it did not achieve the best peak performance on all problems, it has the least overhead with the widest applicability. Furthermore, *Single* achieved the best results on the hardest test problem, suggesting more extensive testing of this method on difficult problems should be performed.

Even though the results appear to be problem independent, *Skip*, *Accumulate*, and *Single* should be tested on a wider range of problem classes to make sure. More advanced techniques for handling or avoiding wasted evaluations may also improve results, such as a modified version of *Single* to allow multiple active genes to be mutated at once. Nevertheless, we feel that the theoretic and empirical evidence sufficiently supports a need to avoid wasting evaluations on actively identical individuals.

References

1. Christensen, S., Oppacher, F.: An Analysis of Koza's Computational Effort Statistic for Genetic Programming. In: Foster, J.A., Lutton, E., Miller, J., Ryan, C., Tettamanzi, A.G.B. (eds.) EuroGP 2002. LNCS, vol. 2278, pp. 182–191. Springer, Heidelberg (2002)
2. Harding, S., Graziano, V., Leitner, J., Schmidhuber, J.: MT-CGP: mixed type cartesian genetic programming. In: GECCO 2012: Proceedings of the Fourteenth International Conference on Genetic and Evolutionary Computation Conference, Philadelphia, Pennsylvania, USA, July 7-11, pp. 751–758. ACM (2012)
3. McDermott, J., White, D.R., Luke, S., Manzoni, L., Castelli, M., Vanneschi, L., Jaskowski, W., Krawiec, K., Harper, R., De Jong, K., O'Reilly, U.M.: Genetic programming needs better benchmarks. In: GECCO 2012: Proceedings of the Fourteenth International Conference on Genetic and Evolutionary Computation Conference, Philadelphia, Pennsylvania, USA, July 7-11, pp. 791–798. ACM (2012)
4. Miller, J.F.: Cartesian genetic programming. In: Cartesian Genetic Programming, ch. 2. Natural Computing Series, pp. 17–34. Springer (2011)
5. Miller, J.F., Smith, S.L.: Redundancy and computational efficiency in cartesian genetic programming. IEEE Transactions on Evolutionary Computation 10(2), 167–174 (2006)
6. Vašíček, Z., Slaný, K.: Efficient Phenotype Evaluation in Cartesian Genetic Programming. In: Moraglio, A., Silva, S., Krawiec, K., Machado, P., Cotta, C. (eds.) EuroGP 2012. LNCS, vol. 7244, pp. 266–278. Springer, Heidelberg (2012)
7. Vassilev, V.K., Miller, J.F.: The Advantages of Landscape Neutrality in Digital Circuit Evolution. In: Miller, J.F., Thompson, A., Thompson, P., Fogarty, T.C. (eds.) ICES 2000. LNCS, vol. 1801, pp. 252–263. Springer, Heidelberg (2000)
8. Walker, J.A., Miller, J.F.: The automatic acquisition, evolution and reuse of modules in cartesian genetic programming. IEEE Transactions on Evolutionary Computation 12(4), 397–417 (2008)
9. Yu, T., Miller, J.: Neutrality and the Evolvability of Boolean Function Landscape. In: Miller, J., Tomassini, M., Lanzi, P.L., Ryan, C., Tetamanzi, A.G.B., Langdon, W.B. (eds.) EuroGP 2001. LNCS, vol. 2038, pp. 204–217. Springer, Heidelberg (2001)

Balancing Learning and Overfitting in Genetic Programming with Interleaved Sampling of Training Data

Ivo Gonçalves[1] and Sara Silva[2,1]

[1] CISUC, Department of Informatics Engineering, University of Coimbra, Portugal
[2] INESC-ID Lisboa, IST, Technical University of Lisbon, Portugal
icpg@dei.uc.pt, sara@kdbio.inesc-id.pt

Abstract. Generalization is the ability of a model to perform well on cases not seen during the training phase. In Genetic Programming generalization has recently been recognized as an important open issue, and increased efforts are being made towards evolving models that do not overfit. In this work we expand on recent developments that showed that using a small and frequently changing subset of the training data is effective in reducing overfitting and improving generalization. Particularly, we build upon the idea of randomly choosing a single training instance at each generation and balance it with periodically using all training data. The motivation for this approach is based on trying to keep overfitting low (represented by using a single training instance) and still presenting enough information so that a general pattern can be found (represented by using all training data). We propose two approaches called interleaved sampling and random interleaved sampling that respectively represent doing this balancing in a deterministic or a probabilistic way. Experiments are conducted on three high-dimensional real-life datasets on the pharmacokinetics domain. Results show that most of the variants of the proposed approaches are able to consistently improve generalization and reduce overfitting when compared to standard Genetic Programming. The best variants are even able of such improvements on a dataset where a recent and representative state-of-the-art method could not. Furthermore, the resulting models are short and hence easier to interpret, an important achievement from the applications' point of view.

Keywords: Genetic Programming, Overfitting, Generalization, Pharmacokinetics, Drug Discovery.

1 Introduction

Genetic Programming (GP) [13] is now a mature technique that routinely produces results that have been characterized as human-competitive [8]. However, a few open issues remain, one of them being the lack of generalization, or overfitting, of the evolved models [12]. Overfitting is said to occur when a model performs well on the training cases but poorly on unseen cases. This indicates

K. Krawiec et al. (Eds.): EuroGP 2013, LNCS 7831, pp. 73–84, 2013.

that the underlying relationships of the whole data were not learned, and instead a set of relationships existing only on the training cases were learned, but these have no correspondence over the whole known cases. Notably, in Koza [7] most of the problems presented did not use separate training and testing datasets, so performance was never evaluated on unseen cases [9]. Other non-evolutionary machine learning methods have dedicated a larger amount of research effort to generalization than GP, although the number of publications dealing with over-fitting in GP has been increasing in the past few years. For a review of the state-of-the-art in avoiding overfitting in GP the reader is referred to [4].

Part of the lack of generalization efforts can be related to another issue occurring in GP - bloat. Bloat can be defined as an excess of code growth without a corresponding improvement in fitness [14]. This phenomenon occurs in GP as in most other progressive search techniques based on discrete variable-length representations. Bloat was one of the main areas of research in GP, not only because its occurrence hindered the search progress but also because it was hypothesized, in light of theories such as Occam's razor and the Minimum Description Length, that a reduced code size could lead to better generalization ability. Researchers had a common agreement that these two issues were related and that counteracting bloat would lead to positive effects on generalization. This, however, has been recently challenged. Contributions show that, on the same problem, bloat free GP systems can still overfit, while highly bloated solutions may generalize well [16]. This leads to the conclusion that bloat and overfitting are in most part two independent phenomena. In light of this finding, new approaches to improve GP generalization ability are needed, particularly ones not based on merely biasing the search towards shorter solutions.

In this work we build on recent developments in this domain. We explore how we can balance keeping overfitting low and still reaching models with general patterns. We do that by interleaving the usage of the training data between a single instance and all the instances. This approach is inspired by a state-of-the-art method to control overfitting called Random Sampling Technique (RST) [4]. In order to experimentally validate our approach, we apply it to hard high-dimensional problems in the field of pharmacokinetics, comparing the results with the ones obtained by standard GP and by RST. The three problems addressed are the prediction of median lethal dose, protein-plasma binding levels, and human oral bioavailability of medical drugs [1]. Section 2 describes the proposed approaches and the experiments conducted. Section 3 presents and discusses the results and section 4 concludes.

2   Approaches and Experiments

This section describes the motivation, the proposed approaches, the experimental parameters and the datasets used.

2.1   Motivation

Using a varying subset of the training data was previously shown to have positive effects. In [2] it was shown that this type of approach could reduce the speed of a GP run and still achieve similar results to the standard GP approach of using all training data in a static manner. In a particular configuration, it was even possible to improve generalization. In [11] the usage of a varying subset of the training data was shown to reduce overfitting in a software quality classification task. [2] used between 10% and 15% of the total training data depending on the variant, while [11] used 50%. More recently, even smaller percentages of the total training data were shown to be able to reduce overfitting and improve generalization. In particular, even using only a single training instance and changing it every generation was shown to be able to achieve these same outcomes. This was shown in [4] in high-dimensional symbolic regression real-life datasets, as well as in artificial datasets in [10] and [3]. In [4] besides the reduced overfitting and improved generalization, it was also shown that the evolved solutions were smaller than those from standard GP.

In this work, we are mainly interested in the idea of choosing the subset of the training data randomly. This kind of approach is called Random Sampling Technique (RST) or Random Subset Selection (RSS). Here, we will use the term RST. Particularly, we build upon the idea of using a single randomly chosen training instance at each generation and balance it with periodically using all the training data. The motivation for this approach is based on trying to keep overfitting low (represented by using a single training instance) and still presenting enough information so that a general pattern can be found (represented by using all training data). We propose two approaches called interleaved sampling and random interleaved sampling that respectively represent doing this balancing in a deterministic or a probabilistic way.

2.2   Interleaved Sampling

This approach is based on deterministically interleaving between using one or all training instances. We propose three variants respectively naming them: interleaved, interleaved single and interleaved all. The first variant is based on using all training instances in the first generation, then changing to a single training instance in the next generation and proceeding with the same interleaving for the remaining generations. As such, and provided that the number of generations is even, this variant always evolves half of the generations with all training instances and the other half with a single instance. The interleaved single variant is based on giving preference to using a single training instance and can consequently be understood as interleaving with a bias towards a single training instance. A parameter is added in order to define how many generations using a single training instance are conducted for each generation where all training instances were used. The values tested for this parameter were 5%, 10%, 15%, 20% and 25%, where each value represents the percentage over the total number of generations. Conversely, the interleaved all variant is based on giving preference to using all training instances. The parameter for this variant is similar to the previous, and in this case defines how many generations using all training instances are conducted for each generation where a single training instance was used. The values tested for this parameter are the same as in the interleaved single variant.

2.3   Random Interleaved Sampling

This approach is based on probabilistically interleaving between using a single or all training instances. At each generation the decision of how many training instances to use is taken. The probability of using a single training instance is given as a parameter. The values tested for this parameter were 5%, 25%, 50%, 75% and 95%. It should be noted that using 100% as a parameter would be equivalent to the RST using a single training instance and changing it every generation. Similarly, using 0% as a parameter would be equivalent to the standard GP approach of always using all training data.

2.4   Parameters and Datasets

The experimental parameters used are provided in Table 1. Furthermore, crossover and mutation points are selected with uniform probability. Fitness is calculated as the Root Mean Squared Error between predicted and expected outputs. Statistical significance of the null hypothesis of no difference was determined with Mann-Whitney U tests at $p = 0.05$. Standard GP and RST 1/1 are used as baselines for comparison. Standard GP uses all the training data at every generation. RST 1/1 is also used as a baseline because it is a representative state-of-the-art method, as recently shown in [4]. It works by randomly choosing a new single training instance at each generation. For each dataset 30 different random partitions are used. Each method uses the same 30 partitions.

Table 1. GP parameters used in the experiments

Runs	30
Population	500
Generations	200
Training - Testing division	50% - 50%
Crossover operator	Standard subtree crossover, probability 0.9
Mutation operator	Point mutation, probability 0.1, mutation probability per node 0.05
Tree initialization	Ramped Half-and-Half, maximum depth 6
Function set	+, -, *, and /, protected as in [13]
Terminal set	Input variables, constants -1.0, -0.5, 0.0, 0.5 and 1.0
Selection for reproduction	Tournament selection of size 10
Elitism	Best individual always survives
Maximum tree depth	17

Experiments are conducted on three multidimensional symbolic regression real-life datasets, all of which on the pharmacokinetics domain. They have already been used in GP studies (e.g. [1]).

Toxicity. The goal of this application is to predict, in the context of a drug discovery study, the median lethal dose (represented as LD50) of a set of candidate drug compounds on the basis of their molecular structure. LD50 refers to the amount of compound required to kill 50% of the considered test organisms (cavies). Reliably predicting this and other pharmacokinetics parameters would permit to reduce the risk of late stage research failures in drug discovery, and enable to decrease the number of experiments and cavies used in pharmacological research [1]. The LD50 dataset consists of 234 instances, where each instance is a vector of 627 elements (626 molecular descriptor values identifying a drug, followed by the known LD50 for that drug). This dataset is freely available at http://personal.disco.unimib.it/Vanneschi/toxicity.txt. We will refer to this dataset as LD50.

Plasma Protein Binding. As in the toxicity application, also here the goal is to predict the value of a pharmacokinetics parameter of a set of candidate drug compounds on the basis of their molecular structure, this time the plasma protein binding level. Protein-plasma binding level (represented as %PPB) quantifies the percentage of the initial drug dose that reaches the blood circulation and binds to the proteins of plasma. This measure is fundamental for good pharmacokinetics, both because blood circulation is the major vehicle of drug distribution into human body and since only free (unbound) drugs can permeate the membranes reaching their targets [1]. The %PPB dataset consists of 131 instances, where each instance is a vector of 627 elements (626 molecular descriptor values identifying a drug, followed by the known %PPB for that drug). We will refer to this dataset as PPB.

Bioavailability. In this dataset the pharmacokinetics parameter to predict is the human oral bioavailability. Human oral bioavailability (represented as %F) is the parameter that measures the percentage of the initial orally submitted drug dose that effectively reaches the systemic blood circulation after passing through the liver. Being able to reliably predict the %F value for a potential new drug is outstandingly important, given that the majority of failures in compounds development from the early nineties to nowadays are due to a wrong prediction of this pharmacokinetic parameter during the drug discovery process [6,5]. The %F dataset consists of 359 instances, where each instance is a vector of 242 elements (241 molecular descriptor values identifying a drug, followed by the known value of %F for that drug). This dataset is freely available at http://personal.disco.unimib.it/Vanneschi/bioavailability.txt. We will refer to this dataset as Bio.

3 Results and Discussion

This section presents and discusses the results achieved. For the remainder of this paper, the terms training and testing fitness are to be interpreted in the following way: training fitness is the fitness of the best individual in the training set; testing fitness is the fitness of that same individual in the testing set. For the purpose of further comparisons we have considered the overfitting measure described in [4]. According to this measure, overfitting is simply calculated as the absolute value of the difference between testing and training fitness. This measure is associated with the intuitive notion that overfitting is related to the discrepancy between the performance of a model on the data seen during the training phase and the unseen data. Tree size is calculated as the number of nodes of a solution. The evolution plots present the results based on the median of the fitness, overfitting, tree size and tree depth of the best individuals in the training data at each generation over 30 runs. These plots can be found in figures 1, 2 and 3.

3.1 Interleaved Single and Interleaved All Variants

The interleaved single and the interleaved all variants are not shown in the evolution plots as they are very similar to, respectively, RST 1/1 and Standard GP. These similarities apply regardless of the parameterization.

For the interleaved single, statistical results confirm that this variant is superior in terms of overfitting reduction, across all datasets, to standard GP, being also superior in testing fitness on the LD50 and the PPB datasets. There is no statistically significant difference in terms of testing fitness on the Bio dataset. The comparisons between the RST 1/1 and standard GP reach the same conclusions. Therefore, the interleaved single variant, in these tested parameterizations, can be seen as equivalent to the RST 1/1. It seems that the effect of presenting all training data with this periodicity to the algorithm is negligible. In terms of tree size and tree depth, the interleaved single variant produces smaller and shallower trees when compared to standard GP. These results are also statistically significant across all datasets.

The interleaved all variant produced similar results to standard GP, across all datasets, in terms of training and testing fitness and overfitting. The statistical results show that there are almost no statistically significant differences between these methods and standard GP. The only statistically significant differences in testing fitness and overfitting occurred on the Bio dataset where standard GP is superior in both measures when compared to parameterizations 15% and 25%. From these results we conclude that providing a bias towards using all training data and periodically using a single instance is not an effective approach of improving generalization and reducing overfitting.

3.2 Interleaved and Random Interleaved Variants

As we can see from the evolution plots, the random interleaved approach has the expected behavior in regard to its parameterization. The closer the parameter is to 100%, the closer the method behaves as the RST 1/1. Conversely, the closer the parameter is to 0%, the closer the method behaves as the standard GP approach. Statistical results confirm that the 5% parameterization is very similar to

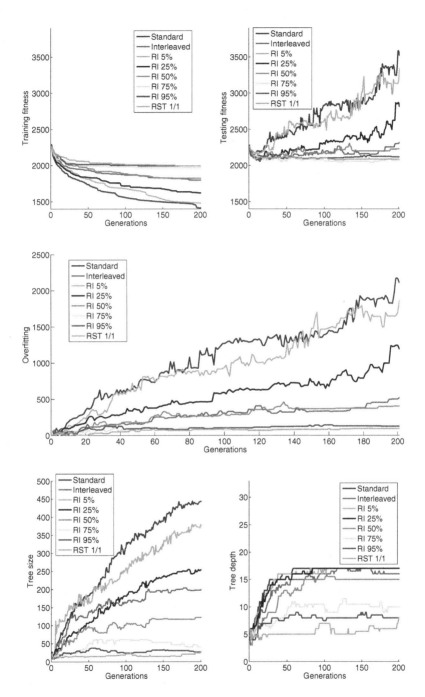

Fig. 1. Training fitness, testing fitness, overfitting, tree size and tree depth evolution plots for: Standard GP, Interleaved, Random Interleaved (RI) 5% 25% 50% 75% 95% and RST 1/1 on the LD50 dataset

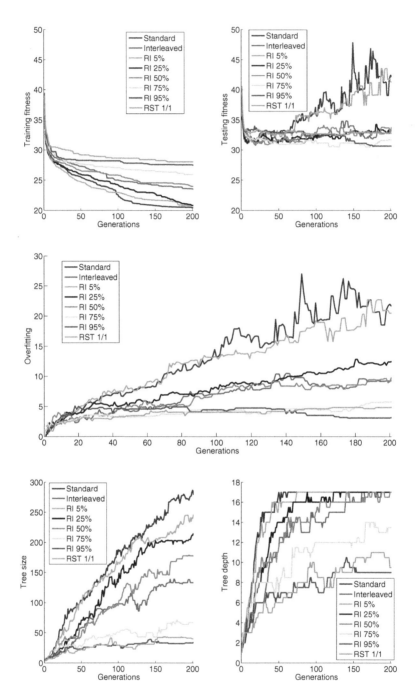

Fig. 2. Training fitness, testing fitness, overfitting, tree size and tree depth evolution plots for: Standard GP, Interleaved, Random Interleaved (RI) 5% 25% 50% 75% 95% and RST 1/1 on the PPB dataset

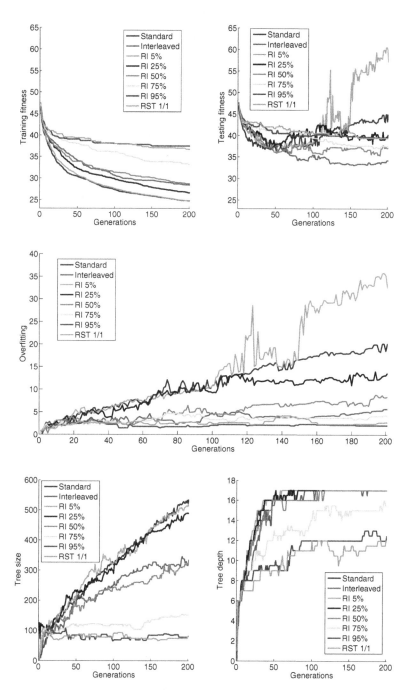

Fig. 3. Training fitness, testing fitness, overfitting, tree size and tree depth evolution plots for: Standard GP, Interleaved, Random Interleaved (RI) 5% 25% 50% 75% 95% and RST 1/1 on the Bio dataset

the standard GP approach and it is unable to improve generalization and reduce overfitting. All other parameterizations are able, with statistical significance, to improve generalization and reduce overfitting over the standard GP approach on the LD50 and PPB datasets. However, only the 50% and the 75% parameterizations can achieve an increase in generalization on the Bio dataset. The RST 1/1 is unable to achieve this same statistically significant result on this dataset. This shows that depending on the dataset, different probabilities of choosing a single training instance may be helpful. Nevertheless, from the results we can see that the most promising area for looking for a good parameterization to a given dataset revolves around the 50% parameterization. The interleaved results are similar to the random interleaved 50%, having also the same statistical significance over the standard GP approach. This was somewhat expected since both methods use on average the same number of generations with a single training instance. As we can see from the RST 1/1 results on the Bio dataset, although it is able to avoid overfitting, it also presents a slow learning of both training and testing data. In comparison, interleaved and random interleaved 50% and 75% are able to increase the rate of learning of the training data while also improving testing fitness. In terms of tree size and tree depth, the interleaved variant and the random interleaved variant with 50%, 75% and 95% parameterizations, produce smaller and shallower trees when compared to standard GP. These results are also statistically significant across all datasets.

3.3   Final Remarks

Overall, and across all the datasets, the methods that showed to be more consistent were: interleaved and random interleaved 50% and 75%. These three methods showed to be superior to standard GP in terms of reducing overfitting and improving generalization. Furthermore, they have also improved generalization where the RST 1/1 and the interleaved single methods could not: the Bio dataset. This dataset showed to be the most difficult of the three in terms of improving the testing fitness over standard GP. These facts allow us to conclude that these three methods are superior to standard GP and more robust than the RST 1/1 approach and hence contribute to an incremental improvement of the state of the art in this field.

From the point of view of the applications, the fact that these methods also produce relatively short models is a major advantage. At the end of the run, random interleaved 75% provides models with median size around 50 for the LD50 and PPB problems, and around 150 for the Bio problem. These are very short models when we consider the dimensionality of the data (626 features for LD50 and PPB, 241 for Bio). For the Bio problem this size is similar to the sizes obtained with the very successful bloat control technique Operator Equalisation (OpEq) [15]. For LD50 it is actually better, i.e. lower, than the sizes obtained by OpEq [16]. For PPB, to our knowledge no results are reported in the literature for the median tree size of the best individual.

4   Conclusions

In this work we expanded on recent developments in terms of overfitting reduction and generalization improvement. These developments have showed that using a small and frequently changing subset of the training data is effective in reducing overfitting and improving generalization. Particularly, we have built upon the idea of using a single randomly chosen training instance at each generation and balance it with periodically using all training data. The motivation for this approach is based on trying to keep overfitting low (represented by using a single training instance) and still presenting enough information so that a general pattern can be found (represented by using all training data). We have proposed two approaches called interleaved sampling and random interleaved sampling that respectively represent doing this balancing in a deterministic or a probabilistic way. Experiments were conducted in three high-dimensional real-life problems on the pharmacokinetics domain. The results have shown that most of the proposed approaches were able to consistently improve generalization and reduce overfitting when compared to the standard GP approach. In particular, three methods have shown these improvements even on a dataset where a state-of-the-art technique failed. These results were confirmed as being statistically significant. From the point of view of the applications, the winning methods have the additional advantage of producing relatively short models, hence easier to interpret.

In conclusion, we have found that both the deterministic and the probabilistic approach of balancing the usage of training data were helpful in improving generalization and reducing overfitting. We have also found that, in most cases, and in order to achieve these improvements, a preference has to be given towards using only a single training instance. The prevalence of this preference is dependent on the dataset but, in general, using a single training instance in more or less half of the generations is enough.

Acknowledgments. This work was partially supported by national funds through FCT under contract Pest-OE/EEI/LA0021/2011. The authors also acknowledge project PTDC/EIA-CCO/103363/2008 from FCT, Portugal. The first author work is supported by Fundação para a Ciência e a Tecnologia (FCT), Portugal, under the grant SFRH/BD/79964/2011.

References

1. Archetti, F., Lanzeni, S., Messina, E., Vanneschi, L.: Genetic programming for computational pharmacokinetics in drug discovery and development. Genetic Programming and Evolvable Machines 8(4), 413–432 (2007)
2. Gathercole, C., Ross, P.: Dynamic Training Subset Selection for Supervised Learning in Genetic Programming. In: Davidor, Y., Männer, R., Schwefel, H.-P. (eds.) PPSN 1994. LNCS, vol. 866, pp. 312–321. Springer, Heidelberg (1994)
3. Gonçalves, I., Silva, S.: Experiments on controlling overfitting in genetic programming. In: Proceedings of the 15th Portuguese Conference on Artificial Intelligence: Progress in Artificial Intelligence, EPIA 2011 (2011)

4. Gonçalves, I., Silva, S., Melo, J.B., Carreiras, J.M.B.: Random Sampling Technique for Overfitting Control in Genetic Programming. In: Moraglio, A., Silva, S., Krawiec, K., Machado, P., Cotta, C. (eds.) EuroGP 2012. LNCS, vol. 7244, pp. 218–229. Springer, Heidelberg (2012)
5. Kennedy, T.: Managing the drug discovery/development interface. Drug Discovery Today 2(10), 436–444 (1997)
6. Kola, I., Landis, J.: Can the pharmaceutical industry reduce attrition rates? Nat. Rev. Drug Discov. 3(8), 711–716 (2004)
7. Koza, J.R.: Genetic Programming: On the Programming of Computers by Means of Natural Selection (Complex Adaptive Systems), 1st edn. The MIT Press (1992)
8. Koza, J.R.: Human-competitive results produced by genetic programming. Genetic Programming and Evolvable Machines 11(3-4), 251–284 (2010)
9. Kushchu, I.: An evaluation of evolutionary generalisation in genetic programming. Artif. Intell. Rev. 18, 3–14 (2002)
10. Langdon, W.B.: Minimising testing in genetic programming. Tech. Rep. RN/11/10, Computer Science, University College London, Gower Street, London WC1E 6BT, UK (2011)
11. Liu, Y., Khoshgoftaar, T.: Reducing overfitting in genetic programming models for software quality classification. In: Proceedings of the Eighth IEEE International Conference on High Assurance Systems Engineering, HASE 2004, pp. 56–65. IEEE Computer Society, Washington, DC (2004)
12. O'Neill, M., Vanneschi, L., Gustafson, S., Banzhaf, W.: Open issues in genetic programming. Genetic Programming and Evolvable Machines 11, 339–363 (2010)
13. Poli, R., Langdon, W.B., McPhee, N.F.: A field guide to genetic programming (2008)
14. Silva, S., Costa, E.: Dynamic limits for bloat control in genetic programming and a review of past and current bloat theories. Genetic Programming and Evolvable Machines 10, 141–179 (2009)
15. Silva, S., Vanneschi, L.: Bloat free genetic programming: Application to human oral bioavailability prediction. International Journal of Data Mining and Bioinformatics 6(6), 585–601 (2012)
16. Vanneschi, L., Silva, S.: Using Operator Equalisation for Prediction of Drug Toxicity with Genetic Programming. In: Lopes, L.S., Lau, N., Mariano, P., Rocha, L.M. (eds.) EPIA 2009. LNCS, vol. 5816, pp. 65–76. Springer, Heidelberg (2009)

Automated Design of Probability Distributions as Mutation Operators for Evolutionary Programming Using Genetic Programming

Libin Hong[1], John Woodward[1], Jingpeng Li[1], and Ender Özcan[2]

[1] Department of Computer Science, University of Nottingham P.R.C.
[2] Department of Computer Science, University of Nottingham U.K.
{Libin.HONG,John.WOODWARD,Jingpeng.LI}@nottingham.edu.cn
Ender.Ozcan@nottingham.ac.uk

Abstract. The mutation operator is the only source of variation in Evolutionary Programming. In the past these have been human nominated and included the Gaussian, Cauchy, and the Lévy distributions. We automatically design mutation operators (probability distributions) using Genetic Programming. This is done by using a standard Gaussian random number generator as the terminal set and and basic arithmetic operators as the function set. In other words, an arbitrary random number generator is a function of a randomly (Gaussian) generated number passed through an arbitrary function generated by Genetic Programming.

Rather than engaging in the futile attempt to develop mutation operators for arbitrary benchmark functions (which is a consequence of the No Free Lunch theorems), we consider tailoring mutation operators for particular function classes. We draw functions from a function class (a probability distribution over a set of functions). The mutation probability distribution is trained on a set of function instances drawn from a given function class. It is then tested on a separate independent test set of function instances to confirm that the evolved probability distribution has indeed generalized to the function class.

Initial results are highly encouraging: on each of the ten function classes the probability distributions generated using Genetic Programming outperform both the Gaussian and Cauchy distributions.

Keywords: Evolutionary Programming, Genetic Programming, Function Optimization, Machine Learning, Meta-learning, Hyper-heuristics, Automatic Design.

1 Introduction

Evolutionary Programming (EP) is one of the branches of Evolutionary Computation and is used to evolve numerical values in order to find a global optimum of a function. The only genetic operator is mutation. The probability distributions used as mutation operators include Gaussian, Cauchy and Lévy, among others.

K. Krawiec et al. (Eds.): EuroGP 2013, LNCS 7831, pp. 85–96, 2013.

In 1992 and 1993, Fogel and Bäck et al. [4][1] indicated that Classical Evolutionary Programming (CEP) with adaptive mutation usually performs better than CEP without adaptive mutation.

In 1996, a new mutation operator, the Cauchy distribution, was proposed to replace the Gaussian distribution. The authors Yao and Yong have done experiments which followed Bäck and Schwefel's algorithm [1]. Fast EP (FEP) [14] uses a Cauchy distribution as mutation operator. The aim of this paper is to develop a Genetic Programming (GP) system which has a function set and terminal set which is capable of (easily) expressing either the Gaussian or Cauchy distribution, and then embracing the search utility of GP to discover more suitable mutation probability distributions.

In recent years, many improvements on EP have been proposed. Improved FEP (IFEP) [13], mixes mutation operators, and uses both Gaussian and Cauchy distributions. Later a mixed mutation strategy (MSEP) [3] was proposed: four mutation operators are used and the mutation operator is selected according to their probabilities during the evolution.

In 2004, EP that uses Lévy probability distribution $L_{\alpha,\gamma}(y)$ as mutation operator was proposed [5]. According to their experimental results, they obtained the following conclusion: Lévy based mutation can lead to a large variation and a large number of distinct values in evolutionary search, in comparison with traditional Gaussian mutation [5]. From 2007, Ensemble strategies with adaptive EP (ESAEP), Novel adaptive EP on four constraint handling techniques, and EP using a mixed mutation strategy were proposed [7][6][3]. Thus research into EP is still very much an active area of research.

This paper proposes a novel method to generate new mutation operators to promote the convergence speed of EP. It applies GP to train EP's mutation operators, and then use the new GP-generated distribution (GP-distribution) as new mutation operator for EP on functions similar (i.e. drawn from the same function class) to functions in the training set, which we now explain.

In previous work on function optimization, typically an algorithm is applied to a *single* function to be optimized. As the algorithm is applied, it learns better values for its best-so-far value. We regard a function instance as a single function drawn from a probability distribution over functions, which we call a *function class*. In this paper we are employing a meta-learning approach consisting of a base-level and meta-level [9] [10]. EP sits at the base-level, learning about the specific function, and GP sits at the meta-level, which is applied across function instances, learning about the function class as a whole. By taking this approach we can say that one mutation operator developed by GP on one function class is suitable for function instances drawn from that class, while another mutation operator is more suited to function instances drawn from a different function class. To phrase it differently, a mutation operator developed on one function class will be able to exploit characteristics of functions that are drawn from that function class.

In Section 2 we describe function optimization and the EP algorithm. In Section 3 we describe how GP is applied to the task of finding a probability distribution which can be used as a mutation operator in EP, and define the Function Classes used in this study are also presented. In Section 4 we compare Gaussian, Cauchy and the GP-distributions found by GP, and plot histograms of GP-distributions. We also list the experimental results. In Section 5 we discuss and explain future work. In Section 6 we summarize and conclude the article.

2 Function Optimization by Evolutionary Programming

Global minimization can be formalized as a pair (S, f), where $S \in \mathbb{R}^n$ is a bounded set on $\mathbb{R}^n$ and $f : S \longrightarrow \mathbb{R}$ is an n-dimensional real-valued function. The aim is to find a point $x_{min} \in S$ such that $f(x_{min})$ is a global minimum on S. More specifically, it is required to find an $x_{min} \in S$ such that

$$\forall x \in S : f(x_{min}) \leq f(x)$$

Here f does not need to be continuous or differentiable but it must be bounded. According to the description by Bäck et al [1], the EP is implemented as follows:

1. *Generate the initial population of p individuals, and set k = 1. Each individual is taken as a pair of real-valued vectors, (x_i, η_i), $\forall i \in \{1, \cdots, \mu\}$. The initialization value of the strategy parameter η is set to 3.0.*
2. *Evaluate the fitness value for each (x_i, η_i), $\forall i \in \{1, \cdots, \mu\}$.*
3. *Each parent (x_i, η_i), $\forall i \in \{1, \cdots, \mu\}$, creates λ/μ offspring on average, so that a total of λ offspring are generated: for i=1, $\cdots$, μ, j=1, $\cdots$, n.*

$$x_i'(j) = x_i(j) + \eta_i(j)D_j \tag{1}$$

$$\eta'(j) = \eta_i(j)exp(\gamma'N(0,1) + \gamma N_j(0,1)) \tag{2}$$

   The above two equations are used to generate new offspring. Objective function is used to calculate the fitness value, the survival offspring is picked up according to the fitness value. The factors γ and γ' have set to $(\sqrt{2\sqrt{n}})^{-1}$ and $(\sqrt{2n})^{-1}$.
4. *Evaluate the fitness of each offspring (x_i', η_i'), $\forall i \in \{1, \cdots, \mu\}$, according to $f(x')$.*
5. *Conduct pairwise comparison over the union of parents (x_i, η_i) and offspring (x_i', η_i'), $\forall i \in \{1, \cdots, \mu\}$. Q opponents are selected randomly from the parents and offspring for each individual. During the comparison, the individual receives a "win" if its fitness is no greater than those of opponents.*
6. *Pick the μ individuals out of parents and offspring, $i \in \{1, \cdots, \mu\}$, that have the most wins to be parents, to form the next generation.*
7. *Stop if the stopping criterion is satisfied; otherwise, k++ and goto Step3.*

If D_j in Eq.(1) is the Gaussian distribution, then the algorithm is CEP. If D_j is the Cauchy distribution, it is FEP [14]. If D_j is the Lévy distribution, it is LEP [5]. Thus this algorithm acts as a template into which we can substitute distributions evolved by GP, which is the contribution of this paper.

3   Genetic Programming to Train Mutation Operators for Function Classes

In this section, we give the details of how we use GP to train an EP mutation operator. In the past, candidate distributions have been nominated by humans and tested on a set of benchmark function instances. Here we automate this process by using GP to generate-and-test the distributions. The research question we are addressing in this paper is the following: is it possible for GP to automatically generate mutation operators (i.e. probability distributions) which can be used in EP to outperform the human generated distributions? As we have a terminal set containing a Gaussian distribution, it is not surprising that we can evolve a new distribution which can outperform a Gaussian distribution. Nor is it surprising that we can evolve a new distribution which can outperform a Cauchy distribution, as a Cauchy distribution can be generated by dividing a Gaussian distribution by another and can easily be generated by GP containing division in its function set.

At this stage we should also point out that we are doing more than "just" parameter tuning. That is, we are not just altering the numerical parameters (mean and variance) of a Gaussian distribution, but actually generating new distributions which do not belong to the Gaussian distribution.

3.1   Genetic Programming and Automatic Design

GP can be considered a specialization of the more widely known Genetic Algorithms (GAs) where each individual is a computer program [8]. GP automatically generates computer programs to solve specified tasks. It is a method of searching a space of computer programs, and therefore is an automatic way of producing computable probability distributions [8]. Over last few years, the application of GP has become more ambitious, and has been applied to other branches like combinatorial optimization [9][2]. However this new direction is probably due largely to the availability faster machines on which our implementations can be executed, rather than any break through or deep understanding of the search mechanisms of GP. In particular GP can be applied to the task of automated design of components of search algorithms [12] [11] though in these cases random search and iterative hill-climbing were used.

3.2   Function Classes

In the past, researchers use particular functions as a benchmark to test the performance of their algorithms. Our work differs markedly in this respect. We define a set of function classes from which functions are drawn from. In this way, we can train an EP mutation operator and tune it to that function class. It would not make sense to apply an EP algorithm (or any other optimization algorithm for that matter) to arbitrary functions and hope for good performance, a consequence of the No Free Lunch theorems.

As an example of a function class $(a \sum_{i=1}^{n} x_i^2)$, where a is a random variable in the range $[1, 2]$, and $f(x) = \sum_{i=1}^{n} x_i^2$ is an instance of a function from this function class (i.e. when $a = 1$). The motivation for defining a function class like this is that we can then evolve a mutation operator which is fit-for-purpose i.e. as a mutation operator on functions drawn from that function class. Evolution is adapting the distribution to fit the environment (function class).

3.3   Algorithm Using GP to Train EP Mutation Operator

Below is the pseudo-code of the training algorithm:

```
1:  Initial gp population
2:  while gpGen < gpMaxGen do
3:     gpPop = 1 /*Set GP iteration*/
4:     while (gpPop < gpMaxPop) do /*Evaluate individuals in GP*/
5:      epIteration = 1   /*Set EP iteration*/
6:      while (epIteration < epMaxIteration) do
7:         Randomly generate a (and b)
8:         Evaluate fitness of pop[gpPop]/*Compute fitness values by EP*/
9:         Set fitness value to fitness[epIteration]
10:        epIteration++
11:     end while
12:     Calculate mean fitness value meanFitness[epMaxIteration]
13:     gpPop++
14:    end while
15:    Select best pop by meanFitness[epMaxIteration]
16:    Crossover pop  /*Crossover pop in GP*/
17:    Mutate pop  /*Mutation pop in GP*/
18: end while
```

The terminal set consists of the Gaussian distribution $N(\mu, \sigma^2)$. We set the value of $\mu = 0$ and the value of σ is randomly assigned from the range $[0, 5]$. The value of μ could be allowed to alter, but it was deemed not necessary in these initial experiments. The value of σ was fixed for a given GP run, but could be allowed to vary between GP programs and within GP programs. We assign the function set as $\{+, -, \times, \div\}$, where $\div$ is protected, if a value a is divided by zero, then the value is a. This simple function set is expressive enough to be able to generate a wide range of functions (and therefore probability distributions). In Step 8, we use EP as fitness function to evaluate the GP-distribution. In Step 9 we assign it the best fitness of each EP run, averaged over the 20 EP runs. When evaluating the fitness value, EP runs 20 times and we calculate the mean value in last generation as fitness value for GP as was done in the original work by Yao [14].

3.4   Unimodal and Multimodal Function Classes

In Table 1, we list all the function classes used in this paper. In the function class suite, f_1-f_7 are unimodal function classes, f_8-f_{10} are multimodal function classes. f_8 is a special case , the f_{min} for function class 8 is not fixed. However for an instance of function class 8, the value of f_{min} is fixed, and depending on the value of a.

Table 1. The 10 function classes used in our experimental studies, where n is the dimension of the function, f_{min} is the minimum value of the function, and $S \subseteq \mathbb{R}^n$. n is 30, a is random number in the range [1, 2], and b is random number from the specified range or N/A.

Function Classes	S	b	f_{min}
$f_1(x) = a \sum_{i=1}^{n} x_i^2$	$[-100, 100]^n$	N/A	0
$f_2(x) = a \sum_{i=1}^{n} \mid x_i \mid + b \prod_{i=1}^{n} \mid x_i \mid$	$[-10, 10]^n$	$b \in [0, 10^{-5}]$	0
$f_3(x) = \sum_{i=1}^{n} (a \sum_{j=1}^{i} x_j)^2$	$[-100, 100]^n$	N/A	0
$f_4(x) = \max_i \{ a \mid x_i \mid, 1 \le i \le n \}$	$[-100, 100]^n$	N/A	0
$f_5(x) = \sum_{i=1}^{n} [a(x_{i+1} - x_i^2)^2 + (x_i - 1)^2]$	$[-30, 30]^n$	N/A	0
$f_6(x) = \sum_{i=1}^{n} (\lfloor ax_i + 0.5 \rfloor)^2$	$[-100, 100]^n$	N/A	0
$f_7(x) = a \sum_{i=1}^{n} i x_i^4 + random[0, 1)$	$[-1.28, 1.28]^n$	N/A	0
$f_8(x) = \sum_{i=1}^{n} -(x_i \sin(\sqrt{\mid x_i \mid}) + a)$	$[-500, 500]^n$	N/A	[-12629.5, -12599.5]
$f_9(x) = \sum_{i=1}^{n} [ax_i^2 + b(1 - cos(2\pi x_i))]$	$[-5.12, 5.12]^n$	$b \in [5, 10]$	0
$f_{10}(x) = -a \exp(-0.2 \sqrt{\frac{1}{n} \sum_{i=1}^{n} x_i^2})$ $- \exp(\frac{1}{n} \sum_{i=1}^{n} \cos 2\pi x_i) + a + e$	$[-32, 32]^n$	N/A	0

4   Experimental Studies

In previous work, most of the authors have tested their algorithms on a benchmark suit of 23 function instances. In this paper, we use the first 10 (see Table 1). This is largely due to the fact that we have to repeatedly run GP to train a mutation operator for each function class. We run EP 20 times with each mutation operator, and use the mean value of all 20 runs as the fitness value for GP. If a mutation operator (GP-distribution) found by GP which has good performance on a function class, it should have good performance on other function instance drawn from that function class.

The new methods we proposed has successfully found a new mutation operator for each function class. All the mutation operators found beat both Cauchy and Gaussian mutation operator. The only function on which good results were not found was f_{10}, but this may be because GP was either over-fitting or under-fitting and is discussed in future work.

4.1   Parameters Setting

A different maximum number of generations is used as a termination criterion in EP as provided in section 4.3. Table 2 provides the rest of the parameter values that we used in our approach. We regard the parameters of EP as fixed for this experiment (in the sense we are comparing a method against others for these EP parameter settings). We are not claiming optimality for the GP parameter settings, which are set rather low compared to traditional values, however we did find in these preliminary experiments that these settings were adequate enough to obtain human competitive results.

Table 2. Parameter settings for GP and EP

Parameter Meanings	Settings	Parameter Name in Section 3.3
Max Generation of GP	5	gpMaxGen
Population Size of GP	9	gpMaxPop
Operators of GP	Crossover Mutation	N/A
GP Function Set	$\{+, -, \times, \div\}$	N/A
GP Terminal Set	$N(0, [0, 5]^2)$	N/A
Number of Iteration of EP	20	epMaxIteration
Population Size of EP	100	N/A
Tournament Size of EP	10	N/A

4.2 Analysis and Comparisons

The best GP-distribution found for each of the ten function classes is listed in Table 3. In our test, μ has a fixed value 0, σ is randomly generated in the range $[0, 5]$. To compare the difference between GP-distributions, Gaussian and Cauchy, we plot all distributions in Fig.1 and Fig.2. For each distribution we plot it for 3000 samples (please note the scale of x-axis).

Table 3. All GP-distributions for function classes

Function Class	Best Distribution Survived in GP (GP-distribution)	Value of σ
$f_1(x)$	$(\div\ (\div\ (-(0\ N(0, \sigma^2)))\ N(0, \sigma^2))\ N(0, \sigma^2))$	0.171281
$f_2(x)$	$N(0, \sigma^2)$	0.010408
$f_3(x)$	$N(0, \sigma^2)$	1.749545
$f_4(x)$	$(+(N(0, \sigma^2)\ (-(\div(\div(+(N(0, \sigma^2)\ N(0, \sigma^2))\ N(0, \sigma^2))$ $N(0, \sigma^2))\ N(0, \sigma^2)))))$	2.962383
$f_5(x)$	$N(0, \sigma^2)$	0.056501
$f_6(x)$	$(+(N(0, \sigma^2)\ (-(N(0, \sigma^2)\ N(0, \sigma^2)))))$	3.879682
$f_7(x)$	$N(0, \sigma^2)$	4.851848
$f_8(x)$	$(\div(\div(\times(\times(N(0, \sigma^2)\ \times (N(0, \sigma^2)N(0, \sigma^2)))\ N(0, \sigma^2))$ $N(0, \sigma^2))N(0, \sigma^2)))$	4.918542
$f_9(x)$	$(\div(N(0, \sigma^2)\ (-(\div(N(0, \sigma^2)\ (-(N(0, \sigma^2)\ N(0, \sigma^2))))$ $N(0, \sigma^2)))))$	0.157557
$f_{10}(x)$	$(+(N(0, \sigma^2)\ (+(N(0, \sigma^2)\ N(0, \sigma^2)))))$	0.276311

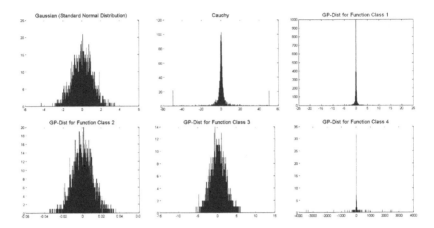

Fig. 1. Histograms of the distributions for 3000 samples

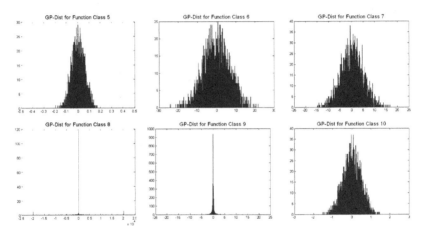

Fig. 2. Histograms of the distributions for 3000 samples

4.3   Test Function Classes

The results in Table 4 show that GP-distribution outperforms both Cauchy and Gaussian on all function classes. The results in Table 5 show that GP-distribution *statistically* outperforms both Cauchy and Gaussian on all function classes except f_{10} at the 0.05 level of confidence. In these initial experiments (which will form the start of a PhD thesis), even by allowing just σ of the Gaussian distribution to be altered we can outperform standard mutation operators on this set of function classes.

Table 4. The results for GP-distribution, FEP and CEP on f_1-f_{10}. All results have been averaged over 50 test runs, where "Mean Best" is the mean best function values found in the last generation, and "Std Dev" is the standard deviation.

Function Class	FEP Mean Best	Std Dev	CEP Mean Best	Std Dev	GP-distribution Mean Best	Std Dev
f_1	1.24×10^{-3}	2.69×10^{-4}	1.45×10^{-4}	9.95×10^{-5}	$\mathbf{6.37\times10^{-5}}$	5.56×10^{-5}
f_2	1.53×10^{-1}	2.72×10^{-2}	4.30×10^{-2}	9.08×10^{-3}	$\mathbf{8.14\times10^{-4}}$	8.50×10^{-4}
f_3	2.74×10^{-2}	2.43×10^{-2}	5.15×10^{-2}	9.52×10^{-2}	$\mathbf{6.14\times10^{-3}}$	8.78×10^{-3}
f_4	1.79	1.84	1.75×10	6.10	$\mathbf{2.16\times10^{-1}}$	6.54×10^{-1}
f_5	2.52×10^{-3}	4.96×10^{-4}	2.66×10^{-4}	4.65×10^{-5}	$\mathbf{8.39\times10^{-7}}$	1.43×10^{-7}
f_6	3.86×10^{-2}	3.12×10^{-2}	4.40×10	1.42×10^{2}	$\mathbf{9.20\times10^{-3}}$	1.34×10^{-2}
f_7	6.49×10^{-2}	1.04×10^{-2}	6.64×10^{-2}	1.21×10^{-2}	$\mathbf{5.25\times10^{-2}}$	8.46×10^{-3}
f_8	-11342.0	3.26×10^{2}	-7894.6	6.14×10^{2}	$\mathbf{-12611.6}$	2.30×10
f_9	6.24×10^{-2}	1.30×10^{-2}	1.09×10^{2}	3.58×10	$\mathbf{1.74\times10^{-3}}$	4.25×10^{-4}
f_{10}	1.67	4.26×10^{-1}	1.45	2.77×10^{-1}	$\mathbf{1.38}$	2.45×10^{-1}

Table 5. 2-tailed t-tests comparing EP with GP-distributions, FEP and CEP on f_1-f_{10}

Function Class	Number of Generations	GP-distribution vs FEP t-test	GP-distribution vs CEP t-test
f_1	1500	2.78×10^{-47}	4.07×10^{-2}
f_2	2000	5.53×10^{-62}	1.59×10^{-54}
f_3	5000	8.03×10^{-8}	1.14×10^{-3}
f_4	5000	1.28×10^{-7}	3.73×10^{-36}
f_5	20000	2.80×10^{-58}	9.29×10^{-63}
f_6	1500	1.85×10^{-8}	3.11×10^{-2}
f_7	3000	3.27×10^{-9}	2.00×10^{-9}
f_8	9000	7.99×10^{-48}	5.82×10^{-75}
f_9	5000	6.37×10^{-55}	6.54×10^{-39}
f_{10}	1500	9.23×10^{-5}	1.93×10^{-1}

Note that if we had only allowed EP to alter σ, then this method would have been regarded as parameter tuning (i.e. σ is simply a parameter of the algorithm). However we are automatically synthesizing new distributions by combining (by adding, subtracting, dividing and multiplying) Gaussian distributions so are engaging in an activity more expressive than tuning a numerical parameter. We have only allowed the Gaussian distributions to vary in their standard deviation, and while it makes complete sense to allow their *means* to be evolved too, this result supports the approach of the automatic design of algorithms, or a component of (in this case probability distributions). As it is sufficient to outperform human designed heuristics. Further work will address the shortcomings of these initial experiments, which we will now consider.

5   Discussion and Future Work

The initial aim of this paper is to build a system which is capable for synthesizing distributions for use as a mutation operator in EP. So far we have only compared it with FEP and CEP which has been successful. Later work therefore will address comparisons with more recent developments in EP including LEP [5], IFEP [13] and MSEP [3].

We have run the GP system for a fixed number of iterations, but have not optimized these parameters. Hence there is further scope for improvement of results in this regard. Further work includes using more sophisticated methods of terminating the meta-search (i.e. GP), such as early stopping to prevent either under-fitting or over-fitting. This is a more crucial issue than with traditional base-level only approaches as each evaluation is itself done over 20 EP runs.

We have defined function classes in terms of a random variable which is a coefficient in the function. This provides a source of related functions to be optimized. Each of these function classes (see Table 1) are either unimodal or multimodal functions. None of the currently defined function classes contain both, so it would be interesting to evolve a distribution capable of performing well on both types of function instances.

In the GP terminal set we used a normal distribution with fixed μ ($\mu=0$) and allowed σ to be set in the training phase. However, just by allowing σ to vary was enough to generate distributions which could beat Gaussian or Cauchy. Due to not allowing μ to vary meant, we could only generate symmetric distributions (see Fig.1 and Fig.2), but this is a reasonable assumption in the knowledge that all of the functions we are optimizing are symmetrical (why would be bias the search in one direction over another). However a hypothesis that comes out of this is the following: if we know a function is symmetrical (due to some real world domain knowledge) then a symmetric mutation operator will outperform an asymmetrical distribution. Similarly if we have little or no knowledge about the functions we are optimizing, then restricting the GP system to only produce symmetric distributions might over-constrain it.

One avenue of further work in GP is always to examine the parameters and components in more detail. In this paper we used a Gaussian distribution in the terminal set, but obviously it would be interesting to see if other distributions would give better results. However, we do not want to get involved in a circular argument, as we could try a Cauchy distribution in the GP terminal set (instead of a Gaussian). However nominating specific distributions (in the context of EP) is what we are trying to avoid in the first place (i.e. the whole point of the paper), and we are just raising the level of abstraction from the base-level to the meta-level [10]. Regardless of this dilemma we have still produced a system which outperforms the two human proposed systems we are comparing with.

6   Summary and Conclusions

EP is a robust method of solving numerical optimization problems. In the past this has involved using probability distributions (Gaussian and Cauchy) nominated by researchers as the mutation operator. In this paper we automatically generate probability distributions using GP, in a meta-learning approach, for use in EP. GP operates at the meta-level and contains a population of probability distributions which are inserted into an EP algorithm operating at the base-level and contains a population of numerical vectors. The fitness of a probability distribution is given by its performance over a number of function instances optimized by it in an EP algorithm. While EP is learning about values of single functions, GP is learning about distributions to be used by EP on functions drawn from a particular function class.

In a deviation from the approach used by other researcher, who tackle single isolated benchmark instances, we tackle function instances drawn from a function class by effectively implementing a probability distribution over function instances. During the training and testing phases the same function is highly unlikely to be seen twice. This is to demonstrate that the mutation operator has learned to generalize to the function class as a whole, rather than to any single instances.

Our initial results are highly encouraging. While we cannot claim that the distributions our method produces outperforms either Gaussian or Cauchy distributions on a single function (due to the statistical nature of EP), we can claim that on all but one function class (f_{10}) our method does produce distributions which statistically outperform the others (at a confidence level of 0.05) and at least does not under-perform on function class f_{10}.

One possible criticism of this method is the long training time required to evolve the distributions. After all we are evolving an evolutionary process itself. One line of future research is to speed-up this method, which is a central question for the GP community. For example, are GP trees the best representation for distributions? However, we claim that the amount of processor time required to generate distributions is still vastly less than the number of man-hours typically used in the design phase of new mutation operators (though of course the two are not directly comparable), and therefore the methodology proposed in this paper is a viable one.

References

1. Back, T., Schwefel, H.P.: An overview of evolutionary algorithms for parameter optimization. Evolutionary Computation 1, 1–23 (1993)
2. Burke, E.K., Hyde, M.R., Kendall, G., Ochoa, G., Ozcan, E., Woodward, J.R.: Exploring Hyper-heuristic Methodologies with Genetic Programming. In: Mumford, C.L., Jain, L.C. (eds.) Computational Intelligence. ISRL, vol. 1, pp. 177–201. Springer, Heidelberg (2009)
3. Dong, H., He, J., Huang, H., Hou, W.: Evolutionary programming using a mixed mutation strategy. Information Science, 312–327 (2007)
4. Fogel, D.B.: Evolving artificial intelligence. PhD thesis, University of California, San Diego (1992)
5. Lee, C.Y., Yao, X.: Evolutionary programming using mutations based on the lévy probability distribution. IEEE Transactions on Evolutionary Computation 8 (2004)

6. Mallipeddi, R., Suganthan, P.N.: Evaluation of novel adaptive evolutionary programming on four constraint handling techniques. In: IEEE Congress on Evolutionary Computation, pp. 4045–4052 (2008)
7. Mallipeddi, R., Mallipeddi, S., Suganthan, P.N.: Ensemble strategies with adaptive evolutionary programming. Information Science, 1571–1581 (2010)
8. Poli, R., Langdon, W.B., et al.: A field guide to genetic programming (2008) ISBN 978-1-4092-0073-4
9. Su Nguyen, M.Z., Johnston, M.: A genetic programming based hyper-heuristic approach for combinatorial optimization. In: Proceedings of the 13th Annual Conference on Genetic and Evolutionary Computation, pp. 1299–1306 (2011) ISBN 978-1-4503-0557-0
10. Woodward, J.: The necessity of meta bias in search algorithms. In: IEEE International Conference on Computational Intelligence and Software Engineering, CiSE (2010)
11. Woodward, J., Swan, J.: Automatically designing selection heuristics. In: ACM Proceedings of the 13th Annual Conference Companion on Genetic and Evolutionary Computation, pp. 583–590 (2011)
12. Woodward, J., Swan, J.: The automatic generation of mutation operators for genetic algorithms. In: ACM Proceedings of the Fourteenth International Conference on Genetic and Evolutionary Computation Conference Companion, pp. 67–74 (2012)
13. Xin Yao, Y.L., Lin, G.: Evolutionary programming made faster. IEEE Transactions on Evolutionary Computation 3, 82–102 (1999)
14. Yao, X., Liu, Y.: Fast evolutionary programming. In: Proceedings of the Fifth Annual Conference on Evolutionary Programming, pp. 451–460. MIT Press (1996)

Robustness and Evolvability of Recombination in Linear Genetic Programming

Ting Hu[1], Wolfgang Banzhaf[2], and Jason H. Moore[1]

[1] Computational Genetics Laboratory, Geisel School of Medicine, Dartmouth College,
Lebanon, NH 03756, USA
{ting.hu,jason.h.moore}@dartmouth.edu
[2] Department of Computer Science, Memorial University,
St. John's, NL, A1B 3X5, Canada
banzhaf@mun.ca

Abstract. The effect of neutrality on evolutionary search is known to be crucially dependent on the distribution of genotypes over phenotypes. Quantitatively characterizing robustness and evolvability in genotype and phenotype spaces greatly helps to understand the influence of neutrality on Genetic Programming. Most existing robustness and evolvability studies focus on mutations with a lack of investigation of recombinational operations. Here, we extend a previously proposed quantitative approach of measuring mutational robustness and evolvability in Linear GP. By considering a simple LGP system that has a compact representation and enumerable genotype and phenotype spaces, we quantitatively characterize the robustness and evolvability of recombination at the phenotypic level. In this simple yet representative LGP system, we show that recombinational properties are correlated with mutational properties. Utilizing a population evolution experiment, we demonstrate that recombination significantly accelerates the evolutionary search process and particularly promotes robust phenotypes that innovative phenotypic explorations.

Keywords: Robustness, Evolvability, Accessibility, Neutrality, Recombination, Genetic Programming.

1 Introduction

In natural systems, the term *evolvability* is usually put forward to describe the capacity of a population to produce heritable and beneficial phenotypic variations [16,25,31]. Although the mechanisms and origins of evolvability are still largely under debate, another pervasive property of natural systems, *robustness*, is often discussed in connection with evolvability and is assigned explanatory power for some of the high evolvability of living systems [18,21]. Despite the fact that most random mutations to genetic material are deleterious, random mutations are the fundamental fuel of long-term evolutionary innovation and adaptation. Robustness enables living systems to remain intact in the face of constant genetic perturbations through allowing genetic variants to expand in

K. Krawiec et al. (Eds.): EuroGP 2013, LNCS 7831, pp. 97–108, 2013.
© Springer-Verlag Berlin Heidelberg 2013

neutral spaces. These neutral spaces are genotypic regions in which mutations do not change phenotype or fitness and are the consequence of a redundant genotype-to-phenotype mapping [32]. Such *neutrality* augments evolvability, by accumulating genetic variations that might be non-neutral under changes of the environmental context [7,8,17,22,35].

A redundant mapping from genotype to phenotype is also pervasive in Genetic Programming (GP), where multiple genotypes encode identical phenotypes. A genetic change to a genotype, either mutation or crossover, is considered as neutral if it does not alter the phenotype or fitness. Extensive investigations and discussions have been carried through on how to characterize and utilize such neutrality in GP [1,3,4,11,28]. It has been recognized that neutrality enables phenotypes to be robust to genetic perturbations [29,36] and, more importantly, that it promotes the evolvability of phenotypes by expanding genotypes in neutral genotypic space without subjecting them to selection pressure [9,13].

In addition to extensive studies on mutational robustness and evolvability, it has been proposed recently in the context of gene regulatory circuits that recombination can create novel phenotypes more efficiently with a much less disruptive effect than mutation [20,33]. It is argued that recombination reorganizes genes and gene circuits and thus has greater phenotypic consequences than point mutation. Meanwhile it is less deleterious since it reuses existing genetic materials. In terms of expanding neutral spaces, recombination is also considered to be able to promote evolvability better than mutation. Neutral genetic variations by mutations are also called cryptic genetic variations that possess potential for creating novel phenotypes [21]. Such mutational robustness provides the quantitative staging ground for long-term adaptation and innovation. Recombination has a powerful effect augmenting those cryptic genetic variations to make qualitative changes [2,23,24].

Recombination has long been the center of the discussion on effective genetic operations in GP [5,19,27,30,34]. Similar to observations in gene regulatory circuits, it is well accepted in GP community that recombination is less destructive and has a larger phenotypic effect compared to point mutation. However, most robustness and evolvability studies in GP only consider mutations, and little has been done on quantifying recombinational robustness and evolvability and investigating the correlation between mutational and recombinational properties.

In a previous study [14], a quantitative characterization of mutational robustness and evolvability was performed in a simple Linear GP (LGP) system, where the entire genotype and phenotype spaces are finite and enumerable. In the current study, we adopt the same LGP system to utilize its compact properties and extend the quantitative metrics to recombination. In particular, we are interested to see whether different phenotypes have varying resilience or innovation potential under recombination. That is, if crossover is applied to a genotype from a given phenotype, is the individual more likely to stay in the same phenotype or to reach a novel phenotype? Are the probabilities to reach different novel phenotypes evenly distributed? Which phenotypes are more accessible from recombining genotypes of other phenotypes? Can recombination promote robust phenotypes to generate high evolvability? We answer these questions by characterizing phenotypic recombinational properties in genotype and phenotype space under a special recombination operator as well as utilizing a population evolution scheme to look into the interplay between mutation and crossover in evolutionary dynamics.

2 Methods

2.1 Linear Genetic Programming on Boolean Search

We consider a simple Linear Genetic Programming system as in the previous study [14]. In the LGP representation, an individual (or computer program) consists of a set of L instructions, which are structurally similar to those found in register machine languages. Each instruction has an operator, a set of operands, and a return value. To further restrict the search space, we use the LGP system on a Boolean search problem where each instruction consists of an operator drawn from the Boolean function set {AND, OR, NAND, NOR}, two Boolean operands, and one Boolean return value. The inputs, operands, and return values are stored in registers with varying read/write permissions. Specifically, R_0 and R_1 are calculation registers that can be read and written, whereas R_2 and R_3 are input registers that are read-only. Thus, a calculation register can serve in an instruction as an operand or a return, but an input register can only be used as an operand. An example program of length $L = 4$ is given here:

$$R_1 = R_2 \ \text{AND} \ R_3$$
$$R_0 = R_2 \ \text{OR} \ R_1$$
$$R_1 = R_1 \ \text{NOR} \ R_2$$
$$R_0 = R_3 \ \text{NAND} \ R_0$$

Instructions are executed sequentially from top to bottom. Prior to program execution, the values of R_0 and R_1 are initialized to FALSE. Registers R_2 and R_3 read two Boolean input values. After program execution, the final value in R_0 is returned as output.

2.2 Genotype and Phenotype Space

We consider each LGP program as a *genotype* and the binary Boolean function f : $\mathbf{B}^2 \to \mathbf{B}$, where $\mathbf{B} = \{\text{TRUE}, \text{FALSE}\}$, represented by the program as its *phenotype*. As described in the previous section, we allow two calculation registers, R_0 and R_1, two input registers, R_2 and R_3, and four possible Boolean operators, AND, OR, NAND, NOR. For the four loci on each instruction, only the two calculation registers can serve as the return (first locus), but all four registers can serve as operands (second and fourth locus), and all four Boolean functions can serve as the operator (third locus), which means there are $2 \times 4 \times 4 \times 4 = 2^7$ possible instructions and thus 2^{28} possible programs of length $L = 4$. These 2^{28} programs

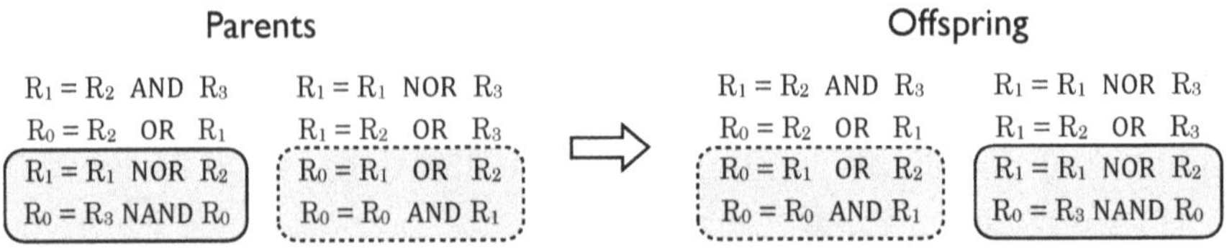

Parents   Offspring

$R_1 = R_2$ AND R_3 $R_1 = R_1$ NOR R_3 $R_1 = R_2$ AND R_3 $R_1 = R_1$ NOR R_3
$R_0 = R_2$ OR R_1 $R_1 = R_2$ OR R_3 $R_0 = R_2$ OR R_1 $R_1 = R_2$ OR R_3
$R_1 = R_1$ NOR R_2 $R_0 = R_1$ OR R_2 $\Rightarrow$ $R_0 = R_1$ OR R_2 $R_1 = R_1$ NOR R_2
$R_0 = R_3$ NAND R_0 $R_0 = R_0$ AND R_1 $R_0 = R_0$ AND R_1 $R_0 = R_3$ NAND R_0

Fig. 1. Symmetric recombination. The crossover point is chosen at half length of a LGP program. Two parent programs (left) swap their third and forth instructions with each other to form two new offspring (right). A offspring is called phenotypically neutral with its parents if it does not map to a novel phenotype different from its parents.

define the finite genotype space mapping to the 16 possible binary Boolean functions $f : \mathbf{B}^2 \to \mathbf{B}$ as phenotypes. Such a highly redundant genotype-to-phenotype mapping suggests great robustness in the system.

We can expect that the distribution of genotypes among different phenotypes is highly heterogeneous. We use s_i to denote the size of a phenotype i, i.e. the total number of genotypes that map to the same phenotype i. s_i ranges from a minimum of 24,832 genotypes (for phenotype EQUAL and NOTEQUAL) to a maximum of 60,393,728 genotypes (for FALSE), occupying between $\ll 1\%$ and 23% of the genotype space, respectively. As examined previously [14], for this particular Boolean LGP system, all phenotypes are connected to each other in the mutational genotypic space. That is, for any given phenotype, there exists a genotype that belongs to this phenotype and can transform to another genotype in any other phenotypes through a point mutation.

2.3   Symmetric Recombination

In the current study, we only consider a single-point recombination [10,12,26] and always choose half of program length as the crossover point (Fig. 1). This allows all offspring resulting from crossover to have the same length as their parents and thus to limit recombination dynamics to within the finite genotype space we have defined. We restrict the crossover point in the current study in order to reduce the computational load of monitoring all possible recombination events. Recombinations are allowed for genotypes within a phenotype and across different phenotypes. Two parent programs generate two offspring through a recombination event.

We investigate crossover events for genotypes from each of the $\binom{16}{2} + 16 = 136$ different unordered phenotype pairs, denoted $\langle i, j \rangle$, where $i, j \in \{1, 2, 3, ..., 16\}$. A phenotype pair $\langle i, j \rangle$ has a finite number $r_{i,j}$ of possible recombination events, i.e. $r_{i,i} = s_i \times (s_i - 1)/2$ if $i = j$ and $r_{i,j} = s_i \times s_j$ otherwise, where s_i is the size of phenotype i as defined previously. Although the genotype space is finite, enumerating all possible recombination events for all pairs of phenotypes would be computationally prohibitive. For instance, there are more than 308 million possible recombination events for choosing two genotypes from even the smallest phenotype EQUAL. Therefore, we sample $S = 1,000,000$ crossover events (without replacement) for genotypes from each phenotype pair $\langle i, j \rangle$. Among all the offspring generated by recombining a parent from phenotype i and a parent from phenotype j, we use $x_{(i,j),k}$ to denote the number of offspring that belong to phenotype k. Since we sample the same number S of crossover events across all possible phenotype pairs, we normalize $x_{(i,j),k}$ by adjusting it for different phenotype pairs, i.e. $x'_{(i,j),k} = \frac{r_{i,j}}{S} \times x_{(i,j),k}$.

2.4   Metrics on Recombinational Properties of Phenotypes

Intuitively, a phenotype is more robust under recombination if its crossover offspring are less likely to be phenotypically different from their parents. We define *recombinational robustness* R of phenotype i as the average fraction of phenotypically neutral offspring over all offspring,

$$R_i = \frac{1}{16} \times \sum_{j=1}^{16} \frac{\sum_{k=i,j} x'_{(i,j),k}}{\sum_{k=1}^{16} x'_{(i,j),k}}. \tag{1}$$

Similar to mutational metrics [6,14,15], we capture recombinational evolvability as the potential to change from one phenotype to another (different) phenotype. Let

$$f_{(i,j),k} = \begin{cases} \dfrac{x'_{(i,j),k}}{\sum_{l \neq i, l \neq j} x'_{(i,j),l}}, & \text{if } k \neq i \text{ and } k \neq j \\ 0, & \text{otherwise} \end{cases} \tag{2}$$

denote the fraction of offspring that result in genotypes of phenotype k by recombining genotypes from phenotypes i and j. We define *recombinational evolvability* E of a phenotype i as

$$E_i = 1 - \sum_{j,k} \left(\frac{f_{(i,j),k}}{\sum_{l,m} f_{(i,l),m}} \right)^2. \tag{3}$$

Since $\sum_{j,k} \frac{f_{(i,j),k}}{\sum_{l,m} f_{(i,l),m}} = 1$ for each i, Eq.(3) describes the diversity of the connections from phenotype i to other phenotypes via recombination. In other words, E_i captures the probability that randomly chosen genotypes from phenotype i generate recombination offspring with distinct phenotypes. This evolvability measure takes on a higher value if a phenotype has a more evenly distributed potential to reach other phenotypes through recombinations.

In addition to measuring the propensity to leave a phenotype, we also use *recombinational accessibility* A_k to describe how easily a phenotype k can be reached via recombination events from other phenotypes, formally defined as,

$$A_k = \sum_{i,j} f_{(i,j),k}. \tag{4}$$

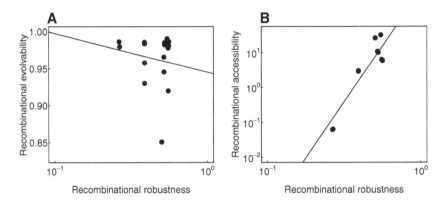

Fig. 2. A) recombinational evolvability and **B**) recombinational accessibility relative to recombinational robustness. Each data point represents a phenotype. Linear-log scale is chosen for **A**) and log-log scale is chosen for **B**) based on their best fitting relationship. The lines show the best fitting curves and provide a guide for the eye.

2.5   Population Evolution

In addition to sampling recombination events in the static genotype and phenotype spaces, we also perform population evolution experiments to investigate the interplay between mutation and recombination in a population under evolution. We choose the least represented phenotype EQUAL as the target phenotype to allow evolution to proceed over a longer time.

A non-overlapping generational evolution model with a fixed population size $|P|$ is adopted in this study. After population initialization, a new generation of offspring is produced sequentially. We randomly choose an individual with replacement, mutate according to a certain rate, and place it into the next generation. This is repeated $|P|$ times until the next generation of the population is filled. When both mutation and recombination are applied, for each generation, we randomly choose two individuals with replacement, cross them over at a given rate, mutate their crossover offspring at a given rate, and place both offspring into the next generation. This is repeated $\frac{|P|}{2}$ times until the next generation of the population is filled. The evolution process is terminated when the target phenotype is reached, and the required number of generations is recorded for each run.

3   Results

3.1   Recombinational Robustness, Evolvability, and Accessibility

Through the extensive sampling, this LGP problem instance is found having complete recombinational connections. That is, for any given phenotype pair, there exist pairs of their genotypes that can generate recombinational offspring of any other phenotypes. Fig. 2 shows the correlations among the recombinational

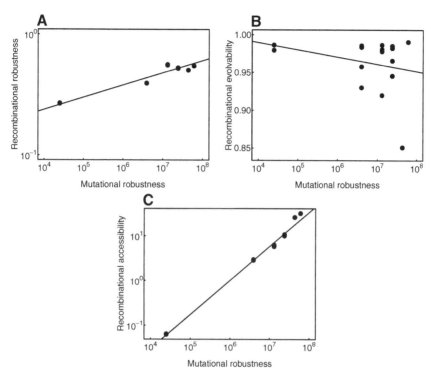

Fig. 3. A) recombinational robustness, **B)** recombinational evolvability, and **C)** recombinational accessibility relative to mutational robustness. Log-log, linear-log, and log-log scales are chosen accordingly based on the best-fitting relationships. Each data point represents a phenotype and the lines depict the best fitting curves.

metrics. Recombinational evolvability is weakly and negatively correlated with recombinational robustness with linear-log fitting $r^2 = 0.02395$, $p = 0.5671$ (Fig. 2-**A**). Phenotypes that have low recombinational robustness are highly evolvable, and robust phenotypes can have either high or low recombinational evolvability. In contrast, recombinational accessibility is strongly and positively correlated with recombinational robustness with a log-log fitting $r^2 = 0.8262$, $p = 1.09 \times 10^{-6}$ (Fig. 2-**B**). This suggests that phenotypes that are resilient to recombination are also very accessible from recombining genotypes of other phenotypes.

3.2   Comparisons of Recombinational and Mutational Measures

We now compare the recombinational measures to the previously investigated mutational measures [14,15]. Fig.3 shows recombinational robustness, evolvability, and accessibility relative to mutational robustness. Recall that phenotypic mutational robustness is defined as the size of a phenotype, i.e. its total number of underlying genotypes.

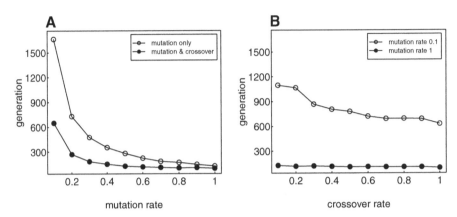

Fig. 4. The generations required to reach the target as a function of **A**) mutation rate and **B**) crossover rate. **A**) Mutation rate varies from 0.1 to 1 and crossover rate is fixed to 1. Two sets of experimental results are included, population evolution with mutation only (circles) and population evolution with both mutation and crossover (solid points). **B**) When both mutation and crossover are applied, we fix mutation rate to 0.1 and 1 and vary crossover rate from 0.1 to 1.

Recombinational robustness is positively correlated with mutational robustness (Fig. 3-**A**), which suggests that mutationally robust phenotypes are also resilient to recombinations ($r^2 = 0.8732$, $p = 1.172 \times 10^{-7}$). Similar to the weak relationship between recombinational evolvability and recombinational robustness, recombinational evolvability is weakly and negatively correlated with mutational robustness (Fig. 3-**B** with $r^2 = 0.06805$, $p = 0.3291$). As seen in the upper-left corner of the figure, less mutationally robust phenotypes that have fewer underlying genotypes are highly evolvable through recombination. Among mutationally robust phenotypes, some are also highly evolvable through recombination, but some only have very biased recombinational connections to other phenotypes. Interestingly, recombinational accessibility has a very strong positive correlation with mutational robustness (Fig. 3-**C**). In addition to the previously found strong positive relationship between mutational robustness and mutational accessibility [14], this very strong correlation ($r^2 = 0.9915$, $p = 7.021 \times 10^{-16}$) suggests that phenotypes with a large number of underlying genotypes are highly accessible from other phenotypes by both mutation and by recombination.

3.3   Population Dynamics Results

We compare two evolution scenarios with mutation only and with both mutation and crossover. Population size is set to 100 for both cases. Fig. 4 shows the population evolution results. Each data point is an averaged value of 100 runs for each configuration. We first vary mutation rate from 0.1 to 1 and fix crossover rate to 1. In general, increasing mutation rate accelerates the search process, and applying both mutation and crossover allows to reach the target faster than

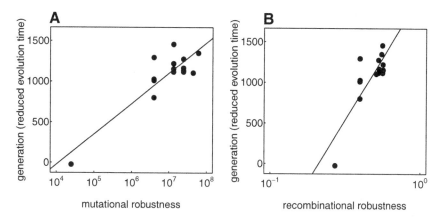

Fig. 5. The reduced evolution time, obtained by comparing mutation-only evolution and mutation-and-crossover evolution, relative to **A**) mutational robustness and **B**) recombinational robustness of the starting phenotypes. Data points represent different starting phenotypes, the line depicts the best linear-log fitting curve.

applying mutation alone. We then fix mutation rate and vary crossover rate (Fig. 4-**B**). Mutation rate is set to 0.1 and 1, and for each fixed mutation rate, crossover rate varies from 0.1 to 1. As seen in the figure, increasing crossover rate also accelerates the evolution process. The trend is more significant for mutation rate 0.1 than for mutation rate 1 in the figure, but it is clearly observable for both cases when one takes a closer look at appropriate scales.

Since it is shown that combining mutation and crossover significantly accelerates evolution, next we are interested to see if this improvement is correlated with the robustness of the starting phenotype. We choose a representative setting with mutation rate 0.1 and crossover rate 1, and obtain the reduced evolution time by taking the difference between mutation-only evolution time and mutation-and-crossover evolution time. As shown in Fig. 5, the reduced evolution time is positively correlated with the starting phenotypic mutational robustness ($r^2 = 0.7756$, $p = 1.513 \times 10^{-5}$) and recombinational robustness ($r^2 = 0.6772$, $p = 1.644 \times 10^{-4}$). This suggests that recombination improves the evolvability of phenotypes, and this improvement is more significant for more robust phenotypes. In other words, recombination promotes robust phenotypes to be more evolvable.

4   Discussion

This study examines the phenotypic robustness and evolvability subject to recombination. Utilizing a simple LGP system that has compact and finite genotype and phenotype spaces allows us to quantitatively characterize robustness and evolvability at the phenotypic level. We also investigate the interplay between mutation and recombination in evolution dynamics by performing a generational population evolution experiment.

The phenotypes of our LGP system have varying recombinational robustness. Some of them are more tolerant to recombinations but some of them are not. Recombination-sensitive phenotypes are found highly evolvable by possessing a relatively evenly distributed potential to reach other phenotypes via recombination. Recombination-robust phenotypes are very accessible from recombining genotypes of other phenotypes. Recombinational robustness is positively correlated with mutational robustness, which suggests that over-represented phenotypes that have a great number of underlying genotypes are robust to both mutation and recombination. These over-represented phenotypes are also very accessible via both mutation and crossover. Through investigating population dynamics, recombination is found to be able to significantly accelerate evolutionary search if added to mutation. This acceleration is more significant when a population is initialized from a more robust phenotype.

Our results agree with findings from biological systems and also provide insights into our own computational systems. The ease of finding a target phenotype considerably depends on whether this target phenotype is over-represented by many genotypes. Less-represented phenotypes might be hard to reach, but they could serve as important bridges accessing other novel phenotypes. Robust phenotypes enhance the innovative power of recombination as they provide rich cryptic genetic variations for phenotypic exploration.

Future work will consider applying different recombinational operations such as a crossover point different from the mid-point adopted in this study or a non-symmetric crossover operation. We want to test if the current observations still hold in other scenarios and if our quantitative measures are sensitive to the choice of recombinational operation. It is also important to extend our quantitative measures to larger and more realistic systems. The results obtained here using a simple LGP system showcase the effectiveness of the quantitative approach and also generate hypotheses on how real and large-scale computational systems could behave. It would be very beneficial to test the scalability of our approach on more complex problem instances. An advantage of using larger-scale problem instances is that evolution will have a longer trajectory, and thus we could make observations on the detailed evolution dynamics at the individual level and see whether crossover leads to the prevalence of robust genotypes/phenotypes. We also would like to include fitness selection in our next step in particular with larger-scale problem instances. Finally, a varying selection pressure may have an impact on the evolution towards high robustness.

Acknowledgments. This work was supported by National Institute of Health (USA) grants R01-LM009012, R01-LM010098, and R01-AI59694 to J.H.M. W.B. acknowledges support from NSERC Discovery Grants, under RGPIN 283304-2012.

References

1. Altenberg, L.: The evolution of evolvability in genetic programming. In: Advances in Genetic Programming, pp. 47–74. MIT Press, Cambridge (1994)
2. Azevedo, R.B., Lohaus, R., Srinivasan, S., Dang, K.K., Burch, C.L.: Sexual reproduction selects for robustness and negative epistasis in artificial gene networks. Nature 440(2), 87–90 (2006)
3. Banzhaf, W.: Genotype-phenotype mapping and neutral variation - a case study in genetic programming. In: Davidor, Y., Männer, R., Schwefel, H.-P. (eds.) PPSN 1994. LNCS, vol. 866, pp. 322–332. Springer, Heidelberg (1994)
4. Banzhaf, W., Leier, A.: Evolution on neutral networks in genetic programming. In: Yu, T., Riolo, R., Worzel, B. (eds.) Genetic Programming Theory and Practice III, ch. 14, pp. 207–221. Springer (2006)
5. Banzhaf, W., Nordin, P., Keller, R.E., Francone, F.D.: Genetic Programming: An Introduction. Morgan Kaufmann (1998)
6. Cowperthwaite, M.C., Economo, E.P., Harcombe, W.R., Miller, E.L., Meyers, L.A.: The ascent of the abundant: How mutational networks constrain evolution. PLoS Computational Biology 4(7), e1000110 (2008)
7. De Visser, J.A.G.M., Hermission, J., Wagner, G.P., Meyers, L.A., Bagheri-Chaichian, H., et al.: Evolution and detection of genetic robustness. Evolution 57(9), 1959–1972 (2003)
8. Draghi, J.A., Parsons, T.L., Wagner, G.P., Plotkin, J.B.: Mutational robustness can facilitate adaptation. Nature 463, 353–355 (2010)
9. Ebner, M., Shackleton, M., Shipman, R.: How neutral networks influence evolvability. Complexity 7(2), 19–33 (2002)
10. Francone, F.D., Conrads, M., Banzhaf, W., Nordin, P.: Homologous crossover in genetic programming. In: Banzhaf, W., Daida, J.M., Eiben, A.E., Garzon, M.H., Honavar, V., Jakiela, M.J., Smith, R.E. (eds.) Proceedings of the Genetic and Evolutionary Computation Conference, pp. 1021–1026 (1999)
11. Galvan-Lopez, E., Poli, R.: An empirical investigation of how and why neutrality affects evolutionary search. In: Cattolico, M. (ed.) Proceedings of the Genetic and Evolutionary Computation Conference, pp. 1149–1156 (2006)
12. Hansen, J.V.: Genetic programming experiments with standard and homologous crossover methods. Genetic Programming and Evolvable Machines 4, 53–66 (2003)
13. Hu, T., Banzhaf, W.: Neutrality and variability: two sides of evolvability in linear genetic programming. In: Rothlauf, F. (ed.) Proceedings of the Genetic and Evolutionary Computation Conference, pp. 963–970 (2009)
14. Hu, T., Payne, J.L., Banzhaf, W., Moore, J.H.: Robustness, Evolvability, and Accessibility in Linear Genetic Programming. In: Silva, S., Foster, J.A., Nicolau, M., Machado, P., Giacobini, M. (eds.) EuroGP 2011. LNCS, vol. 6621, pp. 13–24. Springer, Heidelberg (2011)
15. Hu, T., Payne, J.L., Banzhaf, W., Moore, J.H.: Evolutionary dynamics on multiple scales: a quantitative analysis of the interplay between genotype, phenotype, and fitness in linear genetic programming. Genetic Programming and Evolvable Machines 13, 305–337 (2012)
16. Kirschner, M., Gerhart, J.: Evolvability. Proceedings of the National Academy of Sciences 95, 8420–8427 (1998)
17. Landry, C.R., Lemos, B., Rifkin, S.A., Dickinson, W.J., Hartl, D.L.: Genetic properties influcing the evolvability of gene expression. Science 317, 118–121 (2007)

18. Lenski, R.E., Barrick, J.E., Ofria, C.: Balancing robustness and evolvability. PLoS Biology 4(12), e428 (2006)
19. Luke, S., Spector, L.: A comparison of crossover and mutation in genetic programming. In: Koza, J.R., Deb, K., Dorigo, M., Fogel, D.B., Garzon, M., Iba, H., Riolo, R.L. (eds.) Proceedings of the Annual Conference on Genetic Programming, pp. 240–248 (1997)
20. Martin, O.C., Wagner, A.: Effects of recombination on complex regulatory circuits. Genetics 183, 673–684 (2009)
21. Masel, J., Trotter, M.V.: Robustness and evolvability. Trends in Genetics 26, 406–414 (2010)
22. McBride, R.C., Ogbunugafor, C.B., Turner, P.E.: Robustness promotes evolvability of thermotolerance in an RNA virus. BMC Evolutionary Biology 8, 231 (2008)
23. Neher, R.A., Shraiman, B.I., Fisher, D.S.: Rate of adaptation in large sexual populations. Genetics 184, 467–481 (2010)
24. Otto, S.P.: The evolutionary enigma of sex. The American Naturalist 174(s1), s1–s14 (2009)
25. Pigliucci, M.: Is evolvability evolvable? Nature Review Genetics 9, 75–82 (2008)
26. Platel, M.D., Clergue, M., Collard, P.: Maximum Homologous Crossover for Linear Genetic Programming. In: Ryan, C., Soule, T., Keijzer, M., Tsang, E.P.K., Poli, R., Costa, E. (eds.) EuroGP 2003. LNCS, vol. 2610, pp. 194–203. Springer, Heidelberg (2003)
27. Poli, R., Langdon, W.B.: On the search properties of different crossover operators in genetic programming. In: Koza, J.R., Banzhaf, W., Chellapilla, K., Deb, K., Dorigo, M., Fogel, D.B., Garzon, M.H., Goldberg, D.E., Iba, H., Riolo, R.L. (eds.) Proceedings of the Annual Conference on Genetic Programming, pp. 293–301 (1998)
28. Rothlauf, F., Goldberg, D.E.: Redundant representations in evolutionary computation. Evolutionary Computation 11(4), 381–415 (2003)
29. Soule, T.: Resilient individuals improve evolutionary search. Artificial Life 12, 17–34 (2006)
30. Soule, T., Heckendorn, R.B.: An analysis of the causes of code growth in genetic programming. Genetic Programming and Evolvable Machines 3, 283–309 (2002)
31. Wagner, A.: Robustness, evolvability, and neutrality. Federation of European Biochemical Societies Letters 579(8), 1772–1778 (2005)
32. Wagner, A.: Robustness and evolvability: A paradox resolved. Proceedings of The Royal Society B 275(1630), 91–100 (2008)
33. Wagner, A.: The low cost of recombination in creating novel phenotypes. BioEssays 33(8), 636–646 (2011)
34. White, D.R., Poulding, S.: A Rigorous Evaluation of Crossover and Mutation in Genetic Programming. In: Vanneschi, L., Gustafson, S., Moraglio, A., De Falco, I., Ebner, M. (eds.) EuroGP 2009. LNCS, vol. 5481, pp. 220–231. Springer, Heidelberg (2009)
35. Wilke, C.O.: Adaptive evolution on neutral networks. Bulletin of Mathematical Biology 63, 715–730 (2001)
36. Yu, T., Miller, J.F.: Through the interaction of neutral and adaptive mutations, evolutionary search finds a way. Artificial Life 12, 525–551 (2006)

On the Evolvability of a Hybrid Ant Colony-Cartesian Genetic Programming Methodology

Sweeney Luis and Marcus Vinicius dos Santos

Department of Computer Science, Ryerson University
Toronto, Canada
{sluis,m3santos}@ryerson.ca

Abstract. A method that uses Ant Colonies as a Model-based Search to Cartesian Genetic Programming (CGP) to induce computer programs is presented. Candidate problem solutions are encoded using a CGP representation. Ants generate problem solutions guided by pheromone traces of entities and nodes of the CGP representation. The pheromone values are updated based on the paths followed by the best ants, as suggested in the Rank-Based Ant System (AS_{rank}). To assess the evolvability of the system we applied a modified version of the method introduced in [9] to measure rate of evolution. Our results show that such method effectively reveals how evolution proceeds under different parameter settings. The proposed hybrid architecture shows high evolvability in a dynamic environment by maintaining a pheromone model that elicits high genotype diversity.

Keywords: Ant Colonies, Cartesian Genetic Programming, Rank-Based Ant System, Hybrid Architectures, Evolvability, Dynamic Environments.

1 Introduction

Dynamic problems are those in which the solution changes over time. In such domains, the ability of a population to evolve to a new region in the solution space is key. Tracking a moving optimum or moving from a local to a global optimum is facilitated when the problem representation and optimization methodology interact in ways to provide a high level of evolvability. In natural evolution, evolvability is the capacity for an adaptive response to a dynamic environment (fitness function) [1]. In genetic programming, a machine learning methodology concerned with evolving computer programs, the fitness function is in many cases static, so there is little selection pressure for "evolvability" in the biological sense. In the work presented here we set out to investigate the evolvability of a hybrid methodology that combines the Cartesian Genetic Programming (CGP) [10] representation and the probabilistic techniques for searching the solution space used in Ant Colony Optimization (ACO) [4].

Inspired on the Ants System introduced in [3], Ant Programming (AP) [11] extended ACO to Genetic Programming (GP) tree style representations. The AP

K. Krawiec et al. (Eds.): EuroGP 2013, LNCS 7831, pp. 109–120, 2013.
© Springer-Verlag Berlin Heidelberg 2013

system builds and modifies candidate problem solutions in accordance to the pheromone model referred as *pheromone tree*. The pheromone tree is composed of a number of pheromone tables for each tree node containing the pheromone values for the possible functions and terminals for the corresponding node. Using a similar approach, but based on different pheromone model, Dynamic Ant Programming (DAP) [14] introduced a dynamic tabular pheromone model which holds the pheromone values for the possible functions and terminals at each node and uses a *tabu list* restricting the selection of a non-terminal that has already been selected, thereby enabling the system to create diverse individuals. The pheromone table size changes dynamically in each iteration and nodes with low pheromone levels are deleted. This results in the system creating programs of smaller size on average.

In the work presented here, we propose a methodology that extends to CGP the representations introduced in probabilistic model building GP methodologies introduced in [8,5] and combines it with ACO. We begin by presenting in Section 2 the background materials regarding CGP and ACO. Then, in Section 3 we present how we take advantage of the CGP representation to propose a pheromone model that elicits genotype redundancies which have shown to be crucial for the evolvability of problem solutions [7,16]. We also introduce our learning algorithm, which draws on the Rank-Based Ant System (AS_{rank}) [2], where ants are ranked according to the quality of the CGP genomes they generate and the best ranked ants are used to update the pheromone table. The proposed method is similar to Cartesian Ant Programming (CAP) [6], where a pheromone model is sampled to create the genome of a CGP individual and the Max-Min Ant System (MMAS) [15] is used as the learning algorithm to update the pheromone model. To analyze the evolvability of our system, in Section 3 we propose a variant of the nonsynoymous to synonymous substitution ratio k_a/k_s introduced in [9]. In Section 4 we present the experimental design used to benchmark CAP against our approach. Our results show that in a static environment variability helps our system to converge to an optimal solution and neutrality helps preserve the optimal solution met. In a dynamic environment our system is able to maintain genotype diversity throughout the run which makes it highly adaptable to changes in the environment.

2   Background Materials

CGP is an artificial evolution methodology where the individuals are represented as a graph addressed on the Cartesian co-ordinate system and can be executed as a computer program. CGP distinguishes between genotype and phenotype unlike canonical genetic programming. In CGP, the genotype is a string of integers of fixed size which maps to the phenotype which is an executable graph. The genotype represents the graph's input and output connections. Each node consists of inputs and a function, each of which is represented by an integer number.

A CGP system needs prior definition of the following set of parameters $\{G, n_i,$ $n_o, n_n, F, n_f, n_r, n_c, l\}$, where G is the genotype (fixed set of integers); n_i are the program inputs; n_o is the number of program output connections; n_n is the number of node input connections; F is the set of functions; n_f is the number of functions; n_r is the number of nodes in each row; n_c is number of nodes in each column; l is the level back parameter defining how many previous columns of nodes may have their output connected to the input of a node in the current column. In this paper only feed-forward connectivity is considered. The genotype size is fixed and can be calculated as $n_r * n_c * (n_n + 1) + n_o$.

ACO is a swarm optimization technique inspired by the behavior of some ants species. An ant moves from source to destination guided by the pheromone levels on the available paths the ant can travel. If a path is constantly being used by several ants, then more pheromone gets deposited on that path. Therefore, there is a greater possibility that an ant that comes along this path will choose the path to find its food. Similarly, the lower the pheromone levels on a path the smaller the possibility that an ant will choose that path.

For artificial ants a pheromone model is maintained that holds the pheromone values at each node for the paths possible for the ant to travel from that node. This model is updated after every iteration where the paths traveled by the ant that lead to better solutions have a level of pheromone deposited and the remaining paths have a level of their pheromone value evaporated. Pheromone update is the process where good solutions are rewarded by adding to the level of pheromone on paths chosen to reach that solution and evaporating the pheromone level on paths that did not yield a good solution.

3 Methods

The central hypothesis put forth in this work is that the CGP representation combined with an ACO algorithm that elicits redundancies in genotype to phenotype mapping imparts better evolvability of solutions. In the underlying algorithm, artificial ants iteratively generate quality solutions by updating the pheromone model used to create the programs. The model is updated after each iteration by rewarding the most fit programs of the previous iteration. Such rewarding is achieved by increasing the pheromone level of the inputs and function used in each node, and decreasing the pheromone of unvisited nodes.

Drawing on the work presented in [9] we propose a measurement for rate of evolution. We show that it effectively reflects how evolution is driven by the underlying algorithm, and we perform a study case of the system's evolvability.

Pheromone Model. The pheromone model contains the pheromone values for all available inputs and functions needed in generating a node of the program. All pheromone values are initialized at the start to τ_d for all the available inputs and functions for a node. The inputs that are unavailable to a node have their pheromone value set to zero to refrain them from being selected and generating cyclic graphs, *i.e.*, programs with loops. Table 1 shows an example of a pheromone model for a symbolic regression representation. In the example,

Table 1. Representation of the pheromone model

Node	Input 1					Input 2					Function				Output Node					
	1.0	X	0	1	2	1.0	X	0	1	2	+	-	×	÷	1.0	X	0	1	2	3
0	τ_d	τ_d	0	0	0	τ_d	τ_d	0	0	0	τ_d	τ_d	τ_d	τ_d						
1	τ_d	τ_d	τ_d	0	0	τ_d	τ_d	τ_d	0	0	τ_d	τ_d	τ_d	τ_d	τ_d	τ_d	τ_d	τ_d	τ_d	τ_d
2	τ_d	τ_d	τ_d	τ_d	0	τ_d	τ_d	τ_d	τ_d	0	τ_d	τ_d	τ_d	τ_d						
3	τ_d	τ_d	τ_d	τ_d	τ_d	τ_d	τ_d	τ_d	τ_d	τ_d	τ_d	τ_d	τ_d	τ_d						

$n_i = \{1.0, X\}$, $F = \{+, -, \times, \div\}$, $n_n = 2$, $n_r = 1$, $n_c = 4$, $n_o = 1$ and $l = 3$. These inputs and functions are available for all nodes which are initialized to τ_d at the start.

Genome Creation: Each ant creates an individual's genotype by sampling the pheromone model. The ant samples the pheromone table and selects the appropriate input or function available, for each position in the genotype. The probability p_i that the ant selects a particular input or function i is given by $p_i = \frac{\tau_i}{\sum_{j=1}^{n_n} \tau_j}$, where n_n is the number of available inputs and functions.

Pheromone Update: The pheromone table is updated at the end of every iteration. The ants are ranked according to the quality of the solution they generate. Out of the m ants in each iteration only the $(n-1)$ *best-ranked ants* and the *best ant*, *i.e.*, the ant that produced the best solution so far (this ant could be from the current iteration or from a previous iteration) update the pheromone table as given by the following expression:

$$\tau_{ij}(t+1) = \tau_{ij}(t) + \sum_{r=1}^{n-1}(w - w_r)\Delta\tau_{ij}^r(t) + w\Delta\tau_{best} \tag{1}$$

where: $\tau_{ij}(t)$ is the current pheromone level of input(or function) i at node j at iteration t; w is a constant weight assigned at the start of the experiment; r is the rank of the ant; $w_r = w/(n-r)$; $(w - w_r)$ is the weight calculated that rewards higher ranked ants; and $\Delta\tau_{ij}^r(t)$ is equal to the fitness of rth-best ant, if ant selects input or function i at node j; otherwise it is zero. Analogously, $\Delta\tau_{best}$ is equal to the fitness of best ant.

Measuring Rate of Evolution: The nonsynonymous to synonymous substitution ratio k_a/k_s is a concept used to measure genetic substitution in molecular biology. This measurement has been used in [9] to quantitatively assess evolvability in Linear Genetic Programming (LGP). A change in the genome of an individual that brings about a change in its fitness is known as a *nonsynonymous* change, where as if a genome change does not cause a change in fitness, then it is called a *synonymous* change. We use the same terminology and a similar approach in the work presented here. One key difference, is that in the context of Ants (and Estimation of Distribution Algorithms) changes are brought about by probabilistic sampling of the pheromone table rather than by the application of genetic operators, which is the case in [9].

In our simulated studies we measure the k_a/k_s ratio by observing the changes brought about in the *best-ranked* ants. To determine the value of nonsynonymous (and synonymous) change we compare each individual I and individual J that were brought about by the N best-ranked ants of iteration t and $t-1$, respectively. The value of nonsynonymous change $m_{ak}^I(t)$ on each gene k of each individual I from iteration t is calculated as follows: if gene k did not change, i.e., $I_k = J_k$, then $m_{ak}^I(t) = m_{sk}^I(t) = 0$. Otherwise, if change was *silent*, i.e., individuals I and J have same fitness, then $m_{ak}^I(t) = 0, m_{sk}^I(t) = 1$. If change was not silent, then $m_{ak}^I(t) = 1, m_{sk}^I(t) = 0$.

We compute the number of nonsynonymous substitutions $M_a(t)$ and the number of synonymous substitutions $M_s(t)$ as follows: $M_a(t) = \sum_{i=1}^N m_{ak}^i(t)$, $M_s(t) = \sum_{i=1}^N m_{sk}^i(t)$

Like in [9], we keep a record of all changes to each gene during the iterations of the algorithm. We compute such accumulated numbers of nonsynchronous $c_{ak}(t)$ and synchronous $c_{sk}(t)$ changes in gene k up to iteration t, as follows: initially $c_{ak}(0) = c_{sk}(0) = 0$, for all genes k in the genome. We update these values for each gene k and individual I brought about by the N best-ranked ants of iteration t, as follows: $c_{ak}(t) = c_{ak}(t-1) + m_{ak}^I(t)$, $c_{sk}(t) = c_{sk}(t-1) + m_{sk}^I(t)$.And we compute the *potential* of a gene k being changed nonsynonymously or synonymously (also called the *sensitivity* of a gene) as follows: $n_{ak}(t) = \frac{c_{ak}(t)}{c_{ak}(t)+c_{sk}(t)}$, $n_{sk}(t) = \frac{c_{sk}(t)}{c_{ak}(t)+c_{sk}(t)}$

We add up the sensitivities of all genes in the representation to obtain the total nonsynonymous and synonymous sensitivities $N_a(t)$ and $N_s(t)$: $N_a(t) = \sum_{k=1}^N n_{ak}(t)$, $N_s(t) = \sum_{k=1}^N n_{sk}(t)$

Finally, we compute the nonsynonymous and the synonymous substitution rates k_a and k_s of iteration t as $k_a(t) = M_a(t)/N_a(t)$, $k_s(t) = M_s(t)/N_s(t)$, which enables us to obtain the rate of evolution R_e in iteration t:

$$R_e(t) = k_a(t)/k_s(t) \tag{2}$$

4   Experimental Design and Results

We begin by testing how effectively the rate of evolution reflects the dynamics of the underlying algorithm. We then compare the evolvability of our method with that of CAP in two different environmental conditions: a fixed target and a moving target environment.

4.1   Rate of Evolution under Different Parameter Settings

In this section we describe the experimental setting we have designed to study the influence of different parameter settings on factors related to the Rate of Evolution in a symbolic regression (SR) problem

In these experiments the target expression is the polynomial $x^4 + x^3 + x^2 + x$. The training set, *i.e.*, the fitness cases, consists of 40 equidistant example points in the interval $[-2.0, +2.0]$. Fitness of an individual is computed as the inverse of the accumulated error between the actual example points and the values output by the individual. Formally, let the output of the ith training example be o_i. Let the output of individual g on the ith example from the training set be g_i. Then, for a training set of $n = 40$ examples the fitness f_g of g is calculated as follows: $f_g = \frac{1}{1+\sum_{i=1}^{n} |o_i - g_i|}$

The parameters chosen for this experiment are shown in Table 2. The exponentially weighted moving average method, with a smoothing factor 0.1, is used to smoothen the curves.

Table 2. Parameter values for experiments SR, FTE and MTE

Parameter	Experiment		
	SR	FTE	MTE
n_i	$\{x, 1.0\}$	ditto	ditto
F	$\{+, -, \times, \div\}$	ditto	ditto
Number of Runs	100	ditto	ditto
Number of Iterations	1000	ditto	ditto
Number of Individuals	50	100	100
τ_d	1.0	ditto	ditto
Number of best-ranked ants	10	ditto	ditto
# of equidistant fitness cases	40	ditto	ditto
Interval	$[-2.0, 2.0]$	ditto	ditto

Population Size. In this experiment we alter the population sizes to 50, 100 and 200. From Figure 1(b) we see having a system with a larger population converges to the solution faster than a system with a smaller population.

The rate of evolution (R_e) in Figure 1(a) is synchronous with natural evolutions as it continues to be at the maximum value slightly above 1.0. As the run progresses the value of R_e continues to descend till it reaches *zero* evolution. The system with a larger population size reached *zero* evolution quicker than a system with a smaller population.

Initial Pheromone Level. In this experiment we study the influence of the initial pheromone value on R_e. The initial pheromone level is set to 0.1, 0.5 and 1.0 and analyze the effect on the rate of evolution and average fitness. From Figure 2(b) we see, a setup with a lower initial pheromone level converges to a solution quicker which reflects the findings in [14]. Observing R_e in Figure 2(a) in all conditions the maximum value is around 1.0 and proceeds towards *zero* evolution. With a lower initial pheromone level *zero* evolution reaches quicker than with a setup where the initial pheromone level is higher.

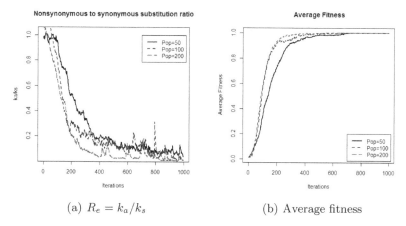

(a) $R_e = k_a/k_s$ (b) Average fitness

Fig. 1. Varying population sizes

4.2   CGP-ACO vs. CAP

Our approach differs from Cartesian Ant Programming (CAP) [6] in two key aspects: the learning algorithm and the method of updating the pheromone model.

CAP uses Max-Min Ant System (MMAS) [15] as the learning algorithm, where the *best ant* updates the pheromone model at the end of the iteration and the unused pheromone trails are subjected to evaporation. In MMAS, the pheromone model is updated according to the equation below:

$$\tau_{ij}(t+1) = (1-\rho)\tau_{ij}(t) + \Delta\tau_{ij}^{best}(t) \tag{3}$$

where: $\tau_{ij}(t)$ is the current pheromone level of input(or function) i at node j at iteration t; ρ is the evaporation rate; $\Delta\tau_{ij}^{best}$ is equal to the fitness of the best ant, if best ant selects input or function i at node j; otherwise it is zero.

In regards to the method of updating the pheromone model, after evaluating the individual, CAP traverses the model beginning from the output nodes and proceeds backwards towards the input nodes, only updating the model for the nodes that appear in the individuals phenotype. As such, only the pheromone values of the used nodes are updated. In our method, however, we update the pheromone model in a forward manner beginning from the input nodes and moving towards the output nodes, updating the pheromone values for all nodes that appear in the individual's genotype.

Fixed Target Evolution (FTE). In this experiment we evolve the expression $x^5 - 2x^3 + x$. Figure 3(d) shows that our approach attains maximum fitness faster with a steady convergence rate throughout the run than the approach used in CAP.

Figure 3(a) shows that our method engenders a high number of nonsynony-mous substitutions from the start of the run, and that number increases after the

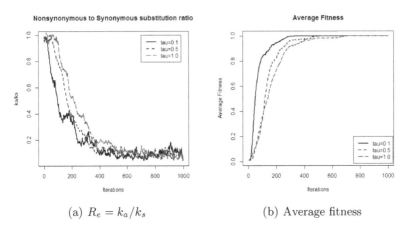

(a) $R_e = k_a/k_s$ (b) Average fitness

Fig. 2. Varying initial pheromone level

system converges to a solution. Using the method of updating the pheromone model as described in CAP, the system fixates on making a maximum number of nonsynonymous substitutions at the start of the run which results in the synonymous substitutions to be low at the start of the run and increase as the system converges to a solution of maximum fitness. In Figure 3(b) we plot the synonymous substitutions which shows us that using the CGP-ACO approach results in making a larger number of substitutions throughout the run which increases after the system converges to a solution. The method used in CAP involves making a fewer number of substitutions compared to the CGP-ACO approach, the system makes most of the substitutions after the system has converged to a solution. The result of the substitutions is seen in the rate of evolvability R_e in Figure 3(c), the CGP-ACO approach has a higher rate of R_e throughout the run where the system converges to *zero* evolvability towards the end of the run. Using the pheromone update method as used in CAP the model the system has a high value of R_e at the start of the run and reaches *zero* evolvability sooner than the CGP-ACO approach.

We conduct the Multiple Hypothesis Testing [13] to compare the performance of the two approaches. We test for the average fitness at different points of the run using a significance level $\alpha = 0.05$. We find CAP has a better performance in the initial stages of the run (at iteration 250, the p-value equals 0.012). However in the middle (at iteration 500, p-value $= 0.58$) and final stages (at iteration 750, p-value $= 0.33$) of the run there is no evidence of statistical difference between the two approaches.

Moving Target Evolution (MTE). In this experiment we create a moving target by increasing the degree n of the polynomial $\sum_{i=1}^{n} x^i$ at regular intervals. We start our target for the first 200 iterations at $i = 3$ where the target expression is $x^3 + x^2 + x$. From iteration 200 to 500 $i = 4$ and iteration 500 onwards $i = 5$.

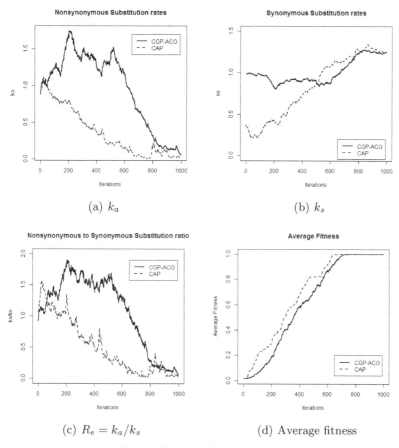

(a) k_a

(b) k_s

(c) $R_e = k_a/k_s$

(d) Average fitness

Fig. 3. FTE: CGP-ACO vs CAP

We use an enhanced version of the AS_{rank} model update method that includes evaporation. We incorporate evaporation to balance the effects of depositing a large amount of pheromone when the target is small which hinders exploration of alternative paths when the target is changed. For this experiment we set the evaporation rate to $\rho = 0.2$.

We emulate CAP's methodology using MMAS as the learning algorithm and with an evaporation rate of $\rho = 0.1$.

In Figure 4(d) we plot the average fitness for both systems. We take note that the convergence of the solution is almost identical for both systems. Analyzing the substitution rates in Figure 4(a) and 4(b) we see that both systems follow a similar trend in evolvability from iteration 0 to 200 where the target is an expression of a lower degree. From iteration 200 to the end of the run, as the target is changed and the degree of the polynomial keeps increasing, we notice that the rate of nonsynonymous substitutions in CAP is greater than in CGP-ACO. Also the number of synonymous substitutions made during this period in CAP is low compared to CGP-ACO. Moreover, Figure 4(d) shows that immediately after the target change CGP-ACO is able to produce solutions with higher fitness than CAP, which makes one wander if the CGP-ACO pheromone model elicits a more diverse genotype than the CAP pheromone model. Figure 4(e) shows that there is strong evidence pointing in that direction. Genotype diversity, in this case, was calculated using the diversity measure introduced by Shapiro in [12] (section 3 of that paper).

To assess the statistical significance we conduct the same Multiple Hypothesis Test as in the previous section (with $\alpha = 0.05$). Testing for the average fitness at different points of the run we find no evidence of statistical difference between the two approaches (at iteration 100, p-value = 0.71; at iteration 350, p-value = 0.3 and at iteration 750, p-value = 0.76). Testing for diversity at different points of the run we find very strong evidence of a statistical difference between the two approaches, showing CGP-ACO elicits higher diversity as the p-value at different points of the run are extremely small.

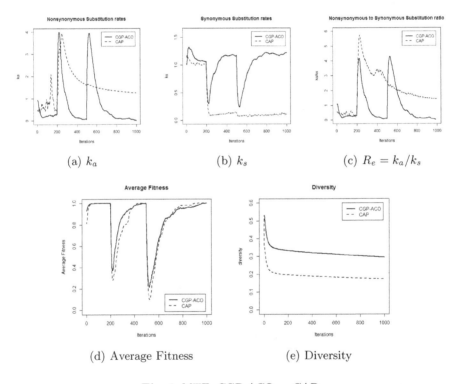

(a) k_a (b) k_s (c) $R_e = k_a/k_s$

(d) Average Fitness   (e) Diversity

Fig. 4. MTE: CGP-ACO vs CAP

5 Conclusion

In this work we introduced a hybrid optimization algorithm that combines Cartesian genetic programming with ant colonies. Using the rate of evolution we tested the evolvability of our system under different parameter settings and compared our results with CAP in two different environmental conditions

Analyzing the results we observed that a lower level of initial pheromone and a bigger population size helps in faster convergence. CGP-ACO has shown to be highly adaptable to the aforementioned environmental conditions. Our results also showed that CGP-ACO is on par with CAP with regards to average fitness of the evolved population. CGP-ACO, however, showed better adaptiveness when faced with a dynamic environment by maintaining a highly diverse genotype population.

The system imposes variability as a driving force when it needs to attain an optimal solution, where as neutrality helps the system preserve an optimal solution. Adaptiveness is a major characteristic of our system as changes in the environment causes the system to reflect those changes in the pheromone model, thus resulting in the creation of individuals that are highly fit for the environmental conditions.

References

1. Altenberg, L.: The evolution of evolvability in genetic programming. In: Advances in Genetic Programming, pp. 47–74. MIT Press, Cambridge (1994)
2. Bullnheimer, B., Hartl, R.F., Strauß, C.: A new rank based version of the ant system - a computational study. Central European Journal for Operations Research and Economics 7, 25–38 (1997)
3. Colorni, A., Dorigo, M., Maniezzo, V.: Distributed Optimization by Ant Colonies. In: European Conference on Artificial Life, pp. 134–142 (1991)
4. Dorigo, M., Birattari, M., Stutzle, T.: Ant colony optimization – artificial ants as a computational intelligence technique. IEEE Comput. Intell. Mag. 1, 28–39 (2006)
5. Ghoulbeigi, E., dos Santos, M.V.: Probabilistic developmental program evolution. In: Proceedings of the 2010 ACM Symposium on Applied Computing, SAC 2010, pp. 1138–1142. ACM, New York (2010)
6. Hara, A., Watanabe, M., Takahama, T.: Cartesian ant programming. In: SMC, pp. 3161–3166 (2011)
7. Harding, S., Miller, J.F., Banzhaf, W.: Smcgp2: self modifying cartesian genetic programming in two dimensions. In: GECCO, pp. 1491–1498 (2011)
8. Holker, G., dos Santos, M.V.: Toward an estimation of distribution algorithm for the evolution of artificial neural networks. In: Proceedings of the Third C* Conference on Computer Science and Software Engineering, C3S2E 2010, pp. 17–22. ACM, New York (2010)
9. Hu, T., Banzhaf, W.: Neutrality and variability: two sides of evolvability in linear genetic programming. In: Proceedings of the 11th Annual Conference on Genetic and Evolutionary Computation, GECCO 2009, pp. 963–970. ACM, New York (2009)
10. Miller, J.F., Thomson, P.: Cartesian genetic programming (2000)
11. Roux, O., Fonlupt, C.: Ant programming: Or how to use ants for automatic programming. In: From Ant Colonies to Artificial Ants 2nd International Workshop on Ant Colony Optimization (2000)
12. Shapiro, J.L.: Diversity Loss in General Estimation of Distribution Algorithms. In: Runarsson, T.P., Beyer, H.-G., Burke, E.K., Merelo-Guervós, J.J., Whitley, L.D., Yao, X. (eds.) PPSN 2006. LNCS, vol. 4193, pp. 92–101. Springer, Heidelberg (2006)

13. Shilane, D., Martikainen, J., Dudoit, S., Ovaska, S.J.: A general framework for statistical performance comparison of evolutionary computation algorithms. Inf. Sci. 178(14), 2870–2879 (2008)
14. Shirakawa, S., Ogino, S., Nagao, T.: Dynamic ant programming for automatic construction of programs. IEEJ Transactions on Electrical and Electronic Engineering TEEE 3, 540–548 (2008)
15. Stützle, T., Hoos, H.H.: MAX-MIN Ant System (November 1999)
16. Woodward, J.R.: Complexity and cartesian genetic programming. In: Mirkin, B., Magoulas, G. (eds.) The 5th Annual UK Workshop on Computational Intelligence, London, September 5-7, pp. 273–280 (2005)

Discovering Subgroups
by Means of Genetic Programming

José M. Luna, José Raúl Romero, Cristóbal Romero, and Sebastián Ventura

Dept. of Computer Science and Numerical Analysis,
University of Cordoba, Rabanales Campus, Albert Einstein building,
14071 Cordoba, Spain
{jmluna,jrromero,cromero,sventura}@uco.es

Abstract. This paper deals with the problem of discovering subgroups
in data by means of a grammar guided genetic programming algorithm,
each subgroup including a set of related patterns. The proposed algorithm combines the requirements of discovering comprehensible rules
with the ability of mining expressive and flexible solutions thanks to
the use of a context-free grammar. A major characteristic of this algorithm is the small number of parameters required, so the mining process
is easy for end-users.

The algorithm proposed is compared with existing subgroup discovery
evolutionary algorithms. The experimental results reveal the excellent
behaviour of this algorithm, discovering comprehensible subgroups and
behaving better than the other algorithms. The conclusions obtained
were reinforced through a series of non-parametric tests.

Keywords: Data mining, subgroup discovery, genetic programming,
grammar guided genetic programming.

1   Introduction

Data mining (DM) is a very popular research area in the field of computer
science. The aim of DM is the discovery of non-trivial information usually hidden
in data. Two are the main tasks in DM, descriptive [10] (mining interesting
patterns and association rules in a dataset) and predictive [11] (obtaining an
accurate classifier). For quite some time now, DM also includes new tasks at the
intersection of descriptive induction and predictive induction, subgroup discovery
(SD) [4] being one of these tasks.

In its original description, SD was defined by *Klösgen* [7] and *Wrobel* [13]
as follows: "Given a population of individuals (customers, objects, etc.) and a
property of those individuals that we are interested in, the task of SD is to find
population subgroups that are statistically most interesting for the user, e.g.,
subgroups that are as large as possible and have the most unusual statistical
characteristics with respect to a target attribute of interest". SD combines the
features of supervised and unsupervised learning tasks, finding explicit subgroups
via rules easily understandable by users. Therefore, these rules should have a

K. Krawiec et al. (Eds.): EuroGP 2013, LNCS 7831, pp. 121–132, 2013.

clear structure and few variables or attributes [5], comprising an antecedent and a consequent, i.e., the left and right hand side of the rule.

Since the concept of SD was firstly introduced, it has been widely studied by many researchers and a number of algorithms have been proposed [1,2,6,8]. Among these algorithms, there exists a number of them that are extensions of classification algorithms, others are extensions of algorithms for mining association rules and, finally, some follow an evolutionary methodology. All these algorithms are detailed in a comprehensive survey on SD approaches [4], where authors also describe a wide variety of quality measures that could be classified as measures of complexity, generality, precision or interest. Complexity measures are related to the interpretability and simplicity of the knowledge extracted from each subgroup. Two measures in this regard are the number of rules and the number of variables of the antecedent. As for the generality measures, they quantify the quality of the subgroups according to the patterns covered, and the most commonly used is support, representing the proportion of the number of transactions satisfying both the antecedent and consequent (target variable). Regarding the precision measures, they include the confidence or reliability of the rule as one of the most commonly used in SD. As far as the interest measures is concerned, a commonly one used in SD is the significance, which indicates the importance of a finding if measured by the likelihood ratio of a rule. Finally, it is also possible to find quality measures trying to obtain a trade-off between generality, interest and precision. An example of this kind of measures is the unusualness of a rule [4].

Recently, the descriptive induction perspective was studied by using a grammar guided genetic programming (G3P) approach [9]. In this approach, authors demonstrated that the use of a grammar to represent association rules allows of mining frequent and reliable rules having an expressive and flexible structure. The goal of this paper is to demonstrate that this interesting feature could be shared with SD, where the interpretability of the extracted knowledge is a major issue for the user. To this end, we propose a G3P approach for mining subgroups statistically interesting for the user, making use of a context-free grammar to represent rules conformant to this grammar. This algorithm, called G3P-SD, provides the possibility of satisfying the SD requirements with the features of G3P. This synergy brings about a novel algorithm which behaves well in terms of statistical measures, discovering subgroups having a simple and flexible structure, and including few variables.

In order to demonstrate the effectiveness of G3P-SD, a series of evolutionary and classic SD algorithms were compared in detail. In this analysis, a number of non-parametric tests were performed, demonstrating the effectiveness of the proposed approach and its ability to discover subgroups including few variables.

This paper is structured as follows: a description of the model proposed as well as its main characteristics is included in Section 2; Section 3 describes the experiments, including the datasets used, the algorithm set-up, and discusses the results obtained; finally, in Section 4, some concluding remarks are outlined.

$G = (\Sigma_N, \Sigma_T, P, S)$ with:

$\quad S \quad = $ Subgroup

$\quad \Sigma_N = \{$Subgroup, Conditions, Class, Condition, Nominal, Numerical $\}$

$\quad \Sigma_T = \{$'AND', 'Attribute', 'Attribute_class', 'value', 'Class_value', '=', 'IN',

$\qquad\quad$ 'Min_value', 'Max_value', 'Class_value' $\}$

$\quad P \quad = \{$Subgroup = Conditions, Class ;

$\qquad\qquad$ Conditions = Condition | 'AND', Condition, Conditions ;

$\qquad\qquad$ Condition = Nominal | Numerical ;

$\qquad\qquad$ Nominal = 'Attribute', '=', 'value' ;

$\qquad\qquad$ Numerical = 'Attribute', 'IN', 'Min_value', 'Max_value' ;

$\qquad\qquad$ Class = 'Attribute_class', '=', 'Class_value'; $\}$

Fig. 1. Context-free grammar expressed in extended BNF notation

2   On the Use of Genetic Programming for Mining Rules in Subgroup Discovery

In this section, the proposed algorithm is described in depth. The strength of this algorithm is its ability to combine the interpretability of using a context-free grammar thanks to G3P with the typical capacity to optimize thanks to the use of evolutionary algorithms. This synergy brings about an approach that discovers comprehensible subgroups having a simple and flexible structure.

2.1   Encoding Criterion

In any G3P algorithm, the individuals or feasible solutions to the problem are represented by means of a genotype and a phenotype. The genotype is presented as a derivation tree structure conformant to a context-free grammar G, providing different shapes and sizes. On the other hand, the phenotype represents the meaning of the tree structure, so the phenotype indicates a rule comprising an antecedent and a consequent.

A context-free grammar could be formally defined as a four-tuple $(\Sigma_N, \Sigma_T, P, S)$, Σ_N being the non-terminal symbol alphabet, Σ_T denoting the terminal symbol alphabet, P standing for the set of production rules, S for the start symbol, and Σ_N and Σ_T being disjoint sets, i.e., $\Sigma_N \cap \Sigma_T = \emptyset$. Any production rule follows the format $\alpha \to \beta$ where $\alpha \in \Sigma_N$, and $\beta \in \{\Sigma_T \cup \Sigma_N\}^*$. Beginning from the start symbol S, each individual is represented in a derivation tree as a sentence conformant to the grammar (see Figure 1). The benefits of using grammars consist in the ability to define syntax constraints, providing expressiveness, flexibility, and the ability to restrict the search space. To obtain individuals, a number of production rules is applied from the set P. This process begins from the start symbol Subgroup, which always has a child node representing the antecedent of the rule, i.e., the conjunction of conditions, and the target attribute or consequent. Considering the grammar defined in this approach, the following

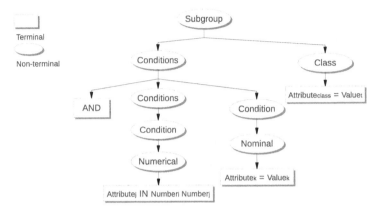

Fig. 2. Sample derivation tree conformant to the grammar defined in the proposed algorithm

language is obtained $L(G) = \{ (AND\,Condition)^n\,Condition \rightarrow Class : n \geq 0 \}$. Therefore, any rule having at least one condition in the antecedent is obtained.

A major characteristic of using grammars is its ability to be adapted to different application domains or problems. Analysing the proposed grammar, it is stated that the algorithm is able to mine any subgroup containing either numerical or nominal features. Given an attribute x and the values $y_1, y_2, ..., y_n$ in the unordered domain D of x, the following expression is valid: $x = y_n$, indicating that x takes the value y_n in D. Furthermore, numerical attributes are used by applying the operator IN, and randomly selecting two feasible values.

For the sake of clarifying the individual representation, it is interesting to show a sample individual generated through the application of a series of production rules from the set P (see Figure 2). The leaf nodes represent terminal symbols according to thee metadata of the dataset used each time. As mentioned above, the phenotype of an individual represents the meaning of the derivation tree, i.e., the rule obtained by eliminating non-terminal genotype symbols. Therefore, focusing on the sample tree depicted, the phenotype represents the following rule:

IF $Attribute_j$ IN $[Number_i, Number_j] \wedge Attribute_k = Value_k$
THEN $Attribute_{class} = Value_t$

2.2 Evaluation of the Derivation Tree Individuals

One of the major tasks in any evolutionary model is the assignment of a fitness value to each solution, determining how close a given solution is to achieve the aim. This task is a core process in SD, which has been studied by many authors [4], originating a wide variety of quality measures.

The goal of the proposed algorithm is not to optimize a specific quality measure but many of them. In the SD task, it is interesting to mine highly related or reliable subgroups of patterns that cover a high percentage of correctly classified examples from the whole set T. We propose the use of support and confidence as measures to calculate the fitness function (see Equation 1) of any subgroup represented as a rule $A \rightarrow C$, A and C state for the antecedent and consequent, respectively. In such a way, a higher fitness function value implies an optimization of generality and precision measures. Additionally, the mere fact of searching for high frequent subgroups implies an optimization in measures of complexity, especially in the number of variables in the antecedent of the rule. Notice that the higher the length of the rule, the lower its support is, i.e., more specific the rule is, so the complexity of the rule is higher.

$$fitness(A \rightarrow C) = \frac{|\{A \cup C \subseteq T\}|}{|T|} * \frac{|\{A \cup C \subseteq T\}|}{|\{A \subseteq T\}|} \qquad (1)$$

2.3   Genetic Operators

In any evolutionary algorithm, the genetic operators play an important role in the search for the best solutions, guiding the searching process to solutions having better fitness values. In this paper, we propose two genetic operators (crossover and mutation) whose main feature is that they do not need a fixed probability to determine whether the genetic operator is applied or not. Instead, these probabilities are adjusted based on the population requirements, i.e., it depends on the diversity of the population, as described below.

Crossover. In this genetic operator (see its pseudocode in Algorithm 1), the goal is to obtain a new individual comprising conditions from two parents. It works by swapping the condition with the lowest frequency in one parent with the

---

Algorithm 1. Proposed crossover operator

Require: *parents*
Ensure: *offsprings*
1: *offsprings* ← ∅
2: **for all** individuals in *parents* **do**
3:     ind_1, ind_2 ← getIndividuals(*parents*)
4:     **if** random() < crossoverProbability **then**
5:         att_1 ← getBestAttribute(ind_1)
6:         att_2 ← getWorstAttribute(ind_2)
7:         $newInd_1$ ← exchange(ind_1,att_1, att_2)
8:         *offsprings* ← *offsprings* ∪ $newInd_1$
9:         $newInd_2$ ← exchange(ind_2,att_1, att_2)
10:        *offsprings* ← *offsprings* ∪ $newInd_2$
11:    **end if**
12: **end for**
13: **return** *offsprings*

Algorithm 2. Proposed mutation operator

Require: *parents*
Ensure: *offsprings*
 1: *offsprings* ← ∅
 2: **for all** individuals in *parents* **do**
 3:    *ind* ← getIndividual(*parents*)
 4:    **if** random() < mutationProbability **then**
 5:       *att* ← getWorstAttribute(*ind*)
 6:       *newAtt* ← newAttribute(*ind,att*)
 7:       *newInd* ← exchange(*ind,att,newAtt*)
 8:       *offsprings* ← *offsprings* ∪ *newInd*
 9:    **end if**
10: **end for**
11: **return** *offsprings*

---

condition with the highest frequency in the other parent. Except for the class or target attribute, any condition could be selected. It does not matter the shape of the tree structure or the domain of the condition to be swapped.

Mutation. The principal aim of this genetic operator is to modify the genotype of an individual in order to change its worst condition (the one having a lower frequency). To do so, the procedure searches for the worst condition of the parent and changes it trying to improve its fitness value. The pseudocode of this genetic operator is shown in Algorithm 2.

As mentioned above, a major feature of the proposed algorithm is its ability to automatically update the genetic operator probabilities, not requiring a pre-fixed parameter. In order to update these probabilities, the algorithm checks, in each generation, whether the average fitness value of the population has increased or decreased. If this value is greater than that calculated in the previous generation, then the crossover probability will be increased since a depth search or exploitation is required. On the contrary, if the average fitness value is less than or equal to that obtained in the previous generation, then the crossover probability should be decreased since it is required to include diversity in the population.

2.4   Proposed Algorithm

In previous subsections, the encoding criterion, the evaluation process, and the genetic operators proposed in the algorithm were described. Now, it is necessary to properly describe the complete evolutionary model, discussing how the different procedures described are combined prompting a promising evolutionary algorithm for SD.

The first interesting procedure to be described is the one responsible for creating the initial population by using the context-free grammar defined in Figure 1 and the metadata extracted from the dataset. The main objective of this initial

procedure is to allow of starting the evolutionary process with quality individuals. To do so, it originates an individual and evaluate it to determine its fitness
function value. If this value is equal to 0, i.e., an invalid individual having a support value or a confidence value of 0, then the procedure creates a new individual
and the invalid one is rejected. Once the created individual has a valid fitness
value, this individual is kept in the population. The procedure continues until
a number of quality individuals is obtained, making the evolutionary process
better since it starts having a high quality population.

The algorithm proposed in this paper is an iterative algorithm that mines
subgroups of an specific target attribute in each iteration (Figure 3 graphically
shows the iterative model). In such a way, its aim is to discover the best subgroups (induced as rules in the form of a derivation tree) for each class or target
attribute. The algorithm runs iteratively a complete evolution of the rules for a

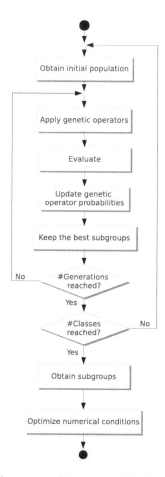

Fig. 3. The flowchart for the proposed iterative G3P algorithm for mining subgroups

specific class, i.e., the individuals evolve along a number of generations in order to obtain the best ones. Once this generational procedure is finished, a new set of individuals satisfying a new class is created. This iterative process is repeated as many times as number of classes or target variable values are available in the dataset.

In each generation of proposed algorithm, a selection procedure working as an elitist selection allows some of the best individuals discovered from the current generation to carry over to the next, unaltered. The fact of selecting the best individuals from a set is not a trivial procedure since it is necessary not only to select the best one but also to select the most representative ones. In such a way, individuals are compared by using Equation 2, considering that two individuals are equivalent if they cover the same instances. Therefore, two individuals are compared by using their vectors of covered instances (V_1 and V_2), where $V_1 \cdot V_2$ is the product of both vectors and $|V_n|$ is the norm of the n-th vector. In this sense, the range of the values is $[0, 1]$, and the closer to one the value is, the more similar these individuals are.

$$comparator(V_1, V_2) = \frac{V_1 \cdot V_2}{|V_1| \cdot |V_2|} \tag{2}$$

For a better understanding, consider two sample rules that cover the following instances (V_1 and V_2) in a sample dataset of ten instances (a logic "1" implies that the rule satisfies the instance, a logic "0" otherwise).

Instances	1 2 3 4 5 6 7 8 9 10
V_1	0 0 1 1 0 0 1 1 1 0
V_2	0 0 0 1 0 0 1 0 1 0

In such a situation, the value of $V_1 \cdot V_2$ is 3, whereas the values of $|V_1|$ and $|V_2|$ are $\sqrt{5}$ and $\sqrt{3}$, respectively. Once these values are obtained, the similarity between these two individuals is defined by Equation 2 as $comparator(V_1, V_2) = 3/(\sqrt{5}*\sqrt{3}) = 0.775$. In consequence, since the range of the values is $[0, 1]$, both individuals tend to cover the same instances.

The aim of SD is the discovery of interesting subgroups for the user, so the fact of giving a huge set of subgroups covering the same instances could not be a good idea. In such a way, we propose the use of a 0.8 threshold to determine whether two subgroups are similar or not. This threshold should be as high as possible, but allowing the extraction of overlapped rules. In SD overlapped subgroups may be interesting since they can show properties of a group from a different perspective.

Finally, once the algorithm reaches the number of target features in the dataset under study, it runs a final procedure to increase or decrease the width of the intervals –if any numeric feature is considered– in order to discover a high quality intervals satisfying more instances or prompting to a more reliable rules. Once this procedure is carried out, the algorithm returns the set of subgroups discovered in each iteration.

3   Experimental Study

In this experimental study, the behaviour of the proposed algorithm — it was written by using JCLEC [12], a Java library for evolutionary computation[1] — is shown with respect to a number of quality measures including measures of complexity, generality, precision and interest. In this experimental stage, a series of evolutionary algorithms were compared in detail, including SDIGA [5], NMEEF-SD [1], and MESDIF [2]. Finally, several non-parametric tests were performed, demonstrating the effectiveness of the proposed approach and its ability to discover subgroups having a low complexity.

Table 1. A set of 12 datasets obtained from the well-known UCI repository

Dataset	$\#Var$	$\#Disc$	$\#Cont$	$\#Class$	$\#Inst$
Australian	14	8	6	2	690
Breast-w	9	9	0	2	699
Bupa	6	0	6	2	345
Car	6	6	0	4	1728
Cleveland	13	0	13	5	303
Diabetes	8	0	8	2	768
Echo	6	1	5	2	131
German	20	13	7	2	1000
Iris	4	0	4	3	150
Led	7	0	7	10	500
Tic-tac-toe	9	9	0	2	958
Vote	16	16	0	2	435

The experimentation was undertaken using 12 datasets from the UCI repository[2]. Table 1 shows the features of each dataset used in this experimental stage, describing the number of variables ($\#Var$), number of discrete attributes ($\#Disc$), number of continuous attributes ($\#Cont$), number of classes ($\#Class$) and number of instances ($\#Inst$). All the experiments were carried out over a ten fold cross validation for each dataset. As far as the evolutionary algorithms are concerned, the optimal parameters are those given by the authors as optimal parameters. On the contrary, the optimal parameters for the proposed algorithm were established from various experimental studies, being a population size of 50 individuals and a maximum number of 100 generations. Notice that there is no probability for the genetic operators.

The results obtained (see Table 2) are the average results obtained from the set of subgroups discovered when running each algorithm thirty times using different seeds each time. Notice that the best results are set in bold typeface.

---

[1] JCLEC is freely available for download from http://jclec.sf.net
[2] Machine learning repository. http://archive.ics.uci.edu/ml/

Table 2. Average results obtained by the evolutionary algorithms using different measures

Dataset	Number of rules				Number of variables				Significance			
	NMEEF-SD	MESDIF	SDIGA	G3P-SD	NMEEF-SD	MESDIF	SDIGA	G3P-SD	NMEEF-SD	MESDIF	SDIGA	G3P-SD
Australian	3.58	10.00	2.64	**2.04**	2.92	3.52	3.28	**2.19**	**23.17**	7.59	16.34	20.92
Breast-w	2.90	11.90	2.52	**2.02**	2.38	2.42	2.43	**2.06**	22.72	19.40	17.32	**23.45**
Bupa	3.46	10.00	2.00	**1.64**	2.22	3.40	2.04	**2.01**	0.88	0.82	0.94	**2.81**
Car	**1.10**	10.40	19.14	**1.10**	**2.00**	3.34	5.10	**2.00**	**37.84**	13.51	1.77	**37.84**
Cleveland	**1.40**	48.26	19.26	1.44	3.00	4.49	5.13	**2.25**	**10.03**	3.95	1.05	6.44
Diabetes	8.38	20.00	**2.00**	2.24	3.46	4.07	2.25	**2.19**	3.20	2.51	5.23	**6.81**
Echo	3.62	19.94	**2.00**	2.26	2.35	3.70	2.65	**2.18**	**1.29**	0.75	1.00	0.83
German	8.80	20.00	8.56	**1.16**	2.77	4.30	4.40	**2.10**	3.07	2.81	0.61	**7.54**
Iris	4.50	8.50	**3.00**	3.04	2.54	2.47	**2.33**	2.51	9.19	6.45	7.97	**9.65**
Led	4.70	78.54	10.04	**4.34**	3.37	3.57	4.55	**3.00**	17.22	17.00	15.99	**17.70**
Tic-tac-toe	**1.00**	6.00	7.90	1.12	**2.00**	3.14	3.98	2.28	5.24	5.00	**6.14**	5.01
Vote	**1.10**	7.86	3.06	2.00	**2.05**	3.44	3.19	2.23	21.97	19.93	18.24	**22.87**
Ranking	2.29	3.83	2.37	**1.5**	2.12	3.45	3.08	**1.33**	1.87	3.5	3.08	**1.54**

Dataset	Support				Confidence				Unusualness			
	NMEEF-SD	MESDIF	SDIGA	G3P-SD	NMEEF-SD	MESDIF	SDIGA	G3P-SD	NMEEF-SD	MESDIF	SDIGA	G3P-SD
Australian	0.78	0.57	0.59	**0.85**	**0.93**	0.80	0.79	0.85	0.17	0.06	0.12	**0.18**
Breast-w	**0.84**	0.71	0.67	0.67	0.95	0.89	0.85	**0.96**	**0.16**	0.11	0.11	0.13
Bupa	0.90	0.59	**0.96**	0.27	0.62	0.51	0.55	**0.86**	0.03	0.01	0.03	**0.05**
Car	**0.43**	0.35	0.04	**0.43**	**1.00**	0.31	0.21	**1.00**	**0.09**	0.02	0.01	**0.09**
Cleveland	0.68	0.49	0.13	**0.72**	**0.86**	0.27	0.12	0.75	**0.13**	0.02	0.01	0.11
Diabetes	**0.86**	0.53	0.81	0.55	0.69	0.69	0.67	**0.79**	0.03	0.02	0.03	**0.07**
Echo	0.62	0.47	**0.70**	0.41	**0.75**	0.58	0.59	0.64	**0.04**	0.02	0.03	0.03
German	**0.74**	0.51	0.17	0.48	0.78	0.64	0.31	**0.88**	0.04	0.02	0.01	**0.07**
Iris	**0.98**	0.84	0.97	0.95	**0.98**	0.92	0.91	0.94	0.19	0.13	0.16	**0.20**
Led	0.78	0.81	0.71	**0.84**	0.62	0.37	**0.72**	0.65	0.06	0.04	0.06	**0.07**
Tic-tac-toe	**0.58**	0.30	0.15	0.56	0.79	0.74	**0.82**	0.77	**0.06**	0.04	0.03	0.05
Vote	**0.94**	0.82	0.80	**0.94**	**0.97**	0.95	0.89	0.95	**0.21**	0.18	0.18	**0.21**
Ranking	**1.58**	3.00	3.04	2.37	**1.66**	3.25	3.33	1.75	**1.70**	3.58	3.25	**1.45**

In order to analyze the results obtained, a series of statistical tests [3] were carried out. The Friedman test is used to compare the results obtained and to be able to precisely analyse whether there are significant differences among the four algorithms. This test first ranks the jth of k algorithms on the ith of N datasets, and then calculates the average rank according to the F-distribution (F_F) throughout all the datasets, and calculates the Friedman statistics. If the Friedman test rejects the null-hypothesis indicating that there are signicant differences, then a Bonferroni-Dunn test is performed to reveal these differences.

The Friedman average ranking statistics distributed according to F_F with $k-1$ and $(k-1)(N-1)$ degrees of freedom for quality measures are: 14.42, 13.55, 12.39, 24.43, 4.27 and 11.12, for the measures number of rules, number of variables, significance, unusualness, support and confidence, respectively. Except for the support measure, none of them belong to the critical interval $[0,(F_F)0.01,3,33 = 4.43]$. Thus, we reject the null-hypothesis that all algorithms perform equally well for these measures. In order to analyse whether there are significant differences among them, the Bonferroni-Dunn test is used to reveal the difference in performance, 1.12 being the critical difference (CD) value for $p = 0.1$; 1.26 for $p = 0.05$; and 1.54 for $p = 0.01$.

The proposed algorithm behaves better than MESDIF and SDIGA at a significance level of $p = 0.01$ (i.e., with a probability of 99%) in all the measures used in this analysis. Once the proposed algorithm is compared to NMEEF-SD, it is not possible to assert that there are significant differences between these two algorithms. However, despite the fact that it is not possible to assert it, the ranking obtained by the proposed algorithm is better than the one obtained by the MESDIF algorithm by almost all the measures under study.

The proposed algorithm obtains the best results for the complexity and interest measures. It also obtains great results in unusualness, which is a trade-off between generality, interest and precision. Therefore, the proposed algorithm appears as a promising proposal for mining comprehensible subgroups and behaving better than the existing algorithms in most of the quality measures.

4   Concluding Remarks

In this paper, a novel G3P algorithm, named G3P-SD, for mining subgroups was presented and described in depth. The aim of this algorithm is to harness the features of G3P to solve the requirements of SD, i.e., the mining of rules having a clear and flexible structure, obtaining interesting subgroups according to a number of quality measures, which could be classified in complexity, generality, precision and interest measures. G3P-SD makes use of a grammar to properly encode the individuals, allowing to carry out the mining process in any domain. The algorithm also defines two genetic operators whose probabilities are self-adapted depending on the quality of the rules discovered in each generation.

A complete experimental study was performed, making an exhaustive comparison between the proposed algorithm and other existing algorithms (NMEEF-SD, MESDIF, and SDIGA). The experimental results, which were backed up with the corresponding non-parametric tests, reveal the effectiveness of G3P-SD, discovering comprehensible subgroups and behaving better than the other algorithms regarding to the measures of complexity, interest, and precision.

Acknowledgments. This work has been supported by the Regional Government of Andalusia and the Ministry of Science and Technology projects P08-TIC-3720 and TIN-2011-22408, respectively, FEDER funds and the Spanish Ministry of Education under the FPU grant AP2010-0041.

References

1. Carmona, C.J., González, P., del Jesus, M.J., Herrera, F.: NMEEF-SD: Nondominated multiobjective evolutionary algorithm for extracting fuzzy rules in subgroup discovery. IEEE Transactions on Fuzzy Systems 18(5), 958–970 (2010)
2. Carmona, C.J., González, P., del Jesus, M.J., Navío-Acosta, M., Jiménez-Trevino, L.: Evolutionary fuzzy rule extraction for subgroup discovery in a psychiatric emergency department. Soft Computing 15(12), 2435–2448 (2011)
3. García, S., Fernández, A., Luengo, J., Herrera, F.: Advanced nonparametric tests for multiple comparisons in the design of experiments in computational intelligence and data mining: Experimental analysis of power. Information Sciences 180(10), 2044–2064 (2010)
4. Herrera, F., Carmona, C.J., González, P., del Jesus, M.J.: An overview on subgroup discovery: Foundations and applications. Knowledge and Information Systems 29(3), 495–525 (2011)
5. del Jesus, M.J., González, P., Herrera, F., Mesonero, M.: Evolutionary fuzzy rule induction process for subgroup discovery: A case study in marketing. IEEE Transactions on Fuzzy Systems 15(4), 578–592 (2007)
6. Kavšek, B., Lavrač, N.: APRIORI-SD: Adapting association rule learning to subgroup discovery. Applied Artificial Intelligence 20(7), 543–583 (2006)
7. Klösgen, W.: Explora: A multipattern and multistrategy discovery assistant. In: Advances in Knowledge Discovery and Data Mining, pp. 249–271 (1996)
8. Lavrač, N., Kavšek, B., Flach, P., Todorovski, L.: Subgroup discovery with cn2-sd. Journal of Machine Learning Research 5, 153–188 (2004)
9. Luna, J.M., Romero, J.R., Ventura, S.: Design and behavior study of a grammar-guided genetic programming algorithm for mining association rules. Knowledge and Information Systems 32(1), 53–76 (2012)
10. Romero, C., Luna, J.M., Romero, J.R., Ventura, S.: RM-Tool: A framework for discovering and evaluating association rules. Advances in Engineering Software 42(8), 566–576 (2011)
11. Romero, C., Ventura, S., Espejo, P., Hervás, C.: Data mining algorithms to classify students. In: Proceedings of the First International Conference on Educational Data Mining, EDM 2008, Montreal, Quebec, Canada, pp. 182–185 (2008)
12. Ventura, S., Romero, C., Zafra, A., Delgado, J.A., Hervás, C.: JCLEC: A java framework for evolutionary computation. Soft Computing 12(4), 381–392 (2008)
13. Wrobel, S.: An Algorithm for Multi-Relational Discovery of Subgroups. In: Komorowski, J., Żytkow, J.M. (eds.) PKDD 1997. LNCS, vol. 1263, pp. 78–87. Springer, Heidelberg (1997)

Program Optimisation
with Dependency Injection

James McDermott and Paula Carroll

Management Information Systems, Quinn School of Business,
University College Dublin, Ireland
jmmcd@jmmcd.net

Abstract. For many real-world problems, there exist non-deterministic
heuristics which generate valid but possibly sub-optimal solutions. The
program optimisation with dependency injection method, introduced here,
allows such a heuristic to be placed under evolutionary control, allowing
search for the optimum. Essentially, the heuristic is "fooled" into using
a genome, supplied by a genetic algorithm, in place of the output of its
random number generator. The method is demonstrated with generative heuristics in the domains of 3D design and communications network
design. It is also used in novel approaches to genetic programming.

1 Introduction

In software engineering, unit testing is the practice of providing known-good
input-output pairs as tests for individual functions. When a function is non-
deterministic, each input does not correspond to a single output, so unit testing
cannot be used. The *dependency injection* design pattern provides a solution:
the random number generator used by the function is shadowed by a source of
non-random numbers, so each input again corresponds to one correct output.

This inspires the idea of searching among the outputs of any non-deterministic
program (NDP) by searching among the sequences of values returned by the non-
random number generator (NRNG). A genetic algorithm (GA) can be used to
supply genomes, and each genome then used as an NRNG, as shown in Fig. 1.
This is *program optimisation with dependency injection* (PODI).

For the remainder of this paper, the goals are to define the PODI idea and to
demonstrate that it can be used for search and optimisation in diverse domains.
Sect. 2, next, describes some related work. The PODI method is defined in
Sect. 3. Several examples of applying PODI in diverse domains are described
in Sect. 4; Sect. 5 analyses the PODI search space; and Sect. 6 gives conclusions.

2 Related Work

Many authors have pursued genetic programming (GP) representations other
than the standard tree-based GP of Koza [9]. Examples include linear GP

K. Krawiec et al. (Eds.): EuroGP 2013, LNCS 7831, pp. 133–144, 2013.

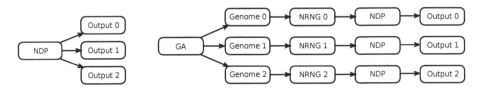

Fig. 1. A non-deterministic program (NDP) can produce multiple outputs (left). In PODI (right), a GA supplies genomes, each giving rise to a non-random number generator (NRNG): given an NRNG instead of an RNG, the NDP produces a *single* output. The GA searches for genomes leading to good outputs.

(LGP) [1], Cartesian GP (CGP) [12], and grammatical evolution (GE) [14]. Each uses a linear genome and a specialised genome-program mapping to produce a program. In PODI, the same idea is used, but any non-deterministic program (NDP) whose output is a program can play the role of the genome-program mapping. PODI can also be used in non-GP domains, using an NDP whose outputs are the objects of the domain's search space.

Another strand of research closely related to PODI is the "programming by optimisation" method [5]. A template program is written by hand, in which some parts are concrete and fixed, and for other parts, alternative algorithms and implementations are provided. Optimisation proceeds by searching among the possible fully concrete programs. The aim is to allow the human programmer to work in the familiar creative domain (writing programs by hand), while the computer carries out the tedious and difficult job of determining which alternatives are faster or more correct in a given context. PODI has a similar goal, in that it allows the programmer to work by programming. However, it does not require a specialised template language, and the search mechanism is different.

3   Method

The PODI representation consists of two parts: a GA to be described below, and a pre-written non-deterministic program (NDP).

Running the NDP produces some output to be evaluated as a candidate solution. Depending on the domain, it could be a string, a vector, a program, or any data structure. Running the NDP multiple times will produce multiple candidate solutions: they will differ because the NDP is non-deterministic. By *injecting* (passing in) an extra argument which will play the role of the random number generator, the NDP can be made deterministic. This new argument is an instance of a non-random number generator (NRNG)[1].

---

[1] An example of dependency injection is given by Peter Norvig: http://www.udacity.com/view#Course/cs212/CourseRev/apr2012/Unit/292001/Nugget/315001

The NRNG has the same interface as a standard random number generator (RNG): `randint(a, b)` returns an integer in $[a, b)$; `random()` returns a floating-point number in $[0, 1)$; `choice(L)` returns an element of the list L; and so on. The NDP can therefore run without modification. However, the values returned by the NRNG are not random, nor even pseudo-random. Instead, they are determined by a stored list of integers which come from a genome[2]. The NDP can therefore be regarded as a mapping from genomes to outputs (such as vectors, programs, or other data structures).

PODI searches using a GA where genomes are variable-length integer arrays. Mutation is per-gene int-flip, and crossover selects one crossover point per parent within the section which was used when the parent was passed to the NDP (compare the *used codons* concept in GE). However, *PODI is not just a GA*. It uses a potentially complex genome-phenotype mapping, the NDP. An NDP can use loops and conditionals to divert control flow, and can call its NRNG any number of times. Therefore there is no direct and fixed correspondence between the genome *loci* and the sequence of NRNG calls. This is the key distinction between PODI and a typical GA. PODI can also do true GP in at least three ways (one is demonstrated in Sect. 4.1, and two in Sect. 4.2).

It might appear that in PODI, the genome's control of the NDP's behaviour is no different from the control that would be exerted by a random seed for a typical RNG. After all, in both cases the input (the genome, or the seed) fully determines the behaviour of the NDP. However, PODI is not random search. The difference is in the fact that *the space of PODI genomes has structure*, whereas the space of random seeds does not. That is, small mutations to a random seed will not result in small changes to the NDP's behaviour, and crossover between a pair of random seeds will not lead to behaviour intermediate between the two. The opposite is true of the PODI operators. This argument is developed with experimental support in Sect. 5.

4 Examples

4.1 Emulating Grammatical Evolution

The PODI framework can be seen as a generalisation of GE. To see this, consider Algorithm 1, a standard method (in non-EC contexts) of deriving a string from

---

[2] It is useful to explain a little of the workings of the NRNG. In an object-oriented language such as Python or Java, the NRNG is a subclass of the language's standard RNG. The NRNG constructor accepts an extra argument, a list of integers, which is stored. Only one method needs to be overridden: in Python, it is the RNG's `random()` method, which is required to return a floating-point value in $[0, 1)$. At every call to `random()`, the next of the stored integers is used. It is divided by the constant `maxval`. This constant usually stores the largest representable integer, such as $2^{31} - 1$. However if the user wishes to use a GA with gene values limited to, say, $[0, 100]$, then `maxval` will be set to 100. The result of the division is in $[0, 1)$, as required, and is returned. Methods other than `random`, such as `randint()` and `choice()`, call `random()`, possibly multiple times, and use its output as needed.

Algorithm 1. *Derive*: derive a string from a grammar.

Require: Grammar $G = (R, S, T)$ where R is a mapping from non-terminal symbols
    to lists of productions, S is a non-terminal start symbol, and T is the terminal set;
Require: Stateful random number generator RNG.
 1: **if** $S \in T$ **then**
 2:    return S
 3: **end if**
 4: $P \leftarrow R[S]$ {# P is a list of items producible from S}
 5: **if** length$(P) = 1$ **then**
 6:    $p \leftarrow P[0]$
 7: **else**
 8:    $p \leftarrow$ RNG.choice(P)
 9: **end if**
10: return Concatenate($[Derive((R, S', T),$ RNG$)$ for S' in $p])$ {# The square brackets
    indicate a *comprehension*: it makes a new list by recursing on each element.}

---

a non-deterministic grammar. It is non-deterministic, thus stretching the strict
definition of "algorithm". Therefore, it can serve as an NDP in PODI. In fact,
PODI with Algorithm 1 mimics the behaviour of GE with the "bucket rule" [7].
Replacing line 8 with the following mimics GE's standard mod rule instead:

  8:   $p \leftarrow P[$RNG.randint$(0, C)$ % length$(P)]$

where C is the maximum value for GE codons, often set to 127 in previous work.

Note that PODI *genes* are in $[0,$ `maxval`$)$, whereas the *codons* returned by
the `randint()` call are in $[0, C)$. Therefore, it is not possible to reproduce a
particular GE run precisely in PODI by setting identical random seeds. Instead,
we wish to demonstrate experimentally that PODI, with the modified version of
Algorithm 1 as the NDP, emulates standard GE behaviour.

For standard GE we use an existing implementation[3]. In both standard GE
and PODI-GE we do not use any special initialisation such as ramped half-
and-half: instead, we randomly initialise the integer-valued genomes. The initial
length is 100 genes. The maximum codon value is 127. Population size is 1000,
the number of generations is 40, the one-point crossover probability is 0.7 (one
crossover point is chosen in *each* parent, within the portion of its genome used
when it was mapped), the per-gene mutation probability is 0.01, the number of
elite individuals is 1, and the tournament size is 3. The fitness function is the
two-dimensional symbolic regression problem

$$f(x, y) = \frac{1}{1 + x^{-4}} + \frac{1}{1 + y^{-4}}$$

used by Pagie and Hogeweg [15]. There are 676 fitness cases distributed in an
even grid across $[-5, 5] \times [-5, 5]$.

---

[3] http://ponyge.googlecode.com

The grammar is as follows (in division, if the denominator is zero, the numerator is returned):

```
<code> ::= function(x, y) <expr>
<expr> ::= <bop>(<expr>, <expr>) | <uop>(<expr>) | <var> | <const>
<bop> ::= add | subtract | multiply | divide
<uop> ::= square | sin | cos
<var> ::= x | y
<const> ::= 0.1 | 0.2 | 0.3 | 0.4 | 0.5
```

The results are shown in Fig. 2: there is a close correspondence in behaviour between the two methods, both in best fitness values and the number of codons used in the best individuals. There are some small differences in overall behaviour, such as PODI-GE spending a few more generations with a wider standard deviation in the number of used codons (generations 31–35 versus generation 33). Re-running the experiment has not demonstrated a trend in this. We conclude that PODI-GE emulates standard GE behaviour.

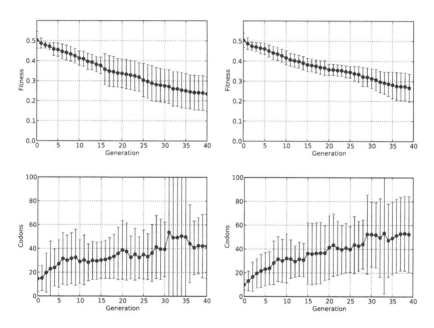

Fig. 2. Mean and standard deviation of best fitness (top) and number of used codons (bottom) across 30 runs. The behaviour of PODI-GE (left) closely matches that of standard GE (right).

4.2 Tree-Based Genetic Programming

PODI can also be used for non-grammatical, tree-based forms of GP. It is sufficient to define an NDP which creates GP-style trees. Many GP initialisation operators are suitable, and we have investigated two.

One is the *grow* operator, which recursively chooses nodes randomly from non-terminals and terminals until the depth reaches a limit, then chooses only from terminals. It is well-known, so to save space we do not describe it in detail.

The other is the *bubble-down* operator [4], which (similar to *grow*) creates a tree one node at a time. A new node is created with a randomly-chosen non-terminal label. It is "bubbled down" through the tree according to randomly-generated *direction* and *slots* values which are associated with the existing and new nodes (see Fig. 3) until it reaches an external position. As yet it lacks children. When the number of nodes plus the number of missing children equals the desired tree size, new nodes are given randomly-chosen *terminal* labels and put in place at external positions in left-to-right order. The direction and slots values, used only during tree generation, are then deleted. A complete implementation of the bubble-down algorithm is available online[4].

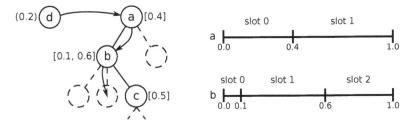

Fig. 3. The bubble-down algorithm. The partially-formed tree so far consists of nodes labelled **a**, **b**, and **c**, with arities 2, 3 and 2. They have randomly-chosen *slots* values, shown in square brackets. A new node has now been created with label **d**, chosen randomly from the non-terminal labels. It has a randomly-chosen *direction* value 0.2 (shown in round brackets). Its slots values are not shown. It must now be bubbled down, and begins at node **a** (top arrow). Since 0.2 lies in slot 0 of node **a** (see right), **d** is bubbled-down to child 0, i.e. it reaches node **b** (middle arrow). The procedure repeats. Node **b** has arity 3, hence 2 slots values, sorted. Since 0.2 lies in slot 1 of node **b** (see right), **d** moves to child 1 (bottom arrow). Since **d** is now external, it stops.

We wish to test PODI where the role of the NDP is played by the grow and the bubble-down algorithms. The test problem is the same symbolic regression problem as in Sect. 4.1, and the settings are the same. The non-terminals and terminals are as in the grammar of that section. For grow, the maximum depth is 6; for bubble-down, the tree size is fixed at 30 nodes. The results are shown in Fig. 4: the mean best fitness for both grow and bubble-down is better than the results shown in Sect. 4.1 for standard GE (t-test with $p < 0.01$).

4.3 Communications Networks

The *ring-spur assignment problem* (RSAP) is a problem in the field of next-generation telecommunications networks. Since this is not an applications paper,

---

[4] Download PODI implemented in Python from `https://github.com/jmmcd/PODI`

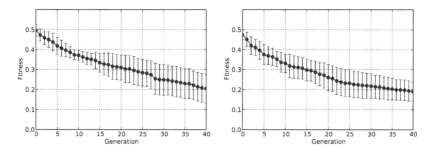

Fig. 4. Results using tree-based GP: mean and standard deviation of the best individual per generation over 30 runs using PODI with *grow* (left), and *bubble-down* (right).

only a brief description will be given. Starting with an existing physical network, the goal is to form a logical overlay network with a resilient structure, of the lowest possible cost. It must consist of a subset of the physical edges, and conform to a "ring-spur" structure (see Fig. 5). The ring-spur structure means that there is one "tertiary" ring; multiple disjoint "local" rings of up to 8 nodes which each intersect with the tertiary ring; and possibly several "spurs", each a single edge connecting one isolated node to a local ring. The cost is the sum of costs of the edges used, with a penalty per spur.

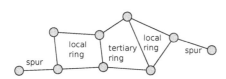

Fig. 5. A valid ring-spur assignment solution: all nodes are included, and the edges form a single tertiary ring intersecting multiple local rings, with some (optional) spurs.

The RSAP was described by Carroll and McGarraghy [3], and integer programming (IP) formulations were given. However for some test problems, the IP method is excessively slow. Kilmartin and Flynn [8] used a variable neighbourhood search method for the problem. They give a non-deterministic initialisation heuristic which attempts to generate valid solutions, and several neighbourhood operators: each generates a new solution, given an existing one.

The initialisation heuristic consists of over 600 lines of Java and works as follows (see [8] for details sufficient for replication). A random node is chosen, and a greedy algorithm over edge costs is used to create a local ring. If it succeeds, the nodes used are removed from the node list. If it fails, the node is removed from the node list and added to a list of spur candidates. The process is repeated: eventually the node list becomes empty. For each spur candidate, a spur is attempted to some local ring. Finally, a tertiary ring is created starting at a random local ring, and again running a greedy algorithm. In the following experiment, this heuristic is used as the NDP of the PODI method.

For comparison, we also implement a naive GA approach. Here, genomes are of length $3m$ where m is the number of physical edges. Each of the first m genes is a bit and determines whether the corresponding edge is used on the tertiary ring. Each of the next m genes determines whether the corresponding edge is used as a spur. Each of the final m genes is an integer and indicates the index of the local ring on which the corresponding edge occurs, or 0 if unused. In this encoding, a large majority of genomes correspond to invalid networks.

Table 1. Results on the RSAP problem. Lower costs are better.

Problem	IP	PODI	GA	Problem	IP	PODI	GA
pdh	1.36e+06	1.36e+06	3.14e+06	dfn-bwin	105810	113818	195473
pioro40	9586 *	9749	None	di-yuan	412300	412300	None
janos-us	16672	23541	None	ta1	1.14e+07	1.29e+07	None
newyork	1.51e+06	1.77e+06	None	sun	694.99	1277.82	None
cost266	1.236e+07	1.65e+07	None	polska	3487	3740	None
atlanta	5.55e+07	1.042e+08	None	giul39	946 *	1021	None
france	20800	26000	None	dfn-gwin	15724	17428	79868
germany50	549150 *	574460	None	norway	596070	808290	None
nobel-eu	None	None	None	janos-us-ca	None	None	None
zib54	None	None	None	ta2	7.38e+07 *	None	None

Table 1 shows results achieved on the problem instances used in previous work [3,8]. The IP results are known to be optimal [3] except where marked *. For PODI and the GA, these are the best (lowest cost) results out of 30 runs, with population 1000 and 100 generations, tournament size 10, crossover probability 0.9, mutation probability 0.05, and elitism of 10 individuals.

For some problems, IP methods show that no valid solution exists (those where IP achieves "None" in Table 1). In a few cases PODI achieves the known optimum. The GA approach is the weakest, usually finding no solution. We conclude that PODI is inferior to the IP method, but because of the use of a domain-specific NDP, it is a better starting point than a naive GA. An applications-oriented paper with full details of this experiment is in preparation.

4.4   Generative 3D Design

The design of 3D structures is an interesting application domain for *interactive* EC. GP has been applied by several authors for this application, e.g. [6]. One line of research used GE to explore spaces of 3D designs such as bridges and pylons consisting of uniform variable-length beams [2,11].

Here, the goal is to explore a space of radially symmetric designs of uniform variable-length beams. An incremental process of hacking and testing led to the creation of an NDP capable of generating many of the desired designs. It is roughly 170 lines long, badly written and difficult to understand, so is not reproduced here in either code or algorithm form[5]. It seems impossible to

---

[5] Download from `https://gist.github.com/4055990`

produce an equivalent parametric model, grammar, or any other explicit representation. Instead, we see this NDP as a black box, *implicitly* defining a design
space amenable to PODI search. Fig. 6 shows a selection of evolved images and
a population after 6 generations. No claim is made that the results are optimal
in any sense: the evolution was driven by interactive aesthetic selection. Instead,
the claim is that the use of the NDP has resulted in a rich and varied search
space (Fig. 6 top). Large numbers of undesired (e.g. non-radially symmetric)
designs, which would be present in typical naive encodings for this problem,
have been eliminated. This greatly improves the interactive evolutionary search.
Also, the PODI operators have been shown to have the capacity to converge the
population (Fig. 6 bottom).

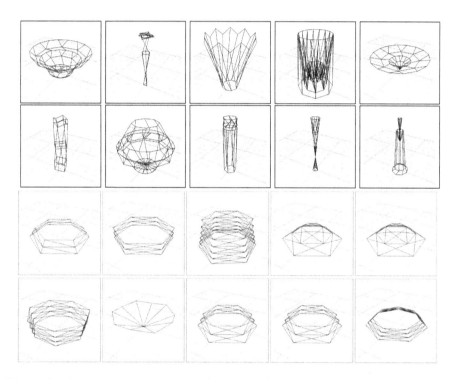

Fig. 6. A selection of evolved results (top 2 rows), demonstrating a wide and varied
search space. A single population (bottom 2 rows), demonstrating some convergence.

5   Analysis: The Structure of the PODI Search Space

We have asserted that the PODI search space of integer arrays has structure, and
in particular that mutation and crossover are useful operators. In experimental
settings, mutation is generally considered useful if it has *locality*, i.e. the semantic
distance between an individual and a mutated version is small [16]; crossover is
considered useful if it is *geometric*, i.e. the semantic distance between parents

Table 2. Median distances between tree-based GP individuals generated using the grow algorithm and the bubble-down algorithm: in all cases, the pairs created by mutation or crossover are closer together than the random pairs. Statistical significance at $p < 0.01$ is indicated by * (see text).

NDP	Distance	Random	Mutation		Crossover	
Grow	Genotype	1e+02	1	*	59	*
Grow	Phenotype	45	5	*	36	*
Grow	Semantic	26	1	*	23	*
Grow	Fitness	0.9	0.011	*	0.62	*
Bubble-down	Genotype	1e+02	1	*	59	*
Bubble-down	Phenotype	72	6	*	61	*
Bubble-down	Semantic	26	0	*	24	*
Bubble-down	Fitness	0.79	0	*	0.59	*

and children is minimised [10]. These properties have been formally defined by Moraglio et al. [13].

The partially converged population of Fig. 6 gives some visual support for the claim that the PODI operators are useful. In order to test the claim experimentally, we will perform many mutations and crossovers on randomly-generated individuals and study the distances between the original and new individuals. Our mutation hypothesis is that the expected semantic distance between an individual and a mutated version is less than that between two randomly-generated individuals. Our crossover hypothesis is that the expected semantic distance between a parent and a child is less than that between two randomly-generated individuals. These relatively weak hypotheses, if proven, are sufficient to show that search with PODI is distinct from random search.

This study is restricted to the GP domain as in Sect. 4.2 (a comparison with GE behaviour is left to future work). For each tree-generating NDP (grow and bubble-down), three methods of creating pairs of individuals are used: random generation of the pair; random generation of the first, and mutation to create the second; and random generation of two parents, crossover to create two children, and then taking all four parent-child pairs. For this experiment one-point mutation is used, rather than a per-gene mutation probability. That is, a mutation changes precisely one gene (as in crossover, the mutation is constrained to occur within the used section of the genome).

Four types of distance between pairs are calculated:

- genome distance is the Levenshtein (edit) distance between genomes;
- phenotype distance is the tree-edit distance between generated trees;
- semantic distance is the Euclidean distance between the vectors of the individuals' values at the fitness cases;
- fitness distance is the difference between the fitness values.

10,000 trials are run for each NDP and each method of creating pairs. Trials where an individual is invalid or a change is genotypically or phenotypically neutral are discarded. Table 2 shows the *median* results (not the mean, because semantics and fitness results are liable to include very large outliers). The low values including zero for the median are not unexpected, since a genotypically or phenotypically non-neutral change can still be neutral in semantics or fitness. In all cases, the mutation and crossover pairs are closer together than the randomly generated pairs. Significance is tested using the Mann-Whitney U test with $p < 0.01$. We conclude that search with PODI is not random search.

6   Conclusions and Future Work

A highly general evolutionary algorithm, *program optimisation with dependency injection*, has been introduced and studied. It has been shown to function as a generalisation of GE, and to be capable of performing tree-based GP in two ways. It has been applied to problems in 3D design and in communications network design, and the structure of its search space has been analysed.

One of the main advantages of EC in general is that it is a useful "black-box" method: it makes many domains amenable to search and optimisation which are inaccessible to some more specialised methods. In a similar way, PODI opens up a broader class of problems to evolutionary approaches. It is not limited to domains where we can define all three typical EC genetic operators (initialisation, crossover and mutation). With PODI, only an NDP is required. Since an NDP is non-deterministic and outputs an object of the solution space without requiring any "parents", it is functionally similar to an *initialisation* operator.

One of the main *dis*advantages of EC in general is that more specialised methods can often out-perform it where they are applicable. An example is gradient-descent methods, which generally out-perform EC when an explicit gradient can be defined on a convex fitness landscape. Similarly, PODI will often be out-performed by specialised methods in particular domains, as we have seen in the RSAP. However, when faced with a new problem or a variant of an existing one such that no existing heuristics have been developed and shown to solve it well, PODI provides a potentially useful starting-point.

PODI is a generative method, in that the NDP is a complex functional mapping from genome to phenotype. The NDP can range from very simple algorithms, such as grow, to complex ones such as those used here for 3D design and communications network design. Both newly-written and third-party programs have been used as NDPs. The NDP can be used as a medium for the expression of domain-specific knowledge. It has the advantage in this regard that directly writing programs (as opposed to creating representations) is a natural way of working for many domain experts.

The results when running PODI on a symbolic regression problem using grow and bubble-down as NDPs are surprisingly good. The latter also offers a potential advantage related to avoiding bloat: tree size can be placed under direct evolutionary control. This idea will be explored in future work.

Acknowledgements. Thanks are due to Erik Hemberg and Edgar Galván-Lopéz for reading drafts, and to anonymous reviewers, and to the authors of [8] for publishing their code.

References

1. Brameier, M., Banzhaf, W.: Linear genetic programming. Springer (2006)
2. Byrne, J., Fenton, M., Hemberg, E., McDermott, J., O'Neill, M., Shotton, E., Nally, C.: Combining Structural Analysis and Multi-Objective Criteria for Evolutionary Architectural Design. In: Di Chio, C., Brabazon, A., Di Caro, G.A., Drechsler, R., Farooq, M., Grahl, J., Greenfield, G., Prins, C., Romero, J., Squillero, G., Tarantino, E., Tettamanzi, A.G.B., Urquhart, N., Uyar, A.Ş. (eds.) EvoApplications 2011, Part II. LNCS, vol. 6625, pp. 204–213. Springer, Heidelberg (2011)
3. Carroll, P., McGarraghy, S.: A decomposition algorithm for the ring spur assignment problem. International Transactions in Operational Research (2012)
4. Hemberg, E., Veeramachaneni, K., McDermott, J., Berzan, C., O'Reilly, U.M.: An investigation of local patterns for estimation of distribution genetic programming. In: Proc. GECCO. ACM (2012)
5. Hoos, H.H.: Programming by optimisation. Tech. Rep. TR-2010, Department of Computer Science, University of British Columbia (2010)
6. Hornby, G.S., Pollack, J.B.: The advantages of generative grammatical encodings for physical design. In: Proc. CEC, pp. 600–607. IEEE (2001)
7. Keijzer, M., O'Neill, M., Ryan, C., Cattolico, M.: Grammatical Evolution Rules: The Mod and the Bucket Rule. In: Foster, J.A., Lutton, E., Miller, J., Ryan, C., Tettamanzi, A.G.B. (eds.) EuroGP 2002. LNCS, vol. 2278, pp. 123–130. Springer, Heidelberg (2002)
8. Kilmartin, P., Flynn, M.: Quantum Annealing in Management Science & Analytics: An investigation of applying QA Techniques to the Ring Spur Assignment Problem. Master's thesis, University College Dublin Business School (2012)
9. Koza, J.R.: Genetic Programming: On the Programming of Computers by Means of Natural Selection. The MIT Press, Cambridge (1992)
10. Krawiec, K., Lichocki, P.: Approximating geometric crossover in semantic space. In: Proc. GECCO, pp. 987–994. ACM, New York (2009)
11. McDermott, J., Byrne, J., Swafford, J.M., Hemberg, M., McNally, C., Shotton, E., Hemberg, E., Fenton, M., O'Neill, M.: String-rewriting grammars for evolutionary architectural design. Environment and Planning B: Planning and Design 39(4), 713–731 (2012), http://www.envplan.com/abstract.cgi?id=b38037
12. Miller, J.F., Thomson, P.: Cartesian Genetic Programming. In: Poli, R., Banzhaf, W., Langdon, W.B., Miller, J., Nordin, P., Fogarty, T.C. (eds.) EuroGP 2000. LNCS, vol. 1802, pp. 121–132. Springer, Heidelberg (2000)
13. Moraglio, A., Krawiec, K., Johnson, C.G.: Geometric Semantic Genetic Programming. In: Coello, C.A.C., Cutello, V., Deb, K., Forrest, S., Nicosia, G., Pavone, M. (eds.) PPSN 2012, Part I. LNCS, vol. 7491, pp. 21–31. Springer, Heidelberg (2012)
14. O'Neill, M., Ryan, C.: Grammatical Evolution: Evolutionary Automatic Programming in an Arbitrary Language. Kluwer Academic Publishers (2003)
15. Pagie, L., Hogeweg, P.: Evolutionary Consequences of Coevolving Targets. Evolutionary Computation 5, 401–418 (1997)
16. Rothlauf, F.: Representations for Genetic and Evolutionary Algorithms, 2nd edn. Physica-Verlag (2006)

Searching for Novel Classifiers

Enrique Naredo, Leonardo Trujillo*, and Yuliana Martínez

Doctorado en Ciencias de la Ingeniería, Departamento de Ingeniería Eléctrica y
Electrónica, Instituto Tecnológico de Tijuana, Blvd. Industrial y Av. ITR Tijuana
S/N, Mesa Otay C.P. 22500, Tijuana B.C., México
{enriquenaredo,ysaraimr}@gmail.com, leonardo.trujillo@tectijuana.edu.mx

Abstract. Natural evolution is an open-ended search process without
an a priori fitness function that needs to be optimized. On the other
hand, evolutionary algorithms (EAs) rely on a clear and quantitative
objective. The Novelty Search algorithm (NS) substitutes fitness-based
selection with a *novelty* criteria; i.e., individuals are chosen based on
their uniqueness. To do so, individuals are described by the behaviors
they exhibit, instead of their phenotype or genetic content. NS has mostly
been used in evolutionary robotics, where the concept of behavioral space
can be clearly defined. Instead, this work applies NS to a more general
problem domain, classification. To this end, two behavioral descriptors
are proposed, each describing a classifier's performance from two different
perspectives. Experimental results show that NS-based search can be
used to derive effective classifiers. In particular, NS is best suited to
solve difficult problems, where exploration needs to be encouraged and
maintained.

Keywords: Novelty Search, Classification, Genetic Programming.

1 Introduction

Research in Evolutionary Computation (EC) has produced search and optimization algorithms that frequently achieve promising new results in diverse domains
[4]. Therefore, the practical value of evolutionary algorithms (EAs) is by now
widely accepted. Nonetheless, for some within the field a conceptual, or even
philosophical, problem remains regarding most EAs. At their core, EAs are simple abstractions of Neo-Darwinian evolution. However, instead of the open-ended
nature of biological evolution, EAs are objective driven, just like any conventional optimization algorithm. Therefore, EAs are expected to converge on a
small subset of local optima within a static fitness landscape.

This difference, however, is not a general one. In fact, some of the earliest
EAs were open-ended techniques [1]. While such EAs are still abstract simplifications of evolution, they do integrate an open-ended feature not present in most
standard algorithms. Open-ended algorithms have mostly been used in specialized domains, such as artificial life environments [10] and interactive search [3].

---

* Corresponding author.

K. Krawiec et al. (Eds.): EuroGP 2013, LNCS 7831, pp. 145–156, 2013.
© Springer-Verlag Berlin Heidelberg 2013

Only recently have open-ended algorithms been proposed to solve mainstream problems. In particular, Lehman and Stanley [5–7] proposed novelty search (NS), an EA where the objective function is abandoned. Instead, selective pressure considers the novelty, or "uniqueness", of each individual by describing its behavior. Thus, fitness in NS is implicitly captured within the behavioral description of each individual. While such an approach might seem counterintuitive, experimental results are promising and show that highly fit solutions can emerge from a search that does not consider fitness explicitly.

Despite the success of NS, it might also appear to be a niche strategy that is well-suited for a small subset of domains. This paper explores the usefulness of NS on a common type of problem: classification. The core element of NS is that each individual is described by a behavioral descriptor, which is then used to measure the novelty that each solution introduces into the search. This paper proposes two behavioral descriptors for a Genetic Programming (GP) classifier. Each descriptor introduces a different behavioral space and corresponding fitness landscapes. Experimental results are encouraging, NS-based classification achieves competitive results compared to a canonical GP. Moreover, the paper analyzes some of the practical considerations that must be accounted for if NS is to be used successfully.

The paper is organized as follows. First, Section 2 describes the NS algorithm. Afterwards, Section 3 presents the proposed NS-based GP algorithm for data classification and two behavioral descriptors for evolved classifiers. Then, Section 4 presents the experiments and an analysis of the results. Finally, a summary of the paper and concluding remarks are given in Section 5.

2   Novelty Search

The main idea behind NS is to eliminate the objective function from a search [5–7]. In other words, evolution is not guided by the measured *quality* of each individual, instead it is guided by a measure of *uniqueness*; i.e., how novel each individual is with respect to what has been found earlier by the search. A known limitation of the traditional objective-based search is a tendency to converge and stagnate on local optima, particularly in multi-modal problems with irregular fitness landscapes. Within EC, diversity preservation techniques are usually incorporated within an EA to overcome the above shortcoming. However, most proposals can be regarded as ad-hoc solutions that must continuously attempt to balance exploration and exploitation during the search . Conversely, through the search for novelty alone, diversity preservation introduces the sole selective pressure during the search.

NS operates based on the concept of behavior, where each individual is described based on the functional behavior it exhibits. Therefore, individuals are described in behavioral space, instead of the more common genotypic, phenotypic or fitness spaces that are used for diversity preservation [13, 14]. Behaviors are expressed by a domain dependent descriptor, such that each individual is mapped to a single point in behavioral space. A behavior implicitly represents the fitness of an individual, providing a fine grained view of its performance or just a different domain specific perspective. Since many individuals in genotypic space express the same behavior, and are thus mapped to the same point in behavioral space, the search for novelty is often feasible. Lehman and Stanley argue that since the number of simple behaviors for any given problem is relatively small, then the search for novelty must necessarily lead to more functionally complex solutions. The concept of behavior as described above is closely related to the concept of semantics in GP [15].

In summary, NS uses a measure of *novelty* to characterize each individual. More precisely, the sparseness of each individual within behavioral space is measured, with respect to other individuals within the population and novel solutions from previous generations. An important observation is that such a measure of novelty is dynamic; i.e., it can produce different results for the same individual depending on the population state and search progress at a given generation. NS measures the sparseness ρ around each individual i, described by its behavioral descriptor $\mathbf{x}$, using the average distance to the k-nearest neighbors in behavioral space, with k an algorithm parameter, given by

$$\rho(\mathbf{x}) = \frac{1}{k} \sum_{i=0}^{k} dist(\mathbf{x}, \mu_i) \, , \qquad (1)$$

where μ_i is the ith-nearest neighbor of $\mathbf{x}$ with respect to distance metric $dist$, a domain-dependent measure of behavioral difference between two descriptors. If the average distance is large then the individual lies within a sparse region of behavioral space and it lies in a dense region when the measure is small.

In NS, sparseness is computed based on the contents of the current population and an archive of individuals that at one moment were considered to be novel. Therefore, an individual is added to the archive if its sparseness is above a minimal threshold ρ_{min}, the second parameter of the NS algorithm. The archive can also mitigate backtracking by the search process. This can also be seen as a shortcoming of the approach, since if the archive grows then a higher computational cost is incurred to compute sparseness. To address this problem, [6] implements the archive as a fixed size FIFO queue.

The NS algorithm provides an open-ended evolutionary approach to solve mainstream scientific and engineering problems. However, since its proposal in [5], and later works [6, 7], most applications of NS have focused on robotics, [5–8]. All of these works are part of a wider area of research known as evolutionary robotics (ER), where evolutionary algorithms are used to solve problems related to robot design and control. Within ER, the topic of evolving a diverse set of behaviors has also been addressed in other ways. For instance, [13, 14] propose to integrate speciation techniques to evolve a diverse set of robot behaviors. A good review on this topic is given by Mouret and Doncieux [9]. Search algorithms that explicitly contemplate behaviors seem well suited for robotics, since most high-level tasks can usually be solved in structurally different ways, guaranteeing multi-modal search spaces.

On the other hand, NS has not been used in most domains. A noteworthy exception is [16], where NS is integrated with an interactive evolutionary system. To the authors knowledge, however, applying NS to mainstream problems is not yet common. The present work proposes the use of NS for a ubiquitous pattern analysis problem, data classification.

3   Classification with Novelty Search

This section presents the proposed behavioral descriptors for GP-based classifiers and discusses the fitness landscape of each.

3.1   Static Range Selection GP Classifier

This work uses the Static Range Selection GP Classifier (SRS-GPC) described by Zhang and Smart [17]. In a classification problem, a pattern $\mathbf{x} \in \mathbb{R}^P$ has to be classified as belonging to a single class from $\Omega = \{\omega_1, ..., \omega_M\}$, where each ω_i represents a distinct class label. Then, in a supervised learning approach the goal is to build a mapping $g(\mathbf{x}) : \mathbb{R}^P \rightarrow \Omega$, that assigns each pattern $\mathbf{x}$ to a corresponding class ω_i, where g is derived based on evidence provided by a training set $\mathcal{T}$ of N P-dimensional patterns with a known classification. In this work, only two-class classification problems are considered. In SRS-GPC, $\mathbb{R}$ is divided into M non-overlapping regions, one for each class. Then, GP evolves a mapping $g(\mathbf{x}) : \mathbb{R}^P \rightarrow \mathbb{R}$, such that the region in $\mathbb{R}$ where pattern $\mathbf{x}$ is mapped to, determines the class to which it belongs. For a two-class problem, if $g(\mathbf{x}) > 0$ then $\mathbf{x}$ belongs to class ω_1, and belongs to ω_2 otherwise. The fitness function is simple, it consists on maximizing the classification accuracy of g.

3.2   Novelty Search Extension of SRS-GPC

As stated above, to apply NS with SRS-GPC the fitness function is substituted by the sparseness measure of Equation 1. Therefore, a proper domain specific behavioral descriptor must be proposed [2]. Two descriptors are proposed next, each inducing a different fitness landscape and behavioral neighborhoods.

Class Descriptor (CD): The training set $\mathcal{T}$ used by SRS-GPC contains sample patterns from each class. Then, for a two-class problem with $\Omega = \{\omega_1, \omega_2\}$ the CD is constructed in the following way. If $\mathcal{T} = \{\mathbf{y}_1, \mathbf{y}_2, ...\mathbf{y}_L\}$, then the behavioral descriptor for each GP classifier K_i is a binary vector $\mathbf{a_i} = (a_1, a_2, ...a_L)$ of size L, where each vector element a_j is set to 1 if classifier K_i assigns label ω_1 to pattern $\mathbf{y}_j$ and is set to 0 otherwise.

Accuracy Descriptor (AD): The second descriptor considers the accuracy of a classifier at a fine scale. If $\mathcal{T} = \{\mathbf{y}_1, \mathbf{y}_2, ...\mathbf{y}_L\}$, then the behavioral descriptor for each GP classifier K_i is a binary vector $\mathbf{b_i} = (b_1, b_2, ...b_L)$ of size L, where each vector element b_j is set to 1 if classifier K_i correctly classifies sample $\mathbf{y}_j$ and is set to 0 otherwise.

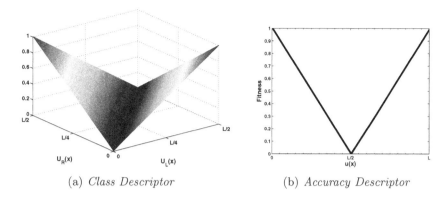

(a) *Class Descriptor*   (b) *Accuracy Descriptor*

Fig. 1. Fitness landscape in behavioral space for each descriptor

While both descriptors are binary vectors of size L, each induces a different fitness landscape in behavioral space. Suppose that the number of training examples from each class is $\frac{L}{2}$, and suppose that they are ordered in such a way that the first $\frac{L}{2}$ elements in $\mathcal{T}$ correspond to class label ω_1. Let $\mathbf{x}$ represent a binary vector, and function $u(\mathbf{x})$ return the number of 1s in $\mathbf{x}$. Moreover, let K_O be the *optimal* classifier that achieves a perfect accuracy on the training set.

Then, the CD of K_O is given by $\mathbf{a}^1 = (1_1, 1_2, ...1_{\frac{L}{2}}, 0_{\frac{L}{2}+1}....0_L)$. The AD of K_O is given by $\mathbf{b}^1$ where $u(\mathbf{b}^1) = L$. Moreover, for a two-class problem, an equally useful solution is to take the opposite (complement) behaviors and invert the classification, such that a 1 is converted to a 0 and vice-versa. These mirror behaviors are $\mathbf{a}^0 = (0_1, 0_2, ...0_{\frac{L}{2}}, 1_{\frac{L}{2}+1}....1_L)$ for the CD and $\mathbf{b}^0$ with $u(\mathbf{b}^0) = 0$ for the AD. The fitness landscapes in behavioral space are depicted in Figure 1.

For a two-class problem with a reasonable degree of difficulty, the initial generations of a GP search should be expected to contain close to random classifiers, with roughly a 50% accuracy. For the CD descriptor, behavioral space is organized on a two dimensional surface, such that one axis u_L considers the number of ones on the left hand side, first $\frac{L}{2}$ bits, of a behavior descriptor $\mathbf{a}$, and u_R considers the remaining $\frac{L}{2}$ bits; see Figure 1(a). Notice that the middle valley of the fitness landscape corresponds to random classifiers, with worst case performance. Hence, NS will push the search towards either of the two global optima, $\mathbf{a}^1$ and $\mathbf{a}^0$ On the other hand, for the AD descriptor, early behaviors will mostly exhibit descriptors with equal proportions of zeros and ones; see Figure 1(b). Then, NS will progressively explore towards two opposite points in behavioral space, $\mathbf{b}^1$ or $\mathbf{b}^0$. The effect on performance of these differences, between the CD and the AD, are explored experimentally in the following section.

Finally, given the above binary descriptors, a natural $dist()$ function for Equation 1 is the Hamming distance, that counts the number of bits that differ between two binary vectors. This similarity measure has been used to measure behavioral diversity in ER [9].

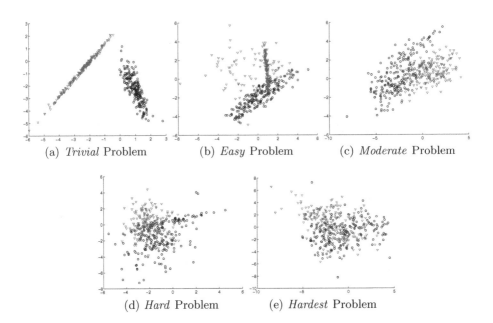

(a) *Trivial* Problem   (b) *Easy* Problem   (c) *Moderate* Problem

(d) *Hard* Problem   (e) *Hardest* Problem

Fig. 2. Five synthetic 2-class problems used to evaluate each algorithm in ascending order of difficulty from left to right

4   Experiments

The performance of the NS-based GP classifier is examined. Several different versions are tested and compared. First, the basic SRS-GPC classifier. Second, the NS variant with CD in two different versions. One configuration uses a novelty archive of unbounded size, while the second one used a FIFO archive with limited size as in [6]. Hereafter, the former is referred to as NS-CD and the latter as NS-CD-L. Similarly, two NS variants with AD are tested, NS-AD and NS-AD-L.

Gaussian Mixture Models are used to generate five random synthetic problems, each with different amounts of class overlap and geometry. All problems are set in the $\mathbb{R}^2$ plane with $x, y \in [-10, 10]$ and 200 sample points were randomly generated for each class. The parameters for the GMM of each class were also randomly chosen, following the same strategy reported in [12]. The five problems are of increasing difficulty, denoted as: *Trivial*; *Easy*; *Moderate*; *Hard*; and *Hardest*; these problems are graphically depicted in Figure 2.

As stated above, five different algorithms are experimentally compared: SRS-GPC, NS-CD, NS-CD-L, NS-AD and NS-AD-L. All algorithms share the same GP representation and genetic operators, a tree-based Koza style algorithm with subtree mutation and crossover. The parameters shared by all algorithms are summarized in Table 1. Additionally, SRS-GPC also uses a keep-best elitism strategy.

Table 1. Parameters for the GP-based search

Parameter	Description
Population size	200 individuals.
Generations	200 generations.
Initialization	Ramped Half-and-Half, with 6 levels of maximum depth.
Operator probabilities	Crossover $p_c = 0.8$, Mutation $p_\mu = 0.2$.
Function set	$\{\,+\,,\,-\,,\,\times\,,\,\div\,,\,\lvert\cdot\rvert\,,\,x^2\,,\,\sqrt{x}\,,\,log\,,\,sin\,,\,cos\,,\,if\,\}$.
Terminal set	$\{x_1,...,x_i,...,x_p\}$, where x_i is a dimension of the data patterns $\mathbf{x} \in \mathbb{R}^n$.
Bloat control	Dynamic depth control.
Initial dynamic depth	6 levels.
Hard maximum depth	20 levels.
Selection	Tournament.

Table 2. Average classification error and standard error of the best solution found by each algorithm on each problem; NS-based algorithms use $k = 15$ and $\rho_{min} = 80$

Problem	SRS-GPC	NS-CD	NS-CD-L	NS-AD	NS-AD-L
Trivial	0.005 ± 0.006	$0.006 \pm 0.008^*$	$0.006 \pm 0.010^*$	$0.002 \pm 0.005^*$	$0.006 \pm 0.007^*$
Easy	0.080 ± 0.026	0.131 ± 0.035	0.128 ± 0.031	0.115 ± 0.034	0.136 ± 0.033
Moderate	0.129 ± 0.030	0.150 ± 0.030	$0.132 \pm 0.041^*$	$0.152 \pm 0.050^*$	$0.133 \pm 0.041^*$
Hard	0.255 ± 0.049	$0.279 \pm 0.044^*$	0.287 ± 0.039	0.282 ± 0.044	$0.272 \pm 0.057^*$
Hardest	0.374 ± 0.048	$0.342 \pm 0.037^*$	$0.381 \pm 0.053^*$	$0.367 \pm 0.049^*$	$0.380 \pm 0.045^*$

Table 3. Average classification error and standard error of the best solution found by each algorithm on each problem; NS-based algorithms use $k = 15$ and $\rho_{min} = 40$

Problem	SRS-GPC	NS-CD	NS-CD-L	NS-AD	NS-AD-L
Trivial	0.005 ± 0.006	$0.004 \pm 0.006^*$	$0.001 \pm 0.004^*$	$0.005 \pm 0.006^*$	$0.005 \pm 0.007^*$
Easy	0.080 ± 0.026	0.124 ± 0.032	0.152 ± 0.124	0.130 ± 0.034	0.134 ± 0.037
Moderate	0.129 ± 0.030	0.153 ± 0.045	$0.180 \pm 0.146^*$	$0.148 \pm 0.044^*$	$0.149 \pm 0.036^*$
Hard	0.255 ± 0.049	$0.281 \pm 0.051^*$	$0.330 \pm 0.155^*$	$0.271 \pm 0.053^*$	$0.271 \pm 0.053^*$
Hardest	0.374 ± 0.048	$0.383 \pm 0.045^*$	$0.406 \pm 0.111^*$	$0.385 \pm 0.050^*$	$0.365 \pm 0.037^*$

For the NS-based algorithms two different parameter settings are used. In particular, two different values for the archive threshold ρ_{min} are used, 40 and 80. Parameter k is set to 15 for all algorithms. Finally, all algorithms were coded using Matlab 2009a and the GPLAB toolbox [11].

For each algorithm, 30 different runs were executed for each problem shown in Figure 2. In each run, the data set is randomly dividing into training and testing sets, with the former containing 70% of the data samples.

First, tables 2 and 3 compare the performance of every algorithm on each problem, considering the test data from each run and presenting the average classification error ± the standard error. In Table 2 the NS-based algorithms use $k = 15$ and $\rho_{min} = 80$, while in Table 3 $k = 15$ and $\rho_{min} = 40$. To verify statistical significance, the Wilcoxon rank-sum test is performed between the control algorithm SRS-GPC and each of the NS algorithms. In tables 3 and 2 an asterisk indicates that the corresponding NS-algorithm achieves statistically

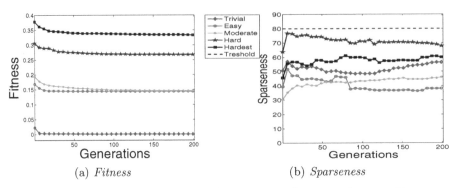

(a) *Fitness*   (b) *Sparseness*

Fig. 3. Evolution of NS-CD with parameters $k = 15$ and $\rho_{min} = 80$

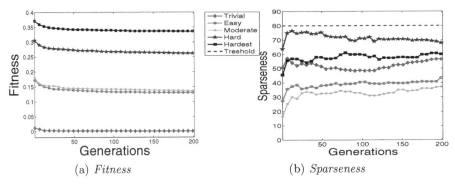

(a) *Fitness*   (b) *Sparseness*

Fig. 4. Evolution of NS-CD-L with parameters $k = 15$ and $\rho_{min} = 80$

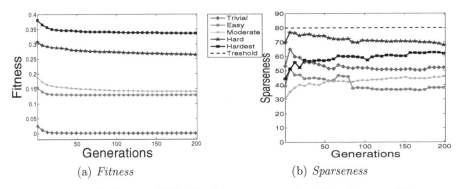

(a) *Fitness*   (b) *Sparseness*

Fig. 5. Evolution of NS-AD with parameters $k = 15$ and $\rho_{min} = 80$

equivalent results with SRS-GPC at the $\alpha = 0.05$ significance level. In general, these results show that AD produces better performance than CD and that limiting the size of the archive does not affect performance, and in some cases improves it. Additionally, a lower ρ_{min} encourages better performance in most algorithms. Moreover, with respect to each problem we can state the following.

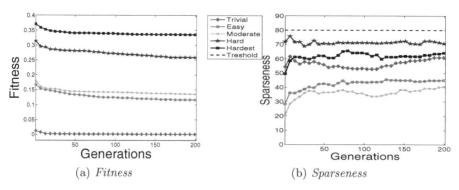

(a) *Fitness*   (b) *Sparseness*

Fig. 6. Evolution of NS-AD-L with parameters $k = 15$ and $\rho_{min} = 80$

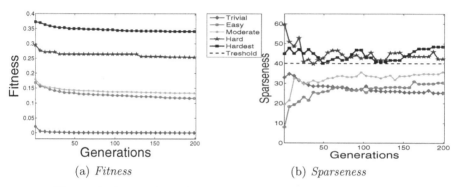

(a) *Fitness*   (b) *Sparseness*

Fig. 7. Evolution of NS-CD with parameters $k = 15$ and $\rho_{min} = 40$

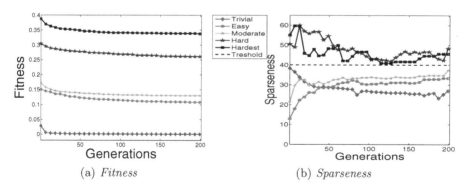

(a) *Fitness*   (b) *Sparseness*

Fig. 8. Evolution of NS-CD-L with parameters $k = 15$ and $\rho_{min} = 40$

First, for the trivial problem, all of the algorithms can solve it nearly perfectly. Second, for the *easy* problem NS produces slightly worse results than standard search. However, both problems are quite easy, far from the type of data generally encountered in real-world scenarios. Finally, for the *moderate* and *hard* problems, the NS-algorithm achieves equal performance with respect to SRS-GPC.

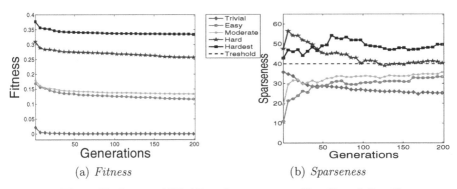

(a) *Fitness*   (b) *Sparseness*

Fig. 9. Evolution of NS-AD with parameters $K = 15$ and $S = 40$

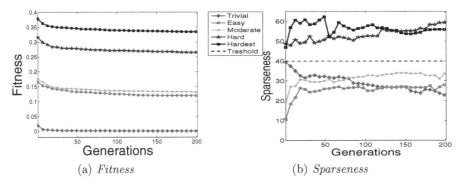

(a) *Fitness*   (b) *Sparseness*

Fig. 10. Evolution of NS-AD-L with parameters $K = 15$ and $S = 40$

Figures 3-10 examines the evolution of the NS-based algorithms. Each figure contains two plots that show averages over all runs; these are: (1) evolution of fitness and (2) evolution of sparseness. First, with respect to the fitness of the best solution at each generation, the difference in performance between each problem is evident and consistent across all algorithms. The second plot in each figure shows the sparseness value associated to the best solution at each generation. A horizontal line in these plots shows the corresponding threshold value, set to 80 in figures 3-6 and set to 40 in figures 7-10. In the former group, on average, the best solution does not reach the threshold. This exhibits the importance of ρ_{min}, if it is not set correctly then the best solution might not be saved in the archive; thus explaining the overall worse performance shown in Table 2. It is apparent that ρ_{min} should be lower, as is the case in figures 7-10. Nonetheless, with $\rho_{min} = 40$ the sparseness value of the best individual rises above the threshold only on the more difficult problems. This illustrates the main assumption behind the usefulness of NS, that random solutions will mostly exhibit bad fitness, and thus good solutions will tend to also be novel ones. Nonetheless, even if the best solution at each generation is not incorporated into the archive, it appears that sufficiently good solutions are saved, based on the test performance summarized in tables 2 and 3, that is mostly equivalent to the standard GP search.

5 Conclusions

This paper uses a GP system based on the NS algorithm to search for data classifiers. To the authors knowledge, the work represents the first attempt to leverage NS to solve a common problem in pattern analysis and recognition, since previous applications of NS were primarily focused on robotic tasks. This line of research follows other recent works where solution behavior [14, 9], or solution semantics [15], are explicitly considered during a population-based search. To do so, two domain-specific behavioral descriptors were proposed, the Class Descriptor and the Accuracy Descriptor. In general, both descriptors appear to produce equivalent performance, in most cases statistically similar to a canonical GP search. Moreover, it appears that NS-based search exhibits the best results when confronted with difficult problems. It seems that the reason for this is that generating a high-quality solution at random is less probable for difficult problems, then the incentive for behavioral exploration is incremented and the search for novelty will indeed lead towards quality during the search. For simple problems, however, the explorative capacity of NS is mostly unexploited or even a detriment to the search; i.e., if random solutions have a high fitness then novelty could easily lead the search towards worse results. Finally, while both descriptors, AD and CD, achieve similar performance on these tests, their differences must be studied and exploited further. In particular, the AD descriptor can only be used in supervised learning problems since it assumes knowledge of a ground truth set or classified samples. The CD descriptor, however, is less restrictive in this sense. Therefore, future work will center on exploring the usefulness of NS on the more difficult problem of non-supervised learning.

Acknowledgments. This research was supported by CONACYT (Mexico) Basic Science Research Grant No. 178323, "*Prediccón de Rendimiento y Dificultad de Problemas en Programación Genética*". First and third authors were supported by PRONABES-DGEST (Mexico) scholarships, respectively No. 20120000634 and No. 20120000735.

References

1. Dawkins, R.: Climbing Mount Improbable. W.W. Norton & Company (1996)
2. Kistemaker, S., Whiteson, S.: Critical factors in the performance of novelty search. In: Proceedings of the 13th Annual Conference on Genetic and Evolutionary Computation, GECCO 2011, pp. 965–972. ACM (2011)
3. Kowaliw, T., Dorin, A., McCormack, J.: Promoting creative design in interactive evolutionary computation. IEEE Transactions on Evolutionary Computation 16(4), 523–536 (2012)
4. Koza, J.: Human-competitive results produced by genetic programming. Genetic Programming and Evolvable Machines 11(3), 251–284 (2010)
5. Lehman, J., Stanley, K.O.: Exploiting open-endedness to solve problems through the search for novelty. In: Proceedings of the Eleventh International Conference on Artificial Life. ALIFE XI. MIT Press, Cambridge (2008)

6. Lehman, J., Stanley, K.O.: Efficiently evolving programs through the search for novelty. In: Proceedings of the 12th Annual Conference on Genetic and Evolutionary Computation, GECCO 2010, pp. 837–844. ACM (2010)
7. Lehman, J., Stanley, K.O.: Abandoning objectives: Evolution through the search for novelty alone. Evol. Comput. 19(2), 189–223 (2011)
8. Lehman, J., Stanley, K.O.: Evolving a diversity of virtual creatures through novelty search and local competition. In: Proceedings of the 13th Annual Conference on Genetic and Evolutionary Computation, GECCO 2011, pp. 211–218. ACM (2011)
9. Mouret, J.B., Doncieux, S.: Encouraging behavioral diversity in evolutionary robotics: An empirical study. Evol. Comput. 20(1), 91–133 (2012)
10. Ofria, C., Wilke, C.O.: Avida: a software platform for research in computational evolutionary biology. Artif. Life 10(2), 191–229 (2004)
11. Silva, S., Almeida, J.: Gplab–a genetic programming toolbox for matlab. In: Gregersen, L. (ed.) Proceedings of the Nordic MATLAB Conference, pp. 273–278 (2003)
12. Trujillo, L., Martínez, Y., Galván-López, E., Legrand, P.: Predicting problem difficulty for genetic programming applied to data classification. In: Proceedings of the 13th Annual Conference on Genetic and Evolutionary Computation, GECCO 2011, pp. 1355–1362. ACM, New York (2011)
13. Trujillo, L., Olague, G., Lutton, E., Fernández de Vega, F.: Discovering Several Robot Behaviors through Speciation. In: Giacobini, M., Brabazon, A., Cagnoni, S., Di Caro, G.A., Drechsler, R., Ekárt, A., Esparcia-Alcázar, A.I., Farooq, M., Fink, A., McCormack, J., O'Neill, M., Romero, J., Rothlauf, F., Squillero, G., Uyar, A.Ş., Yang, S. (eds.) EvoWorkshops 2008. LNCS, vol. 4974, pp. 164–174. Springer, Heidelberg (2008)
14. Trujillo, L., Olague, G., Lutton, E., Fernández de Vega, F., Dozal, L., Clemente, E.: Speciation in behavioral space for evolutionary robotics. Journal of Intelligent & Robotic Systems 64(3-4), 323–351 (2011)
15. Uy, N.Q., Hoai, N.X., O'Neill, M., Mckay, R.I., Galván-López, E.: Semantically-based crossover in genetic programming: application to real-valued symbolic regression. Genetic Programming and Evolvable Machines 12(2), 91–119 (2011)
16. Woolley, B.G., Stanley, K.O.: Exploring promising stepping stones by combining novelty search with interactive evolution. CoRR abs/1207.6682 (2012)
17. Zhang, M., Smart, W.: Using gaussian distribution to construct fitness functions in genetic programming for multiclass object classification. Pattern Recogn. Lett. 27(11), 1266-1274 (2006)

Learning Reusable Initial Solutions for Multi-objective Order Acceptance and Scheduling Problems with Genetic Programming

Su Nguyen[1], Mengjie Zhang[1], Mark Johnston[1], and Kay Chen Tan[2]

[1] Victoria University of Wellington, Wellington, New Zealand
[2] National University of Singapore, Singapore
{su.nguyen,mengjie.zhang}@ecs.vuw.ac.nz,
mark.johnston@msor.vuw.ac.nz, eletankc@nus.edu.sg

Abstract. Order acceptance and scheduling (OAS) is an important issue in make-to-order production systems that decides the set of orders to accept and the sequence in which these accepted orders are processed to increase total revenue and improve customer satisfaction. This paper aims to explore the Pareto fronts of trade-off solutions for a multi-objective OAS problem. Due to its complexity, solving this problem is challenging. A two-stage learning/optimising (2SLO) system is proposed in this paper to solve the problem. The novelty of this system is the use of genetic programming to evolve a set of scheduling rules that can be reused to initialise populations of an evolutionary multi-objective optimisation (EMO) method. The computational results show that 2SLO is more effective than the pure EMO method. Regarding maximising the total revenue, 2SLO is also competitive as compared to other optimisation methods in the literature.

Keywords: genetic programming, scheduling, multiple objective.

1 Introduction

Order acceptance and scheduling (OAS) is an important operation in make-to-order production systems. The aim of OAS is to determine whether to accept or reject orders from customers to optimise the use of the limited capacity of the shop based on requirements (due dates, processing times, etc.) and revenues of the orders. OAS is motivated by practical situations in make-to-order systems such as customised packing material producers [18] or logistic systems where customer selection is important to effectively utilise the available capacity [4]. It is noted that simultaneously dealing with both acceptance and scheduling decisions is necessary to have a proper assessment of the influences of orders on the production activities in the shop. OAS is more challenging than the traditional scheduling problems [1–3, 7, 15, 21, 27] since not only does the processing sequence of orders need to be determined, but also the combination of accepted orders must be decided.

This paper focuses on the OAS problems in the single machine shop with n orders. The goal of OAS is to determine which orders within the n orders are

K. Krawiec et al. (Eds.): EuroGP 2013, LNCS 7831, pp. 157–168, 2013.

accepted (must be processed and delivered) and how the accepted orders are scheduled to optimise certain performance measures. Each order has a release time r_j, a processing time p_j, a due date d_j, a weight/penalty w_j, a maximum revenue e_j, and a deadline $\bar{d}_j$. A specific setup time s_{ij} for order j is incurred if order j is processed immediately after order i (s_{0j} is the setup time of order j in the case that order j is processed first). If the order is completed before the due date d_j, the revenue rev_j obtained from order j is the maximum revenue e_j. Otherwise, rev_j is the remaining revenue after deducting the penalty caused by the tardiness $T_j = \max(0, C_j - d_j)$ from e_j, where C_j is the completion time of order j. Generally, the revenue obtained by an order j can be calculated by $rev_j = e_j I_j - w_j T_j$ in which I_j is 1 if order j is accepted; and 0 otherwise. If orders are finished after their deadline $\bar{d}_j$, no revenue is gained. This problem is the same as those in [18] and [4].

Different methods have been proposed in the literature to deal with OAS. Slotnick and Morton [22] studied OAS in a single machine environment without preemption to maximise the total revenue (which includes costs caused by order lateness). An exact branch and bound method and two heuristic procedures were proposed. The myopic heuristic was shown to be effective and efficient as compared to the branch and bound method which is very computationally expensive. Slotnick and Morton [23] extended their work by considering costs caused by tardiness instead of lateness. Ghosh [10] showed that OAS is NP-hard and proposed two pseudo-polynomial time algorithms and approximate methods to deal with some special cases of this problem. Rom and Slotnick [19] proposed a hybrid genetic algorithm with local search heuristic to handle the same problem which showed very promising results. Oguz et al. [18] investigated OAS with sequence dependent setup times in printing operations for a customised packing material producer and developed a mixed integer linear programming (MILP) formulation. Since optimal solutions can only be obtained for a limited number of orders, Oguz et al. [18] proposed ISFAN, a heuristic based on simulated annealing to handle sequencing decisions. Cesaret et al. [4] proposed a tabu search (TS) method to handle the same problem and the experimental results showed that the proposed TS method outperformed ISFAN especially for instances with a large number of orders. OAS problems in the job shop environment have also been investigated by Wester et al. [26] and Roundy et al. [20]. Different from studies previously discussed, Wester et al. [26] performed a simulation to evaluate different order acceptance strategies when orders arrive according to some stochastic process over time. Roundy et al. [20] examined acceptance decisions when an order arrives to determine whether the production system has the capacity.

1.1   Goals

This paper presents the first work on the multi-objective OAS problem which has not been previously investigated in the literature. We focus on two objectives: (1) total revenue TR $= \sum_{j \in \mathbb{A}} rev_j$ and (2) mean absolute error MAE $= (\sum_{j \in \mathbb{A}} |C_j - d_j|)/n$ where $\mathbb{A}$ is the set of accepted orders. Maximising total revenue is unarguably important for any producers. However, with the current emphasis on the just-in-time (JIT) [6] production concept, where both earliness and tardiness are undesirable, meeting the target job due date would be of significance for the practice of JIT philosophy. The reason is that early jobs increase the inventory costs [5] while tardy jobs result in penalties, such as loss of customer goodwill and damaged reputation [12]. Because of the complexity of this problem, exploring the Pareto front of trade-off solutions is challenging. To deal with this issue, we propose a genetic programming based hyperheuristic (GPHH) method to generate effective reusable initial populations for the evolutionary multi-objective optimisation (EMO) methods. The aim of this approach is to quickly identify potential trade-off solutions to effectively guide the search of the EMO methods to better solutions and reduce their computational cost. This is inspired by the success of GPHH methods [9, 11, 13, 16, 17, 24] for evolving reusable dispatching rules for scheduling problems. These methods employed genetic programming (GP) to evolve dispatching rules which are priority functions based on attributes of jobs and machines to solve the scheduling problems. The results from these studies showed that the dispatching rules are effective even for unseen instances. The proposed GPHH in this paper is similar to that developed by Nguyen et al. [16] to evolve Pareto fronts of non-dominated scheduling policies. However, instead of directly applying the evolved rules [16], we use the evolved rules as the input for EMO methods. In this new approach, we develop a two-stage learning/optimising (2SLO) system to deal with OAS. The first stage performs offline learning to generate resuable non-dominated scheduling rules for OAS. Then the second stage uses EMO methods to solve specific OAS instances based on rules obtained from the first stage.

The research objectives of this paper are as follows.

1. Developing the two-stage learning/optimising system to deal with the multi-objective OAS problem.
2. Developing a GPHH method to learn reusable non-dominated rules for OAS.
3. Developing an EMO method to explore the Pareto front of non-dominated solutions for each specific OAS problem instance.
4. Comparing the performance of the proposed system with other optimisation methods.

1.2 Organisation

The rest of this paper is organised as follows. In Section 2 we describe the proposed 2SLO, GPHH, and EMO methods, and show how scheduling rules are represented in GPHH and how OAS solutions are represented in the proposed EMO method. The performance of the proposed system is compared to those in the literature and the results are shown in Section 3. Finally, we provide the conclusions and discussions for future research in Section 4.

2 Methodology

Fig. 1 presents the conceptual structure of the proposed system. In the first stage, the system applies the proposed GPHH (more details are provided in

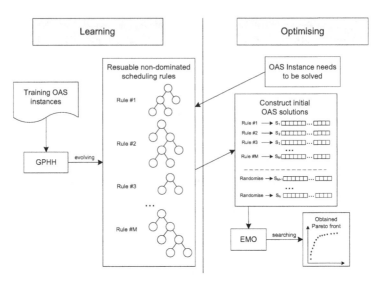

Fig. 1. Conceptual structure of the proposed 2SLO system

Section 2.1) to generate a set of non-dominated scheduling rules. The rules will be evaluated based on a training set of OAS instances. After the non-dominated rules are obtained by GPHH, they are stored in an archive for future use. It is noted that the purpose of this stage is not to find the optimal solutions for any particular OAS instance but to discover effective reusable rules which can help determine potential trade-off solutions when we deal with unseen instances. The reason that GP is used for the learning stage is that the rules generated by GP can be applied to any instance regardless of scale (number of orders) and GP, as an evolutionary computation method, can utilise the available search mechanisms proposed in the literature such as NSGA-II [8], SPEA2 [29], etc. to explore the non-dominated rules.

The second stage of the system is applied whenever an OAS decision needs to be made. In this case, the production planning and control system will collect relevant information of orders to form an OAS instance. The data of this OAS instance will be sent to the archive of reusable rules. Each rule in the archive will construct an OAS solution based on the input data. Solutions constructed by reusable rules are transformed into the form of solutions represented by the proposed EMO method (more details are provided in Section 2.2). After all solutions from rules in the archive are obtained, if these solutions did not fill up the population of the employed EMO method, the remaining solutions are randomly generated. This is to ensure that there are sufficient genetic materials to help explore the whole Pareto front.

It is noted that the second stage does not need to run right after the first stage. In practice, the first stage can be performed whenever the computational resources are available (e.g. overnight or during the weekend). Meanwhile, the EMO method in the second stage is applied immediately when a new OAS instance needs to be solved. Without the input from the learning process in

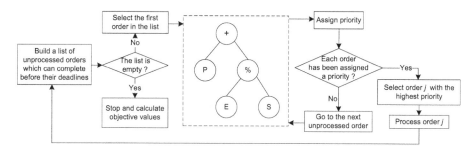

Fig. 2. Representation and evaluation of an evolved scheduling rule

the first stage, the application of the second stage is similar to that of any optimisation method. Different from previous proposed machine learning based evolutionary algorithms [28] where machine learning methods are used as the preprocessing step when solving a particular problem instance, our proposed system takes advantage of OAS features to generate reusable rules through offline learning and thus can reduce the computational cost caused by machine learning methods in the optimising stage.

2.1 GPHH for OAS

The scheduling rules evolved by GP are priority functions to calculate the priorities of orders which determine the sequence in which orders are processed. Fig. 2 shows how a rule is represented by GP and how it can be used to solve an OAS instance. The function and terminal sets used to generate scheduling rules are shown in Table 1. The procedure in Fig. 2 starts by building a list of unprocessed orders which can be processed before their deadlines. Then, the evolved rule calculates the priority of each order in the list using the corresponding information of that order. After priorities are assigned to all orders in the list, the order with the highest priority will be processed (and certainly this order is accepted). The current time of the schedule (ready time to process the next order) is adjusted. The list of unprocessed orders are updated and the procedure stops if no order can be completed before its deadline.

Algorithm 1 shows how the proposed GPHH evolves a set of non-dominated scheduling rules. This algorithm employs the population updating scheme based

Table 1. Terminal and function sets for scheduling rules

Symbol	Description	Symbol	Description
R	release time r_j	P	processing time p_j
E	revenue e_j	W	penalty w_j
S	setup time s_{ij}	d	due date d_j
D	deadline $\bar{d}_j$	t	current time
#	random number from 0 to 1		
Function set		$+,-,\times, \%$ (protected division), If	

Algorithm 1. GPHH to evolve scheduling rules for OAS problems

---

load training OAS instances $\mathbb{D} \leftarrow \{D_1, D_2, \ldots, D_T\}$
randomly initialise the population $P \leftarrow \{\mathcal{R}_1, \mathcal{R}_2, \ldots, \mathcal{R}_N\}$
$\mathcal{P}^e \leftarrow \{\}$ and $generation \leftarrow 0$
while $generation \leq maxGeneration$ **do**
  foreach $\mathcal{R}_i \in P$ **do**
    $\lfloor \ \mathcal{R}_i.objectives \leftarrow$ apply $\mathcal{R}_i$ to each OAS instance $D_k \in \mathbb{D}$
  calculate the crowding distance and ranks for individuals in $P \bigcup \mathcal{P}^e$
  $\mathcal{P}^e \leftarrow select(P \bigcup \mathcal{P}^e)$
  $P \leftarrow$ apply crossover, mutation to $\mathcal{P}^e$
  $\lfloor \ generation \leftarrow generation + 1$
return $\mathcal{P}^e$

---

on crowding distance and non-dominated ranks from NSGA-II [8]. It is noted that other approaches to explore the Pareto front can also be used here but the NSGA-II approach is chosen because of its simplicity and popularity in the EMO literature. At first, a number of training instances are loaded and the initial archive $\mathcal{P}^e$ (parent population) is empty. These training instances will be used to evaluate the performance of an evolved scheduling rule. The initial GP population is created using the ramped-half-and-half method [14]. In each generation of GPHH, all individuals in the population will be evaluated by applying them to solve each training instance. The quality of each individual in the population will be measured by the average values of the objectives across all training instances.

After all individuals have been evaluated, we calculate the crowding distance [8] for each individual. Then, individuals in both archive $\mathcal{P}^e$ and population P are selected to update the archive $\mathcal{P}^e$ based on the crowding distance and the non-dominated rank [8]. The new population will be generated by applying crossover and mutation to the current population. For crossover, GP uses the subtree crossover [14], which creates new individuals for the next generation by randomly recombining subtrees from two selected parents. Mutation is performed by subtree mutation [14], which randomly selects a node of a chosen individual in the population and replaces the subtree rooted at that node by a newly randomly-generated subtree. Binary tournament selection [8] is used to select the parents for the two genetic operations. Based on pilot experiments, the crossover rate and mutation rate used in the three methods are 90% and 10%, respectively, and the maximum depth of GP trees is 8. A population size of 10,000 is used to ensure that there are enough genetic materials to explore the search space of non-dominated rules. The results will be obtained after the proposed method runs for 100 generations. The obtained $\mathcal{P}^e$ is the archive of reusable scheduling rules in 2SLO.

2.2   EMO for OAS

Different from the first stage, the second stage aims to solve a particular OAS instance. In this case, solutions for an OAS instance are represented by arrays

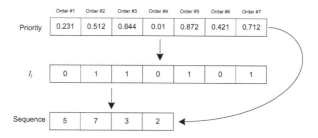

Fig. 3. Representation of OAS solutions

of real numbers (from 0 to 1). An example of an OAS solution is shown in Fig. 3. The dimension of the array is the number of orders n of the OAS instance. Similar to the representation of solutions in pure scheduling problems and that in Rom and Slotnick [19], the real value represents the priority of each corresponding order to determine the sequence in which orders are processed. In our method, the real number array decides both the sequence decisions and acceptance decisions of OAS. In the array, if the value is greater than 0.5, the corresponding order is accepted. After the set of accepted orders are determined, the values corresponding to these orders are treated as the priorities to decide the processing sequence (orders with higher priorities will be processed earlier). This modification is made to maintain a balance between the quality of acceptance decisions and sequencing decisions. It is noted that after the reusable rules are applied, the obtained solutions will be transformed to the form which can be used as the initial solution of NSGA-II. The transformation is performed by assigned random numbers in the range $(0.5, 1]$ to the accepted order such that the orders which are processed earlier have higher values. Random numbers in $[0, 0.5]$ are assigned to other rejected orders.

Since real-code representation is quite popular in the evolutionary computation community, many EMO methods can be employed to search for the Pareto front for a particular OAS instance. Based on our pilot experiments with some popular EMO methods, NSGA-II [8] showed very promising results for the OAS problem in this paper. Therefore, we apply NSGA-II as the EMO method in the optimising stage of Fig. 1. Based on our preliminary experiments, the population size of NSGA-II is 500 and the maximum number of solution evaluations is 100,000. Simulated binary crossover (SBX) and real-parameter mutation [8] are used to generate new solutions with probabilities of 100% and 1% respectively. Binary tournament selection is applied to select solutions for genetic operations.

3   Computational Results

To examine the effectiveness of the proposed 2SLO system (coded in Java and run on Intel i5, 3.10 GHz CPUs), the system is applied to solve the benchmark instances from Casaret et al. [4]. These instances are generated based on tardiness factor τ and due date range R (details about instance generation are provided in [4]).

The test bed contains different sets (each has 10 instances) generated from different combinations of τ and R and the number of orders n. In this paper, we only focus on the sets with the largest number of orders $n = 100$. We use the tuple $\langle \tau, R \rangle$ to indicate the set of 10 instances with tardiness factor τ and due date range R. For the learning stage of 2SLO, we will use the first five instances of a particular set denoted as $\langle \tau, R \rangle^{\mathrm{Tr}}$. In order to investigate the influence of the training set on the reusability of the evolved rules and the performance of the 2SLO system, we will apply the system with three training sets $\langle 0.1, 0.1 \rangle^{\mathrm{Tr}}$, $\langle 0.5, 0.5 \rangle^{\mathrm{Tr}}$, and $\langle 0.9, 0.9 \rangle^{\mathrm{Tr}}$. The performance of the proposed 2SLO system is compared with the pure NSGA-II method (with the same settings as the NSGA-II used in the second stage of 2SLO) by applying them to solve 25 sets of instances (combinations of five values of τ and five values of R) with $n = 100$. The proposed 2SLO system performed 30 independent runs. In each run, a set of resuable rules are obtained and the performance of 2SLO is measured by performing the optimising stage to each test instance 30 times. For each test instance, Pareto fronts obtained by 2SLO and the pure NSGA-II are compared by using the hypervolume ratio (HVR) [25]. The reference Pareto front used to calculate HVR is obtained by extracting non-dominated solutions from all Pareto fronts found by 2SLO and NSGA-II. The solutions obtained by 2SLO regarding the total revenue is also compared to those found by ISFAN [18], MILP, m-ATCS, and TS [4].

3.1   Multi-objective Performance

Table 2 shows the performance of the proposed 2SLO system and that of the pure NSGA-II method. The values in this table are $\overline{\mathrm{HVR}}$ which is the average HVR (higher HVR is better) corresponding to each set of OAS instances. 2SLO-$\langle \tau, R \rangle^{\mathrm{Tr}}$ indicates 2SLO in which GPHH in the first stage uses the training set $\langle \tau, R \rangle^{\mathrm{Tr}}$. Columns min, avg, and max show the minimum, average, and maximum of $\overline{\mathrm{HVR}}$ from 30 independent runs of 2SLO. The results show that the proposed 2SLO methods outperform NSGA-II in many cases with different combinations of τ and R, especially for the case with high τ and R. Comparing the results obtained by 2SLO with different training sets also shows that training sets do have a large impact on the performance of 2SLO. For example, 2SLO trained with $\langle 0.1, 0.1 \rangle^{\mathrm{Tr}}$ provides very good results with the instances with low τ and R. The effectiveness of 2SLO-$\langle 0.1, 0.1 \rangle^{\mathrm{Tr}}$ reduces as τ and R increase (but are still better than NSGA-II in most cases). 2SLO-$\langle 0.5, 0.5 \rangle^{\mathrm{Tr}}$ and 2SLO-$\langle 0.9, 0.9 \rangle^{\mathrm{Tr}}$ are also more effective when they are applied to sets with τ and R close to those of the training set. Examples of Pareto fronts obtained by 2SLO and NSGA-II are provided in Fig. 4. It is obvious that the Pareto fronts obtained by 2SLO are much better than that of NSGA-II. Fig. 4(a) and Fig. 4(b) show that the obtained Pareto fronts are well-spread and close to the reference Pareto front. In Fig. 4(c), although the extreme value for each objective is not found by 2SLO, the Pareto front found by 2SLO contains the most potential compromise solutions since a slight improvement in any objective will rapidly deteriorate the other objective. These experiments have confirmed the effectiveness of the learning/optimising methods in 2SLO to deal with multi-objective OAS problems.

Table 2. Quality of Pareto fronts found by 2SLO (highlighed results indicate that training and test instances come from the same set $\langle \tau, R \rangle$)

τ	R	2SLO-$\langle 0.1, 0.1 \rangle^{\mathrm{Tr}}$			2SLO-$\langle 0.5, 0.5 \rangle^{\mathrm{Tr}}$			2SLO-$\langle 0.9, 0.9 \rangle^{\mathrm{Tr}}$			NSGA-II
		min	*avg*	*max*	*min*	*avg*	*max*	*min*	*avg*	*max*	
0.1	0.1	0.85	0.88	0.91	0.66	0.74	0.81	0.63	0.68	0.72	0.73
	0.3	0.77	0.84	0.89	0.74	0.82	0.88	0.67	0.73	0.80	0.76
	0.5	0.77	0.83	0.89	0.75	0.82	0.88	0.72	0.76	0.82	0.77
	0.7	0.73	0.81	0.87	0.73	0.78	0.86	0.71	0.75	0.80	0.75
	0.9	0.62	0.78	0.84	0.69	0.74	0.81	0.71	0.74	0.79	0.70
0.3	0.1	0.86	0.88	0.90	0.79	0.82	0.86	0.78	0.80	0.81	0.81
	0.3	0.82	0.86	0.90	0.82	0.86	0.89	0.81	0.82	0.85	0.83
	0.5	0.83	0.86	0.90	0.84	0.87	0.90	0.83	0.85	0.88	0.83
	0.7	0.83	0.86	0.90	0.85	0.88	0.91	0.86	0.87	0.90	0.83
	0.9	0.81	0.87	0.90	0.86	0.89	0.91	0.90	0.91	0.93	0.84
0.5	0.1	0.87	0.88	0.91	0.86	0.88	0.90	0.87	0.88	0.89	0.85
	0.3	0.85	0.88	0.91	0.89	0.90	0.92	0.88	0.89	0.90	0.86
	0.5	0.85	0.87	0.90	0.90	0.92	0.93	0.88	0.89	0.91	0.85
	0.7	0.82	0.87	0.90	0.89	0.90	0.91	0.90	0.91	0.93	0.82
	0.9	0.78	0.86	0.90	0.88	0.90	0.92	0.91	0.92	0.93	0.78
0.7	0.1	0.82	0.87	0.89	0.87	0.88	0.91	0.89	0.89	0.90	0.75
	0.3	0.79	0.87	0.90	0.87	0.89	0.90	0.89	0.90	0.91	0.74
	0.5	0.70	0.85	0.89	0.87	0.89	0.90	0.90	0.90	0.92	0.72
	0.7	0.65	0.81	0.87	0.84	0.87	0.89	0.87	0.89	0.90	0.71
	0.9	0.67	0.79	0.86	0.83	0.87	0.88	0.88	0.90	0.91	0.71
0.9	0.1	0.56	0.72	0.79	0.79	0.82	0.86	0.81	0.84	0.85	0.37
	0.3	0.65	0.76	0.85	0.82	0.86	0.88	0.87	0.89	0.90	0.64
	0.5	0.59	0.76	0.83	0.82	0.85	0.87	0.87	0.88	0.89	0.66
	0.7	0.59	0.75	0.81	0.80	0.84	0.86	0.87	0.88	0.90	0.67
	0.9	0.61	0.74	0.80	0.79	0.82	0.84	0.86	0.88	0.89	0.67

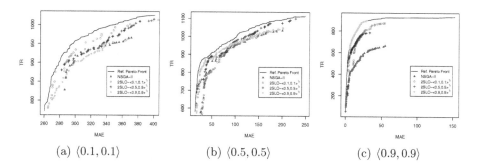

(a) $\langle 0.1, 0.1 \rangle$ (b) $\langle 0.5, 0.5 \rangle$ (c) $\langle 0.9, 0.9 \rangle$

Fig. 4. Examples of Pareto fronts from one run of the EMO methods for three particular problem instances

3.2 Total Revenue

This section will investigate the performance of 2SLO for maximising the total revenue. Table 3 shows the % deviations $(100 \times (UB - TR)/UB)$ from the upper bound (UB), which is determined by MILP and relaxed LP [4] for each OAS instance, of the maximum total revenue in the Pareto fronts obtained by 2SLO and the total revenue obtained by other methods. It is easy to see that the average total revenue obtained by 2SLO is much better than those of MILP (found by the CPLEX solver within 3600 s time limit), m-ATCS, and ISFAN for most combinations of τ and R. 2SLO performs better in the set with τ and R that are close to those of the training set. Although 2SLO performed slightly worse than TS [4] in most cases, it obtained slightly better total revenue in some cases. The reason is that TS is especially designed for maximising total revenue of OAS problems. Moreover, 2SLO focuses on finding the whole Pareto front, which makes it more difficult to find the extreme values for each objectives (as shown in Fig. 4(c)). However, the computational time of 2SLO (for the optimising stage) is much smaller than that of TS in most sets, especially the ones with high τ and R. These results suggest that 2SLO provides good performance on the total revenue objective as compared to the specialised methods proposed in the literature.

Table 3. % Deviations from upper bound of total revenues

τ	R	MILP			m-ATCS			ISFAN			TS			2SLO-0.1			2SLO-0.5			2SLO-0.9			Time (s)	
		a	b	c	a	b	c	a	b	c	a	b	c	a	b	c	a	b	c	a	b	c	2SLO	TS
0.1	0.1	37	44	56	9	15	19	8	9	13	1	2	3	0	1	3	0	2	5	1	5	11	13	16
	0.3	42	51	88	11	17	20	7	9	10	1	2	3	1	2	6	0	1	3	1	4	10	8	17
	0.5	43	51	60	11	14	19	6	9	11	0	1	2	0	2	5	0	1	2	0	2	8	8	10
	0.7	46	54	60	5	11	16	6	9	12	0	0	0	0	1	4	0	0	1	0	1	5	8	6
	0.9	38	60	70	0	6	11	8	12	16	0	0	0	0	0	2	0	0	1	0	0	3	9	3
0.3	0.1	52	62	68	15	19	24	10	12	13	1	2	3	0	3	8	1	4	10	1	7	13	8	22
	0.3	52	64	75	15	18	23	11	13	17	1	2	5	1	4	10	0	3	8	1	6	13	8	20
	0.5	56	66	76	14	18	21	10	14	17	1	2	3	1	5	11	0	2	5	1	5	12	8	16
	0.7	63	73	84	15	20	32	12	14	15	0	1	2	0	4	10	0	1	5	0	3	13	8	9
	0.9	47	66	82	10	15	18	9	13	17	0	0	2	0	2	9	0	1	5	0	2	8	8	7
0.5	0.1	71	77	87	17	22	24	12	16	18	2	3	5	2	7	16	3	8	17	3	10	17	8	25
	0.3	47	61	86	17	23	28	12	15	18	2	3	5	3	7	13	2	5	10	3	9	16	9	28
	0.5	56	70	88	20	24	31	14	17	19	2	3	4	3	8	17	2	4	8	2	8	19	8	20
	0.7	55	71	92	10	23	34	13	17	21	1	2	4	1	6	17	0	3	8	0	5	15	9	15
	0.9	48	66	100	15	24	36	12	18	24	0	2	4	1	6	19	0	3	11	1	5	17	11	12
0.7	0.1	49	67	86	17	22	28	13	17	19	2	4	6	3	8	18	3	8	15	4	9	18	8	33
	0.3	45	57	66	18	24	34	13	17	21	3	6	10	3	9	20	2	9	16	3	10	18	9	26
	0.5	46	55	65	20	26	37	14	18	24	4	6	12	5	12	41	3	9	22	4	11	24	9	22
	0.7	42	60	76	22	31	38	16	19	23	3	7	13	6	15	42	3	11	24	4	12	28	12	26
	0.9	39	53	64	23	31	37	15	18	24	5	8	12	5	16	39	4	12	25	4	12	24	9	17
0.9	0.1	31	37	48	18	22	25	14	17	20	7	9	11	7	16	35	7	13	23	6	13	23	9	29
	0.3	28	40	50	25	31	36	16	20	26	7	13	17	12	27	54	9	20	36	10	18	29	8	26
	0.5	23	38	54	25	33	39	19	21	25	10	15	18	11	29	56	11	22	38	10	20	34	10	21
	0.7	27	38	48	26	36	40	15	21	24	10	15	19	13	29	57	10	21	36	11	19	31	7	22
	0.9	27	35	39	28	35	40	13	21	28	11	15	22	11	28	54	8	22	39	7	18	32	7	17

* a, b, c represent minimum, average and maximum % deviations, respectively
** 2SLO-x represents 2SLO-$\langle x, x \rangle^{Tr}$

4   Conclusions

This paper develops a two-stage learning/optimising system to deal with multi-objective OAS problems. This is the first time that multiple conflicting objectives are considered for OAS. The learning stage of the proposed system helps extract useful information in OAS to build effective scheduling rules. Meanwhile, the optimising stage takes advantage of the reusable rules to initialise populations of EMO methods. The experimental results have shown that the proposed system is effective as compared to other methods in the literature. This confirms the potential of using offline machine learning methods such as GP in this paper to improve the performance of EMO methods. In practical applications of OAS, the learning stage of 2SLO can be employed in a much higher extent than the one in our experiments here. Different combinations of τ and R can be used to train reusable scheduling rules which can be stored in multiple archives. Then, the optimising stage will analyse the instance at hand to decide which archive or combination of archives should be applied. Regarding the optimising stage, we can utilise local search heuristics to further improve the quality of the obtained Pareto fronts.

References

1. Allahverdi, A., Gupta, J.N., Aldowaisan, T.: A review of scheduling research involving setup considerations. Omega 27(2), 219–239 (1999)
2. Bilge, U., Kurtulan, M., Kirac, F.: A tabu search algorithm for the single machine total weighted tardiness problem. European Journal of Operational Research 176(3), 1423–1435 (2007)
3. Boejko, W., Grabowski, J., Wodecki, M.: Block approach-tabu search algorithm for single machine total weighted tardiness problem. Computers & Industrial Engineering 50(1-2), 1–14 (2006)
4. Cesaret, B., Oguz, C., Salman, F.S.: A tabu search algorithm for order acceptance and scheduling. Computers & Operations Research 39(6), 1197–1205 (2012)
5. Cheng, T.C.E., Jiang, J.: Job shop scheduling for missed due-date performance. Computers & Industrial Engineering 34, 297–307 (1998)
6. Cheng, T.C.E., Podolsky, S.: Just-in-Time Manufacturing: An Introduction. Chapman and Hall, London (1993)
7. Choobineh, F.F., Mohebbi, E., Khoo, H.: A multi-objective tabu search for a single-machine scheduling problem with sequence-dependent setup times. European Journal of Operational Research 175(1), 318–337 (2006)
8. Deb, K., Pratap, A., Agarwal, S., Meyarivan, T.: A fast and elitist multiobjective genetic algorithm: NSGA-II. IEEE Transactions on Evolutionary Computation 6(2), 182–197 (2002)
9. Geiger, C.D., Uzsoy, R., Aytug, H.: Rapid modeling and discovery of priority dispatching rules: An autonomous learning approach. Journal of Heuristics 9(1), 7–34 (2006)
10. Ghosh, J.B.: Job selection in a heavily loaded shop. Computers & Operations Research 24(2), 141–145 (1997)
11. Hildebrandt, T., Heger, J., Scholz-Reiter, B.: Towards improved dispatching rules for complex shop floor scenarios: a genetic programming approach. In: GECCO 2010: Proceedings of the 12th Annual Conference on Genetic and Evolutionary Computation, pp. 257–264 (2010)

12. Hino, C.M., Ronconi, D.P., Mendes, A.B.: Minimizing earliness and tardiness penalties in a single-machine problem with a common due date. European Journal of Operational Research 160(1), 190–201 (2005)
13. Jakobović, D., Jelenković, L., Budin, L.: Genetic Programming Heuristics for Multiple Machine Scheduling. In: Ebner, M., O'Neill, M., Ekárt, A., Vanneschi, L., Esparcia-Alcázar, A.I. (eds.) EuroGP 2007. LNCS, vol. 4445, pp. 321–330. Springer, Heidelberg (2007)
14. Koza, J.R.: Genetic Programming: On the Programming of Computers by Means of Natural Selection. MIT Press (1992)
15. Lee, Y.H., Bhaskaran, K., Pinedo, M.: A heuristic to minimize the total weighted tardiness with sequence-dependent setups. IIE Transactions 29(1), 45–52 (1997)
16. Nguyen, S., Zhang, M., Johnston, M., Tan, K.C.: A coevolution genetic programming method to evolve scheduling policies for dynamic multi-objective job shop scheduling problems. In: CEC 2012: Proceedings of the IEEE Congress on Evolutionary Computation, pp. 3261–3268 (2012)
17. Nguyen, S., Zhang, M., Johnston, M., Tan, K.C.: Evolving Reusable Operation-Based Due-Date Assignment Models for Job Shop Scheduling with Genetic Programming. In: Moraglio, A., Silva, S., Krawiec, K., Machado, P., Cotta, C. (eds.) EuroGP 2012. LNCS, vol. 7244, pp. 121–133. Springer, Heidelberg (2012)
18. Oguz, C., Sibel Salman, F., Bilginturk Yalcin, Z.: Order acceptance and scheduling decisions in make-to-order systems. International Journal of Production Economics 125(1), 200–211 (2010)
19. Rom, W.O., Slotnick, S.A.: Order acceptance using genetic algorithms. Computers & Operations Research 36(6), 1758–1767 (2009)
20. Roundy, R., Chen, D., Chen, P., Cakanyildirim, M., Freimer, M.B., Melkonian, V.: Capacity-driven acceptance of customer orders for a multi-stage batch manufacturing system: models and algorithms. IIE Transactions 37(12), 1093–1105 (2005)
21. Selim Akturk, M., Ozdemir, D.: An exact approach to minimizing total weighted tardiness with release dates. IIE Transactions 32(11), 1091–1101 (2000)
22. Slotnick, S.A., Morton, T.E.: Selecting jobs for a heavily loaded shop with lateness penalties. Computers & Operations Research 23(2), 131–140 (1996)
23. Slotnick, S.A., Morton, T.E.: Order acceptance with weighted tardiness. Computers & Operations Research 34(10), 3029–3042 (2007)
24. Tay, J.C., Ho, N.B.: Evolving dispatching rules using genetic programming for solving multi-objective flexible job-shop problems. Computer & Industrial Engineering 54, 453–473 (2008)
25. Van Veldhuizen, D.A., Lamont, G.B.: Multiobjective evolutionary algorithm test suites. In: SAC 1999: Proceedings of the 1999 ACM Symposium on Applied Computing, pp. 351–357 (1999)
26. Wester, F.A.W., Wijngaard, J., Zijm, W.R.M.: Order acceptance strategies in a production-to-order environment with setup times and due-dates. International Journal of Production Research 30(6), 1313–1326 (1992)
27. Yang, W.H.: Survey of scheduling research involving setup times. International Journal of Systems Science 30(2), 143–155 (1999)
28. Zhang, J., Zhan, Z.H., Lin, Y., Chen, N., Gong, Y.J., Zhong, J.H., Chung, H., Li, Y., Shi, Y.H.: Evolutionary computation meets machine learning: A survey. IEEE Computational Intelligence Magazine 6(4), 68–75 (2011)
29. Zitzler, E., Laumanns, M., Thiele, L.: SPEA2: Improving the strength pareto evolutionary algorithm for multiobjective optimization. In: Evolutionary Methods for Design, Optimisation and Control with Application to Industrial Problems, EUROGEN 2001, pp. 95–100 (2002)

Automated Problem Decomposition for the Boolean Domain with Genetic Programming

Fernando E.B. Otero and Colin G. Johnson

School of Computing, University of Kent, Canterbury, UK
{F.E.B.Otero,C.G.Johnson}@kent.ac.uk

Abstract. Researchers have been interested in exploring the regularities and modularity of the problem space in genetic programming (GP) with the aim of decomposing the original problem into several smaller subproblems. The main motivation is to allow GP to deal with more complex problems. Most previous works on modularity in GP emphasise the structure of modules used to encapsulate code and/or promote code reuse, instead of in the decomposition of the original problem. In this paper we propose a problem decomposition strategy that allows the use of a GP search to find solutions for subproblems and combine the individual solutions into the complete solution to the problem.

1 Introduction

Many problems in the genetic programming (GP) literature have demonstrated the scalability issues of GP algorithms—e.g., it is relatively easy to find a solution for the even-4-parity problem [7], while a solution for the even-8-parity problem is much harder to find using a traditional GP. In order to be able to deal with larger and more complex problems, researchers have been interested in exploring the regularities and modularity of the problem space with the aim of decomposing the original problem into several smaller (more tractable) subproblems.

One of the first approaches for exploiting the problem regularities is Koza's Automatic Defined Functions (ADFs) [7,8]. In ADFs, the structure of program trees is defined in a way that subtrees with different roles are evolved in parallel— e.g., there are *function-defining* subtrees and a *result-producing* subtree, which can contain references to the different function-defining subtrees mimicking function calls. Other authors investigated the creation of modules (functions) by identifying subtrees on existing individuals [1,16,15,6]. The main idea is to create modules based on fit or useful subtrees, either encapsulating their functionality or creating parameterised modules.

In this paper, we investigate the use of an automated problem decomposition strategy in the context of GP. The motivation is to use a heuristic to modularise the GP search—i.e., use a GP search to explicitly find solutions to subproblems, which can then be combined to create the solution to the original problem. Therefore, the GP is not concerned with searching for the complete solution; the original problem is decomposed in a series of smaller subproblems.

K. Krawiec et al. (Eds.): EuroGP 2013, LNCS 7831, pp. 169–180, 2013.
© Springer-Verlag Berlin Heidelberg 2013

The remainder of this paper is organised as follows. Section 2 reviews prior efforts to explore the regularities and modularity of the problem space in GP. Section 3 discusses the proposed strategy to modularise the GP search and Section 4 gives details of a specific implementation of this strategy. The computational results are presented in Section 5. Finally, Section 6 concludes this paper and presents future research directions.

2   Background

Automatically Defined Functions (ADFs) were introduced by Koza [7,8] as a technique to explore the regularities and modularities of the problem space in order to deal with complex problems, and it is probably the most popular and studied automatic approach to create modules (sub-routines) in GP. Koza proposed the use of ADFs to decompose the problem into several smaller subproblems. The solution of the original (complete) problem is then obtained by combining the individual solutions to the subproblems. This process, defined by Koza as *hierarchical problem-solving process*, is illustrated in Figure 1. There are three important steps in this process: the first one is where the original problem is decomposed, the second is where the solutions of each subproblem are obtained, and the third one is where the complete solution is built by combining the individual solutions of the subproblems. Koza's ADF approach implements these three steps within a run of a GP algorithm: a modular ADF architecture based on 'function-defining branches' is determined prior to evolving the solutions (decomposition of the problem); the body of each ADF is evolved during the run (subproblem solution search); these ADFs are available to the 'result-producing branch' of candidate solutions (combination of subsolutions), which is also being evolved during the run.

While Koza's ADF approach allows the GP to exploit the problem regularities through a modular architecture, the problem decomposition into an ADF architecture (i.e., number of ADFs, the number of arguments of each ADF) is done manually before the run of the GP. This also includes the definition of the interaction between ADFs—which ADFs are allowed to call which other ADFs. Therefore, the architecture of the candidate solutions is fixed to a pre-defined number of ADFs and the 'result-producing branch'. In [9], a set of architecture altering operations relaxed this restriction, allowing candidate solutions to have a different number of ADFs and each ADF to have a different number of parameters, although the maximum number of ADFs and arguments of each ADF are restricted by user-defined values.

Other works have proposed the creation of modules based on the genetic material from individuals of the population. Koza [7] proposed the use of a subtree *encapsulation* operator. The approach consists in randomly selecting a subtree from a fit individual and creating a terminal primitive to reference the subtree—i.e., a terminal that *encapsulates* the behaviour of the subtree. The motivation is to protect the encapsulated subtree from potential changes as a result of genetic operators, and to facilitate its reuse by allowing the mutation operator to incorporate new references in the population. The terminal primitive created by the encapsulation operator can be seen as a module (function) with no arguments. Angeline and Pollack [1,2] proposed the Genetic Library Builder (GLiB) system, which employs special mutation operators to define new modules based on subtrees from individuals. The first mutation operator is *compression*, which consists of randomly selecting a subtree to define a new module. The newly created module is then stored in a global module library and the occurrence of the subtree is replaced by a reference to the module. The arguments of the module are determined based either on the maximum depth of the module or by the terminal (leaf) nodes used in the subtree. The second mutation operator is *expand*, which consists in expanding the module by replacing its reference with the subtree stored in the module library that defines the module. While module definitions in GLiB are selected at random, Rosca and Ballard [16] proposed a method to create new modules using heuristics to identify 'useful' building blocks: fit blocks (blocks with high fitness value) and frequent blocks (blocks that appear frequently in the entire population). Once a block has been identified and its arguments determined (based on the terminals used in the subtree), its definition is added to the function set as a new function and a replacement operator introduces new individuals using the extended function set.

The idea of identifying building blocks in the population to create a library of modules was extended further to include information accumulated from multiple runs of a GP algorithm. Roberts et al. [15] proposed the use of a *subtree database* to monitor the frequency of use of each subtree during the GP run. At the end of the run, the most frequent subtrees are encapsulated as terminal primitives in a similar manner as the encapsulation operator proposed by Koza [7]. The subsequent runs can then take advantage of the subtree database by using an extended terminal set incorporating the encapsulated subtrees. Keijzer et al. [6] introduced the idea of Run Transferable Libraries (RTL), in which the GP system uses the RTL in two phases: (1) training of the library, where a number of runs is used to refine the randomly generated candidate modules (referred to as Tag Addressable Functions) of the RTL; (2) subsequent runs of the GP use the modules of the RTL. The motivation is that the RTL can be trained in smaller (simpler) problem instances and then be applied to larger (harder) problem instances. A similar idea was used by Christensen and Oppacher [3], where a 'training phase' consisting in generating all small trees in the search space of GP creates a library of useful modules. Christensen and Oppacher's approach explores the fact that there are more solutions of small size for the Santa Fe Trail problem compared to larger ones. The generated modules (small trees) are then used in the search for the complete solution.

Several other approaches for the creation/identification of modules have been proposed in the literature—e.g., in the context of grammar-based GP (grammatical evolution) [4,18], in Cartesian Genetic Programming (CGP) [19] and in GP systems using the Push language [17]; other approaches are discussed in [13]. The majority of approaches for modularity (including the ones discussed above) focus on the discovery of modules rather than on the use of modules to

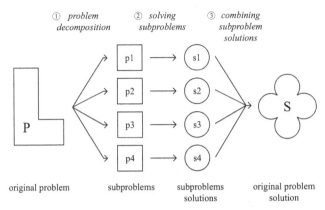

Fig. 1. The hierarchical problem-solving process (adapted from [7]): the original problem P is decomposed in a set of subproblems (step 1); the goal is then to solve each of the subproblems (step 2); finally, the solution S to the original problem P is created by using the solutions to the subproblems (step 3)

decompose the problem into smaller (more tractable) subproblems, relying on the idea that if modules can be created/identified, their usefulness will emerge through the GP search. An indication of this is the fact that modules are usually created/identified during the run of the GP, at the same time that the GP is searching for a solution to the problem. There is no control to check whether different modules are solving different parts of the problem or not, and the quality of the modules is evaluated indirectly by evaluating how well an individual that contains the module reference solves the problem.

This emphasis on the structure of modules to encapsulate code and/or promote code reuse of most previous works in GP modules motivated Jackson and Gibbons [5] to propose the use of *layered learning*—an approach that aims at solving simpler problems in order to deal with harder problems—in the context of GP. The idea is to first use a layer to solve a lower-order version of the original problem. Then, when a solution to the first layer is found, it is converted to a parameterised module. Finally, a second layer is used to search for the solution to the original problem, which can invoke the module created by the first layer. Drawing a comparison with ADFs, the first layer in the layered learning approach can be seen as a function-defining branch and the second layer can be seen as the result-producing branch. The main difference between ADFs and the layered learning approach is that in the latter, all computational effort is first focused in the function-defining branch (layer 1) until it evolved into something potentially useful, and then switched to the result-producing branch (layer 2), while in ADFs both function-defining and result-producing branches are evolved simultaneously. One limitation of the layered learning is the need to manually identify (and specify) a lower-order of the problem to be solved by the first layer. A second limitation is that there is a single decomposition step, and more complex problems may require multiple decomposition steps.

3   Modularisation of the GP Search

The problem-solving procedure of GP can be viewed as a supervised learning procedure:

(1) the training data is represented by a set of input-output pairs, which correspond to the desired behaviour;
(2) the fitness function is used to evaluate how good a candidates solutions' predictions are (i.e., how many correct predictions are made or how close the predictions are to the correct output);
(3) the goal of the GP search is to find a program that can predict the correct output for each of the inputs or, in cases where it cannot find the program that generates the correct output, find one that provides the best fitness score given by the fitness function.

Many supervised learning methods employ a strategy to decompose the problem at hand into smaller subproblems. For example, decision tree induction algorithms usually employ a divide-and-conquer strategy to build a decision tree in a top-down fashion. Starting from the root node, a test is selected to divide the training instances—a descendant of the root node is created for each possible outcome of the test and the training instances are sorted to the appropriate descendant node. This procedure is then repeated for each descendant node using the subset of the training instances associated with the node—a test is selected for each of the descendant nodes to further divide the training instances. Another example is the strategy used by rule induction algorithms. Instead of attempting to create a complete list or set of rules at once, they employ a sequential covering strategy to reduce the problem into to a sequence of simpler problems, each consisting in creating a single rule. The sequential covering is an iterative procedure in which a single rule is created and the training instances correctly classified by the rule are removed from the training data, effectively reducing the search space for the next iterations of the procedure.

Most works in GP focuses on searching for a complete solution. While the use of ADFs (or other module/building block creation method) provides a syntactic modularisation, where different subtrees might focus on different parts of the problem, there is still an evolutionary pressure to solve all parts of the problem at once. McKay [11] argues that this pressure tends to reduce diversity and in some cases prevents the search from converging to an optimal solution. To counteract this effect, McKay uses the concept of partial functions—functions whose values are not defined for some inputs—combined with the use of fitness sharing to promote diversity and allow the GP search to explore subproblem solutions. The use of partial functions can be seen as an explicit attempt to modularise the GP search, i.e., focus the search on solutions of subproblems.

The hierarchical problem-solving process presented by Koza as a motivation to use ADFs is closely related to both divide-and-conquer and sequential covering strategies commonly used in machine learning, although ADFs do not use a heuristic to decompose the problem. The use of layered learning by Jackson and Gibbons [5] can also be seen as a divide-and-conquer, but it involves a single decomposition step represented by the manually identified lower-order version of the original problem. A natural question then arises: *could we apply a heuristic to decompose the problem into smaller problems and use GP to find a solution to subproblems?* Assuming that we successfully decompose the problem and find solutions to the subproblems, we then have a second question: *how do we combine the individual solutions to the subproblems into the complete solution?* In the next section we discuss how we can combine both the sequential covering strategy and the concept of partial functions to modularise the GP search—use GP to solve several smaller subproblems and combine the solutions to create the complete solution to the problem—and address the aforementioned questions.

4   Sequential Covering Genetic Programming

In this section we present the general idea behind the proposed sequential covering GP (SCGP). There are three distinct steps: (i) the decomposition of the problem; (ii) the search for a subproblem solution; and (iii) the combination of subproblem solutions into the complete solution. Figure 2 presents the high-level pseudocode of the SCGP procedure.

The overall SCGP procedure mimics a sequential covering: starting with the complete list of input cases (training data) and an empty *solution tree*,[1] evolves a partial solution using GP, adds the partial solution to the solution tree and removes the cases for which it gives the correct output. The procedure is repeated until there are no input cases remaining. The removal of cases at each iteration effectively changes the search space for the next iterations, which allows the GP to evolve solutions to different parts of the problem—i.e., reduces (decomposes) the problem into a sequence of simpler problems, each consisting in creating a solution for a subset of the input cases.

At each iteration of the SCGP procedure, a partial solution is evolved using a GP.[2] The fitness cases for the GP consists of the available input cases—the ones that have not been correctly predicted previously. The best (fittest) candidate solution evolved by the GP is designated as the partial solution of the iteration. There are two possible outcomes as a result of the GP search: the partial solution produces the correct output for all available input cases (i.e., it is the optimal solution for the subproblem represented by the available input cases), or the partial solution produces the correct output for a subset of the input cases. If the partial solution is the optimal solution for the subproblem, it is added as a leaf component to the solution tree and the SCGP procedure finishes, since the solution tree is able to generate the correct output for all input cases. If the partial solution only solves a subset of the input cases, a *mask selector* is created to combine the newly created partial solution with the remaining solutions of the solution tree. The cases for which the (extended) solution tree gives the correct output are removed and a new iteration of the procedure starts.

---

[1] Here we assume that the solution tree is where all the partial solutions (the solution to individual subproblems) are combined into the complete solution to the problem.

[2] Each iteration of SCGP involves the execution of a GP algorithm, which also evolve for a number of iterations.

1. *training* ← *all input cases*;
2. *solution* ← ∅;
3. **while** |*training*| not empty **do**
4.   *partial* ← *EvolveSolution*(*training*);
5.   **if** *Errors*(*partial, training*) = 0 **then**
6.   *solution* ← *AddLeafComponent*(*partial, solution*);
7.   **else**
8.   *mask* ← *GenerateTestMask*(*partial, training*);
9.   *solution* ← *AddMaskComponent*(*partial, mask, solution*);
10.   **end if**
11.   *training* ← *RemoveCorrectCases*(*solution, training*);
12. **end while**
13. *solution* ← *Simplify*(*solution*); /* `optional` */
14. **return** *solution*;

Fig. 2. High-level pseudocode of the Sequential Covering GP (SCGP)

So far, we have demonstrated how we can use a heuristic to decompose the problem and use a GP to produce the solutions to the subproblems, which answers our first posed question. The remaining issue is how to combine the solutions to the subproblem into a single solution. We have mentioned that individual solutions are structured in a solution tree and combined together using a mask selector. Given that each partial solution in the solution tree is solving a different subproblem, their output vectors (the vector V of the outputs of the partial solution P_i when queried with the input cases C, i.e., $V(P_i) = \{P_i(c_1), \ldots, P_i(c_N)\}$) are complementary.[3] Therefore, a natural way of combining the partial solutions is to combine their output vectors. To that end, we use the semantic crossover proposed by Moraglio et al. [12] to generate *mask selectors*, which act as tests to inform which of the partial solutions to use for a given input.

The geometric semantic crossover [12] is a semantic operator that works on the output vector of two individuals (candidate solutions). For the Boolean domain, the semantic crossover (SGXB) returns an individual $T_3 = (M \wedge T_1) \vee (\overline{M} \wedge T_2)$, where M is a randomly generated boolean crossover mask. The Boolean expression represented by individual T_3 outputs the value of T_1 or T_2 depending on the value of M—i.e., for each input case c, it outputs the value $T_1(c)$ if $M(c)$ evaluates to `true`; otherwise it outputs the value $T_2(c)$. The construction of the individual T_3 is illustrated in Figure 3. We will focus on the Boolean domain from now on; refer to [12] for details of how to apply the semantic crossover in other domains.

Recall that solutions are sequentially discovered by the SCGP procedure, so when a partial solution T_i (the solution created in the i-th iteration) is added to the solution tree, the T_{i+1} solution is unknown. The semantic crossover is usually incomplete, i.e., we do not have two individuals to recombine. To solve

---

[3] There might be overlaps between different vectors, but the important aspect is that for every input case at least one of the vectors provides the correct output.

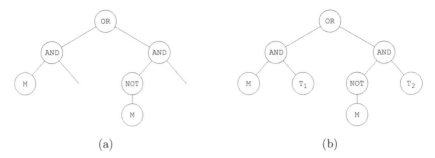

Fig. 3. In (a), the semantic crossover scheme for Boolean functions (M is the randomly generated crossover mask); in (b), the resultant individual T_3 obtained by applying the semantic crossover with individuals T_1 and T_2

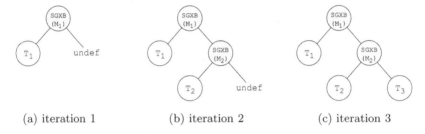

(a) iteration 1   (b) iteration 2   (c) iteration 3

Fig. 4. The sequential solution construction procedure of SCGP: in (a) the solution tree after the first iteration, consisting of the *partial* solution T_1 and an incomplete semantic crossover using mask M_1; (b) the solution tree after the second iteration, after the addition of the *partial* solution T_2 and the incomplete semantic crossover using mask M_2; the complete solution tree, obtained by adding the *partial* solution T_3

this dependency, we use the concept of partial solutions and assume that the solution tree returns an **undef** value for the cases where the mask M_i evaluates to **false**. Therefore, the crossover mask M_i acts as a selector to inform when the output of individual T_i should be used, independently of the other individuals. To ensure this property of the crossover mask, we need to impose a restriction on the creation of the (random) crossover mask M_i: M_i *is a randomly generated boolean crossover mask that, for every input case c, if $M_i(c)$ evaluates to* **true**, $T_i(c)$ *produces the correct output.*

Let us consider a simple example: assume that we would like to search for a boolean function with the following output [1, 1, 0, 1, 0, 1]. The first iteration of SCGP produces an individual T_1 with the output vector [0, 1, 0, 0, 1, 0] (an individual that generates the correct output for input cases 2 and 3). If we generate a crossover mask M_1 that returns **true** for input cases 2 and 3 and add both to the the solution tree, we end up with a partial solution with the output vector [**undef**, 1, 0, **undef**, **undef**, **undef**]. Before we start the next iteration of the SCGP, we remove the input cases for which the solution tree is generating the correct output, so the desired output is [1, -, -, 1, 0, 1] (the positions marked as '-' are not used in the evaluation). This will focus the search on the input cases where the (current) solution tree is not generating the correct output (the input cases for which an `undef` value is generated). The second iteration of SCGP produces an individual T_2 with the output vector [1, 0, 0, 0, 1, 1]. Applying the same procedure to generate a mask M_2 and adding both T_2 and M_2 to the solution tree, we end up with a partial solution with the output vector [1, 1, 0, undef, undef, 1]. Removing the correct input cases, the desired output is [-, -, -, 1, 0, -]. The next iteration of SCGP produces an individual T_3 with the output vector [1, 1, 1, 1, 0, 0]. Since T_3 generates the correct output for the remaining input cases, we don't need to create a crossover mask. Adding T_3 to the solution tree completes the SCGP procedure (there are no input cases for which the solution tree generates an `undef` value) and the solution tree represents the Boolean function with the desired output. The sequential solution construction procedure of SCGP is illustrated in Figure 4.

Note that the sequential construction of the solution avoids the problem of exponential growth of the size of GP individuals and the need for a simplification step [12], observed when semantic operators are used (especially the semantic crossover, since both parents are included in the offspring). The sequential procedure of the SCGP decomposes (reduces) the original problem, and each iteration is searching for a solution to a subproblem. The subproblem solutions are not used during the search of the GP, therefore the size of the current solution tree (the solution being sequentially constructed) does not affect the GP search. On the other hand, the complete solution (solution tree at the end of SCGP) can become syntactically large, depending on the number of iterations required to create the optimal solution. For applications where the size of the complete solution is important, a single simplification step can be used at the end of SCGP.

5   Computational Results

In this section we present the results of the proposed SCGP in two Boolean logic problems.[4] We used a standard tree GP to create a solution at each iteration of SCGP, using a generational scheme with tournament selection (size 5), ramped-half-and-half initialisation, subtree crossover (0.9 probability), subtree mutation (0.1 probability) and elitism (1 individual). We varied the GP parameters population size {10, 50, 100, 500, 1000}, maximum number of iterations {1, 10, 50, 100} and the maximum tree depth {2, 4, 8} to determine their effects on the overall performance of the SCGP. Greater values of the population size and the maximum number of iterations only increased the total number of fitness evaluations without any improvements on the overall performance of SCGP. The only GP parameter that seems to directly affect the performance was the maximum tree depth, where a greater value allows the SCGP algorithm to create a complete solution in a smaller number of sequential covering iterations. The results reported in this section correspond to the runs of SCGP using a GP with a population size of 10, maximum

---

[4] The SCGP algorithm was implemented using the EpochX framework [14].

Table 1. Average (*average ± standard deviation*) number of SCGP iterations and fitness evaluations required by SCGP to create the complete correct (optimal) solution for each problem, calculated over 30 runs. In all problems, the total number of fitness evaluations required is below the allocated maximum (budget) evaluations

problem	avg. SCGP iterations	avg. evaluations	budget
even-5-parity	23.4 ± 2.0	224.2 ± 20.1	320
even-6-parity	46.7 ± 4.4	457.1 ± 44.6	768
even-7-parity	90.5 ± 3.7	895.0 ± 10.4	1792
even-8-parity	181.7 ± 9.3	1814.1 ± 17.3	4096
even-9-parity	374.5 ± 7.5	3735.0 ± 75.4	9216
even-10-parity	767.6 ± 11.5	7666.6 ± 95.0	20480
multiplexer-6	20.9 ± 5.3	199.0 ± 53.4	768
multiplexer-11	136.1 ± 12.4	1350.7 ± 22.4	45056

Table 2. Average percentage (*average ± standard deviation*) of input cases correctly predicted by the best solution for each of the algorithms, calculated over 30 runs

problem	GP	SGP	SSHC	SCGP
even-5-parity	52.9 ± 2.4	98.1 ± 2.1	99.7 ± 0.9	100.0 ± 0.0
even-6-parity	50.5 ± 0.7	98.8 ± 1.7	99.7 ± 0.6	100.0 ± 0.0
even-7-parity	50.1 ± 0.2	99.5 ± 0.6	99.9 ± 0.2	100.0 ± 0.0
even-8-parity	50.1 ± 0.2	99.7 ± 0.3	100.0 ± 0.0	100.0 ± 0.0
even-9-parity	50.0 ± 0.0	99.5 ± 0.3	100.0 ± 0.0	100.0 ± 0.0
even-10-parity	50.0 ± 0.0	99.4 ± 0.2	100.0 ± 0.0	100.0 ± 0.0
multiplexer-6	70.8 ± 3.3	99.5 ± 0.8	99.8 ± 0.5	100.0 ± 0.0
multiplexer-11	76.4 ± 7.9	99.9 ± 0.1	100.0 ± 0.0	100.0 ± 0.0

number of iterations of 1 and maximum tree depth of 8—the combination that produced the best average number of fitness evaluations.

The SCGP was compared against a standard tree GP, semantic GP (SGP) and semantic stochastic hill climber (SSHC), using the same setup as in [12]: GP and SGP using a generational scheme with tournament selection (size 5), crossover and mutation; other parameters set to ECJ's defaults [10]. We selected two standard GP Boolean benchmark problems, the even-parity and multiplexer [7]. These problems present scalability issues for standard GP—solutions for lower-order versions are easily found, while solutions for higher-order versions are not found in most cases using standard GP. The function set used for both problems comprised the Boolean operators {AND, OR, NOT}. All algorithms were allocated a maximum of $2n \times 2^n$ fitness evaluations, where n is the number of input variables of the problem.

Discussion: Table 1 presents the average number of SCGP (sequential covering) iterations and fitness evaluations required by SCGP to create the complete optimal solution for each problem, calculated over 30 runs of the algorithm. In all problems, the total number of fitness evaluation required is below the allocated maximum evaluations. The average number of SCGP iterations can be seen as the number of semantic crossover operations required to create the optimal solution. This shows an interesting aspect of SCGP: while the SGP algorithm applies the semantic crossover selecting two individuals at random, the SCGP algorithm applies the semantic operator in a more directed way. It first selects an individual and the crossover mask, and then tries to evolve the best individual that would fit the remaining input cases to complete the crossover. This advantage is highlighted in the results concerning the average number of training examples correctly predicted by the best solution, presented in Table 2. SCGP is the only algorithm to be able to find the optimal solution in all the problems; neither SGP or SSHC, which also use the semantic crossover, found an optimal solution to all the problems.

6   Conclusions and Future Work

We presented a new problem decomposition strategy in the context of GP. This new strategy relies on a sequential covering approach, commonly used in machine learning, to divide the original problem into smaller subproblems. A GP was used to find solutions for the subproblems and the individual subproblems' solutions are combined using a semantic crossover operator. We conducted experiments in two standard GP Boolean benchmark problems, comparing the SCGP (sequential covering GP) against a standard tree GP, semantic GP (SGP) and semantic stochastic hill climber (SSHC). The proposed SCGP algorithm was the only algorithm to find an optimal solution for all problems within the allocated maximum number of fitness evaluations.

There are several future research directions. The increase in the number of iterations of the GP search did not improve the overall performance of SCGP, which could be an indication that the crossover mask is limiting the use of an individual (one of the individuals in the crossover is only used when the mask evaluates to **true**); it would be interesting to investigate the use of different mask generation procedures. Another approach is to first select the crossover mask, which effectively is responsible to divide the input cases, and then search for each individual to complete the crossover; this would be similar to the top-down approach commonly used by decision tree induction algorithms. Given the nature of the sequential covering solution construction strategy, there is a risk of overfitting the training data. Therefore it will be interesting to investigate how the solutions found by SCGP generalise to unseen input cases. Additionally, a semantic analysis of the crossover masks, responsible for partitioning the input cases, might give interesting insights about the problems (e.g., characterise different regions of the problem space).

Acknowledgements. The authors gratefully acknowledge the financial support from the EPSRC grant EP/H020217/1.

References

1. Angeline, P.J., Pollack, J.B.: The evolutionary induction of subroutines. In: Proc. of the 14th Annual Conference of the Cognitive Science Society, pp. 236–241 (1992)
2. Angeline, P.J., Pollack, J.B.: Coevolving High-level Representations. In: Langton, C. (ed.) Artificial Life III, pp. 55–71. Addison-Wesley (1994), http://www.isrl.uiuc.edu/~amag/langev/paper/angeline94coevolvingHigh.html
3. Christensen, S., Oppacher, F.: Solving the Artificial Ant on the Santa Fe Trail Problem in 20,696 Fitness Evaluations. In: Proc. of GECCO, pp. 1574–1579 (2007)
4. Hemberg, E., Gilligan, C., O'Neill, M., Brabazon, A.: A Grammatical Genetic Programming Approach to Modularity in Genetic Algorithms. In: Ebner, M., O'Neill, M., Ekárt, A., Vanneschi, L., Esparcia-Alcázar, A.I. (eds.) EuroGP 2007. LNCS, vol. 4445, pp. 1–11. Springer, Heidelberg (2007)
5. Jackson, D., Gibbons, A.P.: Layered Learning in Boolean GP Problems. In: Ebner, M., O'Neill, M., Ekárt, A., Vanneschi, L., Esparcia-Alcázar, A.I. (eds.) EuroGP 2007. LNCS, vol. 4445, pp. 148–159. Springer, Heidelberg (2007)
6. Keijzer, M., Ryan, C., Cattolico, M.: Run Transferable Libraries — Learning Functional Bias in Problem Domains. In: Deb, K., Tari, Z. (eds.) GECCO 2004. LNCS, vol. 3103, pp. 531–542. Springer, Heidelberg (2004)
7. Koza, J.R.: Genetic Programming: On the Programming of Computers by Means of Natural Selection. MIT Press (1992)
8. Koza, J.R.: Genetic Programming II: Automatic Discovery of Reusable Programs. MIT Press (1994)
9. Koza, J.R., Bennett III, F.H., Andre, D., Keane, M.: Genetic Programming III: Darwinian Invention and Problem Solving. Morgan Kaufmann (1999)
10. Luke, S.: ECJ: A Java-based Evolutionary Computation Research System (2012), http://cs.gmu.edu/~eclab/projects/ecj/
11. McKay, R.: Partial Functions in Fitness-Shared Genetic Programming. In: Proc. of CEC, pp. 349–356 (2000)
12. Moraglio, A., Krawiec, K., Johnson, C.G.: Geometric Semantic Genetic Programming. In: Coello, C.A.C., Cutello, V., Deb, K., Forrest, S., Nicosia, G., Pavone, M. (eds.) PPSN 2012, Part I. LNCS, vol. 7491, pp. 21–31. Springer, Heidelberg (2012)
13. O'Neill, M., Vanneschi, L., Gustafson, S., Banzhaf, W.: Open issues in genetic programming. Genetic Programming and Evolvable Machines 11, 339–363 (2010)
14. Otero, F., Castle, T., Johnson, C.: EpochX: Genetic Programming in Java with Statistics and Event Monitoring. In: Proc. GECCO Companion, pp. 93–100 (2012)
15. Roberts, S.C., Howard, D., Koza, J.R.: Evolving Modules in Genetic Programming by Subtree Encapsulation. In: Miller, J., Tomassini, M., Lanzi, P.L., Ryan, C., Tetamanzi, A.G.B., Langdon, W.B. (eds.) EuroGP 2001. LNCS, vol. 2038, pp. 160–175. Springer, Heidelberg (2001)
16. Rosca, J., Ballard, D.: Learning by adapting representations in genetic programming. In: Proc. of the IEEE WCCI, pp. 407–412 (1994)
17. Spector, L., Martin, B., Harrington, K., Helmuth, T.: Tag-Based Modules in Genetic Programming. In: Proc. of GECCO, pp. 1419–1426 (2011)
18. Swafford, J., Hemberg, E., O'Neill, M., Nicolau, M., Brabazon, A.: A Non-Destructive Grammar Modification Approach to Modularity in Grammatical Evolution. In: Proc. GECCO, pp. 1411–1418 (2011)
19. Walker, J., Miller, J.: The automatic acquisition, evolution and reuse of modules in cartesian genetic programming. IEEE Transactions on Evolutionary Computation 12(4), 397–417 (2008)

A Multi-objective Optimization Energy Approach to Predict the Ligand Conformation in a Docking Process

Angelica Sandoval-Perez[1,2,*], David Becerra[1,3,*], Diana Vanegas[1], Daniel Restrepo-Montoya[1], and Fernando Nino[1]

[1] Universidad Nacional de Colombia, Bioinformatics and Intelligent Systems Research Laboratory, Bogota, Colombia
[2] Universität Erlangen-Nürnber, Computational Biology, Department Biologie, Erlangen, Germany
[3] McGill University, McGill Centre for Bioinformatics, Montreal, Canada

Abstract. This work proposes a multi-objective algorithmic method for modelling the prediction of the conformation and configuration of ligands in receptor-ligand complexes by considering energy contributions of molecular interactions. The proposed approach is an improvement over others in the field, where the principle insight is that a Pareto front helps to understand the tradeoffs in the actual problem. The method is based on three main features: (*i*) Representation of molecular data using a trigonometric model; (*ii*) Modelling of molecular interactions with all-atoms force field energy functions and (*iii*) Exploration of the conformational space through a multi-objective evolutionary algorithm. The performance of the proposed model was evaluated and validated over a set of well known complexes. The method showed a promising performance when predicting ligands with high number of rotatable bonds.

Keywords: MOEA, rotatable bonds, bonding and non-bonding energy terms.

1 Introduction

Molecular docking can be defined as the prediction of complexes formed by the interaction between two molecules, a receptor and a ligand [2]. Receptors are typically transmembrane molecules involved in a specific biochemical pathway, while ligands are mostly organic molecules that bind to a receptor in such a way that the function of such receptor is modified and/or regulated [17,23].

Computational modelling has contributed to decreasing the time and resources invested in finding molecules with pharmacological activity by helping to elucidate the structural conformation of a molecule inside a living organism, making it a possible computer-aided drug design [13]. However, simulation of receptor-ligand biological systems demands different simplifications and assumptions, either to simulate the binding process or to select the molecules that

---

* These authors contributed equally.

K. Krawiec et al. (Eds.): EuroGP 2013, LNCS 7831, pp. 181–192, 2013.
© Springer-Verlag Berlin Heidelberg 2013

bind to a receptor. Specifically, two that have had a great impact are those on the dynamics of the biological system, and the ones on the energy functions used to calculate the stability of the formed complexes [2,25].

A multi-objective evolutionary algorithm (MOEA) is considered as an adequate approach for the docking problem given the possibility to optimize more than one conflicting objective function simultaneously. By considering different objectives in the fitness function, MOEAs are able to accurately optimize different variables of the modelled system. Previous works have done molecular optimizations using similar multi-objective models [21], but the proposed algorithm implements new alternatives to model the dynamics and energy measures of the receptor-ligand biological system.

Although docking models usually evaluate the energy by using a force field scoring function as a single objective, the proposed model is based on the idea that non-covalent bonds are critical for maintaining the three-dimensional (3D) structure of large molecules [18] and that non-covalent bonds can stabilize unusual conformations in small ligands when they are bound to a receptor causing a detriment in the internal energy. Therefore, a multi-objective optimization approach was chosen to predict protein ligand structures (complexes), where the objective functions to be optimized are the non-bond and bond energy terms.

In the proposed work, the ligand and the receptor are modeled at an atomic level, the ligand as a flexible body and the receptor as a rigid body. Accordingly, the number of rotatable bonds defines the flexibility of the ligand, so that changes occurring in those bonds result in all possible molecular conformations for the ligand. In turn, an MOEA implements a stochastic search of the complexes by performing random changes on contiguous rotatable bonds. The MOEA uses an energy function based on the force fields to predict protein-ligand structures. Then, it optimizes the energy contributions of the non-bonding and bonding energy terms. The proposed model was implemented by adapting some existing software tools combined with others developed in this work. Our approach is flexible to the use of different search algorithms and energy functions; it predicts ligand localizations on the receptor binding site and the ligand conformations that form adequate complexes with the receptor.

2   Methodology

The goal of the proposed approach was to find an energetically stable complex formed between a protein and a ligand. The proposed method involves three main stages which are explained next.

First, the known three-dimensional structures of both molecules were used as data inputs. Specifically, the inputs of the model are: (*i*) a mapping from the cartesian coordinates (algebraic representation) to the rotatable angles (trigonometric representation); the ligand is then represented as an undirected graph (see Fig. 1(a)); (*ii*) the rigid protein modelled by its algebraic representation.

Once the molecular representation is set, the modelling of molecular interactions and the exploration of the conformational space are performed (see Fig.

1(b)). Three important elements of the optimization process need to be defined: the decision space, the objective space and the constraints. The decision space represents all the attainable molecular complexes; the solution is coded as an array representing a possible conformation and configuration of the ligand-receptor system through its torsion angles γi. The objective space contains the images of the solutions to be optimized, and the MOEA optimizes the energy contributions from the bonding and non-bonding terms. In addition, the feasible region is limited by some geometric and energetic constraints.

Finally, a set of energetically stable complexes was obtained, but only one complex (the predicted conformation) was selected. Particularly, the identification of the knees was used as the method to select the predicted complex. This knee identification was based on angles constituted by consecutive predicted conformations (see Fig. 1(c)) [1].

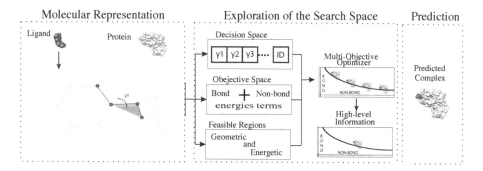

Fig. 1. The proposed methodology

2.1 Molecular Representation

The receptor, which remains rigid, is represented in two ways: (i) as a cavity the ligand fits into and (ii) as an x-, y- and z-axes representation of all atoms. The binding sites were identified by using the DMS program[1] and the sphgen cpp tool from DOCK [15]. It is important to stress that the selected binding sites were the ones with experimental reportes in the literature [3,16,22,24].

In contrast to the receptor, the ligand is considered to be flexible. Consequently, the ligand conformations and configurations are expressed in terms of combinations of rotatable bond angles (see Fig. 1(a)), which makes it easier to track down changes in the ligand's molecular conformations.

A representation of all atoms based on their x, y and z coordinates (algebraic representation) is required to calculate the energy value of the receptor-binding complex. To alternate between the algebraic and the trigonometric representations, the algorithm first defines the number of rotatable bonds in the ligand. These bonds were defined based on the works at [10,19]. Once both of the atoms involved in a rotatable bond are identified, two additional contiguous atoms need

---

[1] http://www.cgl.ucsf.edu/chimera/docs/UsersGuide/midas/dms1.html

to be considered to calculate the dihedral angle; such angles are then computed for each rotatable bond to obtain a trigonometric representation of the molecule.

The ligand trigonometric representation data was arranged using an undirected graph. Thus, each atom is a vertex while covalent bonds are the edges (see Fig. 1(a)). The relevant torsion angles needed are those formed between the four atoms involved in a rotatable bond.

The molecular reconstruction of a conformation consists of finding the new x, y and z coordinates of the atoms after a random change in a torsional angle occurs. Specifically, it is performed by computing the localization of a fourth atom in the graph based on information about their coordinates, the distances between them, the bond angles and the dihedral angles of the three previous atoms. The transformation from the trigonometric to the algebraic representation is done based on the method proposed by Dong and Wu [8].

2.2   Exploration of the Search Space

In any multi-objective problem, two spaces need to be defined: the decision space (the set of all solutions), and the objective space (the objective values). To model any specific problem as an MOEA, three basic sets must be modelled: a set of objective functions, a set of decision variables and a set of constraints [7,21].

Decision Space. In an MOEA, the decision variables are represented as chromosomes that contain the information of the solutions. In this work, the chromosomes represent the conformations and localization of the ligand on the receptor binding site. The complexes are represented as an array of real values that correspond to the location of the ligand with respect to the receptor and to the ligand's conformation through the dihedral angles of rotatable bonds. Specifically, an identifier operator (labeled as ID) models the combinatorial of all possible translations and rotations over each of the x, y and z axes (see Fig. 1(b)).

The ID genetic operator is proposed to modify the variable in the chromosome that models the combinatorial of all 64 possible translations and rotations over each of the x, y and z axes, in order to find the new coordinates of the atoms after random changes in a torsional angle. By using the ID operator it is possible to represent a geometric transformation that consists of a rotation and/or a translation. The genetic operators over the individuals are the ones typically used in an MOEA, except for the ID operator, in which six variables can be mutated: three for translations and three for rotations over the x, y and z axes.

Objective Space. An MOEA was implemented to deal with the conflicting terms in the energy function [11]. The all atoms force fields AMBER [4] and GAFF [26] were selected as the energy functions to be optimized, however, our method is flexible to work with other force fields. The proposed approach does not consider the energy function as a unique value, instead it optimizes the energy contributions from the bonding and non-bonding terms (see Equation 1). The first objective corresponds to the energy contributions from the covalent bonds between the atoms (bonding terms), such as bonds, bond angles and torsion angles (see Equation 2). The second objective is related to the molecular interactions where a covalent bond does not occur, such as electrostatic attractions, repulsion forces, and van der Waals forces (see Equation 3).

$$E_{pair} = E_{bond} + E_{non-bond} \tag{1}$$

$$E_{bond} = \sum_{bonds} k_r(r-r_{eq})^2 + \sum_{angles} k_\theta(\theta-\theta_{eq})^2 + \sum_{dihedral} \frac{v_n}{2} \times [1 + \cos(n\phi - \gamma)] \tag{2}$$

$$E_{non-bond} = \sum_{i<j} \left[\frac{A_{ij}}{R_{ij}^{12}} - \frac{B_{ij}}{R_{ij}^6} + \frac{q_i q_j}{\varepsilon R_{ij}} \right] \tag{3}$$

The NSGA-II [6] algorithm implemented in the Java-based framework jMetal [9] was used to evolve the conformations and localizations of the ligand on the receptor binding site. NSGA-II is a multi-objective evolutionary algorithm which uses an elite-preservation strategy and an explicit diversity-preserving mechanism. NSGA-II creates a random initial population and iteratively improves its quality until some level of acceptability is met. Then, the solutions in the final set are expected to be of high quality and non-dominated with respect to one another (called a Pareto front) [6].

In the proposed method, a high-level analysis algorithm was included in order to choose one of the solutions in the final Pareto front. Such selection focuses on the identification of the knees, i.e., the regions in the Pareto front where small displacements produce a big detriment on at least one of the objectives. To find the knees the method based on angles in [1] was considered.

Feasible Regions. Some steric and geometric constraints define the feasible solutions. Specifically, the steric constraints are represented by the collisions between atoms from the molecule and atoms from the receptor. These collisions are penalized by the scoring function. On the other hand, the geometric constraints are related to infeasible localizations of the ligand, which are defined by delimiting the binding site to such an extent that solutions outside this physical limit can not be generated.

To thoroughly study the performance of the proposed method, some parameters were fixed. The values of those parameters are summarized in Table 1.

2.3   Evaluation of the Proposed Method

The proposed model was evaluated over a set of complexes reported in the literature (see Table 2). These complexes were chosen based on: (1) the proteins involved have a remarkable importance in pharmacology or industry; (2) the molecular structures have a high resolution and (3) the complexes have been widely used in the evaluation of previous methods.

Two aspects were taken into account in the evaluation of the proposed method: The behavior of the Pareto fronts and the Root Mean Square Deviation (RMSD) values of the predicted molecular complexes at different generations of the MOEA. Even though the MOEA is able to obtain a set of solutions, only one experimentally reported complex to perform the evaluation of the method is available at the

Table 1. MOEA's parameters for the proposed approach

Parameter	Value
MOEA algorithm	NSGA-II [6]
Number of evaluations	At most 20000
Population size	100
Fitness Function	Two Objectives (Bond and Non-Bond interactions)
Chromosome	Torsion angles plus the identified operator (ID)
Genetic Operators	SBX Crossover ($\eta_c = 5, p_c = 0.9$)
	Polynomial Mutation ($\eta_m = 10, p_m = 0.01$)
	Rotation and Translation operator

Table 2. Information about the complexes used to test the model

PDB	Atoms	Rotatable bonds	Method	Resolution
1ABE	20	4	X-Ray	1.7
1ACM	26	6	X-Ray	2.8
1BAF	35	4	X-Ray	2.9
1CDG	45	12	X-Ray	2.0

Protein Data Bank[2]. Then, only one solution is selected and compared with its experimental counterpart based on the two mentioned criteria. In addition, since Pareto-optimal solutions for the considered complexes are not known, the volume of the dominated portion of the objective space (i.e., hypervolume) is used as an indicator of the coverage of the Pareto front.

In this work, the Superimpose script included in the set of programs TINKER[3] was used to evaluate how similar the complex conformation predicted by the proposed method was with respect to the one reported in the literature. It is important to stress that only the distances between the atoms of the ligand were taken into account to compare the molecular complexes because the receptor is kept fixed. Furthermore, the reported RMSD is measured without inducing translation or rotation changes in any of the two molecule conformations.

3   Results and Discussion

Figure 2 shows the dynamics of the Pareto fronts at different stages of the algorithm. In addition, Fig. 3 depicts the relation between the RMSD and the energy values for each of the complexes.

The proposed method performed an appropriate exploration of the search space given that it was able to push the initial population in the direction of the Pareto optimal solutions and the volume of the dominated portion of the objective space increased as the algorithm ran (see Fig. 2(a)). In biological terms

---

[2] http://www.rcsb.org/pdb/home/home.do
[3] http://dasher.wustl.edu/tinker/

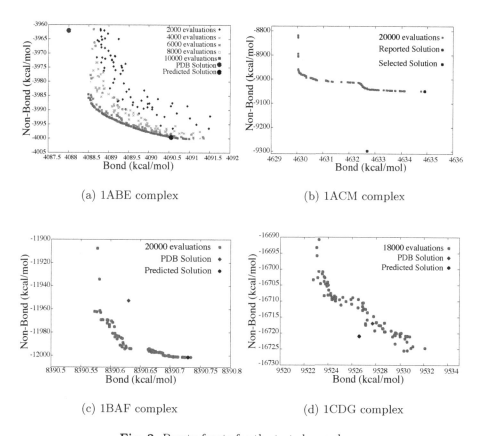

(a) 1ABE complex

(b) 1ACM complex

(c) 1BAF complex

(d) 1CDG complex

Fig. 2. Pareto fronts for the tested complexes

it means that this approach found a balance between the bonding and non-bonding interactions in a receptor-ligand complex.

The diversity of the results in the Pareto fronts was different in each studied complex, but it is important to establish that the parameters of the algorithm were fixed under the same conditions. For example, the diversities of the Pareto fronts in Figs. 2(b), 2(c), and 2(d) were smaller as compared to the ones in Fig. 2(a). This can be explained by the fact that the set of feasible solutions is different for each complex as they have to meet different constraints.

The Pareto fronts also contribute to understand the decision making process. Specifically, the Pareto front in Fig. 2(a) is convex, while the ones in Figs. 2(b), 2(c), and 2(d) lack of convex parts. It is important to highlight that although there are a few individuals in the optimal set presenting high energy levels, the knee-based algorithm was able to discard them. Additionally, the knee-based algorithm was not so sensitive to non-convex parts of the Pareto front, where only the complex reported in Fig. 2(d) showed a clear bias towards the sharpest edge of the Pareto front.

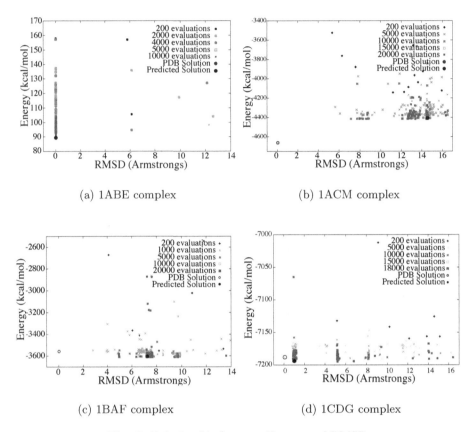

(a) 1ABE complex

(b) 1ACM complex

(c) 1BAF complex

(d) 1CDG complex

Fig. 3. Relationship between Energy and RMSD

The MOEA was able to find molecular complexes with 3D structures relatively close to the ones previously reported (see Figs. 2 and 3). Particularly, in Fig. 3 the search space exploration begins with highly disperse solutions, which converge to lower energy and RMSD values as the number of evaluations increases. Although in the case of the 1ACM complex, the conformations were not close to the reported one (see Fig. 3(b)); such behavior could be related to atom ligand collisions against the protein surface structure (see Fig. 4).

In Fig. 2(b) and 3(b) it can be seen that the algorithm was not able to get close enough to the energy terms of the reported complex. In contrast, the 1BAF complex (see Fig. 2(c) and 3(c)) had a lower energy value with respect to its reported counterpart; then it is worth noting that it is possible to produce lower energy complexes than the ones previously reported. The results for the 1ABE and 1CDG complexes (see Figs. 2(a), 3(a), 2(d) and 3(d)) show the expected behaviour of a Pareto front, where the energy terms of both, predicted and reported conformations, are located very close to each other.

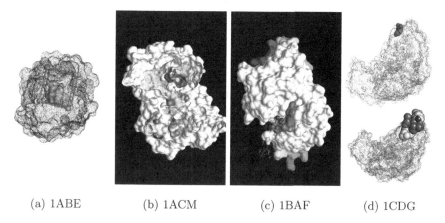

(a) 1ABE   (b) 1ACM   (c) 1BAF   (d) 1CDG

Fig. 4. The best location of the ligands in their corresponding receptors. (a) The receptor surface (black points) and the ligand surface (solid pink body). (b) The receptor (white surface), the reported ligand (pink molecular surface in the middle of the receptor), and the other solutions found by the model (surfaces in other colors). (c) The receptor (white surface) and the ligand: (magenta surface). Atoms and sticks represent other ligand conformations and locations. (d) The complex below shows the possible solutions that were found by the algorithm.

Table 3. Comparison of the RMSD values obtained with different docking models

Approach	1ABE	1ACM	1BAF	1CDG
DOCK [20]	0.20	1.11	– – – – – –	
GOLD [12]	0.86	0.81	6.12	– – –
FLEXX [14]	3.03	0.5 – 1.0	> 3	> 3
Proposed Approach	0.0	7.95	4.93	0.85

The best location of the ligands in their corresponding receptors can be observed in Fig. 4. For the 1ABE complex, the best location for the ligand was inside the binding site because the remaining space is occupied by the receptor (see Fig. 4(a)). Some of the 1ACM and 1BAF conformations fitted inside the binding site, but since the atoms collided, they were penalized and the ligands were located outside the protein surface (see Figs. 4(b) and 4(c)). Figure 4(d) shows that in the cavity of the 1CDG receptor, unlike in 1ACM and 1BAF, there are lesser collisions between atoms from both molecules.

In the prediction of the complexes, it was difficult to establish a relationship between the RMSD errors and energy values, specially when the binding site is a cavity where several collisions between protein and ligand atoms can occur, as it was the case of the 1BAF and 1ACM complexes (see Figs. 4(b) and 4(c)). In contrast, when there are not so many collisions between the protein and ligand in the receptor cavity, as was the case of the 1ABE and 1CDG complexes, the optimization process had a better performance and the predicted complexes were closer to the reported ones (see Figs. 4(a) and 4(d)). A remarkable aspect of the proposed approach is its ability to converge to a set of complexes with similar energy values but different RMSD errors, as shown in Fig. 4(d).

Table 3 shows the comparison between the RMSD values of the complexes predicted by the proposed approach and other docking models. The comparison was carried out using docking models based on evolutionary algorithms to explore the search space, such as DOCK and GOLD, as well as the model FLEXX, which uses a different approach.

It is important to notice that all of the models used in the comparison had at least one energy function based on force fields such as the one used in the proposed approach [5]. The other models also included additional energy and scoring functions to evaluate the geometric complementarity between the receptor and the ligand. However, the predicted complexes had similar RMSD errors for the different models (see Table 3). Only for the 1ACM complex, the RMSD error was higher in the proposed approach than in the other models. In contrast, for the 1ABE complex, the method was able to find a complex with an RMSD equal to 0, which means that the model was able to predict and select the exact complex reported experimentally. For the 1BAF complex, the proposed approach had a similar performance to the other models.

An interesting result was the one obtained for the 1CDG complex, in which the ligand has a high number of rotatable bonds. Generally, docking models have problems in correctly predicting complexes formed with a ligand that had more than seven rotatable bonds [12].

4 Conclusions

This work contributes proposing an optimization energy approach to predict the ligand conformation and configuration in the docking problem. Particularly, we introduced a novel method for predicting molecular complexes based on a multi-objective approach at an atomic conformational level. By analyzing the results, it is possible to establish that the proposed model was capable of optimizing the energy values of complexes formed between a ligand and a receptor.

It can be concluded that: (i) The method proposed for representing small organic molecules is adequate for the search of the conformational space because it reduces the number of variables that need to be considered by the evolutionary algorithm. (ii) The use of an MOEA enabled the identification of molecular complexes with 3D structures relatively close to the ones previously reported for the analyzed structures. (iii) The proposed method was able to find good complexes when the ligand had a high number of rotatable bonds; this is of remarkable importance because other available methods have problems under these situations. (iv) Further work is needed to consider additional scoring functions that evaluate the solutions and penalize collisions; also some geometric constraints can be included to avoid ignoring possible good locations by allowing the exploration of cavities, which either can not be accessible to the solvent or whose shape can produce collisions between the ligand and the receptor.

Acknowledgement. We would like to sincerely thank Nora Martinez for proof-reading this manuscript. AS-P, DB and DR-M are supported by Colciencias's Francisco Jose de Caldas scholarships.

References

1. Branke, J., Deb, K., Dierolf, H., Osswald, M.: Finding Knees in Multi-objective Optimization. In: Yao, X., Burke, E.K., Lozano, J.A., Smith, J., Merelo-Guervós, J.J., Bullinaria, J.A., Rowe, J.E., Tiño, P., Kabán, A., Schwefel, H.-P. (eds.) PPSN 2004. LNCS, vol. 3242, pp. 722–731. Springer, Heidelberg (2004), http://citeseerx.ist.psu.edu/viewdoc/summary?doi=10.1.1.76.9689
2. Brooijmans, N., Kuntz, I.D.: Molecular recognition and docking algorithms. Annu. Rev. Biophys. Biomol. Struct. 32, 335–373 (2003)
3. Brünger, A.T., Leahy, D.J., Hynes, T.R., Fox, R.O.: The 2.9 Å resolution structure of an anti-dinitrophenyl-spin-label monoclonal antibody fab fragment with bound hapten. J. Mol. Biol. 221(1), 239–256 (1991)
4. Case, D., Darden, T., Cheatham Iii, T., Simmerling, C., Wang, J., Duke, R., Luo, R., Crowley, M., Walker, R., Zhang, W., et al.: Amber 10, vol. 32. University of California, San Francisco (2008)
5. Cornell, W.D., Cieplak, P., Bayly, C.I., Gould, I.R., Merz, K.M., Ferguson, D.M., Spellmeyer, D.C., Fox, T., Caldwell, J.W., Kollman, P.: A second generation force field for the simulation of proteins, nucleic acids, and organic molecules. JACS 117(19), 5179–5197 (1995), http://dx.doi.org/10.1021/ja00124a002
6. Deb, K., Pratap, A., Agarwal, S., Meyarivan, T.: A fast and elitist multiobjective genetic algorithm: Nsga-ii. IEEE Transactions on Evolutionary Computation 6(2), 182–197 (2002)
7. Dehuri, S., Cho, S.B.: Multi-criterion pareto based particle swarm optimized polynomial neural network for classification: A review and state-of-the-art. Comp. Sci. Rev. 3(1), 19–40 (2009)
8. Dong, Q., Wu, Z.: A linear-time algorithm for solving the molecular distance geometry problem with exact inter-atomic distances. J. Global Opt. 22(1), 365–375 (2002), http://dx.doi.org/10.1023/A:1013857218127
9. Durillo, J., Nebro, A., Luna, F., Dorronsoro, B., Alba, E.: jmetal: a java framework for developing multi-objective optimization metaheuristics. Departamento de Lenguajes y Ciencias de la Computación, University of Málaga, ETSI Informática, Campus de Teatinos, Tech. Rep. ITI-2006-10 (2006)
10. Hanser, T., Jauffret, P., Kaufmann, G.: A new algorithm for exhaustive ring perception in a molecular graph. J. Chem. Inf. Comput. Sci. 36(6), 1146–1152 (1996)
11. Ishida, M., Asakura, T., Yokoi, M., Saito, H.: Solvent-and mechanical-treatment-induced conformational transition of silk fibroins studies by high-resolution solid-state carbon-13 nmr spectroscopy. Macromolecules 23(1), 88–94 (1990)
12. Jones, G., Willett, P., Glen, R.C., Leach, A.R., Taylor, R.: Development and validation of a genetic algorithm for flexible docking. J. Mol. Biol. 267(3), 727–748 (1997), http://view.ncbi.nlm.nih.gov/pubmed/9126849
13. Kapetanovic, I.M.: Computer-aided drug discovery and development (caddd): in silico-chemico-biological approach. Chemico-Biological Interact. 171(2), 165–176 (2008)

14. Kramer, B., Rarey, M., Lengauer, T.: Evaluation of the FLEXX incremental construction algorithm for protein–ligand docking. Proteins 37(2), 228–241 (1999), http://dx.doi.org/10.1002/(SICI)1097-0134(19991101) 37:2<228::AID-PROT8>3.0.CO;2-8

15. Kuntz, I.D., Blaney, J.M., Oatley, S.J., Langridge, R., Ferrin, T.E.: A geometric approach to macromolecule-ligand interactions. J. Mol. Biol. 161(2), 269–288 (1982)

16. Lawson, C.L., Van Montfort, R., Strokopytov, B., Rozeboom, H., Kalk, K., de Vries, G., Penninga, D., Dijkhuizen, L., Dijkstra, B.W.: Nucleotide sequence and X-ray structure of cyclodextrin glycosyltransferase from *Bacillus circulans* strain 251 in a maltose-dependent crystal form. J. Mol. Biol. 236(2), 590–600 (1994)

17. Lepre, C.A., Moore, J.M., Peng, J.W.: Theory and applications of nmr-based screening in pharmaceutical research. Chem. Rev. 104(8), 3641–3676 (2004)

18. Lodish, H., Baltimore, D., Berk, A., Darnell, J.: Molecular cell biology. WH Freeman, New York (1995)

19. Makino, S., Kuntz, I.D.: Automated flexible ligand docking method and its application for database search. J. Comp. Chem. 18(14), 1812–1825 (1997)

20. Moustakas, D., Lang, P., Pegg, S., Pettersen, E., Kuntz, I.D., Brooijmans, N., Rizzo, R.: Development and validation of a modular, extensible docking program: DOCK5. J. Comput. Aided Mol. Des. 20, 601–619 (2006), http://dx.doi.org/10.1007/s10822-006-9060-4, doi:10.1007/s10822-006-9060-4

21. Nicolaou, C.A., Brown, N., Pattichis, C.S.: Molecular optimization using computational multi-objective methods. Curr. Opin. Drug Discov. Dev. 10(3), 316 (2007)

22. Quiocho, F.A., Vyas, N.K.: Novel stereospecificity of the l-arabinose-binding protein. Nature 310(5976), 381–386 (1984)

23. Sams-Dodd, F.: Target-based drug discovery: is something wrong? Drug Discov. Today 10(2), 139–147 (2005)

24. Stebbins, J., Robertson, D., Roberts, M., Stevens, R., Lipscomb, W., Kantrowitz, E.: Arginine 54 in the active site of *Escherichia coli* aspartate transcarbamoylase is critical for catalysis: A site-specific mutagenesis, nmr, and x-ray crystallographic study. Prot. Sci. 1(11), 1435–1446 (2008)

25. Subasi, E., Basdogan, C.: A new haptic interaction and visualization approach for rigid molecular docking in virtual environments. Presence 17(1), 73–90 (2008)

26. Wang, J., Wolf, R.M., Caldwell, J.W., Kollman, P.A., Case, D.A.: Development and testing of a general amber force field. J. Comp. Chem. 25(9), 1157–1174 (2004)

Semantic Bias in Program Coevolution

Tom Seaton, Julian F. Miller, and Tim Clarke

Department of Electronics
University of York
{tas507,julian.miller,tim.clarke}@york.ac.uk

Abstract. We investigate two pathological coevolutionary behaviours, disengagement and cycling, in GP systems. An empirical analysis is carried out over constructed GP problems and the Game of Tag, a historical pursuit and evasion task. The effects of semantic bias on the occurence of pathologies and consequences for performance are examined in a coevolutionary context. We present findings correlating disengagement with semantic locality of the genotype to phenotype map using a minimal competitive coevolutionary algorithm.

Keywords: Coevolution, Genetic Programming, Semantics, Benchmarks.

1 Introduction

Pathological or unintended behaviours are a well-established issue in the design of coevolutionary algorithms (CoEA) [12]. Coevolutionary pathologies are processes, distinct to coevolutionary systems, that interfere with progress of the search towards a desired goal state. Analysis of these pathological behaviours in systems of minimal complexity has been a principal component of coevolutionary research in genetic algorithm (GA) representations, focusing on both their theoretical basis [4] and mitigation [3]. In this paper, we examine how coevolutionary pathologies can influence progress in coevolutionary forms of genetic programming (GP). Although pathological behaviours have been addressed in GP [8], to our knowledge no studies exist which explicitly recreate these concepts using a quantifiable, controlled approach under program representations. Our intention is to bridge this gap with an initial study demonstrating and analysing pathologies in a minimal form of GP.

Disengagement and cycling are patterns of search behaviour that occur in systems lacking an objective method of fitness evaluation. Informally, coevolutionary algorithms determine a search gradient through the interaction of sets of individuals rather a single individual. Disengagement therefore occurs when an element of the system has entered a state for which no search gradient can be induced by reference to the other coevolving elements. Cycling behaviour occurs when previously visited interactions recur so that the search is led to return repeatedly to a previous set of individuals. The former pathology results in a period of unguided search. The latter pathology wastes computational effort by re-evaluating previously visited states. We postulate that disengagement and

K. Krawiec et al. (Eds.): EuroGP 2013, LNCS 7831, pp. 193–204, 2013.

cycling are particularly significant in coevolutionary systems which use GP representations. Disengagement has been suggested to occur with greater frequency in situations where it is more difficult to make objective progress in some coevolved components than others [1]. Because most GP expressions are far from uniformly represented, such asymmetry may be common. Cycling behaviour is costly because (in general) re-evaluating GP structures is associated with more computation than their binary counterparts. However, it is not presently known which factors in the GP paradigm influence disengagement and cycling behaviours. This empirical work focuses on one possible factor, semantic bias. Research on semantics and the genotype-phenotype map in GP has been a prominent area since GP's inception [11, 14, 20], but it is not clear how previous findings in classical single population GP extend to coevolutionary systems. The experiments described here examine the effect of local and non-local semantic topology on disengagement, cycling and performance in a coevolutionary GP system.

The structure of this paper is as follows. In Section 2, we introduce a set of suitable, simple, benchmark coevolutionary problems. These have been selected to elicit measurable forms of pathological behaviour when using GP in a coevolutionary setting. Section 3 describes our experimental configuration and treatment of parameters. Section 4 summarises the results for each pathological case. The final section discusses how the relationships observed between pathological behaviour, semantic constraints and performance have informed our understanding of coevolution in GP.

2   Benchmark Selection

Few established benchmarks exist for coevolutionary forms of GP. Historically, one natural source of problems has been competitive pursuit and evasion games, where the objective is to develop strategies to intercept or escape an opponent. An example is the *Serengeti* problem, first analysed in GP by Haynes and Sen [5], which presents a classic predator-prey scenario. Strategies are developed for multiple predators ('lions') to capture a prey-agent (a 'gazelle') on a simulated grid-world. *Serengeti* is considered to be difficult to solve without a degree of cooperation between predators [9]. Pursuit and evasion is frequently used in the coevolutionary literature, but has been criticised as a method of benchmarking [2], primarily due to the complexity of interactions between different strategies and the ensuing difficulties when defining measures of progress. However given the breadth of practical applications, it remains an attractive area within which to analyse CoEA, provided a sufficiently simplified problem instance can be defined.

Another commonly employed class of coevolutionary GP problem is a 'game vs. environment' where programs are coevolved for the purpose of controlling an agent in conjunction with an increasingly challenging structure, such as a maze or series of obstacles. The *Tartarus* grid-world game proposed by Teller [17, 18] presents such a situation, in which an agent must manoeuvre a series of blocks into positions around the edges of the world. A more recent example can be found in Cartlidge [1], in which a maze navigation problem was defined where strategies to control robots to escape a maze are coevolved simultaneously with increasingly difficult maps. Both problems are examples of asymmetric problem difficulty in GP (challenging worlds are easier to obtain than good controllers.) However, the utility of established problems such as *Serengeti* and *Tartarus* is questionable when investigating coevolutionary pathologies. Firstly, both *Serengeti* and *Tartarus* lack a clearly defined notion of optimal behaviour or solution concept against which to measure progress. Secondly, their solutions require complex components whose contribution to the problem difficulty is not well understood. Notably, the *Tarturus* game requires that solutions incorporate memory, for example in the form of a finite state machine. It is unclear how these requirements interact with GP performance.

Given the paucity of suitable benchmarks, for this work we introduce two new minimal constructed problems after the style of existing analysis in GA systems, the *GP Greater Than Game* and *Simple Cycler*. These games are designed specifically to explore disengagement and cycling in a GP context. The problems are derived from the concept of GA 'number games' following a similar principle to those analysed in [3] and [19]. We will also consider a more complex historical pursuit and evasion task, the *Game of Tag*.

2.1   Problem Set

GP Greater-Than Game (GP-GTG). To investigate the pathology of disengagement in GP, the GA *Greater-Than* (GT) game described by [1] was generalised to the context of GP representations (GP-GTG). GP-GTG uses two symmetric populations of programs. Each program operates on real values formed from a constrained function set $\{+,-\}$ accepting a single terminal input fixed at unity. Programs have a single output, derived by evaluating the expression at the root node of the program. The outcome of comparing a pair of programs (p, p') is given as a function of the program outputs g. We term this the interaction function:

$$g(p, p') = \begin{cases} 1.0 & o(p) > o(p') \\ 0.5 & o(p) = o(p') \\ 0.0 & o(p) < o(p') \end{cases} \qquad (1)$$

where $o(p)$ and $o(p')$ are the real valued outputs of each program. The expressions are constrained to a maximum depth n, measured from root to terminal nodes. The game is solved after a program is found from the subset of programs which maximises the output.[1]

Simple Cycler (SC). Informally, we define cycling behaviour in coevolutionary GP as exiting and revisiting the same phenotypic state in a program search space. *Simple Cycler* is an elementary game which is designed to simulate measurable, irregular cycles in a coevolutionary GP algorithm. Evolved programs operate on

---

[1] GP-GTG is superficially similar to the GP 'MAX' problem [7]. The key distinction is that programs are evaluated using only their relative rather objective fitness.

boolean values and are constructed from the function set {AND,OR,NOT,IF}, where the IF function accepts three arguments: a condition, response if the condition is true and response if the condition is false. The input is a fixed terminal with value TRUE. Programs are required to output a string of n boolean values (for example, from n selected output nodes). This output is mapped onto an unsigned integer $o \in \{1 : 2^n\}$, using a binary encoding. The interaction function is computed as:

$$g(p,p') = \begin{cases} 1.0 & o(p) > o(p') \text{ except } o(p) = 2^n \text{ and } o(p') = 1 \\ 1.0 & o(p) = 1, \ o(p') = 2^n \\ 0.5 & o(p) = o(p') \\ 0.0 & o(p) < o(p') \text{ except } o(p) = 1 \text{ and } o(p') = 2^n \\ 0.0 & o(p) = 2^n, \ o(p') = 1 \end{cases} \qquad (2)$$

This expression states that the program corresponding to the greatest integer wins, except for the cases where the maximum integer (2^n) value is compared to the minimum integer (1). Therefore under this function all programs can be positioned on a single transitive chain of length 2^n. A cycle is said to occur when a program has changed from a structure corresponding to the smallest integer to the largest and back, traversing the intermediate states. Cycling behaviour is monitored by measuring the average period over a fixed number of generations.

The Game of Tag (GoT). The *Game of Tag* is a two dimensional GP pursuit and evasion game introduced by Reynolds [13]. Games consist of an idealised scenario in which control programs are developed which provide pursuit and evasion strategies. Analogous to the children's game, the objective for each control program is to minimise the length of time during which a program is designated as 'it' (the pursuer). Play occurs between pairs of competitors, which are point objects able to move at a fixed speed over a number of discrete timesteps. No account is made for momentum or limitations in change of heading. If the competitor designated as 'it' enters a certain capture radius of its opponent, the opponent is 'tagged' and the roles are exchanged. Successful programs must simultaneously evolve pursuit and evasion behaviours, depending on their role at that timestep. Effective algorithms should increase the capability of competitors in both roles progressively over time.[2] Our implementation closely follows Reynold's original version. At the start of a game, one competitor is placed at the centre of the two-dimensional play area. The other competitor is placed uniformly at random in a square region with width w centered on this position. Whilst a competitor is in pursuit, it is set to move at twice the speed of the evader. Inputs to each program are restricted to a real-valued vector (x, y) in the local coordinate system of the competitor and a boolean value, which specifies whether the competitor is in pursuit or not at that timestep. Programs provide a single real number output, which is interpreted as an updated heading. A score

---

[2] In this work we do not consider external methods of assisting progress, such as archives. Understanding the components of GP that impact on pathological behaviours may provide systems which are less reliant on these approaches.

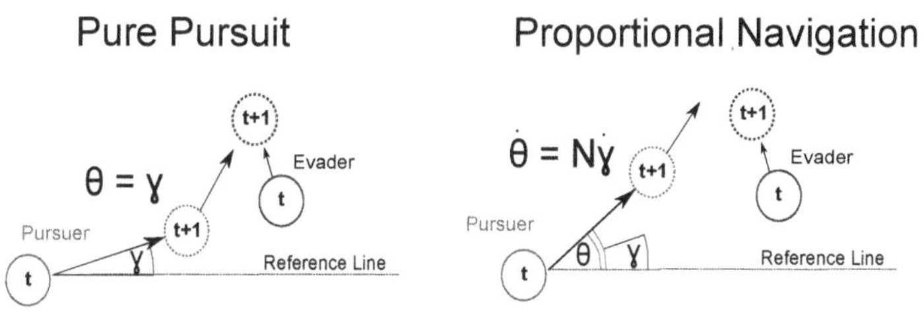

Pure Pursuit   Proportional Navigation

Fig. 1. Pure and proportional navigation pursuit strategies. The pursuer is shown against a fixed trajectory evader is shown over a discrete timestep $t \rightarrow t + 1$.

s is awarded to each competitor at the end of the game, equal to the number of timesteps spent as the evader. During training, the interaction function between two programs is evaluated as the average score obtained over a set of S games. In the first half of the set the first program p begins as the evader and in the second half the initial role is swapped.

$$g(p, p') = \frac{1}{|S|} \sum_{i \in |S|} s_i(p, p') \tag{3}$$

Reynolds assessed the objective quality of competitors by comparison against a robust artificial strategy, pure-pursuit. Competitors implementing pure-pursuit move directly towards their opponent whilst the pursuer and directly away whilst the evader. In the game of tag deviation by either adversary to any other strategy results in poorer performance, because a route other than the shortest path must be traversed (in game-theoretic terms this is a Nash equilibrium.) The present work includes an additional measure of solution quality using a further guidance strategy, proportional navigation. Proportional navigation is a widely applied guidance law, backed by a large body of analysis [15, 22]. The strategy employs the principle that an interception between the trajectories of two objects traveling with fixed speed will occur if the bearing between them is constant. In proportional navigation, the heading is updated at each timestep proportional to a constant N, which controls the magnitude of response (we assume $N=3$, see analysis in [15]). The angle γ gives the heading of the adversary. The angle θ gives the current heading. Angles are measured with respect to the local coordinate system. An example contrasting both strategies is sketched in Figure 1.

3   Experiment

3.1   Algorithm and Representation

An intentionally minimal GP algorithm was used for ease of comparison with other techniques. An integer genotype representation, Cartesian Genetic Programming (CGP), was selected across all problems [10]. Standard CGP uses only a truncation selection strategy followed by uniform mutation without crossover. In addition, CGP has recently been applied to a coevolutionary setting [16].

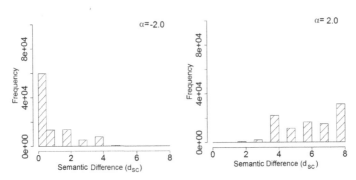

Fig. 2. Example contrasting the effects of the semantic bias on distances of mutated offspring. Illustrated for 10^5 sampled mutation operations in Simple Cycler.

Two populations of CGP programs were initialised uniformly and evaluated through the simplest coevolutionary interaction scheme (complete mixing) in which programs are tested versus all members of the other population P :

$$f(p) = \sum_{p' \in P} g(p, p')$$ (4)

Fitness values are given by the outcomes accumulated over all interactions.

3.2   Semantic Bias

A semantic bias was introduced to the mutation operator. A parameterised technique similar to the methods of Nguyen [11] was used, which has been previously applied to CGP to introduce a syntactic bias in [14]. A metric approximating the semantic difference between programs was defined for each problem, d_{GP-GTG}, d_{SC} and d_{GoT} respectively:

$$d_{GP-GTG} = |o(p) - o(p')|$$ (5)

$$d_{SC} = min \begin{cases} |o(p) - o(p')| \\ 2^n - |o(p) - o(p')|. \end{cases}$$ (6)

$$d_{GoT} = \sum_{K} |\theta(p) - \theta(p')|$$ (7)

Equation 5 is the absolute difference in the output of each program. Equation 6 is the shortest distance measured around the transitive cycle. Equation 7 is the absolute difference between output headings summed over a set of K input vectors to both programs. The set of vectors point to a grid of uniformly distributed fixed positions across the square starting region in the Game of Tag. A sigmoid function is used to bias the probability of mutating to individuals at particular semantic differences. The function gives the probability of accepting a

Table 1. Fixed Algorithm Parameters and Game Properties

Parameter	GP-GTG	SC	GoT
Nodes	20	20	50
Function Set	{+,-}	{AND, OR, NOT, TRUE}	Reynolds [13]
Terminal Set	{0,1}	{TRUE}	$\{x, y, isIt, [0.2{:}1.0]\}$
Mutation Rate	0.05	0.05	0.02
Selection Strategy	4+6 ES	1+1 ES	1+4 ES
Output Type	$o \in \{1 : 2^n\}$	$o \in \{1 : 2^n\}$	$o \in \mathbb{R}$, mapped onto $[0{:}2\pi]$
Populations	2×10	2×1	2×5
Runs	500	200	500
Max Generations	500	1000	500
β	1	1	0.05
Games/Opponent	1	1	Training: 5, Testing: 100
Game length	N/A	N/A	100 timesteps
Startbox Size w	N/A	N/A	7
Pursuer speed	N/A	N/A	2
Evader speed	N/A	N/A	1
Capture radius	N/A	N/A	1

prospective mutated individual, with respect to the semantic distance between parent and child. Control is provided by a pair of parameters $(\alpha, \beta) \in \mathbb{R}^2, \beta \geq 0$. The parameter α alters the slope of the sigmoid function, where $\alpha << 0$ and $\alpha >> 0$ correspond to a bias towards small and large semantic changes in each mutation. The parameter β offsets the function, giving the semantic distance at which there is a 50% chance of accepting a mutation, i.e. $sigmoid(\beta) = 0.5$. An example of the effects of the biased mutation operator on the distribution of mutation distances is illustrated in Figure 2, for SC with $\beta = 1$.

3.3   Summary of Fixed and Variable Parameters

In preliminary experiments, fixed algorithm parameters were tuned independently for each problem to give a locally optimal set of parameters for the CGP system, under no semantic bias ($\alpha = 0$). The range of values given in [10] was used as a basis. The Game of Tag parameters are based on those originally fixed by Reynolds [13]. Following the original work, the root node of all programs evolved in the Game of Tag is seeded with the 'IF-IT' function to provide a separate flow of execution for pursuit and evasion. Because there is no standardised approach to providing constants in CGP, the simplest technique is adopted here: the introduction of a small array of fixed constants as terminal values {0.2, 0.4, 0.6, 0.8, 1.0}. Although a full-factorial analysis of all parameters is outside the feasible scope of this work, in Section 4.2 we test the sensitivity of our experimental outcomes to mutation rate and length of CGP genotype. The offset β was fixed to the minimum semantic difference in the constructed problems and a representative small angular difference of 0.05 revolutions ($18°$) in the GoT, to give semantically local differences in the limit $\alpha << 0$. A summary of all the parameters used in each problem case is given in Table 1.

4   Results

4.1   Disengagement in the GP Greater than Game

The definition in [1] states that two populations can be considered to be disengaged when the variance of the accumulated fitness values across each population is zero. Figure 3 contrasts the probability of disengagement in GP-GTG and the magnitude of expected program output (performance), averaged over all runs as a function of α. A strong sensitivity to the semantic bias was observed. For $\alpha < 0$, the probability of disengagement is high and the evolved program output is low. Performance and disengagement were strongly correlated with the value of α (resp. Spearman 0.99 and -0.95, p $\leq$ 0.005, exact). We infer that using a mutation operator with a high probability of making a small semantic change increases the likelihood of disengagement. Highest performance is observed for this case when the mutation operator is biased towards larger semantic changes.

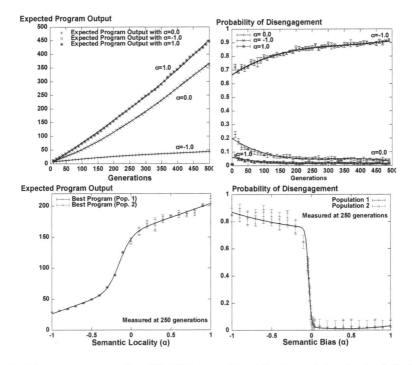

Fig. 3. Disengagement in the GP-GTG case. Top left: Expected output of the best evolved program. Top right: Probability of disengagement. Bottom left: Sensitivity of expected output to semantic locality. Bottom right: Sensitivity of probability of disengagement to semantic locality (reported at 250 generations).

4.2 Periodicity in the Simple Cycler Game

Cycling is characterised by measuring the mean number of generations for each population to transition between the maximum program state 2^n and back. Use of a 1+1 EA ensures that each population is at a single position at any given instance.[3] Figure 4 shows the period obtained over 200 runs, for transitive chains of increasing length. As n is increased, the time to traverse the chain is larger. The effect on cycle rate of mutation rate and α is shown in the bottom two images. Predictably, in the limit of very low mutation rates the cycle frequency tends to zero (no change in state). Biasing the semantic mutation operator towards larger semantic changes ($\alpha \geq 1$) corresponded to longer periods. In the limit of high mutation rates and small α, the average frequency tended to $\sim \frac{1}{2^n}$, or one generation per program state in the transitive chain. The fastest cycling behaviour was apparent in both mutation operators which produced very small semantic changes in programs and also those approaching random search.

4.3 Performance in the Game of Tag

Performance in the Game of Tag was measured by relative evaluation with respect to four pursuit and evasion strategies. These included pure-pursuit (PP) and proportional navigation (PN). In addition, progress was also evaluated against a noisy control (R), which returned a randomised heading for all input vectors. Finally a mixed strategy was defined to give an intermediate quality opponent, which returned either a randomised response or the pure pursuit response with equal probability (PR). Figure 5 (left) shows the expected progress of unbiased CGP against these metrics. Best performance was achieved against the randomised and proportional navigation strategies (evolved strategies are expected to win $\approx 90\%$ of games versus random opponents). Weakest performance is evident against the PP and PR strategies. A modest expected performance ($\approx 20\%$) was observed against the pure pursuit case, though higher success rates were achieved in individual cases, similar to that of Reynolds [13]). A direct comparison with the performance of Reynold's implementation is not possible because only 5 individual runs were reported in the original work. The sensitivity of the CGP algorithm in the Game of Tag to semantic bias was examined. No significant change was observed when measuring against the PP strategy. A weak response was measurable against the PR, R and PN strategies. The measured Spearman correlation coefficients in each case are (PP = -0.17, PR = -0.82, PN = -0.79, R = -0.62) where the correlations in PR, PN and R are significant at $p \leq 0.005$ (exact). Figure 5 (right) shows the change in expected performance at 250 generations for each of the significant results. Best performance was observed at $\alpha = -50$, which corresponds to a strong bias towards small phenotypic changes. However, the net performance change is small ($\approx 5 - 10\%$ difference in win ratio) and the effect of varying semantic locality in this case is marginal.

---

[3] Devising an unambiguous definition of cycling behaviour in larger populations of practical interest is an open issue for GP, which we leave for future debate.

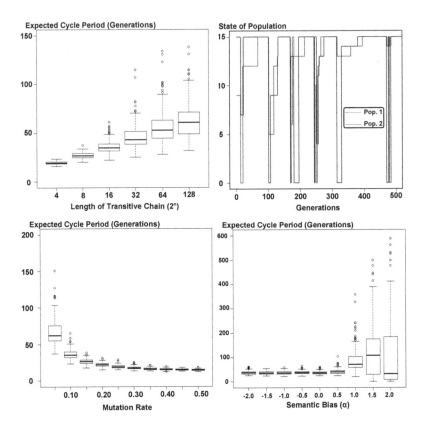

Fig. 4. Cycle rate in the Simple Cycler case. Top left: Scaling of unbiased cycle rate with problem size. Top right: Extract of a coevolutionary run, illustrating irregular cycling in both populations. Bottom left: Response to mutation rate. Bottom right: Response to semantic bias.

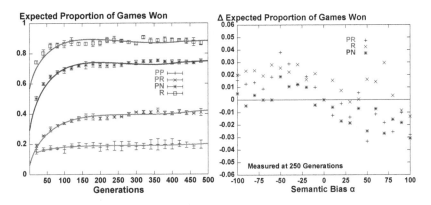

Fig. 5. Game of Tag Performance. Left: Unbiased CGP performance. Right: Sensitivity of performance to semantic bias.

5   Discussion

The strong correlation between performance and disengagement in GP-GTG supports our hypothesis that disengagement is a significant factor in program co-evolution. The probability of disengagement increases for small changes because programs are less likely to be distinguished using the coevolving population. Although we must be wary of generalising too far from this simplified example, the result suggests there may be a tradeoff between the use of semantically local mappings and operators which permit sufficient diversity to ensure populations of programs remain engaged. An interesting result from the Simple Cycler example is the trend towards faster cycling in both random (high mutation rate) and highly local search (small α). Inspection of individual runs showed that this is a consequence of two distinct search behaviours. Under random search, programs do not traverse the chain of states and instead revisit each state with fixed probability. For small n this probability is high, therefore giving a short period. In contrast, when mutations are constrained to programs with a small difference in output, the search tends towards hillclimbing through the intermediate states, also giving fast cycles. The result implies that, because cycling in GP is a pathology which occurs when an algorithm follows a transitive chain of programs, mappings biased towards small semantic changes may worsen this behaviour. Varying semantic bias in the Game of Tag problem introduced only a minor change to performance. We theorise this is due to two issues. Firstly, relative to the constructed problems, the semantic mapping in the Game of Tag is significantly more complex. The relationship between the outcome of a game and changes to program output is not transparent. It is therefore not clear whether our metric for semantic difference is the most suitable for this case. Secondly, the randomised starting configuration introduces noise into each outcome. This reduces the measured likelihood of disengagement in this case because of the increased variation in fitness values.

6   Conclusions and Further Work

These experiments highlight that pathological behaviours are a factor in the performance of coevolutionary forms of GP and that semantic biases in the GP genotype-phenotype map can influence their occurence. We introduced two new constructed problems based on the concept of coevolutionary number games in GA systems. Disengagement in coevolving populations was strongly related to semantic locality. We showed that semantic locality changed the frequency of cycling in a simple GP system. A weak response to semantic bias was also observed in a more realistic coevolutionary system, the Game of Tag. The scope of this work could be extended by analysing further GP algorithms, problem sets and other pathological behaviours which have been characterised in binary representations (for example, overgeneralisation [21]). At present, archiving techniques are used to provide theoretical guarantees of progress in coevolutionary EAs. However, examining the genotype to phenotype map used in methods of GP which have achieved good results without archives [6] may indicate how representations inherently robust to coevolutionary pathologies can be developed.

References

1. Cartlidge, J., Ait-boudaoud, D.: Coevolutionary Optimization. IEEE Transactions on Evolutionary Computation 15(2), 215–229 (2011)
2. Cliff, D., Miller, G.F.: Co-evolution of Pursuit and Evasion II: Simulation Methods and Results. In: From Animals to Animats: Proc. of the Fourth International Conference on Simulation of Adaptive Behaviour. University of Sussex (1995)
3. De Jong, E.: A Monotonic Archive for Pareto-Coevolution. Evolutionary Computation 15(1), 61–93 (2007)
4. Ficici, S.G.: Solution Concepts in Coevolutionary Algorithms. Ph.D. thesis, Brandeis University (2004)
5. Haynes, T., Sen, S., Schoenefeld, D., Wainwright, R.: Evolving multiagent coordination strategies with genetic programming. Tech. Rep. UTULSA-MCS-95-04, The University of Tusla (May 31, 1995)
6. Jaśkowski, W., Krawiec, K., Wieloch, B.: Winning Ant Wars: Evolving a Human-Competitive Game Strategy Using Fitnessless Selection. In: O'Neill, M., Vanneschi, L., Gustafson, S., Esparcia Alcázar, A.I., De Falco, I., Della Cioppa, A., Tarantino, E. (eds.) EuroGP 2008. LNCS, vol. 4971, pp. 13–24. Springer, Heidelberg (2008)
7. Langdon, W., Poli, R.: Foundations of Genetic Programming. Springer (2002)
8. Lipson, H., Bongard, J., Zykov, V.: Co-Evolutionary Methods in System Design and Analysis. In: 15th International CIRP Design Seminar, Shanghai (2005)
9. Luke, S., Spector, L.: Evolving Teamwork and Coordination with Genetic Programming. In: GECCO 1996, pp. 150–156 (July 1996)
10. Miller, J.F. (ed.): Cartesian Genetic Programming, 1st edn. Springer (2011)
11. Nguyen, Q.U.: Examining Semantic Diversity and Semantic Locality of Operators in Genetic Programming. Ph.D. thesis, University College Dublin (2011)
12. Popovici, E., Bucci, A., Wiegand, R.P., De Jong, K.: Coevolutionary Principles. In: Handbook of Natural Computing. Springer, Berlin (2010)
13. Reynolds, C.W.: Competition, Coevolution and the Game of Tag. In: Artificial Life IV, pp. 59–69 (1994)
14. Seaton, T., Miller, J.F., Clarke, T.: An Ecological Approach to Measuring Locality in Linear Genotype to Phenotype Maps. In: Moraglio, A., Silva, S., Krawiec, K., Machado, P., Cotta, C. (eds.) EuroGP 2012. LNCS, vol. 7244, pp. 170–181. Springer, Heidelberg (2012)
15. Shukla, U., Mahapatra, I.R.: The proportional navigation dilemma-pure or true? IEEE Transactions on Aerospace and Electronic Systems 26(2), 382–392 (1990)
16. Šikulová, M., Sekanina, L.: Coevolution in Cartesian Genetic Programming. In: Moraglio, A., Silva, S., Krawiec, K., Machado, P., Cotta, C. (eds.) EuroGP 2012. LNCS, vol. 7244, pp. 182–193. Springer, Heidelberg (2012)
17. Teller, A.: Learning Mental Models. In: Proceedings of the Fifth Workshop on Neural Networks (1993)
18. Trenaman, A.: Concurrent Genetic Programming, Tartarus and Dancing Agents. In: Langdon, W.B., Fogarty, T.C., Nordin, P., Poli, R. (eds.) EuroGP 1999. LNCS, vol. 1598, pp. 270–282. Springer, Heidelberg (1999)
19. Watson, R., Pollack, J.: Coevolutionary Dynamics in a Minimal Substrate. In: GECCO 2001, pp. 702–709. Morgan Kaufmann (2001)
20. Whigham, P.: Search bias, language bias and genetic programming. In: First Annual Conference on Genetic Programming, pp. 230–237. MIT Press (1996)
21. Wiegand, R.P.: An Analysis of Cooperative Coevolutionary Algorithms. Ph.D. thesis, George Mason University (2003)
22. Yuan, L.C.L.: Homing and Navigational Courses of Automatic Target-Seeking Devices. Journal of Applied Physics 19(12), 1122–1129 (1948)

A New Implementation of Geometric Semantic GP and Its Application to Problems in Pharmacokinetics

Leonardo Vanneschi[1,2,3], Mauro Castelli[1,2], Luca Manzoni[3], and Sara Silva[2,4]

[1] ISEGI, Universidade Nova de Lisboa, 1070-312 Lisboa, Portugal
[2] INESC-ID, IST / Universidade Técnica de Lisboa, 1000-029 Lisboa, Portugal
[3] D.I.S.Co., Università degli Studi di Milano-Bicocca, 20126 Milano, Italy
[4] CISUC, Universidade de Coimbra, 3030-290 Coimbra, Portugal
lvanneschi@isegi.unl.pt

Abstract. Moraglio et al. have recently introduced new genetic operators for genetic programming, called geometric semantic operators. These operators induce a unimodal fitness landscape for all the problems consisting in matching input data with known target outputs (like regression and classification). This feature facilitates genetic programming evolvability, which makes these operators extremely promising. Nevertheless, Moraglio et al. leave open problems, the most important one being the fact that these operators, by construction, always produce offspring that are larger than their parents, causing an exponential growth in the size of the individuals, which actually renders them useless in practice. In this paper we overcome this limitation by presenting a new efficient implementation of the geometric semantic operators. This allows us, for the first time, to use them on complex real-life applications, like the two problems in pharmacokinetics that we address here. Our results confirm the excellent evolvability of geometric semantic operators, demonstrated by the good results obtained on training data. Furthermore, we have also achieved a surprisingly good generalization ability, a fact that can be explained considering some properties of geometric semantic operators, which makes them even more appealing than before.

1 Introduction

In the last few years researchers have dedicated several efforts to the definition of Genetic Programming (GP) [5,8] methods or systems based on the semantics of the solutions, where by semantics we generally intend the behaviour of a program once it is executed, or more particularly the set of its output values on input training data [9]. In particular, very recently new genetic operators, called geometric semantic operators, have been proposed by Moraglio et al. [10]. These operators have the interesting property of inducing a unimodal fitness landscape on any problem consisting in finding the match between a set of input data and a set of known outputs (like for instance in regression and classification). As a consequence, in principle all these problems should be easily solvable by GP [8], independently of how complex they are. Nevertheless, as stated by Moraglio et al. [10], these operators have a serious limitation: by construction, they always produce offspring that are approximately the double size of their parents (expressed as the total number of tree nodes), and this makes the size of the individuals in the population grow exponentially with generations. In this way, after a few

K. Krawiec et al. (Eds.): EuroGP 2013, LNCS 7831, pp. 205–216, 2013.

generations the population is composed by individuals so big that the computational cost of evaluating their fitness is unmanageable. This limitation makes these operators impossible to use in practice, in particular on complex real-life applications.

The solution suggested [10] to overcome this drawback is to integrate in the GP algorithm a "simplification" phase, aimed at transforming each individual in the population into an equivalent (i.e. with the same semantics) but smaller one. Even though this is an interesting and challenging study, depending on the language used to code individuals simplification can be very difficult, and it is often a very time consuming task. For this reason, in this paper we propose a different strategy to solve the problem: we develop a GP system incorporating an implementation of geometric semantic genetic operators that makes them usable in practice, and does so very efficiently, without requiring any simplification of the individuals during the GP run. With this system we are able, for the first time, to exploit the great potentialities of the geometric semantic operators on complex real-life problems. In order to experimentally validate our new GP system, we apply it to problems in the field of pharmacokinetics, comparing the results with the ones obtained by standard GP. The two problems addressed are the prediction of human oral bioavailability and protein-plasma binding levels of medical drugs.

The paper is organized as follows: Section 2 presents the state of the art concerning the use of semantics to improve GP. Section 3 describes the geometric semantic operators introduced by Moraglio et al., while Section 4 presents our new GP system that overcomes the current limitations of these operators, making them usable and efficient. Section 5 presents the test problems, the experimental settings and the obtained results, offering in particular a discussion about the generalization ability to out-of-sample data provided by geometric semantic operators. Finally, Section 6 concludes the paper and provides hints for future research.

2   Previous Work on Semantics in GP

Several recent contributions have been aimed at using the notion of semantics to study, or improve, GP. McPhee et al. [9] showed that many applications of crossover often do not have any effect on semantics (i.e., basically crossover tends to produce offspring that have the same behaviour as their parents). These results have cast a shadow on the use of traditional genetic operators, and paved the way to the definition of new, semantic-based, operators. A first step in this direction was made by Beadle and Johnson [2], where semantics is used to define an algorithm called Semantically Driven Crossover. With this method, if the offspring are semantically equivalent to their parents, the children are discarded and the crossover is repeated. This process is iterated until semantically different children are found. The authors argue that this results in increased semantic diversity in the evolving population, and a consequent improvement in the GP performance. Nguyen et al. [13] investigated the role of syntactic and semantic locality of crossover in GP. The results showed that improving syntactic locality reduces code growth, which leads to a slight improvement of the ability to generalize. By comparison, improving semantic locality significantly enhances GP performance, reduces code growth and substantially improves the ability of GP to generalize. This work was the starting point in the search for new operators to directly act on semantics.

Under this perspective, Nguyen et al. [11] proposed Semantics Aware Crossover (SAC), a crossover operator promoting semantic diversity, that was subsequently extended to Semantic Similarity based Crossover (SSC) [14] and to Semantic Similarity based Mutation (SSM) [12]. Krawiec [6] proposed a class of *geometric* crossover operators for GP, i.e. operators aimed at making offspring programs semantically intermediate (medial) with respect to parent programs (a property shared also by the operators considered here). Krawiec and Lichocki [7] have also used a notion of semantic distance to propose a crossover operator for GP that is approximately a geometric crossover

3   Geometric Semantic Operators of Moraglio et al.

While the semantically aware methods cited in the previous section often exhibited superior performance with respect to traditional methods, most of them are indirect: search operators act on the syntax of the parents to produce offspring that are only accepted if some semantic criterium is satisfied. To provide operators able to work directly on the semantic, Moraglio et al. introduced new operators [10] To explain the idea, we first provide an example using Genetic Algorithms (GAs). Let us consider a GA problem in which the target solution is known and the fitness of each individual corresponds to its distance to the target (our reasoning holds for any distance measure used). This problem is characterized by a very good evolvability and it is in general easy to solve for GAs. In fact, for instance, if we use point mutation, any possible individual different from the global optimum has at least one neighbor (individual resulting from its mutation) that is closer to the target than itself, and thus is fitter. So, there are no local optima. In other words, the fitness landscape is unimodal and the fitness-distance correlation [3] is equal to 1, because fitness and distance to the goal are identical, which indicates the problem is easy to solve. Similar considerations hold for many types of crossover, including various kinds of geometric crossover [7].

Now, let us consider the typical GP problem of finding a function that maps sets of input data into known target outputs (regression and classification are particular cases). The fitness of an individual for this problem is typically a distance between its predicted output values and the expected ones (error measure). Now let us assume that we are able to find a transformation on the syntax of an individual whose effect is just a random perturbation of one of its predicted output values. In other words, let us assume that we are able to transform an individual G into an individual H whose output values are like the outputs of G, except for one value, that is randomly perturbed. Under this hypothesis, we are able to map the considered GP problem into the GA problem discussed above, in which point mutation is used. So, this transformation, if known, would induce a unimodal fitness landscape on every problem like the considered one (e.g. regressions and classifications), allowing GP to have a good evolvability on those problems, at least on training data. The same also holds for transformations on pairs of solutions that correspond to GA semantic crossovers.

This idea of looking for such operators is very ambitious and extremely challenging: finding those operators would allow us to directly search the space of semantics, at the same time working on unimodal fitness landscapes. Although not without limitations, the work of Moraglio et al. [10] accomplishes this task, defining new operators that have

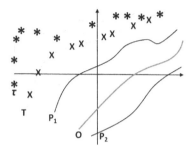

Fig. 1. An illustration of the fact that geometric semantic crossover creates an offspring that is at least not worse than the worst of its parents. In this example, offspring O (which stands between parents P_1 and P_2 in the semantic space by construction) is clearly closer to target T (training points represented by "$\times$" symbols) than parent P_2. In Section 5 we also discuss the geometric properties of this operator on test data, represented by τ (test points represented by "$*$" symbols).

exactly these characteristics. Here we report the definition of the geometric semantic operators as given by Moraglio et al. for real functions domains, since these are the operators we will use in the experimental phase. For applications that consider other types of data, the reader is referred to [10].

Definition 1. (Geometric Semantic Crossover). *Given two parent functions T_1, T_2 : $\mathbb{R}^n \to \mathbb{R}$, the geometric semantic crossover returns the real function $T_{XO} = (T_1 \cdot T_R) + ((1 - T_R) \cdot T_2)$, where T_R is a random real function whose output values range in the interval $[0, 1]$.*

The interested reader is referred to [10] for a formal proof of the fact that this operator corresponds to a geometric crossover on the semantic space, in the sense that it produces an offspring that stands between its parents in this space. We do not report the proof here, but we limit ourselves to remark that, even without a formal proof, we can have an intuition of it considering that the (only) offspring generated by this crossover has a semantic vector that is a linear combination of the semantics of the parents with random coefficients included in $[0, 1]$ and whose sum is equal to 1. Moraglio et al. [10] also prove an interesting consequence of this fact: the fitness of the offspring cannot be worse than the fitness of the worst of its parents. Also in this case we do not replicate the proof here, but we limit ourselves to giving a visual intuition of this property: in Figure 1 we represent a simple two-dimensional semantic space in which we draw a target function T (training points are represented by "$\times$" symbols), two parents P_1 and P_2 and one of their offspring O (which by construction stands between its parents), plus a test set (composed by test points represented by "$*$" symbols) that will be discussed in the final part of Section 5. It is immediately apparent from Figure 1 that O is closer to T than P_2 (which is the worst parent in this case). The generality of this property is proven in [10].

Definition 2. (Geometric Semantic Mutation). *Given a parent function $T : \mathbb{R}^n \to \mathbb{R}$, the geometric semantic mutation with mutation step ms returns the real function $T_M = T + ms \cdot (T_{R1} - T_{R2})$, where T_{R1} and T_{R2} are random real functions.*

Moraglio et al. [10] formally prove that this operator corresponds to a box mutation on the semantic space, and induces a unimodal fitness landscape. Even without a formal proof it is not difficult to have an intuition of it, considering that each element of the semantic vector of the offspring is a "weak" perturbation of the corresponding element in the parent's semantics. We informally define this perturbation as "weak" because it is given by a random expression centred on zero (the difference between two random trees). Nevertheless, by changing parameter ms, we are able to tune the "step" of the mutation, and thus the importance of this perturbation.

We highlight the fact that these operators create offspring that contain the complete structure of the parents, plus one or more random trees and some additional arithmetic operators: the size of the offspring is thus clearly much larger than the size of their parents. The exponential growth of the individuals in the population, demonstrated by Moraglio et al. [10], makes these operators unusable in practice: after a few generations the population becomes unmanageable because the fitness evaluation process becomes unbearably slow. The solution suggested in [10] consists in performing an automatic simplification step after each generation in which the individuals are replaced by (hopefully smaller) semantically equivalent ones. However, this additional step adds to the computational cost of GP and is only a partial solution to the progressive size growth. Last but not least, depending on the particular language used to code individuals and the used primitives, automatic simplification can be a very hard task.

In the next section, we present a novel implementation of GP using these operators that overcomes this limitation, making them efficient without performing any simplification step.

4 Novel Implementation of Geometric Semantic GP

Here we describe the proposed implementation of Geometric Semantic GP. Note that, although we describe the algorithm assuming the representation of the individuals is tree based, the implementation fits any other type of representation.

In a first step, we create an initial population of (typically random) individuals, exactly as in standard GP. We store these individuals in a table (that we call P from now on) as shown in Figure 2(a), and we evaluate them. To store the evaluations we create a table (that we call V from now on) containing, for each individual in P, the values resulting from its evaluation on each fitness case (in other words, it contains the semantics of that individual). Hence, with a population of n individuals and a training set of k fitness cases, table V will be made of n rows and k columns.

Then, for every generation, a new empty table V' is created. Whenever a new individual T must be generated by crossover between selected parents T_1 and T_2, T is represented by a triplet $T = \langle \mathrm{ID}(T_1), \mathrm{ID}(T_2), \mathrm{ID}(R) \rangle$, where R is a random tree and, for any tree τ, $\mathrm{ID}(\tau)$ is a *reference* (or memory pointer) to τ (using a C-like notation). This triplet is stored in an appropriate structure (that we call $\mathcal{M}$ from now on) that also contains the name of the operator used, as shown in Figure 2c. The random tree R is created, stored in P, and evaluated in each fitness case to reveal its semantics. The values of the semantics of T are also easily obtained, by calculating $(T_1 \cdot R) + ((1 - R) \cdot T_2)$ for each fitness case, according to the definition of geometric semantic crossover, and stored in V'. Analogously, whenever a new individual T must be obtained by applying mutation to an individual T_1, T is represented by a triplet $T = \langle \mathrm{ID}(T_1), \mathrm{ID}(R_1), \mathrm{ID}(R_2) \rangle$

(stored in $\mathcal{M}$), where R_1 and R_2 are two random trees (newly created, stored in P and evaluated for their semantics). The semantics of T is calculated as $T_1 + ms \cdot (R_1 - R_2)$ for each fitness case, according to the definition of geometric semantic mutation, and stored in V'. In the end of each generation, table V' is copied into V and erased. All the rows of P and $\mathcal{M}$ referring to individuals that are not ancestors[1] of the new population can also be erased. Note that, while $\mathcal{M}$ grows at every generation, by keeping the semantics of the individuals separated we are able to use a table V whose size is independent from the number of generations.

Summarizing, this algorithm is based on the idea that, when semantic operators are used, an individual can be fully described by its semantics (which makes the syntactic component much less important than in standard GP), a concept discussed in depth in [10]. Therefore, at every generation we update table V with the semantics of the new individuals, and save the information needed to build their syntactic structures without explicitly building them. In terms of computational time, we emphasize that the process of updating table V is very efficient as it does not require the evaluation of the entire trees. Indeed, evaluating each individual requires (except for the initial generation) a constant time, which is independent from the size of the individual itself. In terms of memory, tables P and $\mathcal{M}$ grow during the run. However, table P adds a maximum of $2 \times n$ rows per generation (if all new individuals are created by mutation) and table $\mathcal{M}$ (which contains only memory pointers) adds a maximum of n rows per generation. Even if we never erase the "ex-ancestors" from these tables (and never reuse random trees, which is also possible), we can manage them efficiently for several thousands of generations. Let us briefly consider the cost in terms of time and space of evolving a population of n individuals for g generations. At every generation, we need $O(n)$ space to store the new individuals. Thus, we need $O(ng)$ space in total. Since we need to do only $O(1)$ operations for any new individual (since the fitness can be computed using the fitness of the parents), the time complexity is also $O(ng)$. Thus, we have a linear space and time complexity with respect to population size and number of generations.

The final step of the algorithm is performed after the end of the last generation. In order to reconstruct the individuals, we may need to "unwind" our compact representation and make the syntax of the individuals explicit. Therefore, despite performing the evolutionary search very efficiently, in the end we may not avoid dealing with the large trees that characterize the standard implementation of geometric semantic operators. However, most probably we will only be interested in the best individual found, so this unwinding (and recommended simplification) process may be required only once, and it is done offline after the run is finished. This greatly contrasts with the solution proposed by Moraglio et al. of building and simplifying every tree in the population at each generation online with the search process. If we are not interested in the form of the optimal solution, we can avoid the "unwinding phase" and we can evaluate an unseen input with a time complexity is $O(ng)$. In this case the the individual is used as a "black-box" which, in some cases, may be sufficient.

Excluding the time needed to build and simplify the best individual, the proposed implementation allowed us to evolve populations for thousands of generations with a

---

[1] We abuse the term "ancestors" to designate not only the parents but also the random trees used to build an individual by crossover or mutation.

Id	Individual
T_1	$x_1 + x_2 x_3$
T_2	$x_3 - x_2 x_4$
T_3	$x_3 + x_4 - 2x_1$
T_4	$x_1 x_3$
T_5	$x_1 - x_3$

(a)

Id	Individual
R_1	$x_1 + x_2 - 2x_4$
R_2	$x_2 - x_1$
R_3	$x_1 + x_4 - 3x_3$
R_4	$x_2 - x_3 - x_4$
R_5	$2x_1$

(b)

Id	Operator	Entry
T_6	crossover	$\langle \mathrm{ID}(T_1), \mathrm{ID}(T_4), \mathrm{ID}(R_1) \rangle$
T_7	crossover	$\langle \mathrm{ID}(T_4), \mathrm{ID}(T_5), \mathrm{ID}(R_2) \rangle$
T_8	crossover	$\langle \mathrm{ID}(T_3), \mathrm{ID}(T_5), \mathrm{ID}(R_3) \rangle$
T_9	crossover	$\langle \mathrm{ID}(T_1), \mathrm{ID}(T_5), \mathrm{ID}(R_4) \rangle$
T_{10}	crossover	$\langle \mathrm{ID}(T_3), \mathrm{ID}(T_4), \mathrm{ID}(R_5) \rangle$

(c)

Fig. 2. Illustration of the example described in Section 4. (a) The initial population P; (b) The random trees used by crossover; (c) The representation in memory of the new population P'

considerable speed up with respect to standard GP. Future work will provide a comparison of the execution times of the different methods.

Example. Let us consider the simple initial population P shown in table (a) of Figure 2 and the simple pool of random trees that are added to P as needed, shown in table (b). For simplicity, we will generate all the individuals in the new population (that we call P' from now on) using only crossover, which will require only this small amount of random trees. Besides the representation of the individuals in infix notation, these tables contain an identifier (Id) for each individual ($T_1, ..., T_5$ and $R_1, ..., R_5$). These identifiers will be used to represent the different individuals, and the individuals created for the new population will be represented by the identifiers $T_6, ..., T_{10}$.

The individuals of the new population P' are simply represented by the set of entries exhibited in table (c) of Figure 2. This table contains, for each new individual, a *reference* to the ancestors that have been used to generate it and the name of the operator used to generate it (either "crossover" or "mutation"). For example, the individual T_6 is generated by the crossover of T_1 and T_4 and using the random tree R_1.

Let us assume that now we want to reconstruct the genotype of one of the individuals in P', for example T_{10}. The tables in Figure 2 contain all the information needed to do that. In particular, from table (c) we learn that T_{10} is obtained by crossover between T_3 and T_4, using random tree R_5. Thus, from the definition of geometric semantic crossover, we know that it will have the following structure: $(T_3 \cdot R_5) + ((1 - R_5) \cdot T_4)$. The remaining tables (a) and (b), that contain the syntactic structure of T_3, T_4, and R_5, provide us with the rest of the information we need to completely reconstruct the syntactic structure of T_{10}, which is $((x_3 + x_4 - 2x_1) \cdot (2x_1)) + ((1 - (2x_1)) \cdot (x_1 x_3))$ and upon simplification becomes $-x_1(4x_1 - 3x_3 - 2x_4 + 2x_1 x_3)$.

5 Experimental Study

Problems in Pharmacokinetics. The implementation described in the previous section allows the geometric semantic operators to be used, for the first time, in complex real-life applications. We have chosen two hard regression problems in the field of pharmacokinetics: prediction of human oral bioavailability and prediction of the protein-plasma binding levels of medical drugs. Both have already been tackled by GP in published literature, e.g. [1]. *Human oral bioavailability* (represented as %F) is the parameter that measures the percentage of the initial orally submitted drug dose that effectively reaches the systemic blood circulation after passing through the liver. Being able to reliably predict the %F value for a potential new drug is outstandingly important, given that the majority of failures in compounds development from the early nineties to nowadays are due to inaccurate predictions of this pharmacokinetic parameter during the drug discovery process [4]. The %F dataset consists of 359 instances, where each instance is a vector of 242 elements (241 molecular descriptor values identifying a drug, followed by the known value of %F for that drug). This dataset is freely available from the GP Benchmarks website, gpbenchmarks.org. *Protein-plasma binding level* (represented as %PPB) quantifies the percentage of the initial drug dose that reaches the blood circulation and binds to the proteins of plasma. This measure is fundamental for good pharmacokinetics, both because blood circulation is the major vehicle of drug distribution into human body and since only free (unbound) drugs can permeate the membranes reaching their targets [1]. The %PPB dataset consists of 131 instances, where each instance is a vector of 627 elements (626 molecular descriptor values identifying a drug, followed by the known %PPB for that drug).

Experimental Settings. We have tested our implementation of GP with geometric semantic operators (GS-GP) against a standard GP system (STD-GP). A total of 30 runs were performed with each technique using different randomly generated partitions of the dataset into training (70%) and test (30%) sets. All the runs used populations of 100 individuals allowed to evolve for 2000 generations. It is worth noting that the goal was not to achieve the best possible results, so the parameter settings were not tuned for each technique, save one exception described below. Tree initialization was performed with the Ramped Half-and-Half method [5] with a maximum initial depth equal to 6. The function set contained the four binary arithmetic operators $+$, $-$, $*$, and $/$ protected as in [5]. Fitness was calculated as the root mean squared error (RMSE) between predicted and expected outputs. The terminal set contained the number of variables corresponding to the number of features in each dataset. Tournaments of size 4 were used to select the parents of the new generation. To create new individuals, STD-GP used standard (subtree swapping) crossover [5] and (subtree) mutation [5] with probabilities 0.9 and 0.1, respectively.For GS-GP the mutation rate was 0.5. Preliminary tests have shown that the geometric semantic operators require a relatively high mutation rate in order to be able to effectively explore the search space. The ms step used was 0.001 as in [10]. For both systems, survival was elitist as it always copied the best individual into the next generation. No maximum tree depth limit has been imposed during the evolution.

Experimental Results. The experimental results are reported using curves of the fitness (RMSE) on the training and test sets and boxplots obtained in the following way. For each generation the training fitness of the best individual, as well as its fitness in the test set (that we call test fitness) were recorded. The curves in the plots report the median of these values for the 30 runs. The median was preferred over the mean because of its higher robustness to outliers. The boxplots refer to the fitness values in generation 500, for reasons explained later. In the following text we may use the terms fitness, error and RMSE interchangeably. Plots (a) and (b) of Figure 3 show the evolution of training and test error for STD-GP and GS-GP on the bioavailability problem. They

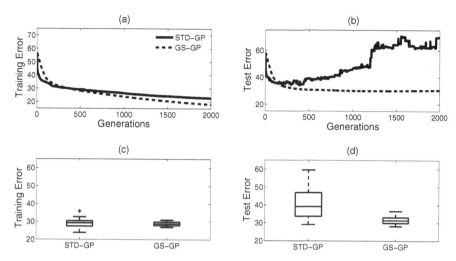

Fig. 3. Results on the bioavailability problem. Evolution of (a) training and (b) test errors for each technique, median of 30 runs. Boxplots of (c) training and (d) test fitness at generation 500. In boxplot (d) STD-GP has three outliers located at 157, 485 and 843 (not shown).

clearly show that GS-GP outperforms STD-GP on both training and test sets. We could informally say that on the training set both techniques "learn well", in the sense that the error curves in plot (a) are steadily decreasing during the whole considered runs, although GS-GP reaches lower error. On the other hand, on the test set, while STD-GP reveals a major loss of generalization ability, GS-GP exhibits a "desirable" behavior where the curve of the test error is regular and monotonically decreasing during the entire evolutionary process. We interpret these results saying that, unlike STD-GP, GS-GP does not overfit the training data on the bioavailability problem. The boxplots (c) and (d) of Figure 3 refer to the fitness values at generation 500, where both techniques have achieved more or less the same training fitness, and GS-GP is not improving test fitness anymore. The boxplots show that GS-GP has less dispersion of results than STD-GP, in particular on the test set. To analyse the statistical significance of these results, a set of tests has been performed. The Kolmogorov-Smirnov test has shown that the data are not normally distributed and hence a rank-based statistic has been used. The Wilcoxon rank-sum test for pairwise data comparison has been used under the alternative hypothesis that the samples do not have equal medians. The p-values obtained were 0.70 when training fitness of STD-GP is compared to training fitness of GS-GP and 6.3×10^{-6} when test fitness of STD-GP is compared to test fitness of GS-GP. Therefore, when using the usual significance level $\alpha = 0.01$ (or even if we use a much smaller one), we can state that at generation 500 the studied techniques have comparable fitness on the training data and GS-GP has significantly lower (i.e., better) fitness than STD-GP on the test data. Plots (a) and (b) of Figure 4 show the evolution of training and test error for STD-GP and GS-GP on the protein-plasma binding problem. As in the bioavailability problem, GS-GP reveals to be superior to STD-GP, this time with a wide difference also on the training set, where GS-GP is able to reach a minimal error. The behaviour on the test set is very similar to the one reported for the bioavailability problem.

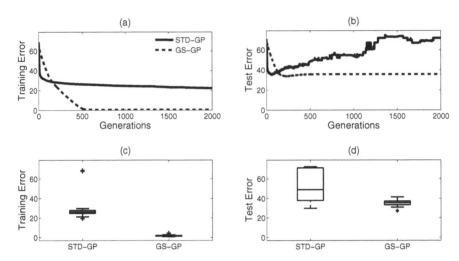

Fig. 4. Results on the protein-plasma binding problem. Evolution of (a) training and (b) test errors for each technique, median of 30 runs. Boxplots of (c) training and (d) test fitness at generation 500. In boxplot (d) STD-GP has six outliers located at 236, 259, 339, 456, 4402 and 5441 (not shown).

The boxplots (c) and (d) of Figure 4 once again refer to the values measured in generation 500, which is more or less the point when GS-GP has stabilized its fitness values both in training and test data. They show similar characteristics to the ones observed on the bioavailability problem, with GS-GP once again exhibiting a lower dispersion of results then STD-GP. They also show that GS-GP performs better than STD-GP in both training and test data. Using the same statistical tests as before, the comparative p-values obtained on the protein-plasma binding problem were 3.0×10^{-11} when training fitness of STD-GP is compared to training fitness of GS-GP and 5.1×10^{-6} when test fitness of STD-GP is compared to test fitness of GS-GP. This allows us to conclude that on the protein-plasma binding problem GS-GP outperforms STD-GP both on the training and test set in a statistically significant way.

Discussion. The good results that GS-GP has obtained on training data were expected: the geometric semantic operators induce an unimodal fitness landscape, which facilitates evolvability. On the other hand, on a first analysis, we have been surprised by the excellent results we have obtained on test data. These results even appeared a bit counterintuitive to us: we were expecting that the good evolvability on training data would entail an overfitting of those data.

However, an explanation of the excellent generalization ability shown by GS-GP on the two studied applications, we have realized one feature of geometric semantic operators that was not so obvious previously. Namely, the geometric properties of those operators hold *independently of the data* on which individuals are evaluated, and thus they hold also on test data. In other words, geometric semantic crossover produces an offspring that stands between the parents also in the semantic space induced by test data. As a direct implication, following exactly the same argument as Moraglio et al. [10], each offspring is, in the worst case, not worse than the worst of its parents on the test set. This can be seen by looking back at Figure 1, where a simple test set τ is drawn (testing data are represented by "$*$" symbols) and where it is clear that offspring O is closer to data in τ than parent P_2. Analogously, as it happens for training data, geometric semantic mutation produces an offspring that is a "weak" perturbation of its parent also in the semantic space induced by test data (and the maximum possible perturbation is, again, expressed by the ms step). The immediate consequence for the behaviour of GS-GP on test data is that, while geometric semantic operators do not guarantee an improvement in test fitness each time they are applied, they at least guarantee that the possible worsening of the test fitness is bounded (by the test fitness of the worst parent for crossover, and by ms for mutation). In other words, *geometric semantic operators help control overfitting*. Of course overfitting may still happen, as seen in plot (b) of Figure 4 for GS-GP (slight but visible), but there are no big "jumps" in test fitness like the ones observed in plots (b) of Figures 3 and 4 for STD-GP. We remark that, without the novel implementation that allowed us to use geometric semantic GP on these complex real-life problems, this interesting property would probably remained unnoticed.

6   Conclusions and Future Work

New genetic operators, called geometric semantic operators, have been proposed for genetic programming (GP). They have the extremely interesting property of inducing a unimodal fitness landscape for any problem consisting in matching input data to known target outputs (regression and classifications are instances of this general problem). This should make all the problems of this kind easily evolvable by GP. Nevertheless, as demonstrated in the literature, in their first definition these new operators have a strong limitation that makes them unusable in practice: they produce offspring that are larger than their parents, and this results in an exponential growth of the size of the individuals in the population. In this paper we have proposed a novel implementation of GP that uses the geometric semantic operators in a very efficient manner, in terms of computational time and memory. This new GP system evolves the semantics of the individuals without explicitly building their syntax. It does so by keeping a set of trees (of the initial population and the random ones used by geometric semantic crossover and mutation) in memory and a set of pointers to them, representing the "instructions" on how to build the new individuals. Thanks to this compact representation, it was possible to explore, for the first time, the great potential of geometric semantic GP to solve complex real-life problems. We have used two problems in the field of pharmacokinetics: the prediction of human oral bioavailability and the prediction of protein-plasma binding levels of medical drugs. The experimental results demonstrate that the new system outperforms standard GP. Besides the fact that the new GP system has excellent results on training data (which was expected, given that its fitness landscape is unimodal), we were surprised by its excellent generalization ability on the studied applications, which in retrospect can be explained by considering the geometric properties of the new operators. This encourages us to pursue the study: besides additional experimental validations on new data and different applications, we plan to orient our future activity towards more theoretical studies of the generalization ability of geometric semantic GP. In particular, we are interested in studying the "shape" of the functions produced by semantic GP with respect to the one generated by standard GP, and how this influences the generalization ability. On the more practical side, we are interested in comparing the runtime performance of geometric semantic GP with standard GP also considering the effect of a simplification phase at the end of the algorithm for when a "black-box" individual cannot be used.

Acknowledgments. This work was supported by national funds through FCT under contract Pest-OE/EEI/LA0021/2011 and by projects EnviGP (PTDC/EIA-CCO/103363/2008) and MassGP (PTDC/EEI-CTP/2975/2012), Portugal.

References

1. Archetti, F., Lanzeni, S., Messina, E., Vanneschi, L.: Genetic programming for computational pharmacokinetics in drug discovery and development. Genetic Programming and Evolvable Machines 8, 413–432 (2007)
2. Beadle, L., Johnson, C.: Semantically driven crossover in genetic programming. In: Proc. of the IEEE World Congress on Comput. Intelligence, pp. 111–116. IEEE Press (2008)
3. Jones, T., Forrest, S.: Fitness distance correlation as a measure of problem difficulty for genetic algorithms. In: Proceedings of the Sixth International Conference on Genetic Algorithms, pp. 184–192. Morgan Kaufmann (1995)
4. Kennedy, T.: Managing the drug discovery/development interface. Drug Discovery Today 2(10), 436–444 (1997)
5. Koza, J.R.: Genetic Programming: On the Programming of Computers by Means of Natural Selection. MIT Press, Cambridge (1992)
6. Krawiec, K.: Medial Crossovers for Genetic Programming. In: Moraglio, A., Silva, S., Krawiec, K., Machado, P., Cotta, C. (eds.) EuroGP 2012. LNCS, vol. 7244, pp. 61–72. Springer, Heidelberg (2012)
7. Krawiec, K., Lichocki, P.: Approximating geometric crossover in semantic space. In: GECCO 2009, July 8-12, pp. 987–994. ACM (2009)
8. Langdon, W.B., Poli, R.: Foundations of Genetic Programming. Springer (2002)
9. McPhee, N.F., Ohs, B., Hutchison, T.: Semantic Building Blocks in Genetic Programming. In: O'Neill, M., Vanneschi, L., Gustafson, S., Esparcia Alcázar, A.I., De Falco, I., Della Cioppa, A., Tarantino, E. (eds.) EuroGP 2008. LNCS, vol. 4971, pp. 134–145. Springer, Heidelberg (2008)
10. Moraglio, A., Krawiec, K., Johnson, C.G.: Geometric Semantic Genetic Programming. In: Coello Coello, C.A., Cutello, V., Deb, K., Forrest, S., Nicosia, G., Pavone, M. (eds.) PPSN XII, Part I. LNCS, vol. 7491, pp. 21–31. Springer, Heidelberg (2012)
11. Nguyen, Q.U., Nguyen, X.H., O'Neill, M.: Semantic Aware Crossover for Genetic Programming: The Case for Real-Valued Function Regression. In: Vanneschi, L., Gustafson, S., Moraglio, A., De Falco, I., Ebner, M. (eds.) EuroGP 2009. LNCS, vol. 5481, pp. 292–302. Springer, Heidelberg (2009)
12. Quang, U.N., Nguyen, X.H., O'Neill, M.: Semantics based mutation in genetic programming: The case for real-valued symbolic regression. In: Matousek, R., Nolle, L. (eds.) 15th Intern. Conf. on Soft Computing, Mendel 2009, pp. 73–91 (2009)
13. Uy, N.Q., Hoai, N.X., O'Neill, M., McKay, B.: The Role of Syntactic and Semantic Locality of Crossover in Genetic Programming. In: Schaefer, R., Cotta, C., Kołodziej, J., Rudolph, G. (eds.) PPSN XI. LNCS, vol. 6239, pp. 533–542. Springer, Heidelberg (2010)
14. Uy, N.Q., Hoai, N.X., O'Neill, M., McKay, R.I., Galvan-Lopez, E.: Semantically-based crossover in genetic programming: application to real-valued symbolic regression. Genetic Programming and Evolvable Machines 12(2), 91–119 (2011)

A Grammar-Guided Genetic Programming Algorithm for Multi-Label Classification

Alberto Cano, Amelia Zafra, Eva L. Gibaja, and Sebastián Ventura

Department of Computer Science and Numerical Analysis
University of Cordoba, 14071 Cordoba, Spain
{acano,azafra,egibaja,sventura}@uco.es

Abstract. Multi-label classification is a challenging problem which demands new knowledge discovery methods. This paper presents a Grammar-Guided Genetic Programming algorithm for solving multi-label classification problems using IF-THEN classification rules. This algorithm, called G3P-ML, is evaluated and compared to other multi-label classification techniques in different application domains. Computational experiments show that G3P-ML often obtains better results than other algorithms while achieving a lower number of rules than the other methods.

Keywords: Multi-label classification, grammar-guided genetic programming, rule learning.

1 Introduction

Classification is a common task in supervised learning. Traditional classification associates a single label to the examples from a set of disjoint labels L. This problem is known as binary classification when $|L| = 2$ whereas it is known as multi-class classification when $|L| > 2$. Multi-label classification [16] is a classification paradigm where examples are simultaneously associated with a set of labels $Y \subseteq L$. Nowadays, many different challenging applications motivate multi-label classification methods [2,6,12,15,22]. According to Tsoumakas et al. [16], the existing methods for multi-label classification are grouped in two main categories: algorithm adaptation and problem transformation.

Algorithm adaptation methods extend traditional algorithms in order to handle multi-label data directly [3,23]. Problem transformation methods transform the multi-label classification problem into one or more single-label classification problems, which can be solved using traditional classifiers. Binary Relevance (BR) and Label Powerset (LP) are two of the most applied problem transformation methods.

On the one hand, BR employs a single-label classifier for each label, resulting in $|L|$ independent binary classifiers. However, it assumes label independency and ignores label correlations that exist in the data. On the other hand, LP generates each unique combination of the original labels as a new label. LP transformation directly takes into account label correlations but suffers from the large number of label subsets, the majority of which are associated with very few examples.

K. Krawiec et al. (Eds.): EuroGP 2013, LNCS 7831, pp. 217–228, 2013.
© Springer-Verlag Berlin Heidelberg 2013

Genetic Programming (GP) [11] is a learning methodology belonging to the family of evolutionary computation [21] and it has valuable characteristics such as its great flexibility for representing solutions, and the fact that a priori knowledge is not needed about the statistical distribution of the data (data distribution free). These characteristics convert GP into a paradigm of growing interest for obtaining classification rules [8] showing that GP is a mature field that efficiently achieves low error rates in supervised learning. These results suggest that it would be interesting to adapt this paradigm to multi-label classification and check its performance, since GP has not been applied to multi-label classification yet.

This paper presents a new Grammar-Guided Genetic Programming (G3P) [20] algorithm called G3P-ML to deal with multi-label classification. G3P-ML obtains a set of IF-THEN classification rules which provide a natural and human-understandable representation of the knowledge discovered.

The proposal employs a context-free grammar, which establishes a formal definition of the syntactical restrictions of the problem to be solved and its possible solutions, so that only grammatically correct individuals are generated. The comprehensibility of the knowledge discovered has been an area of growing interest and this comprehensibility is currently considered to be just as important as obtaining high predictive accuracy. This way, the user can understand the system's results and combine them with his/her knowledge to make a well-informed decision, rather than blindly trusting the incomprehensible output of a black box system. Therefore, G3P-ML has the advantage of being able to add comprehensibility and clarity to the knowledge discovery process.

The proposal is analyzed, evaluated and compared to other rule-based multi-label classification techniques in a collection of multi-label data sets. Experimental results shows that G3P-ML often obtains better results than the other algorithms while keeping the number of rules lower than the other methods, i.e., providing more simple and comprehensible classifiers.

The paper is structured as follows. Section 2 describes the proposed algorithm. Section 3 evaluates and compares our algorithm to rule-based techniques implemented in six data sets. Section 4 presents the experimental study setup. Finally, Section 5 presents the conclusions of this work.

2   G3P-ML Algorithm

This section presents the algorithm, the individual and the classifier representation, the genetic operators, the fitness function and the evolutionary process.

2.1   Individual Representation

G3P-ML employs an individual = IF-THEN rule representation. The IF part of the rule (antecedent) contains a logical combination about the values of predicting attributes, and the THEN part (consequent) contains the predicted class for the concepts satisfied by the antecedent of the rule. The rule determines whether an example is considered to belong to the class from the consequent. The antecedent represents the individual genotype, while the phenotype represents the entire rule that is applied to the examples. Figure 1 shows the rules' grammar.

$\langle S \rangle \rightarrow \langle cmp \rangle \mid OR \langle S \rangle \langle cmp \rangle \mid AND \langle S \rangle \langle cmp \rangle$
$\langle cmp \rangle \rightarrow \langle op\_num \rangle \langle variable \rangle \langle value \rangle \mid \langle op\_cat \rangle \langle variable \rangle \langle value \rangle$
$\langle op\_num \rangle \rightarrow \geq \mid > \mid < \mid \leq$
$\langle op\_cat \rangle \rightarrow = \mid \neq$
$\langle variable \rangle \rightarrow$ *Any valid attribute in dataset*
$\langle value \rangle \rightarrow$ *Any valid value*

Fig. 1. Grammar used for representing the individuals' genotypes in G3P-ML

2.2   Classifier Representation

The classifier provided by G3P-ML is a rule base that consists of several IF-THEN classification rules obtained from the evolutionary process. The predicted labels for an example are the aggregation of the consequents from the rules whose antecedent satisfies the example. The number of rules is undetermined and the evolutionary process is responsible to discover the most appropiate ones. This classification model induction is shown in Figure 2.

IF rule$_1$ *covers* example $THEN$ example *belongs to label$_i$*
IF rule$_2$ *covers* example $THEN$ example *belongs to label$_j$*
IF rule$_3$ *covers* example $THEN$ example *belongs to label$_k$*

Example *belongs to* $\{label_i, label_j, label_k\}$

Fig. 2. Multi-label classifier by means of IF-THEN classification rules

2.3   Initialization

The initialization process generates the initial population. Our algorithm employs a simple and commonly used approach to generate the individuals by means of the context-free grammar. This approach employs the production rules of the language defined by the grammar, generating only valid individuals and guaranteeing that the syntax tree generated adopts the size set by the user between a maximum and minimum number of derivations.

The creation of a new individual consists of two steps: the former selects a valid derivation value for the current individual, the latter derivates the production rules to generate the syntax tree within the selected number of derivations. The derivations of the production rules start with the initial symbol of the grammar (axiom), and then choose one of the available productions for this axiom. The process continues derivating the non-terminal symbols of the production rules until all the non-terminal symbols have been derivated to terminal ones.

The choice of the production rules to generate new individuals is not made totally at random. In order to guarantee that the syntax tree generated is valid and uses the appropriate number of derivations, the algorithm calculates a selection probability for each symbol according to the allowed number of derivations.

2.4   Genetic Operators

G3P-ML uses two genetic operators to generate new individuals in a given generation of the evolutionary algorithm. These operators are based on selective crossover and selective mutation as proposed by Whigham [19], and their basic principles and functioning are briefly described in this section.

Crossover Operator. The crossover operator creates new rules by mixing the contents of two parent rules. To do so, a non-terminal symbol is chosen at random with uniform probability from among the available non-terminal symbols in the grammar and two sub-trees (one from each parent) are selected whose roots coincide with the symbol adopted or with a compatible symbol.

All non-terminal symbols (excepting the root symbol) have the same probability of being selected as the symbol from which swap the sub-trees. On the other hand, in order to reduce bloating, if one of the new offspring surpasses the maximum size allowed, one of the two parents is randomly selected to pass, without modification, to the next generation. If both offspring surpass this size or at least one of them does not contain a symbol compatible with the chosen symbol, the crossover is aborted and both parents are reproduced.

Mutation Operator. The mutation operator is responsible for preventing the loss of genetic diversity in the population, which is highly significant in the genetic convergence process. It produces small random changes in an individual to engender a new offspring and continue the search process. This operator randomly selects the node in the tree where the mutation is to take place. If the node is terminal symbol, it will be replaced by another compatible terminal. More precisely, two nodes are compatible if they are derivations of the same non-terminal.

When the selected node is a non-terminal symbol, the subtree underneath this node will substitute any other valid derivation subtree as a result. For that reason, a new production of the grammar is derived for this non-terminal symbol. The procedure used to generate this subtree is the same as the one used to create new individuals and guarantees that the individual does not exceed the maximum size allowed.

2.5   Fitness Function

The fitness function measures the effectiveness of the rule represented by an individual. The results of the matching of the rules and the examples from the data set are used to build the confusion matrix, which is a table with two rows and two columns that reports the number of true positives (T_P), false positives

(F_P), true negatives (T_N), and false negatives (F_N). There are several measures to evaluate the quality of the rules using the data from the confusion matrix. Our fitness function combines two commonly used indicators, namely precision and recall. Precision measures the number of examples correctly labelled as belonging to the class divided by the number of examples that the rule has considered as belonging to the label, whereas recall, also called sensitivity in some fields, measures the number of examples correctly labelled as belonging to the class divided by the number of examples that belong to the label.

$$Precision = \frac{T_P}{T_P + F_P} \qquad Recall = \frac{T_P}{T_P + F_N}$$

$$Fitness = F\text{--}Measure = 2 \cdot \frac{Precision \cdot Recall}{Precison + Recall}$$

The fitness function computes the harmonic mean of precision and recall, known as the F-Measure. The goal of the algorithm is to maximize both precision and recall, which evaluate different and conflicting characteristics in the classification process. In addition, to ensure the better simplicity of the rules, for equally fitness rules, the simplest with the lower number of conditions prevails.

2.6   Evolutionary Algorithm

The algorithm is run several times to find classification rules, focussing each run on a particular label, and labelling as negative examples all the examples relative to the other classes. Therefore, the minimum number of runs required to cover all the labels is equal to the number of labels $|L|$. However, one rule may not be sufficient to cover the majority of the examples of a label. In that case, the algorithm focusses on learning rules over the uncovered examples from that label. This behaviour is controlled by a parameter which defines the minimum label coverage. The algorithm will continue finding rules for the label until its minimum coverage has been achieved. Once a rule is learned, it is necessary to evaluate its suitability for being included in the classifier, by checking its own coverage. Thus, the algorithm also defines a parameter for the minimum coverage of the rules. When the minimum label coverage has been exceeded or the rule learned does not achieve the minimum coverage required, the algorithm continues with the next label until all the labels have been covered.

The main steps of our algorithm are based on a classical generational and elitist evolutionary algorithm. A population of classification rules is initially generated following the initialization procedure described in Section 2.3. The population is evaluated using the fitness function described in Section 2.5. The main loop of the algorithm is composed of the following phases. First, the parent selection phase where individuals are selected by means of binary tournaments. Then, the recombination and mutation processes described in Section 2.4 are carried out with a certain degree of probability, obtaining the offspring, whose individuals are evaluated. Finally, the population is updated by direct replacement, that is, the resulting offspring replace the current population. The algorithm employs elitism to keep the best individual.

The algorithm run finishes when one of the four following conditions is met. Two of them are related to the minimum coverage: the accumulated coverage of the current label exceed the minimum required, or if the rule coverage does not achieve the minimum required. The other two are related to evolutionary performance: the maximum number of generations is reached or if the best individual in the population achieves the optimal of the fitness function. Once the run has finished, the best individual (rule) obtained is appended to the classifier.

3   Experimental Study

This section describes the details of the experiments performed to evaluate the capabilities of the proposal and compare it to other ML classification methods.

3.1   Problem Domains

Six data sets are used in the experiments to evaluate the proposal and compare to other methods. The data sets have been selected from the MULAN [17] and KEEL [1] repository website and they are very varied in their degree of complexity, number of labels, number of attributes, and number of examples.

Table 1 summarises the information about these data sets, including the label cardinality and density which indicate how multi-labelled a dataset is. Label cardinality is the average number of labels of the examples in D whereas label density of D is the average number of labels in D divided by $|L|$.

Table 1. Data sets information

Data set	Examples	Attributes	Labels	Cardinality	Density
Emotions	593	72	6	1.8684	0.3114
Enron	1702	1001	53	3.3783	0.0637
Genbase	662	1186	27	1.2522	0.0463
Medical	978	1449	45	1.2453	0.0276
Scene	2407	294	6	1.0739	0.1789
Yeast	2417	103	14	4.2370	0.3026

3.2   Comparison of the Algorithms and Experimental Settings

MULAN is built on top of WEKA [10] and it provides the Binary Relevance (BR) and Label Powerset (LP) transformation methods to prepare the multi-label data for the classical classifiers. There are three well-known classification algorithms from WEKA that produce classification rules: J48 [13], JRIP [4], and PART [9]. The problem transformation methods together with the base classifiers result in the BR-J48, BR-JRIP, BR-PART, LP-J48, LP-JRIP, and LP-PART combinations. The parameters for the base classifiers are the default provided by WEKA.

Our proposal has been implemented in the JCLEC software [18] and its main parameters are shown in Table 2. All experiments are repeated with 10 different seeds and the average results are shown in the result tables. The data sets are partitioned using the 10-fold cross-validation procedure.

Table 2. G3P-ML parameters

Parameter	Value	Parameter	Value
Population size	1000	Parents selector	Binary tournament
Number of generations	250	Maximum tree depth	100
Crossover probability	95%	Minimum label coverage	90%
Mutation probability	30%	Minimum rule coverage	5%

4   Results

This section presents and discusses the experimental results from the experimental studies, which evaluate and compare our method to the different algorithms.

In order to analyse the results from the experiments, some non-parametric statistical tests are used to validate the results. The Iman and Davenport test is performed to evaluate whether there are significant differences in the results. This useful non-parametric test, recommended by Demsar [5], is applied to rank the algorithms over the data sets according to the F-distribution. When the Iman and Davenport test indicates that the results are significantly different, the Bonferroni–Dunn post hoc test [7] is used to find the significant differences occurring between algorithms in the multiple comparison.

Table 3 shows the average Hamming loss [14] results (to minimize) from the 10-fold cross validation test folds for the different methods (rows) and data sets (columns). The Hamming loss considers the prediction error (an incorrect label is predicted) and missing error (a label is not predicted) at the same time. G3P-ML often obtains the best results with the lowest Hamming loss value whereas LP-J48 obtains the worst results. The difference is especially noticeable in Emotions, Genbase and Medical datasets.

The Iman and Davenport statistic (distributed according to the F-distribution with 6 and 30 degrees of freedom) is 11.9127 for Hamming loss. This test establishes an F-distribution value $= 2.4205$ for a significance level of alpha $= 0.05$. This value is lower than the statistic critical value 11.9127. Thus, the test rejects the null hypothesis and therefore it can be said that there are statistically significant differences between the Hamming loss results of the algorithms.

Figure 3 shows the application of the Bonferroni–Dunn test to the Hamming loss with alpha $= 0.05$, whose critical difference is 3.2901. This graph represents a bar chart, whose values are proportional to the mean rank obtained from each algorithm. The critical difference value is represented as a thicker horizontal line and those values that exceed this line are algorithms with significantly different results than the control algorithm, which is G3P-ML. Therefore, the

Table 3. Hamming loss results from the test folds of the 10-fold cross-validation

Data set	Emotions	Enron	Genbase	Medical	Scene	Yeast
G3P-ML	**0.1587**	**0.0515**	**0.0002**	**0.0052**	0.1161	0.2906
BR-J48	0.2510	0.0603	0.0011	0.0114	0.1289	0.2499
BR-JRIP	0.2522	0.0564	0.0012	0.0118	**0.1132**	**0.2158**
BR-PART	0.2529	0.0668	0.0014	0.0124	0.1170	0.2203
LP-J48	0.2749	0.0711	0.0711	0.0142	0.1415	0.2786
LP-JRIP	0.2869	0.0652	0.0050	0.0154	0.1292	0.2633
LP-PART	0.2653	0.0737	0.0025	0.0157	0.1358	0.2907

Table 4. Accuracy results from the test folds of the 10-fold cross-validation

Data set	Emotions	Enron	Genbase	Medical	Scene	Yeast
G3P-ML	**0.4999**	**0.3898**	**0.9896**	0.7328	0.5559	0.4426
BR-J48	0.4491	0.3883	0.9862	**0.7333**	0.5526	0.4353
BR-JRIP	0.4362	0.3604	0.9851	0.7031	0.5700	0.4403
BR-PART	0.4274	0.3780	0.9834	0.7164	0.5938	**0.4620**
LP-J48	0.4396	0.3521	0.3521	0.7209	0.5952	0.4108
LP-JRIP	0.4255	0.2645	0.9650	0.6876	**0.6279**	0.4332
LP-PART	0.4589	0.3312	0.9766	0.6927	0.6128	0.3904

algorithms right beyond the critical difference from the proposal value are significantly worse. Observing this figure, G3P-ML obtains statistically significantly better results than all Label Powerset methods. On the other hand, G3P-ML achieves better results than Binary Relevance methods, but the differences are lower than the statistical critical difference.

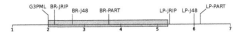

Fig. 3. Bonferroni–Dunn test for Hamming loss

Table 4 shows the average example-based accuracy results. The accuracy differences are less significant and valuable in this case. G3P-ML achieves the highest average accuracy, followed closely by BR-PART. On the other hand, LP-JRIP obtains among the worst results, and LP-J48 fails most of the predictions in Genbase.

The Iman and Davenport statistic is 1.7741 for the accuracy. Thus, it accepts the null-hynothesis that all algorithms perform equally well respect to accuracy.

Table 5 and Table 6 show the example-based precision and recall results. G3P-ML does not achieve a high precision when compared with the other methods since their policy is very conservative, i. e., they run away from the risk of failing predictions. This behaviour manages them to maintain a high precision, but at the cost of a much lower recall. On the other hand, G3P-ML obtains the highest recall.

Table 5. Precision results from the test folds of the 10-fold cross-validation

Data set	Emotions	Enron	Genbase	Medical	Scene	Yeast
G3P-ML	0.5687	0.4535	0.9966	0.7952	0.6059	0.4842
BR-J48	0.5988	0.5649	0.9947	0.8395	0.6978	0.6014
BR-JRIP	**0.6175**	**0.5972**	**0.9970**	**0.8544**	**0.7561**	**0.7011**
BR-PART	0.6066	0.5159	0.9927	0.8251	0.7328	0.6712
LP-J48	0.5452	0.4749	0.4749	0.7699	0.6182	0.5387
LP-JRIP	0.5291	0.4124	0.9706	0.7391	0.6510	0.5675
LP-PART	0.5748	0.4497	0.9920	0.7409	0.6342	0.5192

Table 6. Recall results from the test folds of the 10-fold cross-validation

Data set	Emotions	Enron	Genbase	Medical	Scene	Yeast
G3P-ML	**0.7495**	**0.7096**	**0.9930**	**0.8519**	**0.7722**	**0.8188**
BR-J48	0.5879	0.5133	0.9914	0.8062	0.6445	0.5753
BR-JRIP	0.5406	0.4573	0.9882	0.7568	0.6354	0.4970
BR-PART	0.5521	0.5379	0.9907	0.7956	0.6800	0.5527
LP-J48	0.5496	0.4660	0.4660	0.7480	0.6163	0.5430
LP-JRIP	0.5360	0.2947	0.9665	0.7036	0.6483	0.5527
LP-PART	0.5758	0.4483	0.9800	0.7264	0.6319	0.5145

The Iman and Davenport statistic is 14.8425 for precision and 13.2278 for recall, both lower than the statistic critical value. Figure 4 shows the application of the Bonferroni–Dunn test to the precision and recall. BR-JRIP obtains the highest precision ranking, and BR transformations demonstrate to perform much better than LP ones, which achieves similar results than G3P-ML. G3P-ML obtains the highest recall ranking, and always obtains better recall results than the other methods. On the other hand, BR-JRIP, which obtained the best precision ranking, now obtains significantly lower ranking regarding to the recall values. Since precision and recall are conflicting characteristics, none of the algorithms is clearly performing better than the others and therefore the harmonic mean of precision and recall (F-Measure) is used to evaluate together, which represents a balance among them.

Table 7 shows the macro and micro averaged F-Measures [16]. G3P-ML often achieves better F-Measure values than the other methods whereas Label Powerset transformations obtain the worst.

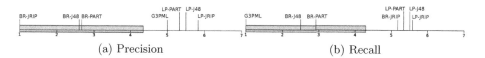

(a) Precision   (b) Recall

Fig. 4. Bonferroni–Dunn test for the precision and recall

Table 7. F-measure results from the test folds of the 10-fold cross-validation

Data set		Emotions	Enron	Genbase	Medical	Scene	Yeast
G3P-ML	Macro	**0.6261**	**0.5319**	**0.9958**	0.8065	0.6497	**0.4783**
	Micro	**0.6347**	**0.5360**	**0.9913**	0.7772	0.6310	0.5913
BR-J48	Macro	0.5849	0.4272	0.9942	**0.8426**	0.6481	0.4529
	Micro	0.5942	0.5107	0.9883	**0.7936**	0.6379	0.5817
BR-JRIP	Macro	0.5569	0.4156	0.9951	0.8185	0.6678	0.4025
	Micro	0.5706	0.5060	0.9876	0.7760	0.6635	0.5841
BR-PART	Macro	0.5534	0.4157	0.9941	0.8205	**0.6831**	0.4224
	Micro	0.5817	0.4980	0.9857	0.7760	**0.6719**	**0.6024**
LP-J48	Macro	0.5431	0.3617	0.3617	0.8017	0.6159	0.4246
	Micro	0.5580	0.4371	0.4371	0.7394	0.6051	0.5407
LP-JRIP	Macro	0.5227	0.3060	0.9500	0.7835	0.6501	0.4143
	Micro	0.5361	0.3174	0.9447	0.7102	0.6379	0.5599
LP-PART	Macro	0.5580	0.3413	0.9807	0.7827	0.6321	0.3986
	Micro	0.5752	0.4228	0.9733	0.7152	0.6211	0.5180

The Iman and Davenport statistic is 5.7692 and 10.7009 for the F-Measure, both lower than the statistic critical values. Figure 5 shows the application of the Bonferroni–Dunn test to the F-Measure.

(a) Macro-averaged   (b) Micro-averaged

Fig. 5. Bonferroni–Dunn test for the F-Measure

Table 8 shows the average number of rules from the classifiers. Classification with rule-based systems comes with two contradictory requirements in the obtained model: the complexity and the exactness (accuracy, precision, recall, F-Measure). The higher number of rules, the more capability to faithfully represent the data, but also the more complexity of the rule base and therefore the lower interpretability and comprehensibility of the model and knowledge discovered. It is interesting to highlight these results and compare the number of labels from the data sets with the number of rules employed by the classifiers. G3P-ML obtains classifiers with a significantly lower number of rules than the other methods. On the other hand, BR-J48 obtains the highest number of rules.

Figure 6 shows the application of the Bonferroni–Dunn test to the number of rules. G3P-ML obtains statistically significantly better results than BR-J48, BR-PART, and LP-J48. On the other hand, G3P-ML achieves better results than BR-JRIP, LP-JRIP and LP-PART, but the differences are lower than the statistical critical difference.

Table 8. Number of rules results from the 10-fold cross-validation

Data set	Emotions	Enron	Genbase	Medical	Scene	Yeast
G3P-ML	**12.6**	227.1	26.6	**69.0**	**14.8**	**34.3**
BR-J48	209.8	2390.9	54.2	257.3	429.7	1504.1
BR-JRIP	75.6	364.6	54.0	160.6	93.1	116.8
BR-PART	98.1	2164.8	66.7	252.8	168.0	242.6
LP-J48	134.8	537.0	537.0	143.3	262.7	653.4
LP-JRIP	78.6	**176.4**	**23.7**	99.7	97.9	312.2
LP-PART	120.7	517.8	31.6	157.9	186.2	616.4

Fig. 6. Bonferroni–Dunn test for the number of rules

5   Conclusion

In this paper we presented a new Grammar-Guided Genetic Programming algorithm, called G3P-ML, for solving multi-label classification problems using comprehensible IF-THEN classification rules. Our proposal is compared to other rule-based multi-label classification techniques, considering the problem transformation techniques for multi-label data, over six data sets. Experimental results show that our proposal obtains better results than other algorithms in most of the performance metrics considered. Moreover, it achieves the lowest number of rules and therefore the more simplicity and interpretability of the knowledge model extracted. The results were validated using non-parametric statistical tests, whose reports support the better performance of our proposal. Another interesting conclusion obtained in this study, it is that BR problem transformations have demonstrated to perform much better than LP ones, achieving better results in all the metrics evaluated. However, they produce classifiers with a high number of rules, considering the number of labels.

Acknowledgments. This work has been supported by the Regional Government of Andalusia and the Ministry of Science and Technology, projects P08-TIC-3720 and TIN-2011-22408, FEDER funds, and FPU grant AP2010-0042.

References

1. Alcalá-Fdez, J., Fernandez, A., Luengo, J., Derrac, J., García, S., Sánchez, L., Herrera, F.: KEEL Data-Mining Software Tool: Data Set Repository, Integration of Algorithms and Experimental Analysis Framework. Journal of Multiple-Valued Logic and Soft Computing 17, 255–287 (2011)
2. Boutell, M.R., Luo, J., Shen, X., Brown, C.M.: Learning multi-label scene classification. Pattern Recognition 37(9), 1757–1771 (2004)

3. Chen, B., Ma, L., Hu, J.: An improved multi-label classification method based on svm with delicate decision boundary. International Journal of Innovative Computing, Information and Control 6(4), 1605–1614 (2010)
4. Cohen, W.W.: Fast Effective Rule Induction. In: 12th International Conference on Machine Learning, pp. 1–10 (1995)
5. Demšar, J.: Statistical Comparisons of Classifiers over Multiple Data Sets. Machine Learning Research 7, 1–30 (2006)
6. Diplaris, S., Tsoumakas, G., Mitkas, P.A., Vlahavas, I.P.: Protein Classification with Multiple Algorithms. In: Bozanis, P., Houstis, E.N. (eds.) PCI 2005. LNCS, vol. 3746, pp. 448–456. Springer, Heidelberg (2005)
7. Dunn, O.J.: Multiple Comparisons Among Means. Journal of the American Statistical Association 56(293), 52–64 (1961)
8. Espejo, P.G., Ventura, S., Herrera, F.: A survey on the application of genetic programming to classification. IEEE Transactions on Systems, Man, and Cybernetics, Part C: Applications and Reviews 40(2), 121–144 (2010)
9. Frank, E., Witten, I.H.: Generating Accurate Rule Sets Without Global Optimization. In: 15th International Conference on Machine Learning, pp. 144–151 (1998)
10. Hall, M., Frank, E., Holmes, G., Pfahringer, B., Reutemannr, P., Witten, I.H.: The WEKA Data Mining Software: An Update. SIGKDD 11, 10–18 (2009)
11. Koza, J.: Genetic Programming: On the Programming of Computers by Means of Natural Selection. MIT Press (1992)
12. Ngan, P.S., Wong, M.L., Lam, W., Leung, K.S., Cheng, J.C.: Medical data mining using evolutionary computation. Artificial Intelligence in Medicine 16(1), 73–96 (1999)
13. Quinlan, J.R.: C4.5: Programs for Machine Learning. Morgan Kaufmann Publishers, San Francisco (1993)
14. Schapire, R.E., Singer, Y.: BoosTexter: A Boosting-based System for Text Categorization. Machine Learning 39, 135–168 (2000)
15. Trohidis, K., Tsoumakas, G., Kalliris, G., Vlahavas, I.: Multilabel classification of music into emotions. In: 9th Int. Conf. on Music Information Retrieval (2008)
16. Tsoumakas, G., Katakis, I.: Multi-label classification: An overview. International Journal of Data Warehousing and Mining 3(3), 1–13 (2007)
17. Tsoumakas, G., Katakis, I., Vlahavas, I.: Mining Multi-label Data. In: Data Mining and Knowledge Discovery Handbook, pp. 667–685 (2010)
18. Ventura, S., Romero, C., Zafra, A., Delgado, J.A., Hervás, C.: JCLEC: A Java Framework for Evolutionary Computation. Soft Computing 12, 381–392 (2007)
19. Whigham, P.A.: Schema theorem for context-free grammars. In: 2nd IEEE Conference on Evolutionary Computation, vol. 1, pp. 178–181 (1995)
20. Wong, M.L., Leung, K.S.: Data Mining Using Grammar Based Genetic Programming and Applications. Kluwer Academic Publisher (2000)
21. Yu, X., Gen, M.: Introduction to Evolutionary Algorithms. Springer (2010)
22. Zhang, M.L., Zhou, Z.H.: Multilabel neural networks with applications to functional genomics and text categorization. IEEE Transactions on Knowledge and Data Engineering 18, 1338–1351 (2006)
23. Zhang, M.L., Zhou, Z.H.: Ml-knn: A lazy learning approach to multi-label learning. Pattern Recognition 40, 2038–2048 (2007)

Global Top-Scoring Pair Decision Tree for Gene Expression Data Analysis

Marcin Czajkowski and Marek Kretowski

Faculty of Computer Science, Bialystok University of Technology
Wiejska 45a, 15-351 Białystok, Poland
{m.czajkowski,m.kretowski}@pb.edu.pl

Abstract. Extracting knowledge from gene expression data is still a major challenge. Relative expression algorithms use the ordering relationships for a small collection of genes and are successfully applied for micro-array classification. However, searching for all possible subsets of genes requires a significant number of calculations, assumptions and limitations. In this paper we propose an evolutionary algorithm for global induction of top-scoring pair decision trees. We have designed several specialized genetic operators that search for the best tree structure and the splits in internal nodes which involve pairwise comparisons of the gene expression values. Preliminary validation performed on real-life micro-array datasets is promising as the proposed solution is highly competitive to other relative expression algorithms and allows exploring much larger solution space.

Keywords: evolutionary algorithms, decision tree, top-scoring pair, classification, gene expression, micro-array.

1 Introduction

DNA chips [16] may be used to assist diagnosis and to discriminate cancer samples from normal ones [17]. Extracting accurate and simple decision rules that contains marker genes are of great interest for biomedical applications. However, finding a meaningful and robust classification rule is a real challenge, since in different studies of the same cancer, diverse genes consider to be marked [23].

Dimensionality and redundancy are one of the most typical statistical problems that often occur with micro-array analysis. In particular, we are faced with the *"small N, large P problem"* [27] of statistical learning. The number of samples (denoted by N) comparing to the number of genes (P) remains quite small as N usually does not exceeded one or two hundreds where P is usually several thousands. The high ratio of features/observations may influence the model complexity and can cause the classifier to over-fit the training data. Furthermore, most of genes are known to be irrelevant so the gene selection prior to classification should be considered [17] to: simplify calculations, decrease model complexity and often to improve accuracy of the following classification.

Recently, a large number of supervised solutions have been described in literature for micro-array classification, including: nearest neighbors [8], neural

K. Krawiec et al. (Eds.): EuroGP 2013, LNCS 7831, pp. 229–240, 2013.
© Springer-Verlag Berlin Heidelberg 2013

networks [3], Support Vector Machine [20] and random forests [7]. Most of machine learning methods provide "black box" decision rules, which usually involve many genes combined in a highly complex fashion and therefore are difficult to interpret from medical point of view. There is a need for simple models like decision trees or rule extraction systems which may actually help in understanding and identifying casual relationships between specific genes.

In this paper we propose a hybrid solution called Global Top-Scoring Pair Decision Tree ($GTSPDT$) that combines the power of evolutionary approach, relative expression algorithms and decision trees. It combines different top-scoring extensions, eliminates their restrictions and allows exploring much larger solution space. Evolutionary algorithm (EA) globally searches for the best tree structure and tests which involve pairwise comparisons of the gene expression values. The general structure of our solution follows a typical framework of EA with an unstructured population and a generational selection. We have designed several specialized operators to mutate and cross-over individuals and a fitness function that helps mitigating the over-fitting problem.

The rest of the paper is organized as follows. In the next section the relative expression algorithms and decision tree classifiers for gene expression analysis are briefly recalled. Section 3 describes in detail the $GTSPDT$ solution and section 4 presents preliminary experimental validation on real-life micro-array datasets. In the last section, the paper is concluded and possible future works are sketched.

2   Background and Motivation

In this section the decision trees and the family of top-scoring algorithms are presented and their application for gene expression data is discussed.

2.1   Decision Trees

Decision trees (also known as classification trees) [22] represent one of the main techniques of classification analysis in data mining and knowledge discovery. They predict the class membership (dependent variable) of an instance using its measurements of predictor variables.

In the literature, there are several attempts to use decision trees for the classification analysis on gene expression data. In [8] the author compares some classification principles, among which there is the CART system and in [28] the application of C4.5, bagged and boosted decision trees are presented. In [32] the author compares decision trees with SVMs on gene expression data and concludes that bagging and boosting decision tress perform as well as or close to SVM algorithms. However ensemble methods and decision trees with complex multivariate tests based on linear or non-linear combination splits are much more difficult to understand or interpret by human experts. Although higher accuracy than single-tree solutions, their potential for scientific modeling of underlying processes is limited.

2.2   A Family of Top-Scoring Algorithms

Relative expression algorithms [10] are simple yet powerful classifiers. The use of the ordering relationships for a small collection of genes has potential for identify gene-gene interactions with plausible biological interpretation and direct clinical applicability [15]. The most popular solution is called Top-Scoring Pair (TSP) [10] and has many applications in identifying marker genes in micro-array datasets [26] or as a feature selection in more complex classifiers [32]. In addition, the TSP solution is parameter free, data driven learning approach that is invariant to any simple transformation of data like normalization and standardization.

TSP is extended in two main directions, each having its pros and cons. First technique called $k-TSP$ [29] increases the number of top-scoring pairs included in the final prediction. This solution was later extended by weight pairwise comparisons $Weight\ k-TSP$ [4] and Top-Scoring Pair Decision Tree ($TSPDT$) [5]. Different approaches called Top-Scoring Triplet (TST) [15] and Top-Scoring 'N' (TSN) [19] search for more than two ordering relationships between genes. Multiple implementation of these solutions may be found as R package [31].

Top-Scoring Pair. The TSP method proposed by Donald Geman [10] is based on pairwise comparisons of gene expression values. Discrimination between two classes depends on finding pairs of genes that achieve the highest ranking value called "score". Consider a gene expression profile consisting of P genes and N samples participating in the training micro-array dataset. Let the data be represented as a $P \times N$ matrix in which expression value of u-th gene from v-th sample is denoted as x_{uv}. Each row represents observations of a particular gene over N training samples, and each column represents a gene expression profile composed from P genes. Each profile has a true class label denoted $C_m \in C = \{C_1, \ldots, C_M\}$. For the simplicity of calculations it is assumed that there are only two classes ($M = 2$) and profiles with indexes from 1 to N_1 ($N_1 < N$) belong to the first class (C_1) and profiles from range $\langle N_1 + 1, N \rangle$ to the second class (C_2).

The TSP method focuses on gene pair matching (i, j) $(i, j \in \{1, \ldots, P\}, i \neq j)$ for which there is the highest difference in probability p of an event $x_{in} < x_{jn}$ $(n = 1, 2, \ldots, N)$ between class C_1 and C_2. For each pair of genes (i, j) two probabilities are calculated $p_{ij}(C_1)$ and $p_{ij}(C_2)$:

$$p_{ij}(C_1) = \frac{1}{|C_1|} \sum_{n=1}^{N_1} I(x_{in} < x_{jn}),$$

$$p_{ij}(C_2) = \frac{1}{|C_2|} \sum_{n=N_1+1}^{N} I(x_{in} < x_{jn}),$$

where $|C_m|$ denotes a number of profiles from class C_m and $I(x_{in} < x_{jn})$ is the indicator function defined as:

$$I(x_{in} < x_{jn}) = \begin{cases} 1, & \text{if } x_{in} < x_{jn} \\ 0, & \text{if } x_{in} \geq x_{jn} \end{cases}$$

TSP is a rank-based method, so for each pair of genes (i, j) the "score" denoted Δ_{ij} is calculated as:

$$\Delta_{ij} = |p_{ij}(C_1) - p_{ij}(C_2)|.$$

In the next step of the algorithm, pairs with the highest score are chosen.

There should be only one top pair in the TSP method, however it is possible that multiple gene pairs achieve the same top score. In that case a secondary ranking, based on the rank differences in each class and samples, is used to eliminate draws.

$$\gamma_{ij}(C_1) = \frac{\sum_{n=1}^{N_1}(x_{in} - x_{jn})}{|C_1|},$$

$$\gamma_{ij}(C_2) = \frac{\sum_{n=N_1+1}^{N}(x_{in} - x_{jn})}{|C_2|}.$$

For each pair of genes (i, j) the second ranking is calculated and pair with the highest score τ_{ij} is chosen:

$$\tau_{ij} = |\gamma_{ij}(C_1) - \gamma_{ij}(C_2)|,$$

The TSP prediction is made by comparing the relation between expression values of two genes (i, j) marked as "top-scoring pair" in new test sample w. If we observe that $p_{ij}(C_1) \geq p_{ij}(C_2)$ and $x_{iw} < x_{jw}$, then TSP votes for class C_1, however if $x_{iw} \geq x_{jw}$ then TSP votes for class C_2. An opposite situation is when $p_{ij}(C_1) < p_{ij}(C_2)$, cause if $x_{iw} < x_{jw}$ TSP votes for C_1 and if $x_{iw} \geq x_{jw}$ TSP chooses C_2.

Top-Scoring Extensions. There are two main ways to extend the TSP solution: application of multiple pairs of genes or comparison relationships for more than two genes. One of the solutions that uses the first approach is $k-TSP$ [29] which applies no more than k top-scoring pairs in classification. The parameter k can be set up a priori or can be determined by a cross-validation. Next, the $k-TSP$ classifier uses no more than k top scoring disjoint gene pairs that have the highest score and simple majority vote for a final decision.

The $Weight\ k-TSP$ [4] solution modifies rankings of $k-TSP$ and calculates the ratio of two genes in order to find optimal top-scoring pairs.

Solution called $TSPDT$ [5] is a hybrid of $k - TSP$ and a top-down induced decision tree [24]. At first, a test analogous to the $k - TSP$ method is searched for the root node. Then, the set of instances is split according to decision of the best pair (or pairs) of genes in the current node and then each derived subset goes to the corresponding branch. The process is recursively repeated for each branch until leaf node is reached.

Different approach for the TSP extension is discussed in [15] where authors focused on the predicting germline BRCA1 mutations in breast cancer. A three-gene version of relative expression analysis called Top-Scoring Triplet (TST) [15] was proposed as potentially more discriminating than TSP since there are six possible orderings that must be analyzed.

Next, the general idea of pairwise or triplet rank comparisons was proposed in [19]. The top-scoring N (TSN) algorithm uses generic permutations and dynamically adjust the size to control both the permutation and combination space available for classification. Variable N denotes the size of the classifier, therefore in the case where $N = 2$ the TSN algorithm simply reduces to the TSP method and when $N = 3$, the TSN can be seen as TST. The classifier's size can be chosen by a user or by an internal cross-validation that checks classification accuracy for the different values of N (on a training data, in a range specified by the user) and selects the classifier with the highest score.

2.3   Motivation

There are two main drawbacks of TSP extensions. The first one is enormous computational requirements because the general complexity of aforementioned algorithms is $O(k * P^N)$, where k is the number of top-scoring groups, P is the number of features and N is the size of group of genes which ordering relationships is compared. There are some attempts of improving TSP performance by parallelization the algorithm and using graphic processing unit (GPU) for calculations [18], however the parameters k or/and N must be small (upper limit of the test was equal: $N = 4$, $k = 1$ but only when P was significantly reduced by the feature selection).

The second drawback is finding accurate value of the parameters k and N. In TSP extensions they are defined by the user or determined by internal cross-validation. However, it is time consuming and decreases the set of instances which is already very small. In addition, it is also not clear which extension should be prefered: $k - TSP$ or TSN. It should be noted that the $k - TSP$ algorithms cannot replace the TSN with $N > 2$ as the $k - TSP$ has restriction to use only disjoint gene pairs. On the other side, the $k - TST$ or $k - TSN$ were not proposed in the literature, probably because of it's huge complexity.

In the $TSPDT$ system $k - TSP$ algorithm is calculated in each non-terminal tree node, therefore the general complexity must be multiplied by the number of internal nodes. In addition, the $TSPDT$ like most of practical decision-tree inducers is based on heuristics such as greedy approach where locally optimal decisions are made in each node and cannot guarantee to return optimal classifier.

Previously performed research showed that decision trees [11,6], extension of TSP [4] and hybrid solution called $TSPDT$ [5] may be successfully applied to the gene expression data. In this paper we would like to unite aforementioned extensions of TSP through the evolutionary approach. We propose a hybrid solution called Global Top-Scoring Pair Decision Tree ($GTSPDT$) that combines the power of evolutionary approach, relative expression algorithms and decision trees.

Our goal is to improve classification accuracy and help in identifying genomic "marker interactions". Evolutionary algorithm searches for the best tree structure and tests which involve multiple pairwise comparisons of the gene expression values. The number of top-scoring pairs applied in each split is determined by the evolution and by removing restrictions on disjoint gene pairs, the splits may compare relationships for more than two genes like in TSN. Application of evolutionary algorithms to the TSP solutions can decrease computation time and allows to explore larger solution space.

3   Global Top-Scoring Pair Decision Tree

General structure of $GTSPDT$ follows a typical framework of evolutionary algorithms [21] with an unstructured population and a generational selection.

Representation. Decision trees are quite complicated tree structures, in which number of nodes, type of the tests and even number of test outcomes are not known in advance. Therefore, representing individuals in their actual form (as potential tree-solutions) seems more adequate than encoding them in the fixed-size (usually binary) chromosomes.

Figure 1 illustrates the single individual. Each test in a non-terminal node is composed of a group of top-scoring pairs. Similarly to $TSPDT$ and $k-TSP$, the final decision in each node depend on a simple majority voting where each top-scoring pair vote has the same weight. Therefore, the TST solution can be represented by the 3 top-scoring pairs that involve only three genes. In the analogous way, TSN, $k-TSP$ or even a variation $k-TSN$ representation can be found by the $GTSPDT$. In every node information about learning vectors associated with the node is also stored. This enables the algorithm to perform more efficiently local structure and tests modifications during applications of genetic operators.

Initialization. Initial population could be generated randomly to cover the entire range of possible solutions, however due to the large solution space, seeding the initial population with good solutions may speed up evolutionary search. Each individual in the initial population is generated by the classical top-down,

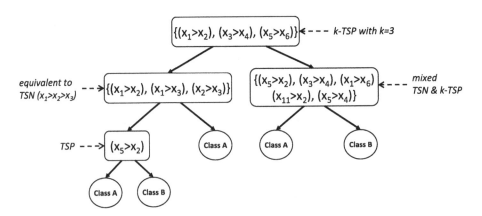

Fig. 1. An example representation of a single individual with different tests in internal nodes

greedy approach. Split in each internal node is based on a mixed dipole strategy [13] and constructed as follows. Among feature vectors located in the node two objects from different classes are randomly chosen. Next, an effective top-scoring pair test (one pair of genes which separates this two objects) constructed on randomly selected attributes constitute a split. The recursive partitioning is finished when the node is pure (all training objects in the node are from the same class) or the number of objects is lower than the predefined value (default value: 5).

Selection and Termination Condition. Ranking linear selection [21] is applied as a selection mechanism. In each iteration, single individual with the highest value of fitness function in current population is copied to the next one *(elitist strategy)*. Evolution terminates when the fitness of the best individual in the population does not improve during the fixed number of generations (default value: 1000). In case of a slow convergence, maximum number of generations is also specified (default value: 10000), which allows to limit the computation time.

Genetic Operators. To maintain genetic diversity, we have proposed two specialized genetic operators corresponding to the classical mutation and cross-over. Each evolutionary iteration starts with randomly choosing the operator type where the default probability to select mutation equals 0.8 and to select cross-over equals 0.2. Both operators have impact on the tree structure and the tests in non-terminal nodes. After each operation it is usually necessary to relocate learning vectors between parts of the tree rooted in the altered node. This can cause that certain parts of the tree does not contain any learning vectors and has to be pruned.

Cross-over starts with selecting positions in two affected individuals. We have adapted three variants of recombination [13]:

- subtrees starting in the selected nodes are exchanged;
- tests associated with the nodes are exchanged (only when non-terminal nodes are chosen);
- branches which start from the selected nodes are exchanged in random order (only when non-terminal nodes are chosen).

Mutation solution starts with randomly choosing the type of node (equal probability to select leaf or internal node). Next, the ranked list of nodes of the selected type is created and a mechanism analogous to ranking linear selection is applied to decide which node will be affected. Depending on the type of node, ranking takes into account two elements:

- location (level) of node. It is evident that modification of the test in the root node affects whole tree and has a great impact, whereas mutation of an internal node in lower parts of the tree has only a local impact. Therefore, internal nodes in lower parts of the tree are mutated with higher probability;
- classification accuracy of the node - worse in terms of prediction accuracy leaves and internal nodes are mutated with higher probability (homogeneous leaves are not included).

Each leaf can be transformed into an internal node with a new dipole test, similar to one used in population initialization. As for the internal nodes, we have propose a few variants of mutation:

- node can be transformed (pruned) into a leaf,
- test in node is replaced by new top-scoring pair,
- one of the attributes from top-scoring pair is replaced by random one which effectively separates at least two objects in the node,
- new top-scoring pair is added or removed from the test in the node,
- tests between father and son exchanged,
- all subtrees are replaced with randomly chosen one.

Fitness Function. Specification of a suitable fitness function is one of the most important and sensitive element in the design of evolutionary algorithm. It drives the evolutionary search process and measures how good a single individual is in terms of meeting the problem objective. Direct minimization of the prediction error measured on the learning set usually leads to the over-fitting problem. In typical top-down tree inducers it is partially mitigated by a stopping condition and an application of the post-pruning [9].

In case of evolutionary induced classification trees, we need to balance the reclassification quality and the complexity of the tree. A similar idea is used in cost complexity pruning in the CART system [2]. The fitness function is maximized and has the following form:

$$Fitness(T) = Q_{Reclass}(T) - \alpha \cdot (2 * S(T) + K(T)),$$

where $Q_{Reclass}(T)$ is the reclassification quality of the tree T, $S(T)$ is the size of the tree expressed as a number of nodes, K is the number of unique genes that were used to build the classifier and α is the relative importance of the complexity term specified by user (default value is 0.05). Penalty associated with the classifier complexity increases proportionally with the tree size and the number of different genes that constitute the top-pairs to prevent over-fitting.

It should be noticed that there is no optimal value of α for all possible datasets and tuning it may lead to the improvement of results for the specific problem. Further research to determine the appropriate value of complexity penalty term for proposed solution is required and other commonly used measures such as Akaikes information criterion (AIC) [1] or Bayesian information criterion (BIC) [25]should be considered.

4   Results and Discussions

Performance of classifiers was investigated on public available micro-array datasets, summarized in Table 1. We have extend previous comparison of TSP-family algorithms [5] by enclosing the accuracy and the size of proposed solution $GTSPDT$. To check and compare results of other popular decision trees and rule classifiers on analyzed data please also refer to [5].

Table 1. Details of Kent Ridge Bio-medical gene expression datasets

Datasets	Symbol	Attributes	Train	Test
Breast Cancer	BC	24481	34/44	12/7
Central Nervous System	CNS	7129	21/39	-
Colon Tumor	CT	6500	40/22	-
DLBCL vs Follicular Lymphoma	DF	6817	58/19	-
Leukemia ALL vs AML	LA	7129	27/11	20/14
Lung Cancer Brigham	LCB	12533	16/16	15/134
Lung Cancer University of Michigan	LCM	7129	86/10	-
Lung Cancer - Totonto, Ontario	LCT	2880	24/15	-
Ovarian Cancer	OC	15154	91/162	-
Prostate Cancer	PC	12600	52/50	27/8

Datasets and Setup. Proposed solution was tested on Kent Ridge Bio-medical Repository [12] and the datasets refer to the studies of human cancer, including: leukemia, colon tumor, prostate cancer, lung cancer, breast cancer, ovarian cancer etc. If datasets, described in Table 1 were not pre-divided into the training and the testing sets we use typical 10-fold cross-validation. To ensure stable results, for all datasets average score of 10 runs is shown.

In the experiments, we have compared proposed solution with TSP, $k-TSP$ and $TSPDT$. The maximum number of top-scoring pairs (parameter k) for $k-TSP$ and $TSPDT$ was set to 9. Classification was performed with default parameters for all algorithms through all datasets and was preceded by a step known as feature selection, where a subset of relevant features is identified. We decided to use popular method called Relief-F [14] for micro-array analysis with its default parameters and 1000 features subset size.

Comparison of Top-Scoring Family Algorithms Methods. Table 2 summaries classification performance for the proposed solution TSP, $k-TSP$, $TSPDT$ and $GTSPDT$. Preliminary results show that on most of datasets, the classification accuracy increased (or did not change) when decision trees with TSP were applied. However, for some datasets, like Colon Tumor, both decision tree solutions did not work well which may suggest over-fitting to the training data. In general $GTSPDT$ managed to increase classification accuracy (average on all datasets over 3%). The greatest improvement of $GTSPDT$ can be noticed on the Lung Cancer datasets. According to the Friedman test, there is a statistically significant difference (p-value of 0.0019) in the accuracy between TSP and $GTSPDT$.

Number of internal nodes and the average number of top-scoring pairs used in $GTSPDT$ classifier presented in Table 2 allows to compare the sizes of tested solutions. The TSP algorithm uses only one pair of genes and $k-TSP$ no more than 9 pairs. The $TSPDT$ tree uses no more than $k=9$ pairs in each internal node, so this value must be multiplied by the tree size. The proposed solution managed to slightly decrease the tree size comparing to $TSPDT$ and used less pairs of genes in each internal node (an average: 2.2).

Table 2. Comparison of top-scoring algorithms, including accuracy, number of internal nodes and the number of gene pairs

Datasets	Classifiers accuracy and size of the solution						
	TSP	k-TSP	TSPDT		GTSPDT		
	accuracy	accuracy	nodes	accuracy	nodes	pairs	accuracy
BC	52.63	68.42	2.0	78.95	1.1	2.9	77.37
CNS	49.00	58.50	3.0	63.00	1.1	3.1	65.00
CT	83.64	88.93	2.0	84.88	1.8	2.6	82.26
DF	72.75	87.82	1.6	95.25	1.4	3.2	97.70
LA	73.53	91.18	1.0	91.18	1.0	1.0	91.18
LCB	76.51	83.89	1.0	83.89	1.0	2.5	93.02
LCM	95.87	95.23	1.1	97.77	1.0	1.1	98.96
LCT	50.92	58.42	2.4	55.33	1.6	2.7	78.46
OC	99.77	100.00	1.0	100.00	1.0	1.0	99.60
PC	76.47	91.18	2.0	94.12	2.2	1.9	91.76
Average	73.11	82.36	1.7	84.44	1.3	2.2	87.53

5   Conclusion

In this paper we propose the $GTSPDT$ system for solving classification problems on micro-array data. The evolutionary approach of the hybrid solution combines the power of decision trees and popular top-scoring algorithms. EA globally searches for the best tree structure and the top-scoring pairs which are used as splitting tests in non-terminal nodes. We have designed several specialized operators to mutate and cross-over individuals (trees) and a fitness function that helps mitigating the over-fitting problem. The $GTSPDT$ solution is highly competitive to other relative expression algorithms in terms of accuracy and the model complexity. It can explore much larger permutation and combination space and therefore has potential to discover new biological connections between genes.

In this paper we only focus on the general concept of $GTSPDT$. We do not enclose any biological aspects of the rules generated by proposed system or case studies on particular datasets. Furthermore improvement is still required. Application of local optimizations (memetic algorithms), new specialized operators and self-adaptive parameters should speed up convergence of the evolutionary algorithm. We also want to test different fitness functions based on e.g. information criterion and extended $GTSPDT$ to handle cost-sensitive and multi-class problems. More work on preprocessing datasets, gene selection and using additional problem-specific knowledge is also required to improve $GTSPDT$ classification and rule discovery.

Acknowledgements. This work was supported by the grant S/WI/2/13 from Bialystok University of Technology.

References

1. Akaike, H.: A New Look at Statistical Model Identification. IEEE Transactions on Automatic Control 19, 716–723 (1974)
2. Breiman, L., Friedman, J.: Classification and Regression Trees. Wadsworth Int. Group (1984)
3. Cho, H.S., Kim, T.S.: cDNA Microarray Data Based Classification of Cancers Using Neural Networks and Genetic Algorithms. Nanotech 1 (2003)
4. Czajkowski, M., Kretowski, M.: Novel Extension of $k - TSP$ Algorithm for Microarray Classification. In: Nguyen, N.T., Borzemski, L., Grzech, A., Ali, M. (eds.) IEA/AIE 2008. LNCS (LNAI), vol. 5027, pp. 456–465. Springer, Heidelberg (2008)
5. Czajkowski, M., Kretowski, M.: Top Scoring Pair Decision Tree for Gene Expression Data Analysis. In: Software Tools and Algorithms for Biological Systems. Advances in Experimental Medicine and Biology, vol. 696, pp. 27–35 (2011)
6. Czajkowski, M., Grześ, M., Kretowski, M.: Multi-Test Decision Trees for Gene Expression Data Analysis. In: Bouvry, P., Kłopotek, M.A., Leprévost, F., Marciniak, M., Mykowiecka, A., Rybiński, H. (eds.) SIIS 2011. LNCS, vol. 7053, pp. 154–167. Springer, Heidelberg (2012)
7. Diaz-Uriarte, R., Alvarez de Andres, S.: Gene selection and classification of microarray data using random forest. BMC Bioinformatics 7, 3 (2006)
8. Dudoit, S.J., Fridlyand, J.: Comparison of discrimination methods for the classification of tumors using gene expression data. Journal of the American Statistical Association 97, 77–87 (2002)
9. Esposito, F., Malerba, D., Semeraro, G.: A comparative analysis of methods for pruning decision trees. IEEE Transactions on Pattern Analysis and Machine Intelligence 19(5), 476–491 (1997)
10. Geman, D., d'Avignon, C., Naiman, D.Q., Winslow, R.L.: Classifying gene expression profiles from pairwise mRNA comparisons. Statistical Applications in Genetics and Molecular Biology 3(19) (2004)
11. Grześ, M., Kretowski, M.: Decision Tree Approach to Microarray Data Analysis. Biocybernetics and Biomedical Engineering 27(3), 29–42 (2007)
12. Kent Ridge Bio-medical Dataset Repository, http://datam.i2r.a-star.edu.sg/datasets/index.html
13. Kretowski, M., Grześ, M.: Evolutionary Induction of Mixed Decision Trees. International Journal of Data Warehousing and Mining 3(4), 68–82 (2007)
14. Kononenko, I.: Estimating Attributes: Analysis and Extensions of RELIEF. In: Bergadano, F., De Raedt, L. (eds.) ECML 1994. LNCS, vol. 784, pp. 171–182. Springer, Heidelberg (1994)
15. Lin, X., Afsari, B., Marchionni, L., Cope, L., Parmigiani, G., Naiman, D., Geman, D.: The ordering of expression among a few genes can provide simple cancer biomarkers and signal BRCA1 mutations. BMC Bioinformatics 10(256) (2009)
16. Lockhart, D.J., Winzeler, E.A.: Genomics, gene expression and DNA arrays. Nature 405, 827–836 (2000)
17. Lu, Y., Han, J.: Cancer classification using gene expression data. Information Systems 28(4), 243–268 (2003)
18. Magis, A.T., Earls, J.C., Ko, Y., Eddy, J.A., Price, N.D.: Graphics processing unit implementations of relative expression analysis algorithms enable dramatic computational speedup. Bioinformatics 27(6), 872–873 (2011)
19. Magis, A.T., Price, N.D.: The top-scoring 'N' algorithm: a generalized relative expression classification method from small numbers of biomolecules. BMC Bioinformatics 13(1), 227 (2012)

20. Mao, Y., Zhou, X.: Multiclass Cancer Classification by Using Fuzzy Support Vector Machine and Binary Decision Tree With Gene Selection. Journal of Biomedicine and Biotechnology, 160–171 (2005)
21. Michalewicz, Z.: Genetic Algorithms + Data Structures = Evolution Programs, 3rd edn. Springer (1996)
22. Murthy, S.: Automatic construction of decision trees from data: A multidisciplinary survey. Data Mining and Knowledge Discovery 2, 345–389 (1998)
23. Nelson, P.S.: Predicting prostate cancer behavior using transcript profiles. Journal of Urology 172, 28–32 (2004)
24. Rokach, L., Maimon, O.: Top-down induction of decision trees classifiers - A survey. IEEE Transactions on Systems, Man, and Cybernetics - Part C 35(4), 476–487 (2005)
25. Schwarz, G.: Estimating the Dimension of a Model. The Annals of Statistics 6, 461–464 (1978)
26. Shi, P., Ray, S., Zhu, Q., Kon, M.A.: Top scoring pairs for feature selection in machine learning and applications to cancer outcome prediction. BMC Bioinformatics 12(375) (2011)
27. Simon, R., Radmacher, M.D.: Pitfalls in the use of DNA microarray data for diagnostic and prognostic classification. Journal of the National Cancer Institute 95, 14–18 (2003)
28. Tan, A.C., Gilbert, D.: Ensemble machine learning on gene expression data for cancer classification. Applied Bioinformatics 2, 75–83 (2003)
29. Tan, A.C., Naiman, D.Q.: Simple decision rules for classifying human cancers from gene expression profiles. Bioinformatics 21, 3896–3904 (2005)
30. Quinlan, R.: Inductive knowledge acquisition: A case study, vol. 9, pp. 157–173. Addison-Wesley (1987)
31. Yang, X., Liu, H.: Top Scoring Pair based methods for classification (BigTSP R package) (2012), http://cran.r-project.org
32. Yoon, S., Kim, S.: k-Top Scoring Pair Algorithm for feature selection in SVM with applications to microarray data classification. Soft Computing - A Fusion of Foundations, Methodologies and Applications, 151–159 (2009)

Asynchronous Evaluation Based Genetic Programming: Comparison of Asynchronous and Synchronous Evaluation and Its Analysis

Tomohiro Harada[1] and Keiki Takadama[2]

[1] The University of Electro-Communications, Japan
Research Fellow of the Japan Society for the Promotion of Science DC
harada@cas.hc.uec.ac.jp
[2] The University of Electro-Communications, Japan
keiki@inf.uec.ac.jp
http://www.cas.hc.uec.ac.jp

Abstract. This paper compares an asynchronous evaluation based GP with a synchronous evaluation based GP to investigate the evolution ability of an asynchronous evaluation on the GP domain. As an asynchronous evaluation based GP, this paper focuses on Tierra-based Asynchronous GP we have proposed, which is based on a biological evolution simulator, Tierra. The intensive experiment compares TAGP with simple GP by applying them to a symbolic regression problem, and it is revealed that an asynchronous evaluation based GP has better evolution ability than a synchronous one.

Keywords: genetic programming, tierra, asynchronous evaluation, symbolic regression.

1 Introduction

Conventional *Evolutionary Algorithms (EAs)* like *Genetic Algorithms (GAs)* [4] and *Genetic Programmings (GPs)* [8] search solution by generating population through a reproduction and a deletion based on evaluations of all individuals at the same time. In contrast to this, EAs such as *Differential Evolution (DE)* [14], and *MOEA/D* [16] are recently attracted attention, and their high search abilities have been revealed. The common feature of these approaches is to *asynchronously* evolve individuals independent of other individuals, unlike the conventional approaches requires evaluations of all other individuals.

From the viewpoint of GPs, it is assumed that the asynchronous evaluation has advantages for the program evolution because (1) the asynchronous evaluation based GP can delete incomplete programs which include infinite loops or multiple-loops and (2) can reproduce faster executed programs which is desired to evolve. Focusing on these advantage, the previous researches have proposed *Tierra-based Asynchronous Genetic Programming (TAGP)* [5,6,11] as a novel GP approach that asynchronously evaluates and evolves programs, which is based on a biological evolution simulator, Tierra [12], proposed by T. S. Ray.

K. Krawiec et al. (Eds.): EuroGP 2013, LNCS 7831, pp. 241–252, 2013.

The purpose of this paper is to analyze the difference between the synchronous evaluation and the asynchronous evaluation and to investigate the better evolution ability of the asynchronous evaluation on the GP domain. Toward this purpose, this paper compares TAGP as the asynchronous evaluation based GP with simple steady-state GP (SGP) [13] as the synchronous evaluation based GP. The experiment is conducted with the assembly language program and applies these two methods to a symbolic regression problem which is well known and easy benchmark.

This paper is organized as follows. Section 2 discusses the difference between the synchronous and the asynchronous evaluation EAs and clarifies the advantage of the asynchronous evaluation on the GP domain. Section 3 explains a biological evolution simulator, Tierra, which is base of TAGP, and Section 4 explains the algorithm of TAGP. Section 5 conducts an experiment to compare TAGP with SGP and shows its result. Section 6 discusses the result and analyzes the difference of two methods, and Section 7 finally gives conclusions and future works.

2 Motivation

It is usual that conventional *Evolutionary Algorithms (EAs)* like *Genetic Algorithms (GAs)* [4] and *Genetic Programmings (GPs)* [8] search solution by generating new population through a reproduction and a deletion based on evaluations of all individuals in a current population. These approaches require to evaluate all individuals before the reproduction and the deletion at the same time, because selection is conducted based on the evaluations. Therefore, it is necessary for the conventional EAs to synchronize evaluations of all individuals in a population.

In contrast to this, EAs like *Differential Evolution (DE)* [14], and *MOEA/D* [16] are recently attracted attention. The common feature of these approach is that each individual in population independently generates a child and next population is generated from them, unlike the conventional EAs. When generating children, evaluations of all individuals are unnecessary, and children can be generated only based on evaluation of a focused or a few other individual(s). From this feature, since these approaches need not synchronize evaluations of all individuals, they can asynchronously evolve each individual.

This paper defines the former EAs as *synchronous evaluation based EAs (SEEAs)*, while the latter as *asynchronous evaluation based EA (AEEAs)*. In previous researches, it has been revealed that the AEEAs has better search ability than the SEEAs. One main reason is independent evolution of individuals. Since evolving individual independently contributes to maintain diversity of a population, the AEEAs can search a large area and are prevented from falling into the local optimal. Additionally, one more advantage of the AEEAs is to be easily able to parallelize algorithms. Since the AEEAs evolve each individual not considering other individuals or using a part of other evaluation, they can decrease overhead of parallelization [15] [2].

As a novel GP approach which applies the asynchronous evaluation, the previous researches have proposed *Tierra-based Asynchronous Genetic Programming (TAGP)* [5,6,11] which is based on a biological evolution simulator, Tierra [12], proposed by T. S. Ray. The advantage to apply the asynchronous evaluation to GP, without mentioned above, is (1) deletion of incomplete programs, and (2) priority reproduction of faster program because of the feature of the program evolution.

(1) Deletion of incomplete programs. When evolving programs including loops, it is possible that programs which cannot be evaluated are generated with genetic operators because of an infinite loop or a multiple-loop. Since the SEEAs require all evaluations in a population to generate next population, it is usual to restrict upper execution steps and to impose a penalty on programs which exceed the limitation. It is, however, difficult to appropriately configure the restriction and the penalty. On the other hand, the AEEAs can continue to evolve programs even if program which does not finish its execution because all programs are independently evaluated and programs can be reproduced without waiting for other program evaluation.

(2) Priority reproduction of faster program. In program evolution, since programs which can be executed faster are usually evaluated better, it is expected that giving a lot of reproduction chance to such programs performs effective. Since the AEEAs can reproduce programs in order of finishing execution, faster executed programs can be naturally given a lot of reproduction chance.

To verify the feature and the advantage of the asynchronous evaluation in GP, this paper compares TAGP as the AEEA with simple steady-state GP (SGP) [13] as the SEEA.

3   Tierra

Tierra [12] proposed by T. S. Ray is a biological evolution simulator, where digital creatures are evolved through a cycle of a self-reproduction, deletion and genetic operators such as a crossover or a mutation. Digital creatures live in a memory space corresponding to the nature land on the earth, and they are implemented by a linear structured computer program such as the assembly language to reproduce (copy) themselves to a vacant memory space. CPU time corresponding to energy like actual creatures is given to each creature, and they execute instructions of a self-reproduction program within allocated CPU time. Since given CPU time is shorter for execution time of programs, all programs are executed in parallel. Lifespan of a program is decided with a *reaper* mechanism. All programs are arranged in a queue, named as *reaper queue*, and a reproduced program is added to the end of the reaper queue. While program execution, a program which can correctly execute its instruction moves its position in the reaper queue to lower, while one which cannot correctly execute its instruction moves its position to upper. Then, when a memory space is filled, a program which is at a top of the reaper queue is deleted from the memory. Due to the reaper mechanism, programs which cannot reproduce themselves within allocated CPU time or include some incorrect instructions are deleted from the memory, while creatures which can reproduce themselves propagate in the memory.

As results of such evolution, Tierra generates, for example, programs, called *parasite*, which reproduce themselves by using other program's instructions, or ones, called *hyper-parasite*, which have immunity to the *parasites*. Note that this evolution is not pre-programmed in Tierra but is caused by *emergence* [9]. As the final stage of Tierra, programs which have shorter program size or have efficient algorithm are generated, which require less CPU time than an initial program to reproduce themselves [1].

4   Tierra-Based Asynchronous Genetic Programming

4.1   Overview

The previous researches focus on the feature of Tierra that can evolve programs, *i.e.*, digital creatures, with asynchronous execution, and have proposed a novel GP based on Tierra mechanism, named as *Tierra-based Asynchronous Genetic Programming (TAGP)* [5, 6, 11]. To apply Tierra to evolving programs with a given task, the previous research introduces *fitness* commonly used in EAs to evaluate programs, and also introduces reproduction and deletion mechanisms depending on *fitness* into Tierra. This is because it is impossible to give any purposes to programs in Tierra whose purpose is only to reproduce themselves, and reproduction and deletions is decided depending on self-reproduction.

Figure 1 shows an image of TAGP. TAGP firstly starts from one program which completely accomplishes the given task. Programs which consist of a linear structured instructions and some registers are stored in a limited memory space. Each program executes a small number of instructions, which is preconfigured, *e.g.*, three instructions, to simulate a parallel execution. All programs are arranged on *reaper queue* which controls lifespan of programs. When an execution of one program is finished, *i.e.*, all instructions in its program are executed, its fitness is evaluated depending on its execution result, and the reproduction and the reaper queue control are conducted. Then if a memory is filled with programs, programs which are arranged at the upper of the reaper queue are removed from the memory while a vacant memory space exceeds a certain threshold, *e.g.*, 20% of a memory, and its space become free.

4.2   Algorithm

TAGP evolves programs through the following selection, reaper queue control, reproduction, and deletion algorithms. The algorithm of TAGP is shown in Algorithm 1. In Algorithm 1, *prog.acc_fit* and *prog.fitness* respectively indicate accumulated and evaluated fitness of evaluated fitness, and $rand(0, 1)$ indicates random real value between 0 to 1.

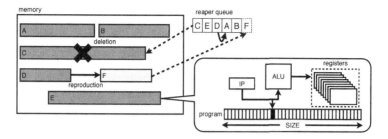

Fig. 1. An image of TAGP

Selection and Reaper Queue Control. When an execution of one program is finished, its fitness is evaluated depending on its register value. Each program accumulates fitness in every evaluations, and whether a program is selected or not is determined based on the accumulated fitness. Here the maximum fitness is represented as f_{max}, and if the accumulated fitness of a program exceeds f_{max}, it is selected as a reproduction candidate, and f_{max} is subtracted from its accumulated fitness (the 1st and 2nd lines in Algorithm 1). While if not, a program is not selected. Depending on this selection condition, a program which completely accomplishes the given task, *i.e.*, its fitness is equal to f_{max}, is invariably reproduced. High fitness programs are easy to be reproduced because the accumulated fitness frequently exceeds f_{max}, while low fitness ones are hard to satisfy this condition. Then, a position in the reaper queue of a program that satisfies the selection condition becomes lower than the current one, *i.e.*, its deletion probability decreases (the $3^{rd} \sim 5^{th}$ lines), while one that does not satisfies the condition becomes upper, *i.e.*, its deletion probability increases (the $20^{th} \sim 22^{nd}$ lines). The move distance is determined by the move rate represented as P_{down} and P_{up} which are calculated as the following equation based on fitness,

$$P_{down}(f) = \frac{f}{f_{max}} \times P_r, \ P_{up}(f) = \frac{f_{max} - f}{f_{max}} \times P_r, \tag{1}$$

where P_r is the maximum probability of P_{down} and P_{down}, which is preconfigured. Depending on these equations, higher fitness programs are arranged on lower position in the reaper queue, *i.e.*, survive long, while lower ones are arranged on upper, *i.e.*, are easily removed.

Reproduction. Programs which are selected depending on the selection condition become a reproduction candidate. To reproduce better program asynchronously, TAGP only compares two programs which are recently evaluated. A better program generates a offspring with the genetic operator such as a crossover and a mutation, and is reproduced to a vacant memory space which is larger than a program size of the offspring (the $6^{th} \sim 7^{th}$ lines). Additionally, to preserve programs which can accomplish the given task, the elite preserving strategy [7] is applied (the $8^{th} \sim 15^{th}$ lines). Concretely, if a current program is evaluated as f_{max}, it is compared with one which is recently evaluated as f_{max}.

Algorithm 1. The algorithm of TAGP

1: **if** $prog.acc\_fit \geq f_{max}$ **then**
2:     $prog.acc\_fit \leftarrow prog.acc\_fit - f_{max}$
3:     **repeat**
4:         down reaper queue position
5:     **until** $rand(0, 1) < P_{down}(prog.fitness)$
6:     reproduce better program of $prog$ and $prev\_prog$ with genetic operators
7:     $prev\_prog \leftarrow prog$
8:     **if** $prog.fitness = f_{max}$ **then**
9:         **if** $prog$ is better than $prev\_elite$ **then**
10:            reproduce $prog$ without any genetic operators
11:        **else**
12:            reproduce $prog$ with genetic operators
13:        **end if**
14:        $prev\_elite \leftarrow prog$
15:    **end if**
16: **else**
17:    **if** $rand(0, 1) < rand(\dfrac{prog.fitness}{f_{max}}, 1)$ **then**
18:        remove $prog$ from memory
19:    **end if**
20:    **repeat**
21:        up reaper queue position
22:    **until** $rand(0, 1) > P_{up}(prog.fitness)$
23: **end if**

Then if the current one is better, it is reproduced as an elite program *without* the genetic operators to preserve better program, while even if not, it is reproduced *with* the genetic operators. TAGP employs four genetic operators, a crossover, a mutation, and an instruction insertion/deletion. The crossover operator combines a reproduced program with previously reproduced program. The mutation operator changes one random instruction in a reproduced program to other random instruction. The insertion operator inserts one random instruction into a reproduced program, while the deletion operator removes one instruction selected at random in a reproduced program.

Deletion. TAGP conducts two deletion. One is a reaper queue based deletion which is conducted during the reproduction process. If a vacant memory space is not found during the reproduction process, programs which is arranged upper in the reaper queue are removed until a total vacant memory space becomes grater than a certain threshold, which is preconfigured and is usually set as 20% of the memory. This deletion remove elder and lower fitness program depending on the reaper queue control.

While another deletion is a *natural death* which is applied to programs which do not satisfied the selection condition. The natural death mechanism is employed in *sugarscape* [3], and removes program according to the $17^{th} \sim 19^{th}$ line in Algorithm 1, where $rand(a, 1)$ indicates random real value between $a(\leq 1)$ to 1. This deletion remove lower fitness program even if the memory is not filled.

5   Experiment

To validate the effectiveness of the AEEA, and to analyze the difference of the AEEA and the SEEA, this paper compares TAGP and simple steady-state GP (SGP) [13] by applying two methods to a symbolic regression problem.

5.1   Example and Settings

This paper applies these methods to a symbolic regression problem. Concretely, we use *Quartic* [8] which is well known and easy benchmark problem represented as $f(x) = x^4 + x^3 + x^2 + x$. As a training set, we use 16 data point from $x = \{0, 1, \ldots, 15\}$. Fitness is evaluated as the following equation

$$fitness = f_{max} - \frac{1}{N} \sum_{i=1}^{N} |f(x_i) - res_i|, \tag{2}$$

where f_{max} indicates the maximum fitness, N indicates the number of the training data, *i.e.*, 16 in this experiment, $f(x_i)$ indicates the function value calculated from x_i, while res_i indicates the execution result of a program in respect to the input value x_i.

This paper employs a program written by actual assembly language embedded on PIC16 micro-controller unit [10] developed by Microchip Technology Inc.. This is 12bits word assembly language, and has 33 simple instructions which consist of add-subtract, logical, bit, and branch operations. Note that since this language does not include a multiplication instruction, calculating multiplication has to combine some instructions and loop structures.

Parameter settings in this experiment are shown in Table 1, 2, and 3. This experiment compares the AEEA and the SEEA with the same number of the evaluations. Both of TAGP and SGP employ same parameters for the crossover, mutation, insertion, and deletion rate, while two point crossover is employed, and the maximum fitness is set as 100. In SGP, the population size is set as 100, and the upper execution steps are restricted to 50000 and if execution steps exceed, its fitness becomes 0. While in TAGP, the memory size is set as 6400, 12800, and 25600 instructions, the deletion removes programs until the total vacant memory exceeds 20% of the memory size, while P_r which is the maximum probability of P_{down} and P_{up}, is set as 0.9. Note that the maximum program size is configured as 256 and the population size of SGP is configured as 100, an allocated memory space of SGP is $256 \times 100 = 25600$, which is the same size with the maximum memory size of TAGP.

The experiment conducts 30 trials in both GPs, and to evaluate the effectiveness of the proposed method, we compare an average number of the execution steps of the best program in the memory/population to evaluate whether an faster program is generated.

Table 1. Common parameter settings

Parameter	value
# of evaluations	200 × 5000
Crossover rate	0.8
Mutation rate	0.05
Insertion rate	0.05
Deletion rate	0.05
Crossover method	Two point crossover
Max. program size	256
f_{max}	100

Table 2. Parameter settings of SGP

Parameter	value
Population size	100
Upper execution steps	50000

Table 3. Parameter settings of TAGP

Parameter	value
	6400
Memory size	12800
	25600
Removing threshold	20% of memory
P_r	0.9

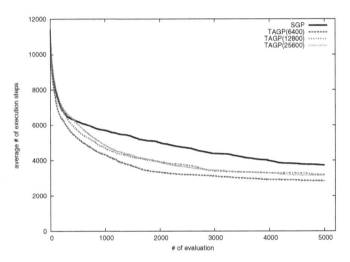

Fig. 2. The result of the average number of the execution steps

5.2 Result

Figure 2 shows the average number of the execution steps in each GP and each memory size. In Figure 2, the abscissa indicates the number of the evaluations, while the ordinate indicates the average number of the shortest execution steps of the maximum fitness program. The solid line shows the result of SGP, while the dotted lines show the results of TAGP of the different memory sizes. Note that all evolved programs can correctly solve the given problem. As shown in Figure 2, in all memory sizes of TAGP, the average execution step is less than the one of SGP. This result indicates that TAGP performs better evolution ability than SGP. Concretely, in contrast to the evolution of SGP slows down at about 500 evaluations, TAGP keeps evolving programs and can generate the efficient program which finishes the execution about 3000 steps. Comparing the difference between the memory sizes of TAGP, smaller memory space get better evolution

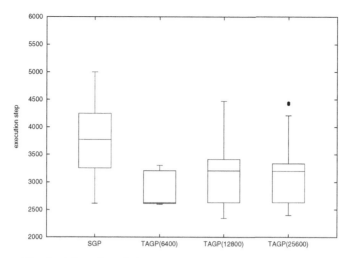

Fig. 3. A boxplot of the execution steps for each GP method

ability. From these results, it is revealed that TAGP has better evolution ability than SGP on the symbolic regression problem, and additionally, the smaller memory size accelerates the program evolution.

Figure 3 shows a boxplot of the execution steps finally given by the best program in the memory/population after 200×5000 evaluations. In Figure 3, the abscissa indicates the difference of the GP methods, while the ordinate indicates the execution steps finally given by the best program in the memory/population. As shown in Figure 3, it is indicated that the execution step of evolved programs with TAGP is shorter than 3500, while the one with SGP is weighted from 3200 to 4200. Focusing on the difference between the memory size of TAGP, the variability of the execution steps is small in the case that the memory size is 6400, while in the case that the memory size is 12800 and 25600, shorter execution step programs which is about 2300~2400 are generated that are not generated with small memory size TAGP or SGP. From these results, it is revealed that TAGP can generate shorter execution step programs than SGP, and the small memory size enables stable program evolution, while the large memory size enables to generate shorter step programs than the small memory size or SGP.

6   Discussion

The average program size of the best program in the memory/population is shown in Figure 4. In Figure 4, the abscissa indicates the number of the evaluation, while the ordinate indicates the average program size of the maximum fitness and the shortest execution steps program. The solid line shows the result of SGP, while the dotted lines show the results of TAGP of the different memory sizes. As shown in Figure 4, the average program size increases at the early evolution period. This is because the program evolution of this problem mainly

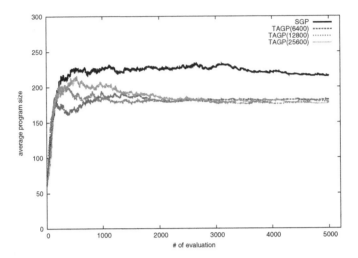

Fig. 4. The result of the average program size

expand loop structures. Since a loop expansion can reduce a number of judge of a termination condition, it decreases the execution steps. Comparing TAGP with SGP, although TAGP decreases the program size after size increasing, SGP keeps large program size. From the viewpoint of the program size, since the maximum program size is limited to 256, programs which is larger than the limit cannot be generated. However, although it is required to expand loops to evolve program in this experiment, a large program cannot expand its loop because of the size limitation. Therefore, since it is hard for a large program to be evolved by expanding the loops unless become small by removing inefficient instructions, the program evolution of SGP which keeps large program size slows down. In contrast to this, since TAGP can decreases the program size and leaves space for the evolution, TAGP can keep evolving the program. The reason why TAGP can decrease the program size is that TAGP restricts the large program size because of controlling the population based on the memory size, where the smaller program easily survives.

Finally, to clarify the difference of the diversity between TAGP and SGP, the standard deviation of the execution steps in the memory/populaiton is shown in Figure 5. In Figure5, the abscissas indicate the number of the evaluation, while the ordinates indicate the average of the standard deviation of the execution steps in the memory/population. The solid line shows the result of SGP, while the dotted lines show the results of TAGP of the different memory sizes. As shown in Figure 5, the standard deviation of the execution steps in TAGP is larger than the one in SGP, which indicates that the diversity of the programs in TAGP is larger than the one in SGP. This is because since TAGP selects programs based on fitness and execution completion, faster programs have selection probability even if they are not the best, in contrast to SGP selects programs with absolute comparison based on fitness and actual execution steps where it is very hard

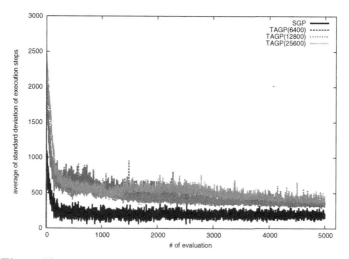

Fig. 5. The average of the standard deviation of the execution steps

for slower programs to be selected. This feature is the common advantage of the AEEA approaches to be able to preserve the diversity of population because of the asynchronous evaluation. It is revealed that the asynchronous evaluation also contributes better evolution ability in the GP domain.

7   Conclusion

This paper focused on the asynchronous evaluation on the GP domain, analyzed the difference between the synchronous and the asynchronous evaluation based GPs. Concretely, this paper compares TAGP as the asynchronous evaluation based GP we proposed with simple steady-state GP as the synchronous evaluation based GP. The intensive experiment is conducted to investigate the effectiveness of the asynchronous evaluation on the GP domain by applying these two methods to the symbolic regression problem. The experiment has revealed that TAGP has better evolution ability than SGP, and the small memory size accelerates the program evolution, while the large memory size generates shorter execution step programs than the small memory or SGP. The reason of this improvement is that TAGP can naturally restrict to generate the larger size program because of the memory size based population control, while TAGP can also preserve the diversity of the population because of the asynchronous evaluation.

The following issues should be pursued in the near future: (1) experiments on other benchmark problems such as boolean and classification and a comparison with other GP methods, and (2) an improvement of evolution ability of TAGP.

Acknowledgments. This work was supported by JSP KAKENHI Grant Number 249376.

References

1. ATR Evolutionary Systems Department: Artificial Life and Evolutional System. Tokyo Denki University Press (1998)
2. Durillo, J.J., Zhang, Q., Nebro, A.J., Alba, E.: Distribution of Computational Effort in Parallel MOEA/D. In: Coello, C.A.C. (ed.) LION 2011. LNCS, vol. 6683, pp. 488–502. Springer, Heidelberg (2011), http://dx.doi.org/10.1007/978-3-642-25566-3_38
3. Epstein, J.M., Axtell, R.L.: Growing Artificial Societies: Social Science from the Bottom Up (Complex Adaptive Systems), 1st printing edn. The MIT Press (November 1996), http://www.amazon.com/exec/obidos/redirect?tag=citeulike07-20&path=ASIN/0262550253
4. Goldberg, D.E.: Genetic Algorithms in Search, Optimization and Machine Learning, 1st edn. Addison-Wesley Longman Publishing Co., Inc., Boston (1989)
5. Harada, T., Otani, M., Matsushima, H., Hattori, K., Sato, H., Takadama, K.: Robustness to Bit Inversion in Registers and Acceleration of Program Evolution in On-Board Computer. Journal of Advanced Computational Intelligence and Interlligent Informatics (JACIII) 15(8), 1175–1185 (2011)
6. Harada, T., Otani, M., Matsushima, H., Hattori, K., Takadama, K.: Evolving Complex Programs in Tierra-based On-Board Computer on UNITEC-1. In: 2010 61st World Congress on International Astronautical Congress (IAC) (2010)
7. Jong, D., Alan, K.: An Analysis of the Behavior of a Class of Genetic Adaptive Systems. Ph.D. thesis, Department of Computer and Communications Sciences, University of Michigan (1975)
8. Koza, J.: Genetic Programming On the Programming of Computers by Means of Natural Selection. MIT Press (1992)
9. Langton, C.G.: Artificial Life. Addison-Wesley (1989)
10. Microchip Technology Inc.: PIC10F200/202/204/206 Data Sheet 6-Pin, 8-bit Flash Microcontrollers. Microchip Technology Inc. (2007), http://ww1.microchip.com/downloads/en/DeviceDoc/41239D.pdf
11. Nonami, K., Takadama, K.: Tierra-based Space System for Robustness of Bit Inversion and Program Evolution. In: SICE, 2007 Annual Conference, pp. 1155–1160 (2007)
12. Ray, T.S.: An approach to the synthesis of life. Artificial Life II XI, 371–408 (1991)
13. Reynolds, C.W.: An evolved, vision-based behavioral model of coordinated group motion. In: Proc. 2nd International Conf. on Simulation of Adaptive Behavior, pp. 384–392. MIT Press (1993)
14. Storn, R., Price, K.: Differential Evolution - A Simple and Efficient Heuristic for Global Optimization over Continuous Spaces. J. of Global Optimization 11(4), 341–359 (1997), http://dx.doi.org/10.1023/A:1008202821328
15. Tasoulis, D., Pavlidis, N., Plagianakos, V., Vrahatis, M.: Parallel differential evolution. In: Congress on Evolutionary Computation, CEC 2004, vol. 2, pp. 2023–2029 (June 2004)
16. Zhang, Q., Li, H.: MOEA/D: A Multiobjective Evolutionary Algorithm Based on Decomposition. IEEE Trans. Evolutionary Computation 11(6), 712–731 (2007)

How Early and with How Little Data? Using Genetic Programming to Evolve Endurance Classifiers for MLC NAND Flash Memory

Damien Hogan, Tom Arbuckle, and Conor Ryan

Computer Science and Information Systems,
University of Limerick,
Ireland
{damien.t.hogan,tom.arbuckle,conor.ryan}@ul.ie

Abstract. Despite having a multi-billion dollar market and many operational advantages, Flash memory suffers from a serious drawback, that is, the gradual degradation of its storage locations through use. Manufacturers currently have no method to predict how long they will function correctly, resulting in extremely conservative longevity specifications being placed on Flash devices.

We leverage the fact that the durations of two crucial Flash operations, *program* and *erase*, change as the chips age. Their timings, recorded at intervals early in chips' working lifetimes, are used to predict whether storage locations will function correctly after given numbers of operations. We examine how **early** and with how **little** data such predictions can be made. Genetic Programming, employing the timings as inputs, is used to evolve binary classifiers that achieve up to a mean of 97.88% correct classification. This technique displays huge potential for real-world application, with resulting savings for manufacturers.

Keywords: Genetic Programming, Binary Classifier, Flash Memory.

1 Introduction

The NAND Flash memory [19] market is projected to be worth US$24 billion for 2013 [23], with recent application areas such as smart-phones, tablet PCs, and Solid State Drives (SSDs) continuing to increase market value. NAND Flash memory, which is used primarily for data storage, is more expensive than traditional forms of memory such as hard-disk drives (HDDs) but offers numerous advantages including faster performance and lower power consumption. However, a significant drawback is that storage locations (cells) in Flash devices have a limited working lifetime, and slowly degrade [6] through repeated use, eventually becoming unreliable. A difficulty posed by this is the fact that the rate at which cells wear out varies significantly between devices and even between cells within the same device.

In Flash devices, data is read and programmed one *page* (group of bytes) at a time, but is erased a *block* (group of pages) at a time. Programming and then

K. Krawiec et al. (Eds.): EuroGP 2013, LNCS 7831, pp. 253–264, 2013.
© Springer-Verlag Berlin Heidelberg 2013

erasing a block is known as a program/erase (p/e) *cycle*, and the longevity of a block, its *endurance*, is measured by the number of p/e cycles it completes before it becomes unreliable. It is hugely time consuming to measure the endurance of blocks since they must be cycled to destruction in order to find the actual number of cycles completed. This means it is not economical for manufacturers to perform tests to accurately specify endurance, resulting in extremely conservative estimates being used for the specifications of Flash devices.

Since manufacturers cannot be sure of the actual number of p/e cycles blocks within their devices will complete, a significant amount of internal redundancy, known as *over-provisioning*, must be included in items such as SSDs. This ensures that when the weakest blocks fail, others will be available to take their place and maintain the specified capacity. A technique to allow manufacturers predict the quality of blocks without requiring time consuming tests would mean that the endurance specification of Flash devices could be increased.

As the blocks within Flash devices are p/e cycled, the cells within them degrade, making it easier to program and erase them. This results in the time taken to perform these operations decreasing as the number of cycles completed increases. In previous work [13], we established that the duration of the program and erase operations could be used to predict the quality of blocks. In particular, Genetic Programming (GP) [17] was used to evolve binary classifiers which predicted whether blocks would successfully complete a predefined number of cycles based only on program and erase timing information. That work, essentially a proof-of-concept, investigated only timing data recorded upon completion of 1,000 and 10,000 p/e cycles.

The research presented in this paper, in collaboration with partners in industry, extends our previous work and investigates the effect of using timing information recorded at many different p/e cycling intervals. A significant component of this research is the destructive testing of blocks on actual Flash devices in order to accumulate data to train and test the classifiers. This paper confirms that program and erase times can be used as an indication of the endurance capability of a block, and, going beyond our previous results, that the number of cycles at which the times are recorded has a significant effect on predictions made. The results illustrate that endurance predictions can be made **early** in the lifecycles of the chips and show how **little** data is needed to do so. They establish the success of this approach and its huge potential for real-world application.

This paper comprises the following sections: Background, Related Research, Destructive Testing of Flash Devices, Evolving Endurance Classifiers Using GP, Results, Future Work, and Conclusions.

2   Background

Flash memory [4] is a non-volatile, solid state, form of memory. Non-volatile memory retains its contents when power is removed, while solid-state memory has no moving parts, being purely electronic in nature. The advantages of Flash over HDDs include faster read and write speed, lower power consumption, greater durability, lower noise emission, and lower weight. However, Flash-based devices remain significantly more expensive and offer much smaller storage capacities than HDDs.

Data is stored within Flash devices in cells whose main component is a floating gate transistor [15]. An insulating oxide layer maintains the charge on the floating gate even when power is removed, with the level of charge determining the bit or bits stored by that cell. A cell is programmed by placing charge on its floating gate, while it is erased by removing charge from the gate. This requires electrons to be forced through/over the transistor's insulating oxide layer and on to the floating gate using techniques such as Fowler-Nordheim (FN) tunneling [9]. However, these operations gradually degrade the oxide layer until eventually the cell can no longer reliably store charge.

Flash often uses multi-step approaches to operations. That is, to program a value, a voltage is repeatedly applied until the operation succeeds. If a certain number of retries has been reached and the operation has not succeeded, then program failure is deemed to occur. Due to the manner in which the oxide degrades, it becomes progressively *easier* to program (and erase) a location, so the time taken to perform these operations decreases. However, once the degradation has reached a certain level, it is no longer possible to store data at that location.

Traditional forms of Flash memory store one bit per cell, and are known as single-level cell (SLC) Flash. SLC cells are regarded as programmed if their charge exceeds a particular voltage threshold and erased if it does not. However, in order to increase capacity, the standard has now become multi-level cell (MLC) Flash which stores 2 bits per cell. Rather than having a single threshold like SLC cells, MLC implements three thresholds in order to differentiate between 4 voltage levels representing 00, 01, 10, and 11. This requires the ability to program and sense precise amounts of charge, reducing the margin for error associated with the single threshold in SLC and resulting in the necessity for advanced error correcting code (ECC) [20].

ECC is required to detect and correct single bit errors occurring within NAND Flash memory. The MLC NAND Flash devices examined in this paper implement 12-bit per 528 byte ECC meaning they are capable of correcting 11,915 single bit errors per storage block. As the cells within blocks degrade, the number of errors detected in data read from the blocks increases until eventually the number of errors correctable through ECC is exceeded and the block must be marked as bad and removed from service.

3 Related Research

It is important to be able to characterise Flash memory behaviour, given the various reliability issues to which Flash is prone [10]. Earlier work on characterising Flash [11,7] showed both that program times vary predictably with wear and that erase times are dependent upon it. More recent work has studied the effects of baking the chips at temperature and p/e cycling [21] as well as the complex error patterns [5] that Flash exhibits during its working lifetime.

Predictions of performance can then be based on characterisations. For example, testing of chips followed by analysis of measurements of their latency has been used for predicting endurance [3], and models of trapped charge [8] and of the lifetimes of the tunnel oxide [16] have been employed similarly. A recent paper by Grupp et al. [12] characterises the performance of 45 chips from six manufacturers to make predictions of the future tradeoffs to be made as a result of the drive towards increasing NAND Flash chips' capacity.

Concerning the use of evolutionary computation, including GP, to solve problems related to non-volatile memory, there are still comparatively few publications. Our recent papers (project sketch [2,1]) show how GP can be used to predict NAND Flash endurance (trial results [13]) and retention [14]. Genetic Algorithms can also optimise the operating parameters of NOR memory [22].

4   Destructive Testing of MLC NAND Flash Devices

This research is unique in that the data used for the machine learning phase of the process is acquired through the destructive testing of MLC NAND Flash chips. Over the course of approximately one month, blocks within six Flash devices were p/e cycled until failure using a purpose built Flash test platform, capable of measuring errors and the duration of program and erase operations.

The endurance of random blocks within the test devices was evaluated by p/e cycling them until failure. Each block was repeatedly programmed and erased until the number of errors, or bit-error-rate (BER), recorded in data read from the block exceeded the number of errors correctable through ECC. The BER was calculated by writing a specific data pattern to the block and immediately reading it back, recording the number of single bit differences introduced by this action. The BER and the *average* program and erase timings since the previous interval were recorded upon completion of 10 p/e cycles, 500 cycles, 1,000 cycles, and every 1,000 cycles thereafter until the BER surpassed the maximum level of ECC. Recording the average timing information meant, for example, that the program and erase values recorded at 1,000 cycles were the average values for all program and erase operations performed between 501 and 1,000 cycles.

Fifty blocks were randomly selected and tested from each of six test devices. All devices were of the same specification and from the same manufacturer, with two devices being selected from each of three different production batches. However, on completion of the hardware testing phase of the research, one test block was found to be bad (faulty) resulting in the accumulation of a data-set describing 299 blocks.

4.1   Data Analysis

The duration of program and erase operations serves as input data to a binary classifier evolved using GP. This classifier predicts whether test blocks will function correctly beyond some predefined number of cycles, or decision boundary. Our goal is to investigate the effect of using different combinations of timing information as input data when evolving classifiers. In particular, since we know the program and erase times decrease as blocks degrade, we investigate how **early** in the lifecycles of the chips such predictions can be made. We also examine how **little** timing data is required for these predictions.

Fig. 1 shows the distribution of endurance values recorded from 299 randomly selected blocks across six MLC NAND Flash devices. The violin plot shows the minimum, maximum, median (white dot), all data points within the first and third percentiles (black rectangle), and also the density distribution (grey shaded area). The endurance not only varies significantly between blocks on different devices but also between blocks within the same device. It should be noted that the endurance values recorded from blocks on two of the chips (both from the same production batch) were easily distinguishable from the endurance values from the remaining four chips since their endurance was significantly lower than the rest. The values recorded from these two 'weaker' chips can be identified in the region with high density to the left of the violin plot.

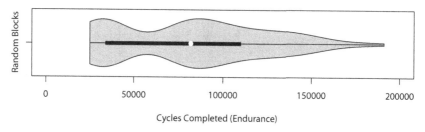

Fig. 1. The violin plot shows the distribution of the endurance values evaluated across all six test chips. This varied between a minimum of 25,000 and a maximum of 191,000 cycles, having a mean value of 81,615 and a median of 82,000.

Fig. 2a and Fig. 2b show the distribution of program and erase times recorded at regular intervals up to 10,000 cycles. The plots highlight the variation in values recorded from blocks at each interval and also the fact that the program and erase time for each block decrease as the device is p/e cycled. At the point when blocks were deemed to have failed, the program time was, on average, approximately 18% faster than the initial recorded program time for each block. However, the pattern displayed by the erase time differed from that of the program time in that it initially decreased (on average by approximately 34%) before later increasing significantly and finishing on average 27% slower than the initial recorded erase time. It is important to note, however, that since only timing information recorded up to the completion of 10,000 cycles is being used in our GP experiments, the increase in erase time will not be applicable here (and is not visible in Fig. 2b) since it only occurs later in the lifetime of blocks.

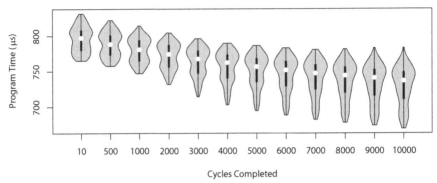

(a) Distribution of the program times at regular intervals up to 10,000 cycles.

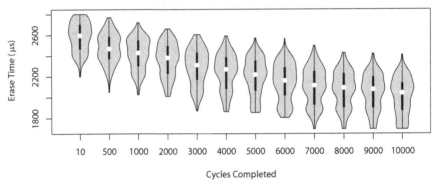

(b) Distribution of the erase times at regular intervals up to 10,000 cycles.

Fig. 2. Distribution of Program and Erase operation durations

5   Evolving Endurance Classifiers Using GP

GP is a member of the Evolutionary Algorithms family of machine learning techniques while binary classifiers divide data-sets into two groups, assigning each item to be a member of one group or the other. This research utilises GP to evolve binary classifiers to identify blocks that will still function correctly upon completion of some predefined number of p/e cycles, or decision boundary. In particular, we investigate how **early** in a block's lifetime (and with how **little** data) accurate classifications can be made of its potential endurance.

Prior to starting the GP process, the data set was randomly divided into four equal parts, or folds. Data points from each of the six chips were distributed as equally as possible across the four folds. This 4-fold cross validation process permitted training and testing on four different compositions of the data set. Each composition used three different folds for training data with the remaining fold providing test data. Following the training phase, the single best performing individual was chosen to be evaluated using the testing data. The test data results across all four folds were averaged since the system may have performed better on some folds than others.

Decision boundaries denote the number of cycles at which the classifications of blocks or data-points change from pass to fail. If they have successfully completed at least that number of cycles, they achieve a pass. Otherwise, they are considered to have failed. The five decision boundaries listed in Table 1 allow the evaluation and comparison of different inputs across a number of decision boundaries with each providing a different composition of pass/fail data-points.

Table 1. Five decision boundaries provided a wide range of pass/fail rates

Decision Boundary	Data Points Pass	Data Points Fail
35,000 Cycles	~75%	~25%
50,000 Cycles	~66%	~34%
82,000 Cycles	~50%	~50%
98,000 Cycles	~34%	~66%
110,000 Cycles	~25%	~75%

The inputs available for use in these GP experiments are the program and erase times recorded at regular intervals up to 10,000 cycles. As listed in Table 2 over the page, a number of sets of input combinations were tested, with 'No Ref.' (no *reference points*, see below) being the program and erase times (just two inputs) at each interval up to and including 10,000 cycles. The second set of tests, 'pt10, et10 Ref.', used four inputs; the first two remained fixed at 10 cycles, essentially forming reference points with the second two being formed in turn by the various intervals available. By using four inputs, the system could learn from the rate of change of the pair of program times and the pair of erase times. The 'pt1k, et1k Ref.' input combinations followed the same pattern as the previous set but used the timing information recorded at 1,000 cycles as a fixed reference point. Finally, 'pt10k, et10k Ref.' took the opposite approach and retained the 10,000 cycles inputs in every batch of runs while selecting the remaining two inputs from the other available intervals. Every combination of inputs was used to evolve classifiers for all five decision boundaries.

ECJ [18], a Java-based evolutionary computation research system, was used to perform the GP experiments described above. Thirty GP runs were performed per fold, giving a total of 120 GP runs for every set of inputs on each of the five decision boundaries. Table 3 lists the GP parameters used for all the experiments.

6   Results

Fig. 3 shows the results for the test-sets listed in Table 2. The 'No Ref.' line in Fig. 3a shows the results achieved when using just two inputs, with no reference points, meaning the system could not learn from the rate of change. In this case, the x-axis represents the number of cycles from which the input data is taken.

Table 2. Classifier Inputs: A total of 43 input combinations were evaluated

No.	No Ref.	pt10, et10 Ref.	pt1k, et1k Ref.	pt10k, et10k Ref.
			Inputs	
1	p10, e10	p10, e10, p500, e500	p1k, e1k, p2k, e2k	p10, e10, p10k, e10k
2	p500, e500	p10, e10, p1k, e1k	p1k, e1k, p3k, e3k	p500, e500, p10k, e10k
3	p1k, e1k	p10, e10, p2k, e2k	p1k, e1k, p4k, e4k	p1k, e1k, p10k, e10k
4	p2k, e2k	p10, e10, p3k, e3k	p1k, e1k, p5k, e5k	p2k, e2k, p10k, e10k
5	p3k, e3k	p10, e10, p4k, e4k	p1k, e1k, p6k, e6k	p3k, e3k, p10k, e10k
6	p4k, e4k	p10, e10, p5k, e5k	p1k, e1k, p7k, e7k	p4k, e4k, p10k, e10k
7	p5k, e5k	p10, e10, p6k, e6k	p1k, e1k, p8k, e8k	p5k, e5k, p10k, e10k
8	p6k, e6k	p10, e10, p7k, e7k	p1k, e1k, p9k, e9k	p6k, e6k, p10k, e10k
9	p7k, e7k	p10, e10, p8k, e8k	p1k, e1k, p10k, e10k	p7k, e7k, p10k, e10k
10	p8k, e8k	p10, e10, p9k, e9k		p8k, e8k, p10k, e10k
11	p9k, e9k	p10, e10, p10k, e10k		p9k, e9k, p10k, e10k
12	p10k, e10k			

Table 3. Tableau showing GP parameters and settings

Parameter	Details		
Objective	Correctly classify data points using a given boundary.		
Terminal Set	Program and erase timing information, See Table 2. $\Re$, where the ephemeral random integer constant ($\Re$) ranges over the interval [-100, +100].		
Function Set	+, -, *, %		
Fitness	The percentage of data points correctly classified.		
Generations	100	Population	1000
Crossover Rate	0.8	Mutation Rate	0.15
Reproduction Rate	0.05	Max Tree Depth	10

We can see from this plot that, using a decision boundary of 35,000 cycles, inputs of *pt10* and *et10* reached approximately 83.5% while, at the right hand side of the plot, *pt10000*, *et10000* achieved around 87.75% correct classification.

The remaining three lines represent the batches of tests performed when using a pair of fixed inputs to allow the system to learn from the rate of change. In these cases, the x-axis represents the two variable inputs. The 'pt10, et10, Ref.' line in Fig. 3a shows the effect of changing the third and fourth inputs while the first two inputs (*pt10*, and *et10*) remain static. The left most point on this line shows the results with inputs of *pt10*, *et10*, *pt500*, and *et500* while, as we move from left to right along the x-axis, the success rate initially decreases (at *pt10*, *et10*, *pt1000*, *et1000*). However, we can see that as the two variable inputs are taken from incrementally higher levels of cycling, the classification success rate steadily increases, reaching its highest point at *pt10*, *et10*, *pt10000*, *et10000*.

Fig. 3a and Fig. 3b show that at the two lower boundaries, classifiers evolved without reference points are capable of achieving reasonable results (>80%). As can be seen in Fig. 3b, using just the timing information recorded at 500 cycles

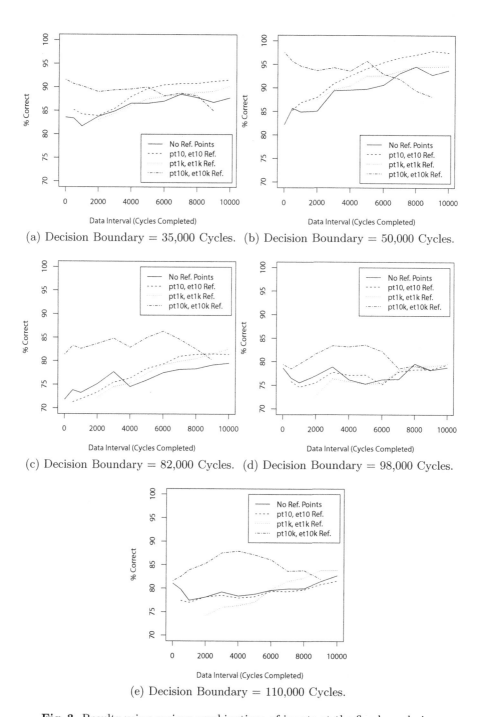

(a) Decision Boundary = 35,000 Cycles. (b) Decision Boundary = 50,000 Cycles.

(c) Decision Boundary = 82,000 Cycles. (d) Decision Boundary = 98,000 Cycles.

(e) Decision Boundary = 110,000 Cycles.

Fig. 3. Results using various combinations of inputs at the five boundaries (two inputs - *pt500, et500*), almost 86% of the blocks are correctly classified at a boundary of 50,000 cycles. This result shows the potential of this approach since, even with so **little** data, we can predict the future status of blocks at such an **early** stage in their lifetime. However, still better results are possible if a fixed reference point is used to allow the system to learn from the rate of change of the program and erase times. Table 4 presents a summary of the best results achieved for each decision boundary. These results show that a mean of 91.56% correct classification was reached for the 35,000 cycle decision boundary while at the 50,000 cycles boundary a mean of 97.88% was achieved.

Table 4. The best results achieved for each decision boundary

Decision Boundary	Best Inputs	Result
35,000 Cycles	pt10, et10, pt10000, et10000	91.56 %
50,000 Cycles	pt10, et10, pt9000, et9000	97.88 %
82,000 Cycles	pt6000, et6000, pt10000, et10000	86.36 %
98,000 Cycles	pt5000, et5000, pt10000, et10000	83.60 %
110,000 Cycles	pt4000, et4000, pt10000, et10000	87.93 %

The three higher decision boundaries proved more difficult than the earlier ones. Fig. 3c, Fig. 3d, and Fig. 3e show that in order to evolve classifiers for boundaries later in the lifetime of blocks, the system must also train on data recorded after the completion of larger numbers of cycles. However, care must be taken to ensure the data intervals, or inputs, are not too close together since in this case they do not provide enough information about the rate of change of the program and erase time.

We have investigated the use of combinations of timing information from various intervals up to 10,000 cycles. Excellent results were achieved when identifying weak blocks (blocks which will complete fewer than 50,000 cycles). Huge potential is also shown at higher boundaries considering a mean classification rate of 87.93% was achieved using inputs recorded as early as 4,000 and 10,000 cycles to predict the status of test blocks after the completion of 110,000 cycles.

7   Future Work

Having established that the current technique provides excellent classification results at lower decision boundaries, identifying 'weak' chips, we will proceed to enhance the system in order achieve a reliable estimate of the number of cycles at which a test block will fail. Switching from a classification to a regression approach, we will use GP to provide an initial rough estimate of the number of cycles a block will complete based on timing data taken early in the block's lifetime. Moreover, as the block continues to be used, and more timing information at later numbers of cycles becomes available, we will verify that the calculated time-to-failure becomes more accurate.

8   Conclusions

Our previous work confirmed that program and erase timing information could be used as a predictor for block endurance. This paper expands on that work and shows that the number of cycles completed when timing information is recorded has a significant effect on the quality of the evolved classifier.

In total, 43 combinations of timing inputs were examined for each of five decision boundaries. Results show that the use of timing data recorded **early** in the lifetime of blocks allows the evolution of excellent classifiers at lower decision boundaries. For example, a mean of 97.88% of blocks were correctly classified using previously unseen test data at a boundary of 50,000 cycles. Indeed, even when using as **little** as a timing data pair recorded at 500 cycles, almost 86% of the blocks can be correctly classified at this boundary. The results also confirm that better classifier performance is achieved in these tests when using four inputs. The first pair act as points of reference so that the system can determine the rate of change of the program and erase times using the second pair of inputs. The findings at higher decision boundaries are also extremely encouraging. Using only inputs up to 10,000 cycles, a mean success rate of 87.93% was achieved to predict the operating status of test blocks after the completion of 110,000 cycles.

We have proposed a technique to allow manufacturers to optimise the use of existing Flash chips without requiring any modifications to the underlying hardware. Successful classification of chips will allow manufacturers to increase their specified endurance values and also, by reducing over-provisioning, increase the specified capacity of devices which use Flash memory (such as SSDs).

Acknowledgements. The authors thank the numerous reviewers for their helpful comments. This research was funded by Enterprise Ireland under contract IP/2008/0591.

References

1. Arbuckle, T., Hogan, D., Ryan, C.: Optimising Flash Memory for Differing Usage Scenarios: Goals and Approach. In: Lee, G., Howard, D., Ślęzak, D., Hong, Y.S. (eds.) ICHIT 2012. CCIS, vol. 310, pp. 137–140. Springer, Heidelberg (2012)
2. Arbuckle, T., Hogan, D., Ryan, C.: Optimising Flash non-volatile memory using machine learning: A project overview. In: Proceedings of the 5th Balkan Conference on Informatics (BCI 2012), pp. 235–238 (2012)
3. Boboila, S., Desnoyers, P.: Write endurance in Flash drives: Measurement and analysis. In: 8th USENIX Conference on File and Storage Technologies (FAST 2010), San Jose, California, pp. 115–128 (2010)
4. Brewer, J., Gill, M.: Nonvolatile Memory Technologies with Emphasis on Flash (A Comprehensive Guide to Understanding and Using Flash Memory Devices). Wiley-IEEE Press (2008)
5. Cai, Y., Haratsch, E., Mutlu, O., Mai, K.: Error patterns in MLC NAND Flash memory: Measurement, characterization, and analysis. In: Design, Automation Test in Europe Conference Exhibition (DATE 2012), pp. 521–526 (2012)

6. Cappelletti, P., Bez, R., Cantarelli, D., Fratin, L.: Failure mechanisms of Flash cell in program/erase cycling. In: Technical Digest, International Electron Devices Meeting (IEDM 1994), San Francisco, CA, USA, pp. 291–294 (1994)

7. Desnoyers, P.: Empirical evaluation of NAND Flash memory performance. SIGOPS Oper. Syst. Rev. 44, 50–54 (2010)

8. Fayrushin, A., Lee, C., Park, Y., Choi, J., Choi, J., Chung, C.: Endurance prediction of scaled NAND Flash memory based on spatial mapping of erase tunneling current. In: 3rd IEEE International Memory Workshop (IMW 2011), pp. 1–4 (2011)

9. Fowler, R.H., Nordheim, L.: Electron emission in intense electric fields. Proceedings of the Royal Society of London. Series A 119(781), 173–181 (1928)

10. Ghidini, G.: Charge-related phenomena and reliability of non-volatile memories. Microelectronics Reliability 52, 1876–1882 (2012)

11. Grupp, L.M., Caulfield, A.M., Coburn, J., Swanson, S., Yaakobi, E., Siegel, P.H., Wolf, J.K.: Characterizing Flash memory: anomalies, observations, and applications. In: Proceedings of the 42nd Annual IEEE/ACM International Symposium on Microarchitecture, MICRO 42, pp. 24–33. ACM, New York (2009)

12. Grupp, L., Davis, J., Swanson, S.: The bleak future of NAND Flash memory. In: Proceedings of the 10th USENIX Conference on File and Storage Technologies, San Jose, California, pp. 17–24 (2012)

13. Hogan, D., Arbuckle, T., Ryan, C.: Evolving a storage block endurance classifier for Flash memory: A trial implementation. In: Proc. 11th IEEE Int. Conference on Cybernetic Intelligent Systems (CIS 2012), pp. 12–17 (2012)

14. Hogan, D., Arbuckle, T., Ryan, C., Sullivan, J.: Evolving a retention period classifier for use with Flash memory. In: Proc. 4th Int. Conf. on Evolutionary Computation Theory and Applications (ECTA 2012), pp. 24–33 (2012)

15. Kahng, D., Sze, S.: A floating-gate and its application to memory devices. The Bell System Technical Journal 46(6), 1288–1295 (1967)

16. Kitahara, Y., Hagishima, D., Matsuzawa, K.: Reliability of NAND Flash memories induced by anode hole generation in floating-gate. In: International Conference on Simulation of Semiconductor Processes and Devices (SISPAD 2011), pp. 131–134 (2011)

17. Koza, J.R.: Genetic Programming: On the Programming of Computers by Means of Natural Selection. The MIT Press (1992)

18. Luke, S.: ECJ 20. A Java-based evolutionary computation research system (2010), http://cs.gmu.edu/~eclab/projects/ecj/

19. Micheloni, R., Crippa, L., Marelli, A.: Inside NAND Flash Memories. Springer (2010)

20. Micheloni, R., Marelli, A., Ravasio, R.: Error Correction Codes for Non-Volatile Memories. Springer (2010)

21. Moon, J., No, J., Lee, S., Kim, S., Yang, J., Chang, S.H.: Noise and interference characterization for MLC Flash memories. In: International Conference on Computing, Networking and Communications (ICNC 2012), pp. 588–592 (2012)

22. Sullivan, J., Ryan, C.: A destructive evolutionary algorithm process. Soft Computing – A Fusion of Foundations, Methodologies and Applications 15, 95–102 (2011)

23. Trendforce: eMMC and SSD to contribute to 15% NAND Flash output value growth in 2013 (2012), http://press.trendforce.com/en/node/4931 (accessed January 11, 2013)

Examining the Diversity Property
of Semantic Similarity Based Crossover

Tuan Anh Pham[1], Quang Uy Nguyen[2],
Xuan Hoai Nguyen[3], and Michael O'Neill[4]

[1] Centre of Information Technology, Military Academy of Logistics, Vietnam
[2] Faculty of IT, Military Technical Academy, Vietnam
[3] IT Research and Development Center, Hanoi University, Vietnam
[4] Natural Computing Research & Applications Group,
University College Dublin, Ireland
{anh.pt204,quanguyhn,nxhoai}@gmail.com, m.oneill@ucd.ie

Abstract. Population diversity has long been seen as a crucial factor for the efficiency of Evolutionary Algorithms in general, and Genetic Programming (GP) in particular. This paper experimentally investigates the diversity property of a recently proposed crossover, Semantic Similarity based Crossover (SSC). The results show that while SSC helps to improve locality, it leads to the loss of diversity of the population. This could be the reason that sometimes SSC fails in achieving superior performance when compared to standard subtree crossover. Consequently, we introduce an approach to maintain the population diversity by combining SSC with a multi-population approach. The experimental results show that this combination maintains better population diversity, leading to further improvement in GP performance. Further SSC parameters tuning to promote diversity gains even better results.

Keywords: Genetic Programming, Semantic, Diversity, Locality.

1 Introduction

Similar to other evolutionary algorithms, it has been found for Genetic Programming (GP) that there two crucial properties that strongly affect its performance, namely, the diversity of a population [4,8] and the locality of operators [5,14]. The diversity of a population, which is directly affected by search operators, represents its ability to explore different parts of the search space while the locality of an operator exhibits its ability to focus on exploiting a specific area of the search space. Intuitively, these two properties seem to be contradictory. It means that an approach that maintains high diversity in the population often has low locality in search operators and vice versa.

In a recent work [10], Uy et al. proposed a new semantic based crossover for GP, Semantic Similarity based Crossovers (SSC), with the main objective to improve the locality of the standard subtree crossover. It has been shown [10] that SSC achieved its objective and increased locality in the crossover operator leading to a significant improvement in GP performance. To counter the

K. Krawiec et al. (Eds.): EuroGP 2013, LNCS 7831, pp. 265–276, 2013.
© Springer-Verlag Berlin Heidelberg 2013

effect of reducing search diversity while enforcing locality, SSC also forbid the exchange of two semantically equivalent subtrees. However, there are still three open questions related to SSC [10], which are:

1. How the diversity of the population is impacted by SSC with its focus on operator locality?
2. Is there a way to reduce this impact on diversity while maintaining SSC locality?
3. If we can balance operator locality with population diversity will we then see additional gains in the performance of GP?

This paper tries to address these three questions. We first analyse the diversity of GP populations when the crossover operator is SSC. We then propose an approach to retain the population diversity by combining SSC with multi-population Genetic Programming. The remainder of the paper is organised as follows. In the next section, we briefly review the previous work on diversity in GP. Section 3 details Semantic Similarity based Crossovers. The experimental settings are detailed in Section 4. The results of the experiments are presented and discussed in Section 5. Finally, Section 6 concludes the paper and highlights some potential future work.

2   Related Work

It is widely believed that maintaining high population diversity is important for evolutionary algorithms [4]. Rapid loss of diversity, especially semantic diversity, has been suggested as the main cause for premature convergence of GP evolutionary search [12]. Consequently, GP systems may be trapped into local optima. When considering the diversity in GP populations, it is important to distinguish between two types of diversity. The first is syntactic or genotypic diversity and the second is the behavioural or phenotypic diversity. In this paper, we will focus on the later type of diversity. We argue that the second type of diversity is more critical to GP's behaviour than the first, as it is easy to find programs that are all syntactically distinct, yet have identical semantics.

Controlling (syntactic) diversity has been considered since the early days of GP. Much of earlier work focused on the initialisation phase of GP. Koza introduced the well-known Ramped-Half-and-Half technique for creating the initial GP population to reduce the occurrence of duplicated trees [6]. O'Reilly and Oppacher [11] and Poli and Langdon [12] tested various crossover operators to study their impact on syntactic diversity, They showed that standard crossover (SC) often leads to loss of diversity, hence is not an ideal operator.

Rosca [13] proposed a method to measure semantic diversity in GP population using phenotype entropy. Langdon [7] used (explicit) fitness sharing to preserve diversity. It clusters the population into a number of groups, based on their similarity with respect to a fitness-based metric. Members of the same group are penalized by being forced to share fitness, while isolated individuals retain their full fitness. McKay [9] used implicit fitness sharing, in which the reward for each fitness case is shared by all individuals that give the same output.

More recently, semantic diversity has received more attention from GP researchers. Burke et al. [2] conducted an analysis on the effect of different diversity measures on fitness. They showed that there is a strong correlation between entropy and the edit distance on the one hand, and change in fitness on the other. Gustafson et al. [4] examined the possible effects of sampling both unique structures and behaviours in GP. The behaviour sampling results helped to explain previous diversity research and suggest new ways to improve search. Similarly, Looks [8] proposed a new method for sampling semantically unique individuals in GP, by generating a number of unique minimal programs, then combining random programs with these minimal programs to generate the population. He argued that it increases the behavioral diversity of the population, leading to significant gains in GP performance. Beadle and Johnson proposed Semantic Driven Crossover (SDC) [1]. In SDC, the semantic equivalence of the offspring produced by crossover with their parents is checked by transforming them to Reduced Ordered Binary Decision Diagrams (ROBDDs). If two trees reduce to the same ROBDD, they are semantically equivalent. If the offspring are equivalent to their parents, they are discarded and the crossover is restarted. This process is repeated until semantically new children are found. The authors argued that this results in increased semantic diversity in the evolving population, and a consequent improvement in GP performance. Overall, promoting diversity, especially semantic diversity, is important and often leads to beneficial results.

3   Methods

This section briefly presents Semantic Similarity based Crossover (SSC) more details of SSC could be found in [10]

3.1   Measuring Semantics

The *Sampling Semantics* of any (sub)tree could be defined as follows:

Let F be a function expressed by a (sub)tree T on a domain D. Let P be a set of points sampled from domain D, $P = \{p_1, p_2, ..., p_N\}$. Then the *Sampling Semantics* of T on P on domain D is the set $S = \{s_1, s_2, ..., s_N\}$ where $s_i = F(p_i), i = 1, 2, ..., N$.

The values of two parameters N and P are dependent on problem. In this paper, N is set as the number of fitness cases of problems (20 points), and we choose the set of points P uniformly randomly from the problem domain.

Based on sampling semantics (SS), *Sampling Semantics Distance* (SSD) between two subtrees could be defined. Let $U = \{u_1, u_2, ..., u_N\}$ and $V = \{v_1, v_2, ..., v_N\}$ be the SS of $Subtree_1(St_1)$ and $Subtree_2(St_2)$ on the same set of evaluating values, then the SSD between St_1 and St_2 is defined as follows [10]:

$$SSD(St_1, St_2) = \frac{|u_1 - v_1| + |u_2 - v_2| + ... + |u_N - v_N|}{N} \qquad (1)$$

Thanks to SSD, a relationship between two subtree called *Semantic Similarity* is defined. Two subtrees are semantically similar on a domain if their SSD on the same set of points in that domain lies within a positive interval. The formal definition of semantic similarity (SSi) between subtrees St_1 and St_2 is as follows:

$$SSi(St_1, St_2) = \textbf{if } \alpha < SSD(St_1, St_2) < \beta$$
$$\textbf{then } \text{true}$$
$$\textbf{else } \text{false}$$

here α and β are two predefined constants, known as the *lower* and *upper bounds* for semantic sensitivity, respectively. In this paper, we set $\alpha = 10^{-4}$ and $\beta = 0.4$ which are good values found in the previous experiments [10].

3.2 Semantic Similarity Based Crossover

In [10], SSC was proposed to improve the locality of crossover. It was an extension of Semantic Aware Crossover [17] in two ways. Firstly, when two subtrees are selected for crossover, their semantic similarity, rather than semantic equivalence as in SAC, is checked. Secondly, as semantic similarity is more difficult to satisfy than semantic equivalence, so repeated failures may occur. Thus SSC uses multiple trials to find a semantically similar pair, only reverting to random selection after passing a bound on the number of trials. Algorithm 1 shows how SSC operates in detail. In our experiments, the value of Max_Trial was set to 12, with this value having been calibrated by earlier experiments as the value for its good performance [10].

4   Experimental Settings

To investigate the diversity property of SSC, we used eight real-valued symbolic regression problems. The problems and training data are shown in Table 1. These functions were taken from previous work on using semantics based operators in GP [10].

The GP parameters used for our experiments are shown in Table 2. It should be noted that the raw fitness is the mean of absolute error on all fitness cases. Therefore, the smaller values are better. For each problem and each parameter setting, 100 runs were performed.

We divided our experiments into two sets. The first is to analyse the diversity property of SSC and the second aims to test a method for maintaining diversity of the population by combining SSC with multi-population GP.

Algorithm 1. Semantic Similarity based Crossover

---

select Parent 1 P_1;
select Parent 2 P_2;
Count=0;
while *Count<Max_Trial* **do**
    choose a random crossover point $Subtree_1$ in P_1;
    choose a random crossover point $Subtree_2$ in P_2;
    generate a number of random points (P) on the problem domain;
    calculate the SSD between $Subtree_1$ and $Subtree_2$ on P
    if *$Subtree_1$ is similar to $Subtree_2$* **then**
        execute crossover;
        add the children to the new population;
        return true;
    else
        Count=Count+1;

if *Count=Max_Trial* **then**
    choose a random crossover point $Subtree_1$ in P_1;
    choose a random crossover point $Subtree_2$ in P_2;
    execute crossover;
    return true;

---

5   Results and Discussion

This section first analyses the diversity property of SSC and then introduce a method for maintaining the diversity of the population using SSC. After that, the issue of parameter tuning of SSC is addressed.

5.1   Diversity Analysis

As previously discussed, phenotypic diversity is often more important than genotypic diversity, in this paper, we analyse the diversity property of SSC using the phenotypic measurement proposed in Rosca [13]. The population phenotypic diversity is measured as

$$E(P) = -\sum_k p_k.log(p_k) \qquad (2)$$

where the population is partitioned according to fitness value, and p_k is the proportion of the population that have the fitness value in the fitness partition k^{th}. In this experiment we partitioned the population into 10 equal parts from the smallest fitness value to the greatest.

Figure 1 shows how the diversity of the population changed in GP with SSC (shorthanded as SGP) and GP with standard crossover for functions $F2$ and

Table 1. Symbolic Regression Functions

Functions	Training Data
$F1 = x^3 + x^2 + x$	20 random points $\subseteq$ [-1,1]
$F2 = x^4 + x^3 + x^2 + x$	20 random points $\subseteq$ [-1,1]
$F3 = x^5 + x^4 + x^3 + x^2 + x$	20 random points $\subseteq$ [-1,1]
$F4 = x^6 + x^5 + x^4 + x^3 + x^2 + x$	20 random points $\subseteq$ [-1,1]
$F5 = (x+1)^3$	20 random points $\subseteq$ [-1,1]
$F6 = cos(3x)$	20 random points $\subseteq$ [-1,1]
$F7 = 2sin(x)cos(y)$	20 random points $\subseteq$ [-1,1]
$F8 = x^4 - x^3 + y^2/2 - y$	20 random points $\subseteq$ [-1,1]

Table 2. Run and Evolutionary Parameter Values

Parameter	Value
Population size	500
Generations	50
Selection	Tournament
Tournament size	3
Crossover probability	0.9
Mutation probability	0.05
Initial Max depth	6
Max depth	15
Max depth of mutation tree	5
Non-terminals	+, -, *, / (protected version),
	sin, cos, exp, log (protected version)
Terminals	X, 1
Raw fitness	mean absolute error on all fitness cases
Trials per treatment	100 independent runs for each value

$F4$ [1]. It can be seen from the figure that as the evolution progressed the population diversity decreased and population diversity of SGP was constantly lower than GP. It is understandable as the main objective of SSC is to improve the locality of crossover in GP, i.e to generate children that are not largely different from their parents. This results confirm our intuition that GP with SSC has to sacrifice some diversity for its contradictory counterpart - locality.

5.2   Maintaining Diversity for SSC

The previous subsection showed that using SSC in GP results in the loss of population diversity. Therefore, improving its diversity while maintaining its

---

[1] The figures for other test functions are similar and due to space limits, they are not shown here.

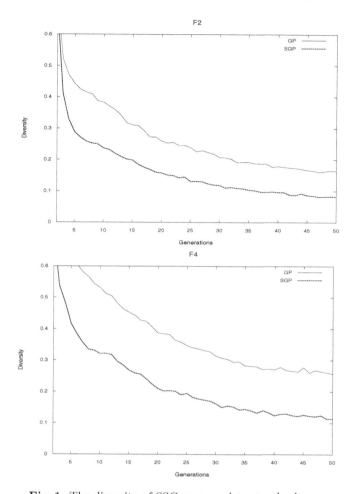

Fig. 1. The diversity of SSC compared to standard crossover

locality is potentially performance advantageous. To achieve this objective it is tempting to combine SSC with some diversity promotion mechanism which does not modify the crossover operator (e.g., a mechanisms that operates on the population structure). In this paper, we combine a multi-population approach with SSC to improve the diversity of SGP.

The idea of dividing a large population into several sub-populations is not new in itself e.g., see [15], which describes an island model approach. Individuals are allowed to migrate among sub-populations with a given frequency. This model helps to explore different parts of the search space through different sub-populations and maintaining diversity within a subpopulation thanks to the introduction of immigrants. The island model for GP was empirically studied [3,16] and the authors showed that it helped to improve GP performance by improving the diversity of GP population.

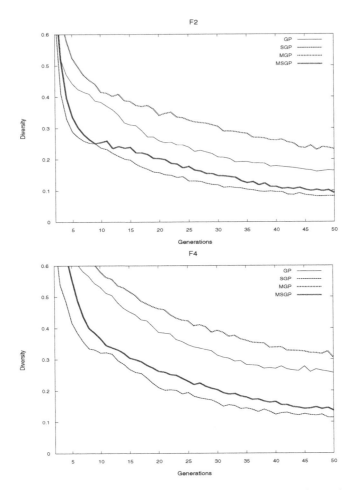

Fig. 2. The diversity of SSC in multi-population GP compared to other methods

In order to implement multi-population GP, some parameters need to be tuned. These parameters include the number of subpopulations, the number of the individuals that migrate among subpopulations and the frequency for migrating individuals. In this paper, these values were calibrated by experiments and the values for the good performance of multi-population GP are as follows: 10 subpopulations, 20 individuals in each subpopulation were migrated to others, and the frequency for migrating individuals is 2.

We implemented SSC in a multi-population GP with the above configuration and the resultant system is labelled MSGP in the following results. Figure 2 presents the comparative population diversity of four tested systems, GP, SGP, MGP (GP with muti-population) and MSGP (GP with multi-population and SSC) [2]. It can be observed from Figure 2 that MGP maintained higher diversity

---

[2] Again, we only show the results for $F2$ and $F4$ due to space limits.

than standard GP. This is consistent with the previous results in [16]. What is more important is that by combining SSC with MGP (MSGP), we could maintain the higher diversity in the population compared to SGP. Although the improvement of diversity of MSGP compared to SGP was not remarkably significant, this enhancement led to the better performance of SSC as shown in the following.

To compare the performances of all systems in the experiments, we use two classic metrics namely mean of the best fitness and the number of successful runs. These results are shown in Table 3 and Table 4.

Table 3. Number of successful runs

Methods	F1	F2	F3	F4	F5	F6	F7	F8
GP	46	12	9	1	4	36	11	0
MGP	58	34	14	7	7	62	18	0
SGP	65	28	19	8	15	48	45	0
MSGP	68	35	29	13	19	65	54	0

Table 4. Mean best fitness of four methods. Note that the values are scaled by 10^2.

Methods	F1	F2	F3	F4	F5	F6	F7	F8
GP	1.30	1.56	1.61	2.03	2.64	1.85	3.10	13.7
MGP	0.96	1.27	1.35	1.69	1.99	1.35	1.73	10.6
SGP	0.81	0.99	1.01	1.26	1.43	1.02	1.37	9.80
MSGP	0.62	0.85	0.90	1.01	1.21	0.93	0.95	9.21

It can be seen from these tables that implementing SSC in a multi-population GP helped to further improve the performance of SSC. Obviously, the number of successful runs of MSGP was always greater than those of SGP and the quality of solutions found by MSGP was also better than ones of SGP. We also statistically tested the significance of the results in Table 4 using a Wilcoxon signed rank test with a confidence level of 95%. The statistical results show that all the improvements of MSGP, MGP and SGP over standard GP are significant. However, MSGP performance is not significantly better than SGP and MGP though it is the best method among four tested systems in terms of the number of runs which solved the problem in each instance.

5.3   Tuning SSC Parameters for Better Diversity

The previous section showed that MSGP helped to improve the performance of GP compared to SGP, nevertheless, the margin of the improvement, in terms of mean best fitness, was not remarkable. The reason may lie in the fact that MSGP had only slightly higher population diversity than SGP and still rather lower than standard GP. Therefore, we hypothesized that by reducing the value of Max_Trial in SSC we can further increase its diversity and this potentially lead to further improvements of MSGP performance. We tested this hypothesis by conducting an experiment with smaller values of Max_Trial, namely 6, 8, and 10. MSGP with these configurations are denoted as MSGP6, MSGP8 and MSGP10 respectively. We measured the performance of these MSGP configurations and compared them with other systems in the previous subsection. The results are shown in Table 5 and Table 6 [3].

Table 5. Number of successful runs of three new configurations

Methods	F1	F2	F3	F4	F5	F6	F7	F8
GP	46	12	9	1	4	36	11	0
MGP	58	34	14	7	7	62	18	0
SGP	65	28	19	8	15	48	45	0
MSGP	68	35	29	13	19	65	48	0
MSGP6	74	39	26	17	20	68	50	0
MSGP8	68	43	36	23	15	68	54	0
MSGP10	68	52	32	17	21	58	51	0

Table 6. Mean best fitness of three new configurations. Note that the values are scaled by 10^2.

Methods	F1	F2	F3	F4	F5	F6	F7	F8
GP	1.30	1.56	1.61	2.03	2.64	1.85	3.10	13.7
MGP	0.96	1.27	1.35	1.69	1.99	1.35	1.73	10.6
SGP	0.81	0.99	1.01	1.26	1.43	1.02	1.37	9.80
MSGP	0.62	0.85	0.90	1.01	1.21	0.93	0.95	9.21
MSGP6	**0.26**	**0.52**	**0.68**	0.90	**1.04**	**0.60**	**0.86**	9.17
MSGP8	**0.27**	**0.54**	**0.55**	0.86	**1.12**	**0.54**	**0.65**	9.20
MSGP10	**0.26**	**0.42**	**0.67**	0.87	**0.96**	**0.68**	1.01	**9.04**

It can be seen from these tables that the new configurations of MSGP helped to improve the performance of GP to a further extent. The number of successful runs of MSGP6, MSGP8 and MSGP10 was often greater than MSGP and the mean best fitness was usually far smaller than that of MSGP. We also statistically

---

[3] We also measured the performance of SGP6, SGP8, SGP10 and their performances are inferior to SGP12. These results are consistent with the results in [10].

tested the significance of improvement of the results in Table 6 using a Wilcoxon signed rank test with a confidence level of 95%. In this table, if a result of MSGP6, MSGP8 and MSGP10 is significantly better than the result of SGP, it is printed in bold face. The results of statistical tests show that in most cases, the improvement of MSGP6, MSGP8 and MSGP10 over SGP is statistically significant.

6   Conclusions and Future Work

In this paper, we investigated the diversity property of Semantic Similarity based Crossover (SSC). Since SSC aims to improve locality, it may lead to the loss of diversity and the experimental results presented in the paper confirmed this. We then proposed an approach to maintain diversity for SSC by combining it with multi-population GP (MSGP). We tested the new method on eight symbolic regression problems and the results showed that multi-population GP with SSC has higher diversity than standard GP with SSC (SGP). This led to the superior performance of MSGP to SGP. However, the improvement was not significant. Then, we tuned the parameter of SSC to achieve higher diversity and resulted in better performance of MSGP.

There are a number of areas for future work which arise from this paper. First, we want to test more values of Max_Trail of SSC to figure out the suitable values for a class of problems. Second, we would like to combine SSC with other methods for promoting diversity such as fitness sharing [7] to see if it gains further improvement. Last but not least, we aim to investigate the impact of this method on some more difficult problems such as text summarization, time series prediction, etc. For these problems, we predict that maintaining high diversity along with locality is critical for GP performance.

Acknowledgments. This work was funded by The Vietnam National Foundation for Science and Technology Development (NAFOSTED), under grant number 102.01-2011.08. Michael O'Neill is grateful for the financial support of Science Foundation Ireland under grant numbers 08/IN.1/I1868 and 08/SRC/FM1389.

References

1. Beadle, L., Johnson, C.: Semantically driven crossover in genetic programming. In: Proceedings of the IEEE World Congress on Computational Intelligence, pp. 111–116. IEEE Press (2008)
2. Burke, E.K., Gustafson, S., Kendall, G.: Diversity in genetic programming: An analysis of measures and correlation with fitness. IEEE Transactions on Evolutionary Computation 8(1), 47–62 (2004)
3. Fernandez, F., Tomassini, M., Vanneschi, L.: An empirical study of multipopulation genetic programming. Genetic Programming and Evolvable Machines 4(1), 21–51 (2003)
4. Gustafson, S., Burke, E.K., Kendall, G.: Sampling of Unique Structures and Behaviours in Genetic Programming. In: Keijzer, M., O'Reilly, U.-M., Lucas, S., Costa, E., Soule, T. (eds.) EuroGP 2004. LNCS, vol. 3003, pp. 279–288. Springer, Heidelberg (2004)

5. Hoai, N.X., McKay, R.I., Essam, D.: Representation and structural difficulty in genetic programming. IEEE Transaction on Evolutionary Computation 10(2), 157–166 (2006)
6. Koza, J.: Genetic Programming: On the Programming of Computers by Natural Selection. MIT Press, MA (1992)
7. Langdon, W.B.: Genetic Programming and Data Structures: Genetic Programming + Data Structure = Automatic Programming! Kluwer Academic, Boston (1998)
8. Looks, M.: On the behavioral diversity of random programs. In: GECCO 2007: Proceedings of the 9th Annual Conference on Genetic and Evolutionary Computation, July 7-11, vol. 2, pp. 1636–1642. ACM Press (2007)
9. McKay, B.: An investigation of fitness sharing in genetic programming. The Australian Journal of Intelligent Information Processing Systems 7(1/2), 43–51 (2001)
10. Nguyen, Q.U., Nguyen, X.H., O'Neill, M., McKay, R.I., Galvan-Lopez, E.: Semantically-based crossover in genetic programming: application to real-valued symbolic regression. Genetic Programming and Evolvable Machines, 91–119 (2011)
11. O'Reilly, U.M., Oppacher, F.: Program Search with a Hierarchical Variable Length Representation: Genetic Programming, Simulated Annealing and Hill Climbing. In: Davidor, Y., Männer, R., Schwefel, H.-P. (eds.) PPSN 1994. LNCS, vol. 866, pp. 397–406. Springer, Heidelberg (1994)
12. Poli, R., Langdon, W.B.: On the search properties of different crossover operators in genetic programming. In: Genetic Programming: Proceedings of the Third Annual Conference, pp. 293–301. Morgan Kaufmann (1998)
13. Rosca, J.P.: Entropy-driven adaptive representation. In: Proceedings of the Workshop on Genetic Programming: From Theory to Real-World Applications, July 9, pp. 23–32 (1995)
14. Rothlauf, F.: Representations for Genetic and Evolutionary Algorithms, 2nd edn. Springer (2006)
15. Tenese, R.: Parallel genetic algorithms for a hypercube. In: Greenstette, J.J. (ed.) Genetic Algorithms and Their Applications: Proceedings of the Second International Conference on Genetic Algorithms, pp. 177–183. Lawrence Erlbaum
16. Tomassini, M., Vanneschi, L., Fernández, F., Galeano, G.: A Study of Diversity in Multipopulation Genetic Programming. In: Liardet, P., Collet, P., Fonlupt, C., Lutton, E., Schoenauer, M. (eds.) EA 2003. LNCS, vol. 2936, pp. 243–255. Springer, Heidelberg (2004)
17. Nguyen, Q.U., Nguyen, X.H., O'Neill, M.: Semantic Aware Crossover for Genetic Programming: The Case for Real-Valued Function Regression. In: Vanneschi, L., Gustafson, S., Moraglio, A., De Falco, I., Ebner, M. (eds.) EuroGP 2009. LNCS, vol. 5481, pp. 292–302. Springer, Heidelberg (2009)

Author Index